W9-CSK-861

PROVENCE

Signpost Guides

Titles in this series include:

- Andalucía and the Costa del Sol
- Bavaria and the Austrian Tyrol
- Brittany and Normandy
- Burgundy and the Rhône Valley
- California
- Canadian Rockies, Alberta and British Columbia
- Catalonia and the Spanish Pyrenees
- Dordogne and Western France
- England and Wales
- Florida
- Ireland
- Italian Lakes and Mountains with Venice and Florence
- Languedoc and South-west France
- Loire Valley
- New England
- New Zealand
- Provence and the Côte d'Azur
- Scotland
- Tuscany and Umbria
- Vancouver and British Columbia
- Washington DC and Virginia, Maryland and Delaware
  and

- Selected Bed and Breakfast in France (annual edition)

For further information about these and other Thomas Cook publications, write to Thomas Cook Publishing, PO Box 227, Units 19–21, The Thomas Cook Business Park, Coningsby Road, Peterborough PE3 8XX, United Kingdom.

Signpost
Guides

PROVENCE

The best of Provence and the Côte
d'Azur from the landscapes that
inspired Van Gogh and Cézanne
to the glitzy resorts of the
Mediterranean and the magnificent
remains of Arles, Nîmes and Orange

Andrew Sanger

The
Globe
Pequot
Press

Thomas Cook
Publishing

Published by Thomas Cook Publishing
A division of Thomas Cook Holdings Ltd
PO Box 227, Units 19–21
The Thomas Cook Business Park
Coningsby Road
Peterborough PE3 8XX
United Kingdom

Telephone: +44 (0)1733 416477
Fax: +44 (0)1733 416688
E-mail: books@thomascook.com

For further information about
Thomas Cook Publishing, visit our website:
www.thomascook.com

ISBN 1-841573-36-1

Published in the USA by
The Globe Pequot Press
PO Box 480
Guilford, Connecticut 06437
USA

ISBN 0-7627-2651-2

Text: © 2003 Thomas Cook Publishing
Maps and diagrams:
Road maps supplied and designed by Lovell Johns Ltd., OX8 8LH
Road maps generated from Bartholomew Digital Database
© Bartholomew Ltd., 1999
City maps prepared by RJS Associates, © Thomas Cook Publishing

Head of Publishing: Donald Greig

Written, researched and updated by: Andrew Sanger
Series Editor: Edith Summerhayes
Project Editor for second edition: Fay Franklin
Motorway information, page 29: Andrew Roast

All rights reserved. No part of this publication may be reproduced, stored in a retrieval system or transmitted, in any form or by any means, electronic, mechanical, recording or otherwise, in any part of the world, without the prior permission of the publisher. Requests for permission should be addressed to Thomas Cook Publishing, PO Box 227, Units 19–21, The Thomas Cook Business Park, Coningsby Road, Peterborough PE3 8XX in the UK, or the Globe Pequot Press, PO Box 480, Guilford, Connecticut 06437, USA, in North America.

Although every care has been taken in compiling this publication, and the contents are believed to be correct at the time of printing, Thomas Cook Holdings Ltd cannot accept responsibility for errors or omissions, however caused, or for changes in details given in the guidebook, or for the consequences of any reliance on the information provided.

The opinions and assessments expressed in this book do not necessarily represent those of Thomas Cook Holdings Ltd.

Readers are asked to remember that attractions and establishments may open, close or change owners or circumstances during the lifetime of this edition. Descriptions and assessments are given in good faith but are based on the author's views and experience at the time of writing and therefore contain an element of subjective opinion which may not accord with the reader's subsequent experience. Any changes or inaccuracies can be notified to the Commissioning Editor at the above address.

About the author

Andrew Sanger is a well-established freelance travel journalist who has, over the last 20 years, contributed hundreds of travel articles to British national newspapers and magazines. He has also written 25 guidebooks, most about regions of France. From 1991 to 1999 Andrew was editor of French Railways' travel magazine *Top Rail*, and has twice been a winner at the prestigious annual Travelex Travel Writers' Awards in London (1994 and 1996).

Andrew's recent guidebook titles include *Languedoc & Roussillon* (1997), *South-West France* (1998), *Exploring Israel* (2000), and pocket guides to *Lanzarote* (1999), *Channel Hopping* (1999), *Brussels and Bruges* (2000) and *Tenerife* (2000), *Signpost Burgundy and the Rhône Valley* (2000) and *Signpost Loire Valley* (2002).

Andrew has had a long and close involvement with France, starting with his primary education at the Lycée Français in London. He began to visit France on his own from the age of 14, when he travelled by train to the Massif Central. His next trip was to Six-Fours-les-Plages, on the Mediterranean coast, which he chose 'purely because of the name' and promptly fell in love with. Since then he reckons to have walked, cycled, driven and travelled by train over almost the whole of France, with accommodation ranging from mobile homes to 5-star hotels, from sleeping rough to luxury villas – as well as acquiring a home of his own, in the heart of a medieval village near Montpellier.

'While living in the south of France, I worked as vineyard labourer, English teacher and anything else that came to hand. For a time I was employed as a truck driver delivering high-quality cheeses, milk and dairy products to the village shops. A lot of the journeys were done partly at night, so they would have their fresh milk in the morning – I got to know those inland mountain roads like the back of my hand! I loved the light and the silence of the Mediterranean countryside at dawn. And I think I'm still pretty good at driving down a village street so narrow you have to fold in the wing mirrors. It was hard work, but I never could get rid of the feeling that it was all one long holiday. When making deliveries, I'd finish as soon as I could to allow time for a spell on the beach before going back to the depot. None of the other drivers was interested in the beach!'

Acknowledgements

The author would like to thank British Airways, for their assistance, Eurotunnel, for the fastest Channel crossings, Rail Europe/Motorail, for the easiest way to the South, Bernard and Diana Eder, for the house and Gerry and Josh, for coming with me.

Contents

About Signpost Guides

Thomas Cook's Signpost Guides are designed to provide you with a comprehensive but flexible reference source to guide you as you tour a country or region by car. This guide divides Provence into touring areas – one per chapter. Major cultural centres or cities form chapters in their own right. Each chapter contains enough attractions to provide at least a day's worth of activities – often more.

Star ratings

To make it easier for you to plan your time and decide what to see, the principal sights and attractions are given a star rating. A three-star rating indicates an outstanding sight or major attraction. Often these can be worth at least half a day of your time. A two-star attraction is worth an hour or so of your time, and a one-star attraction indicates a site that is good but often of specialist interest.

Chapter contents

Every chapter has an introduction summing up the main attractions of the area, and a ratings box, which will highlight the area's strengths and weaknesses – some areas may be more attractive to families travelling with children, others to wine-lovers visiting vineyards, and others to people interested in finding castles, churches, nature reserves or good beaches.

Each chapter is then divided into an alphabetical gazetteer, and a suggested tour. You can select whether you just want to visit a particular sight or attraction, choosing from those described in the gazetteer, or whether you want to tour the area comprehensively. If the latter, you can construct your own itinerary, or follow the authors' suggested tour, which comes at the end of every area chapter.

The gazetteer

The gazetteer section describes all the major attractions in the area – the villages, towns, historic sites, nature reserves, parks or museums that you are most likely to want to see. Maps of the area highlight all the places mentioned in the text. Using this comprehensive overview of the area, you may choose just to visit one or two sights.

One way to use the guide is simply to find individual sights that interest you, using the index, overview map or star ratings, and read what our authors have to say about them. This will help you decide whether to visit the sight. If you do, you will find plenty of practical information, such as the street address, the telephone number for enquiries and opening times.

Alternatively, you can choose a hotel, perhaps with the help of the accommodation recommendations contained in this guide. You can

Symbol Key

- ❶ Tourist Information Centre
- ❷ Advice on arriving or departing
- ❷ Parking locations
- ❷ Advice on getting around
- ❷ Directions
- ❶ Sights and attractions
- ❷ Accommodation
- ❶ Eating
- ❷ Shopping
- ❷ Sport
- ❷ Entertainment

Practical information

The practical information in the page margins, or sidebar, will help you locate the services you need as an independent traveller – including the tourist information centre, car parks and public transport facilities. You will also find the opening times of sights, museums, churches and other attractions, as well as useful tips on shopping, market days, cultural events, entertainment, festivals and sports facilities.

then turn to the overall map on page 10 to help you work out which chapters in the book describe those cities and regions that lie closest to your chosen touring base.

Driving tours

The suggested tour is just that – a suggestion, with plenty of optional detours and one or two ideas for making your own discoveries, under the heading *Also worth exploring*. The routes are designed to link the attractions described in the gazetteer section, and to cover outstandingly scenic coastal, mountain and rural landscapes. The total distance is given for each tour, as is the time it will take you to drive the complete route, but bear in mind that this indication is just for the driving time: you will need to add on extra time for visiting attractions along the way.

Many of the routes are circular, so that you can join them at any point. Where the nature of the terrain dictates that the route has to be linear, the route can either be followed out and back, or you can use it as a link route, to get from one area in the book to another.

As you follow the route descriptions, you will find names picked out in bold capital letters – this means that the place is described fully in the gazetteer. Other names picked out in bold indicate additional villages or attractions worth a brief stop along the route.

Accommodation and food

In every chapter you will find lodging and eating recommendations for individual towns, or for the area as a whole. These are designed to cover a range of price brackets and concentrate on more characterful small or individualistic hotels and restaurants. In addition, you will find information in the *Travel facts* chapter on chain hotels, with an address to which you can write for a guide, map or directory. The price indications used in the guide have the following meanings:

€   budget level
€€   typical/average prices
€€€   de luxe

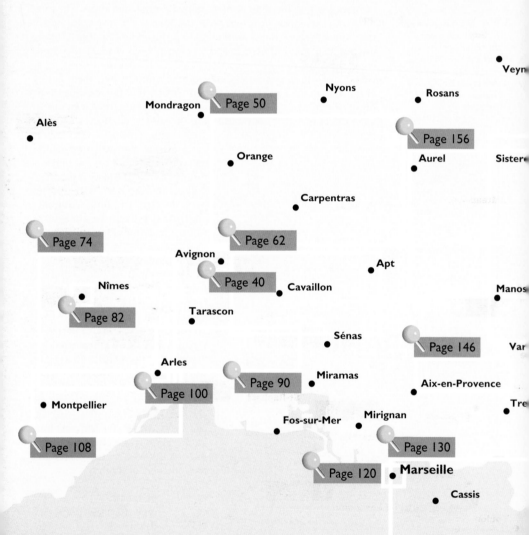

Veyn

Nyons

Rosans

Mondragon   Page 50

Alès

Page 156

Orange

Aurel   Sister

Carpentras

Page 74

Page 62

Avignon

Page 40

Apt

Nîmes   Cavaillon

Manos

Page 82

Tarascon

Sénas

Page 146

Var

Arles

Page 90

Page 100   Miramas

Aix-en-Provence

Montpellier

Tre

Mirignan

Page 108

Fos-sur-Mer

Page 130

Page 120   Marseille

Cassis

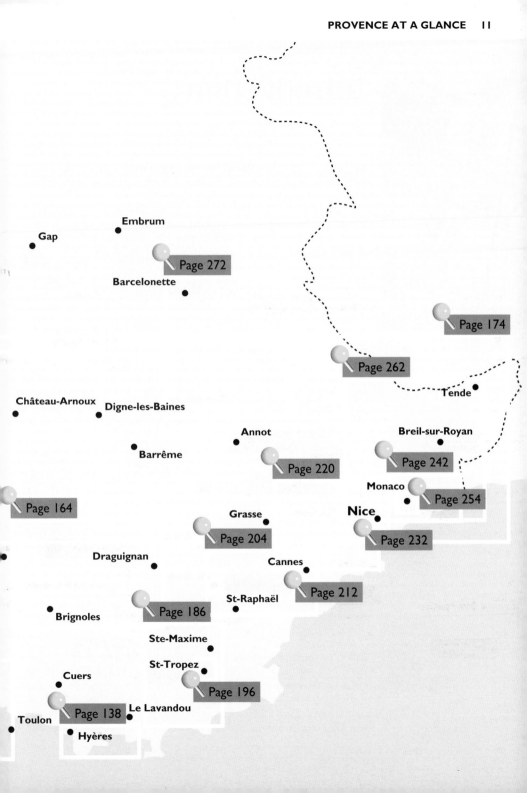

Embrum

Gap

Page 272

Barcelonette

Page 174

Page 262

Tende

Château-Arnoux   Digne-les-Baines

Annot   Breil-sur-Royan

Barrême   Page 242

Page 220   Monaco

Page 254

Page 164   Nice

Grasse   Page 232

Page 204

Draguignan   Cannes

Page 212

Brignoles   St-Raphaël

Page 186

Ste-Maxime

St-Tropez

Cuers   Page 196

Page 138   Le Lavandou

Toulon

Hyères

Introduction

Above
Nice

An invisible frontier somewhere in the Rhône valley, somewhere south of Valence and north of Orange, separates two utterly different countries. One is France; the other, Provence.

As soon as France is left behind, you slip into another landscape, a warmer, more comfortable climate and a way of life which is both more enthusiastic and more leisurely. The most fascinating, barely definable quality of this new country is *sunlight*. Everything is vivid, brilliantly illuminated. The rocky hills appear scoured clean. That clear, crystal light has produced, and attracted, the greatest of modern artists – Picasso, Cézanne, Van Gogh and others.

During the long summer months, millions of people come here, some with a rucksack, some with a Rolls-Royce. They pour down the Rhône valley and cover the coast from Marseille to Monaco. And yet strangely the deep heart of Provence is little visited. It feels as if it has no connection with the dazzling world of the Côte d'Azur.

Much of the countryside remains untouched – wild hills of dense evergreen scrub, narrow roads winding close to cliff edges, sudden dramatic views – but every inch of fertile soil is farmed, with dozens of different crops packed in together, vines, purple lavender, peppers, courgettes and flowers.

Every village seems to have been arranged deliberately; the way the houses step down the hills, among trees and terraces, is exquisite. And somehow all these places manage to be simultaneously provincial and cosmopolitan, simple yet sophisticated. Carpentras, Vaison-la-Romaine, Forcalquier, Apt and Manosque, for example, are little towns that couldn't be more 'nowhere', and yet all have this curious characteristic. The local people themselves seem to have it. Perhaps it comes from long history: Provence has seen it all. Forcalquier, it turns out, was in its time a great political and cultural centre. But that was hundreds of years ago.

The cities, too, from Nîmes to Nice, seem modern enough, with apartment blocks, furniture warehouses, hypermarkets and high-tech industries around the outskirts, yet underneath the tarmac is ancient Rome. Marseille was founded by the ancient Greeks.

It is hard to avoid history in Provence. Invited by the people of this region to come in and help fight off an uncivilised Celtic attack from the north, the Romans decided to stay put, and (having dealt with the Celts) made the whole place into a province of Rome. Hence the name, and hence, too, the great number of Roman theatres, temples, monuments, roads and bridges, preserved by good weather and sturdy construction in almost perfect condition. The majestic power and beauty of the Pont du Gard, built simply to carry fresh water into Nîmes, is the supreme example. Strong, overbearing, forceful, efficient, it reveals much of the nature of the Romans and their civilisation.

After the 5th-century Roman withdrawal, Provence broke up into principalities, counties and duchies. The northern Celts occupied the rest of France, from which the South constantly asserted its independence. Nevertheless, through the complexities of inheritance, in 1481 Provence became part of the kingdom of France. In 1539, French was made the official language, and in the end, it was the Revolution which truly united France and Provence, although the people of the South have continued their fight to be different.

For years the region suffered from the ruthless efforts of the northern establishment to eradicate the various 'heresies', culture and language of Provence. This process, by wholesale slaughter and by encouraging mass emigration, caused the impoverishment which lasted until this century. Strange, then, that today Provence is almost synonymous with good living, and the Côte d'Azur with highlife.

Prosperity and poverty are inseparable here. Narrow alleys open into elegant squares. Damp backstreets run parallel to leafy boulevards busy with cafés and shops. Grand 17th-century mansions with imposing doorways and balconies line streets barely wide enough for a single car. Turning a corner, you suddenly walk into a quiet paved square with its fountain. Even along the rich, sybaritic, azure coast, turn off a flamboyant promenade and you'll find a vegetable market or a tangle of backstreets where the shutters could do with a lick of paint.

Below
Cannes

Follow the country roads to some extraordinary sights, such as the strange village of Roussillon standing on top of a hill of dazzling red and yellow ochre, or the awesome Grand Canyon of the Verdon, 1000m of rock rising up sheer from a tortuous stream. Along the way, the small towns and villages have as much character and history as the cities, but are free of their crowds and traffic. In any of them, after a few minutes sitting in the shade at an outdoor table you feel like staying the rest of your life.

Yet for all its history and its natural wonders, by far the most impressive thing in Provence remains the climate and the style of life it has created. Everything is in the open. Every town and village is built with plenty of outdoor living space, somewhere to play *boules* in a quiet square. Cafés and restaurants put their tables on the pavement and from morning till night, people sit there, eating, drinking, talking. Massive *platanes*, plane trees, provide the essential shade, trunks mottled by peeling bark, branches heavy with foliage. Provence, at peace after a long and turbulent past, celebrates light, art and life – *la vie en plein air*, life in the open air.

Travel facts

Accommodation

Accommodation in Provence and the Côte d'Azur ranges from some of the world's most palatial 5-star hotels to overcrowded campsites, and everything in between. There are hundreds of small, moderately priced, independent family-run hotels. Every little town, and many a tiny village, has at least one clean, adequately comfortable, unpretentious hotel, or sometimes a *restaurant avec chambres* (restaurant with rooms). Standards range from the extremely basic to the height of elegance and luxury. Prices are normally for the room, not per person. A star system operates, but many hotels fall well short of even a single star (expect to pay under €25), while others far exceed the requirements for the maximum grade '4-star Luxe' (expect to pay over €150). Most are 2–3 stars (expect to pay around €50–€70). There are plenty of self-catering villas and apartments, too, but prices are high and you won't find many bargains unless you look inland.

Outside high season (July–August), booking hotels far ahead is rarely essential; except in popular holiday areas, it is usually sufficient to phone a few days before to reserve a room.

The major international hotel chains are represented in Provence and on the Côte d'Azur. The big French chains, all with several hotels in the region, include:

• **Campanile** – popular national chain of motels with restaurant; reliable, all identical, mid-price.
• **Formule 1, Etap Hotel, Balladins, Bonsaï, Liberté, Première Classe** – all economy motels; modern but minimalist.
• **Ibis** – modern, functional, town hotels; mid- to low-budget.
• **Méridien** – smart, modern high-quality chain.
• **Sofitel** – luxurious modern hotels.

Useful French hotel and restaurant federations include:
• **Relais & Châteaux** – independently owned; top of the market, old-fashioned luxury and (especially those designated as 'Relais Gourmand') with excellent food. Free handbook from French Government Tourist Offices abroad.
• **Relais Routiers** – truckdrivers' stops; inexpensive roadside restaurants generally with a few basic rooms above. Recognisable by a blue and red circular sign outside.
• **Relais du Silence** – top-quality hotels in especially quiet locations. Bookable online at *www.silencehotel.com*
• **Logis et Auberges de France** – a great resource; almost 5000 small, unpretentious, family-run independent hotels, nearly all with a good

Web sites for further info

www.fr-holidaystore.co.uk/ tourops Tour operators specialising in France.

www.logis-de-france.fr/us/index.htm English-language pages of Logis de France site.

www.francetourism.com French Tourist Office site in the US with useful accommodation and trip-planning pages.

www.provencetourism.com The regional tourist office site with booking information for hotels and other accommodation.

www.gites-de-france.fr/eng/index.htm Gîtes de France site.

Above
The Hôtel Negresco, Nice

Camping

France has over 11000 approved campsites. They're graded with stars: anything above 2 stars will have hot showers and good facilities. *Camping à la Ferme*, campsites on farms, tend to be more basic. Four-star and the even better 4-star 'Grand Comfort' sites have excellent amenities, a play area, a shop, and sports facilities, often including a swimming-pool. *Castels et Camping*, mainly in superb locations, is a federation of top-quality camps (web: *www.les-castels.com*).

inexpensive restaurant (half of them specialise in regional dishes). Rooms are adequate, reasonably priced. Free handbook from French Government Tourist Offices abroad.

- **Gîtes** are simple cottages rented as inexpensive self-catering vacation accommodation. They're bookable in the UK on *08705 360 360*, or online at *www.gites-de-france.fr*
- **Villages des Vacances** (holiday villages), either for all the family or for children only, are popular with the French. Details from national and regional tourist offices.
- **Chambres d'Hôtes** ('guest rooms'), usually announced by a simple handmade sign on a front gate, are homely bed & breakfast stop-overs (often with evening meal too), in ordinary family homes in rural areas.
- **Café-Couette** is a scheme to pre-book bed & breakfast at ordinary homes and *chambres d'hôtes*. Bookable in France; *tel: 01 42 94 92 00; fax: 01 42 94 93 12*. Find them online at *www.cafe-couette.com*

Airports

Nice Côte d'Azur and Marseille Marignane are the principal regional airports of Provence, receiving daily scheduled international and internal flights (*see Getting to Provence and the Côte d'Azur on page 27*). Local airports used mainly for internal flights (sometimes in summer only) are Avignon Caumont, Cannes-Mandelieu, Monaco Monte Carlo, Nîmes, St-Raphaël-Fréjus and Toulon-Hyères.

Children

Children in France will strike their British, American and Australasian counterparts (and their parents) as very well behaved and fairly strictly disciplined. Children are expected to sit quietly at table and eat grown-up food. On the other hand, there are plenty of facilities and entertainments for kids and – so long as they know how to behave – they are welcomed everywhere.

Climate

The long, warm, dry summer, from around mid-April to mid-October, has average daytime temperatures in the coastal region and river valleys generally above 20°C (reaching 28°C in July and August). Temperatures are lower at higher altitudes. Occasional heavy storms are a feature of the later summer and autumn.

In winter it's cold inland, with snow in the Mediterranean Alps. On or near the coast, it is generally mild, with rainy or cloudy days, January and February being the coldest and wettest months.

A cool, dry north wind – the *Mistral* – can blow for several days at a time in any season, either as a gentle but persistent refreshing breeze in summer or as a strong icy blast in winter.

If you've a taste for adventure...

...look out for the next Signpost.

- Andalucía and the Costa del Sol
- Bavaria and the Austrian Tyrol
- Brittany and Normandy
- California
- Canadian Rockies
- Catalonia and the Spanish Pyrenees
- Dordogne and Western France
- Florida
- Ireland
- Italian Lakes and Mountains
- Languedoc and South-West France
- Loire Valley
- New England
- New Zealand
- Provence and the Côte d'Azur
- Scotland
- Vancouver and British Columbia
- Burgundy and the Rhône Valley
- England and Wales
- Tuscany and Umbria
- Washington DC, Virginia, Maryland and Delaware

Thomas Cook

Publishing

Available from all quality booksellers, Thomas Cook branches and direct from Thomas Cook Publishing. Give us a call on **+44 (0) 1733 416477**, or email: publishing-sales@thomascook.com to order your copy today!

ⓘ Thomas Cook
Travellers Cheques
free you from the hazards
of carrying large amounts
of cash. Thomas Cook
Foreign Exchange Bureaux
provide full foreign
exchange facilities and will
change currency and
traveller's cheques (free of
commission in the case of
Thomas Cook Travellers
Cheques). They can also
provide emergency
assistance in the event of
loss or theft of Thomas
Cook Travellers Cheques.

Currency

France is part of the EU's 12-country 'euro zone', throughout which
the currency is the euro (€), divided into 100 euro cents (which – in
France only – are also officially known as centimes). There are notes of
5, 10, 20, 50, 100, 200 and 500 euro, and coins of 1 and 2 euro, and of
1, 2, 5, 10, 20 and 50 cents. Notes and coins are interchangable
between countries in the zone despite each country's coins having its
own designs on one side.

Euros are readily available from all ATMs (Cash Dispensers), using
credit cards and debit cards displaying the appropriate international
symbols.

If entering or leaving France with more than €7600 in cash, it must
be declared to Customs.

Customs regulations

Non-EU citizens aged over 15 and spending less than 6 months in
France may be able to reclaim VAT (TVA in French) on any items
costing over €350 purchased for export. At the time of the purchase,
present your passport and ask for a *bordereau* form. On leaving France,
have the *bordereau* validated by French Customs.

For travellers returning to the UK and other EU countries there are no
restrictions, except that all goods brought back must be for personal
consumption and must be legal for private possession. In the UK, HM
Customs & Excise still maintain (unenforceable) limits on the amount
of alcoholic drinks and tobacco that will be considered reasonable 'for
personal use'. These propose up to 90 litres of wine, 10 litres of spirits
and 800 cigarettes. More information on: *www.hmce.gov.uk*

For visitors entering France there are no limits on legal articles for
ordinary personal use.

Drinking

In Provence, as elsewhere in France, drink plays a vital part in life, but
it is rare to see a local person drunk. The French usually drink to
enhance appetite, conversation and companionship. In any bar or
brasserie, not only alcoholic and soft drinks are served but also coffee
(including decaffeinated), hot chocolate, tea and herbal tea.

Drinks
de l'eau mineral – mineral water
gazeuese or *plat* – sparkling or still
bière – any name-brand German or Belgian beer
demi or *pression* – a glass of draught lager-style beer
café – espresso (the French keep going with frequent shots all day)
café crème (usually *grand crème*) – coffee with milk (the French
usually drink this only for breakfast)

Electricity

The power supply in France is 220 volts. Circular 2-pin plugs are used.

Entry formalities

Travellers from the USA, New Zealand and Canada do not need a visa for visits of less than 90 days. Australians and South Africans must apply for a visa from a French Embassy. UK and other EU members do not need a visa to travel in France.

déca – decaf
thé (nature, citron or *au lait)* – tea (black, with lemon, or with milk)
tissane – herb tea
chocolat chaud – hot chocolate
Miky – cold chocolate drink
pastis – a Provençal favourite: anis-flavoured spirit, served with a jug of iced water to mix
Suze, Noilly Prat, Dubonnet and *Martini* – popular brand-name aperitifs
Panaché – shandy: mixed beer and lemonade
Coca – Coca Cola
diabolo menthe (green) or *diabolo grenadine* (red) – lemonade mixed with brightly coloured syrup.
jus d'ananas, jus de poire – pineapple juice or pear juice are both popular
jus d'orange – bottled orange juice
orange pressé – freshly squeezed orange juice
Orangina – fizzy orange drink
sirop – fruit flavoured sweet drink served in either still or fizzy water
vin (rouge/blanc/rosé/doux/mousseux) wine – (red/white/rosé/sweet /sparkling). No need to ask for dry wine – it's all dry unless you specify sweet
pichet – carafe
See also Wines, page 36.

Eating out

Most French eating places offer a choice of about three *menus*, that is, *prix fixe* (fixed price) set meals and *à la carte*, a list of dishes individually priced. Typical *menu* prices might be €17, €25, €35. The variation in price doesn't reflect differences in quality but in the number of courses and difficulty of preparation. In general, to get the best out of a French restaurant, order one of the *menus*. Prices will usually be higher if you pick and choose from the *carte*. The day's menus are always displayed outside the restaurant.

Prices must include service and all taxes. It's not necessary to give any extra tip, though a few cents is often left for the waiter on a café table. *Vin compris* means wine included (usually about a quarter or third of a litre of house wine per person); *boisson comprise* suggests you may have some drink other than wine.

Away from resorts and big cities, it can be difficult to find something to eat outside normal mealtimes. The lunch break lasts from 1200 to about 1400. Sunday lunch, often taken *en famille* at a local restaurant, lasts until 1500. Dinner hours are a little more flexible, usually from 1900–2200, though 2000 is still the usual time to start. *Brasseries* are bars which generally serve food at any time. A *salon de thé* serves pastries and other light snacks with tea or coffee between meals.

Festivals

Major and minor festivals and *festins* (local celebrations, usually saints' days) take place all over Provence throughout the year. Highlights include:

Mid-Feb/mid-Mar: Lemon Festival, Menton

3rd Sun in Feb: Mimosa procession, Bormes-les-Mimosas

Shrove Tue: Carnival and Battle of the Flowers, Nice

May: Film Festival, Cannes

24–25 May: Gypsy Festival, Les Saintes-Maries-de-la-Mer

Jul: Opera and Music Festival, Aix

July: Drama, Dance and Music Festival, Avignon

July: Chorégies International Music Festival, Orange

Start of Aug: Lavender Procession, Digne

Sun nearest 22 Oct: Blessing of the Sea, Les Saintes-Maries-de-la-Mer

Food
(regional specialities)

See *Setting the scene, pages 36–7*.

Above
Celebrating the grape harvest in Grimaud

Health

It's usually possible to see a general practitioner without an appointment, or to phone to request a visit. For doctors, medicines and hospital treatment, payment must be made on the spot. Keep receipts – you will need them when claiming reimbursement, whether through Form E111 (available to UK citizens – instructions on the form and accompanying leaflet) or from your travel insurance.

Information

• **UK** *Maison de France (French Government Tourist Office), 178 Piccadilly, London W1V 0AL; tel: 0891 244123; fax: 020 7493 6594.*
• **Ireland** *Maison de France (French Government Tourist Office), 38 Lower Abbey Street, Dublin 1; tel: 1 703 4046; fax: 1 874 7324.*
• **USA** *Maisons de France (French Government Tourist Offices) 676 N. Michigan Avenue, Chicago, IL 60611-2819; fax: (312) 337-6339; 9454 Wilshire Boulevard, Suite 715, Beverly Hills, CA 90212-2967; fax: (310) 276-2835; 444 Madison Avenue, 16th Floor (between 49 and 50th Street), New York, NY 10022-6903; fax: (212) 838-7855.*
• **Australia** *Maison de France (French Government Tourist Office), BNP Building, 12 Castlereagh Street, Sydney, NSW 2000; tel: (61) 2 231 5244; fax: (61) 2 221 8682.*
• **Comités Régionaux du Tourisme (Regional Tourism Comittees) in Provence** *CRT Provence-Alpes-Côte d'Azur, Espace Colbert, 14 rue Sainte-Barbe, 13001 Marseille; tel: 04 91 39 38 00; CRT Riviera-Côte d'Azur, 55 Promenade des Anglais, 06011 Nice; tel: 04 93 37 78 78; Provence International – Maison du Tourisme, 2 rue Beauvau, 13001 Marseille; tel: 04 91 39 56 56; fax: 04 91 39 56 00; e-mail: pati@provencetourism.com*

Provence on the Web

www.beyond.fr Quirky personal tourist material gathered about everywhere behind the Riviera.

www.crt-paca.fr/eng/accueil_flash.jsp?LNGID=eng English-language pages on the official CRT website of the PACA (Provence-Alpes and Côte d'Azur) region.

www.focusguides.com/newsfrance.htm News, links and features.

www.info.france-usa.org Informative French Embassy site.

www.monaco-tourism.com 'Welcome to Monaco' site for visitors.

www.ambafrance-ca.org/english Interesting French Embassy site in Canada provides information, news, links.

www.provenceweb.fr The regional tourist office site.

Insurance

UK citizens should travel with Form E111 entitling reimbursement of part of any medical expenses incurred, as well as travel insurance covering medical emergencies. Other visitors are advised to have full medical cover as part of their travel insurance policy. It is compulsory for motorists to have third-party insurance (see *page 25*).

Maps

Tourist offices have free city and country maps printed in French and sometimes in English. City brochures usually have a map of the city printed inside. Michelin green maps 113 (Montpellier-Marseille), 114 (Côte d'Azur-Var) and 115 (Côte d'Azur-Alpes-Maritimes) cover all of Provence and the Côte d'Azur in detail. The annual Michelin motoring atlas is useful for touring in Provence and further afield. The Michelin *Atlas Autoroutier* (Motorway Atlas) is a handbook detailing facilities, junctions, etc, on the *autoroutes*. IGN regional maps are an alternative to Michelin, and IGN local large-scale maps are ideal for walking.

Museums

Basic opening times for most museums in the region are 0900–1200, 1400–1800, closed Mon or Tue and some national holidays, with many variations (sometimes with different opening times on different days and different months). Hours are often extended July–August.

National Parks and Regional Nature Parks

www.parcs-naturels-regionaux.tm.fr Website of the Fédération des Parcs Naturels Régionaux de France (French Regional Nature Parks).

The offices of the region's parks are:

Parc National du Mercantour *Head office: 23 rue d'Italie, Nice 06006; tel: 04 93 16 78 88; e-mail: mercantour.cpa@espaces-naturels.fr; www.parc-mercantour.com*

Information at the park: *Maison du Parc, Villa la Sapinière, Barcelonette; tel: 04 92 81 21 31.*

Parc Naturel Régional de Camargue *Mas du Pont de Rousty – Route des Stes-Maries de la Mer – 13200 Arles; tel: 04 90 97 10 40; fax: 04 90 97 12 07. Tourism information: tel: 04 90 97 86 32; e-mail: infos@biosfera.fr; www.biosfera.fr/camargue/camarweb/pnrchova.htm*

Parc Naturel Régional du Lubéron *60 place Jean Jaurès – BP 122 – 84404 Apt Cedex; tel: 04 90 04 42 00; fax: 04 90 04 81 15; e-mail: info@parc-du-luberon.com; www.parc-du-luberon.org*

Parc Naturel Régional du Verdon *Mairie – BP 14 – 04360 Moustiers-Ste-Marie; tel: 04 92 74 63 95; fax: 04 92 74 63 94; e-mail: info@parcduverdon.fr; www.parcduverdon.fr*

Left
The Picasso Museum, Antibes

Opening times

• **Shops:** typically Tue–Sat 0900–1200 or 1230, 1500–1900. Food shops may open earlier in the morning, but later in the afternoon, and some (especially *pâtisseries*) open on Sunday morning. In resorts, shops may keep longer hours and stay open all day, seven days a week.
• **Department stores:** Mon–Sat 0900–1830 (often with one or more later evenings per week).
• **Hypermarkets:** Mon–Sat 0900–2200.
• **Banks:** either Mon–Fri or Tue–Sat 0900–1200, 1400–1700, with local variations. Banks always close on local and national holidays.
• **Petrol stations:** usually daily around 0700–2200.
• **Post offices:** Mon–Fri 0800–1900, Sat 0800–1200. Stamps and envelopes can usually be bought from newsagents.
• **Tourist offices:** usually Mon–Sat 0900–1200, 1400–1800. Longer hours, and no midday closing, in season.
• **Businesses:** Mon–Fri 0900–1200, 1400–1800.
• **Bars:** 0700 or 0800 to 2300 or 2400. Some stay open later, especially in resorts.
• **Restaurants:** 1200–1400, 1900–2200. Most restaurants have one or more days off per week.
• **Churches:** usually daily 0900–1700.

Packing

Bring a hat, sunglasses, light clothes and cool footwear. If you're planning to visit up-market night spots, casinos or classical concerts, a smart dress, jacket or smart casual wear could be appropriate. Beachwear is never worn away from the beach. A light sweater is always useful as it can be cool even on summer evenings. In winter, take a thick sweater and coat.

Postal services

Postcards and letters are charged at the same rate for all EU destinations, with delivery within a few days. Stamps are available in newsagents and tobacconists. Airmail rates for letters to other destinations are much higher and items have to be weighed at a post office (indicated by a PTT sign). Letter boxes are yellow.

Reading

• *Travels in the South of France*, Stendhal – detailed if clinical observation of towns in the 1820s.
• *The Count of Monte Cristo*, Alexandre Dumas – a masterpiece of thrills, adventure and revenge, focused on the Château d'If prison and a Mediterranean island.

Public holidays

1 Jan – New Year's Day
Mar/Apr – Easter Monday
1 May – Labour Day
8 May – VE Day
May – Ascension
May/Jun – Pentecost
(Whit Monday)
14 Jul – National Day
(France only)
15 Aug – Assumption
1 Nov – All Saints
11 Nov – Armistice Day
25 Dec – Christmas

Where national holidays
fall on a Sunday, the next
day is taken as a holiday
instead.

Public transport

Town buses – called *bus*,
they are available in all
cities from about
0700–2100.

Trains – useful for
excursions, the coastal line
offers spectacular views,
with stations at all towns.
Similar useful and scenic
rail services are the
Digne–Nice line and
Nice–Tende line.

Ferries – frequent ferries
link offshore islands to the
nearest mainland harbours.
For the Iles d'Or
(Porquerolles, Port Cros,
Ile de Levant) depart from
Cavalaire, le Lavandou,
Port d'Hyères or Toulon.

- *Tender is the Night*, F Scott Fitzgerald – fashionable, wealthy Americans having a bad time on the Riviera during the 1920s.
- *Lettres de mon Moulin*, Alphonse Daudet – cult reading in France, the 'letters' from the windmill near les Baux de Provence are insightful, sometimes amusing, sometimes poignant accounts of Provençal life in the 1860s.
- *Jean de Florette* and *Manon des Sources*, Marcel Pagnol – evocative Provençal peasant dramas which became classic films.
- *J'Accuse*, Graham Greene – exposé of the organised crime and political corruption in Nice.
- *Monsieur, Livia, Constance, Sebastian and Quinx*, five books by Lawrence Durrell – collectively called the Quincunx or Avignon Quintet. Set in and around Avignon during the Nazi occupation.
- *Bonjour Tristesse*, Françoise Sagan – the teenage author's bestseller about the Esterel coast in the 1950s.
- *Aspects of Provence*, James Pope-Hennessy – a personal look at the region by a cultured traveller in the 1950s.
- *A Year in Provence*, Peter Mayle – about second-homers in the Lubéron, followed by similar sequels.

Sport

- **Bullfighting** – two types, *corrida* (Spanish) and *course à la cocarde* (Provençal), are both wildly popular among locals indifferent to the small matter of cruelty to animals, especially in the Camargue, Nîmes and Arles.
- **Cycling** – locals like it, so do visitors, and the Tour de France attracts huge crowds as it passes through the region every July.
- **Diving** – for both scuba and skin-diving, the Riviera is popular, especially off the *calanques* and islands between Hyères and Marseille.
- **Golf** – there are many excellent golf courses on the Côte d'Azur and a short distance inland. Among the best is the Royal Mougins, at Mougins, near Cannes.
- **Motor Racing** – the Monte Carlo Rally (Jan) and the Monaco Grand Prix (May) are highlights of the spectator sporting calendar.
- **Pétanque** – emblematic of Provençal life, it's the favourite game of local men (women rarely play it), and resembles a sort of casual bowls played with small shiny metal balls on any dusty piece of flat ground in the shade. Rules are simple, but playing it is tricky.
- **Riding** – ride a white horse – it's the speciality of the Camargue.
- **Rock-climbing** – in the river gorges and on coastal cliffs, especially the Grand Canyon du Verdon and the *calanques* near Marseille.
- **Skiing** – in Provence? Yes, there are ski resorts in the Provence Alps, not an hour away from the Riviera, notably Isola 2000.
- **Watersports** – the region's major sporting activity with sailing on lakes, canoeing on the rivers, and sailing or windsurfing at the coast. All waterside resorts have facilities for equipment hire and tuition.

Safety and security

Crime is soaring in Nice and Marseille, where it is best to remain in the main tourist areas. The other towns and rural areas included here are generally very safe. However, it is wise to take certain precautions: do not wear ostentatious jewellery, openly handle large sums of cash, or leave anything of value on view in cars. To call Police, dial 17.

Tipping

Restaurants – included, not necessary
Bars – included, not necessary, but a few cents is normal
Taxis – €1
Hotels, room service – included, not necessary
Tour guides – €1
Toilet attendants – 20 cents

Toilets

Usually called *WC* (pronounced Veh-Seh) or *Toilettes*. Free or small charge in bars. Small charge for attended public toilets, no charge if not attended. Many are automatic self-cleaning, charging 20 cents (these can be dangerous for children).

Telephones

With few exceptions, public phones require a pre-paid phone card (available from newsagents and other shops).
Directory enquiries: 12; Operator: 13.

To call the UK from France, the international dialling code is 00 44. The code for Australia is 00 61, USA and Canada 00 1, New Zealand 00 64. Calling from the UK or any other country, the code for France is 00 33.

Time

France observes Central European Standard Time and Central European Daylight Saving Time. These are one hour ahead of GMT and 5 hours ahead of US Eastern Standard Time throughout the year. French Daylight Saving Time ('Summer Time') starts at 0200 on the last Sunday in March and ends at 0300 on the last Sunday in October.

Travellers with disabilities

For parking, the orange card scheme applies in France. Vehicles modified for a disabled driver and showing 'disabled' on the registration document are entitled to lower *autoroute* tolls.

Accessibility information for tourists is available from: **Association des Paralysés de France**, 17 blvd Auguste Blanqui, 75013 Paris; *tel: 01 40 78 69 00*.
CNFLRH, 236bis rue de Tolbiac, 75013 Paris; *tel: 01 53 80 66 66*.
RADAR, 12 City Forum, 250 City Road, London EC1V 8AF; *tel: 020 7250 3222*.

Wine tasting

Touring in wine country, you'll see signs at the Cave Coopérative (local communal winery), at vineyard gates, or at the end of their access roads, offering *dégustation* or tasting. Take them up on it. It's usually free of charge, and is an opportunity to taste several varieties. You don't need to be a wine expert, and there's no obligation to buy – though it may be polite to buy at least one bottle after a tasting session.

Driver's guide

Breakdowns

Hazard warning lights are compulsory (or a warning triangle – motoring organisations recommend you to have both). On *autoroutes*, use the emergency phones provided; an approved recovery vehicle will be sent and a fixed fee charged (around €70). On other roads, members of motoring organisations with European cover should contact their emergency phone number. Those without European cover should simply make contact with a local garage.

Car hire

Car hire is very widely available all over France from both major international and local firms. Prices are generally higher than in other countries. Do-it-yourself car hire is much more expensive than taking it as part of a package.

Documents

Insurance and car registration papers, and a driving licence must always be carried when driving. A full UK or other western European or US driving licence is accepted. The minimum driving age for a car or motorcycle is 18.

Accidents

If you have an accident you must stop the vehicle immediately but with minimum obstruction to traffic. If anyone has been injured, or either party is under the influence of alcohol, the police must be called. French motorists will probably complete a *constat* (an insurance form verifying the facts) and all parties must sign to show that it is an accurate account. Non-French motorists should simply exchange details with the other parties.

It's worth knowing that if a motor accident involves a pedestrian under 16 or over 70, or a severely disabled person, they cannot be held responsible for the accident.

If the accident is due to a bad road surface or faulty traffic light, a claim may be made against the Ponts et Chaussées authority.

A hitch-hiker may claim against his driver even if he or she is not responsible for the accident.

Caravans and camper vans

On hills, watch out for signs applying a lower speed limit for caravans. Before setting out, check that brake and other cables to the caravan are firmly in place and correctly adjusted, and that caravan tyres are of the same size and type and in sound condition. The make and serial number of a caravan must be clearly displayed. Remember that stopping overnight in a caravan or camper van is only permitted at campsites or other authorised locations. This is strictly applied in Provence, where equipment is liable to peremptory confiscation. Caravans and camper vans are not allowed to stop at all in Monaco, even during the day.

Driving conditions

Motorways (A) are called *autoroutes* in French – they are of high standard, with frequent service stations where food and sometimes accommodation is available. Main roads (N or RN) are called *routes nationales*. Secondary roads (D) are called *routes départementales:* the extensive network of clearly marked, straight, well-maintained D roads in France makes it easy to avoid busy main highways.

Main highways are generally well maintained and of high standard and are kept clear in snowy weather. Roads in town may be of poor standard, and are often cobbled. While locals may ignore cobbles and drive normally over them, it would be wiser to protect your car's suspension by driving gently on cobbled streets. Some country lanes,

Drinking and driving laws

In France the maximum legal level of alcohol in the blood is 0.05 per cent. Depending on the amount of excess, penalties range from on-the-spot fines, impounding the vehicle, confiscation of driving licence, etc, up to prison sentences of varying severity.

Fuel

Regular unleaded (*essence sans plomb*), high-octane unleaded (*super sans plomb*) and diesel (*gasoil or diesel*) are all widely available. Leaded petrol is hard to find.
Credit cards are widely accepted at petrol stations, but not universally; be sure to know your PIN number as customers are sometimes required to 'verify' the card by tapping in their PIN on a keypad. Traveller's cheques cannot usually be used to pay for petrol.

Insurance

Third-party insurance is compulsory.
Comprehensive insurance issued by UK insurers is valid in the EU (a Green Card is no longer required, though a few insurers still wish to be informed that you are going abroad).

too, may be of poor standard. In summer, *autoroutes* in Provence are notorious for dense traffic and jams. Roadside panels warn of dates to avoid because exceptionally heavy traffic is expected.

It's important to understand the *priorité à droite* rule, the main cause of accidents involving foreign drivers in France. The rule is this: drive on the right and always give way to anything approaching from the right, except where signs indicate to the contrary. There is one other exception: vehicles emerging from private property don't have priority over traffic on the public highway.

Be especially careful where two major highways merge – watch for priority signs, and in towns, where traffic coming from side roads on your right will effectively drive out as if it has a 'green light' even if you are on the main road.

Most roundabouts now give priority to vehicles already on the roundabout (as in the UK). On approaching these roundabouts you will see signs *Vous n'avez pas la priorité* and/or *Cédez le passage*. If there are no such signs, the usual priority rule applies, so traffic already on the roundabout has to give way to traffic entering it. Remember to go round the roundabout in an anticlockwise direction.

Right
Mont Ste-Victoire

Lights

Dipped lights and main beam must be adjusted to avoid dazzling oncoming drivers when driving on the right. Dipped lights must also be used in rain and poor visibility as well as after dark. Motorcycles over 125cc must use a dipped headlight at all times.

Parking

In town centres, cars parked in no-parking zones are generally quickly towed away without warning. Kerbside signs always make it clear what the parking regulations are in each street.

Speed limits

Speed limits reflect road conditions, and variable limits are used on some busy roads, so watch signs. In normal circumstances, limits are generally 50kph (31mph) in town, 90kph (55mph) out of town. The limit is generally 110kph (68mph) on dual carriageways, and 130kph (80mph) on motorways (sometimes lower on toll-free motorways). Motorways often have a minimum fast lane speed limit of 80kph (49mph). Signs sometimes indicate lower speed limits for wet weather or fog, and new drivers (first two years) must also keep to limits about 10kph lower than indicated.

Information

Bison Futé provides traffic information and organises alternative routes (Routes Bis) to avoid congestion. It publishes an annual map, available free from tourist offices and some gas stations.

- For Bison Futé's up-to-the-minute traffic information, *tel: 08 26 022 022* (20 cents/minute).
- Visit *www.bison-fute.equipement.gouv.fr* and click on the map for regional traffic news.
- For RAC Motoring Advice in the UK, *tel: 0906 4701 740.*

Police

Law enforcement in France is perfunctory and severe. Most minor offences, including speeding, not stopping at a Stop sign, overtaking where forbidden and not wearing a seat belt, are punishable by an immediate on-the-spot fine of around £100. Issuing a receipt is part of the on-the-spot procedure – always be sure to get one, and keep it carefully. More serious motoring offences such as drink-driving are liable to impounding of the car, heavy fines, or imprisonment.

Seat belts

Seat belts must be worn at all times in both the front and back of the car, except in older vehicles which do not have seat belts fitted. Children under 10 are not allowed to travel in the front seats (except for babies up to 9 months weighing under 9kg and seated in a rear-facing baby seat). Even in rear seats, all children must use seat belts. NB: Although children over a certain age may travel in the front of a car, remember that airbags can kill a child or small adult.

Security

Ensure tyres are in good condition and properly inflated – worn tyres can incur on-the-spot fines. Motorcyclists must wear a helmet. Spectacle wearers are advised to carry a spare set. It is also wise to carry spare bulbs for the lights. Take extra care when overtaking – driving on the right with a right-hand drive makes it difficult to see oncoming traffic. Crime is not a big problem in Provence, except in Nice and Marseille, but it's a wise precaution everywhere to put all valuables out of sight when leaving your car parked.

Tolls

Tolls are levied on most *autoroutes*, except by-passing large cities. They are especially high in the Côte d'Azur region, particularly for short hops. Credit cards can be used to pay motorway tolls; signatures are not normally required. Traveller's cheques cannot usually be used for tolls.

Getting to Provence and the Côte d'Azur

From the UK

Option one: Just get in your car and go. Dozens of operators cross the Channel each day and *autoroutes* (motorways) run direct from the ferry terminals. The 1200-km drive to the Riviera takes under 12 hours. This works well in low season, but from May to October you're likely to have trouble finding hotel accommodation 'on spec'. It's also far from being the cheapest way to go.

Option two: Book a self-drive package holiday. Highly available and good value for money, all packages include Channel crossings and accommodation (whether hotel, self-catering, or camping in pre-erected tents) in Provence. Some include hotel stops *en route*. The cheapest packages may use poor-quality campsites in unattractive areas, while the most expensive put you up in good hotels on the Côte d'Azur. Before you book, look carefully at a regional map to be clear which resorts are offered, where they are and what they are like. When reading brochures you will see that many of the locations are far from the sea. Several companies, for example, offer 'Côte d'Azur' accommodation at Ste-Anastasie-sur-Issole, a village 48km inland from the less interesting stretch of coast at Toulon and Hyères. However, a short drive inland, of say 10km, is worthwhile as it allows you to choose lower-priced accommodation while remaining within easy reach of the beaches.

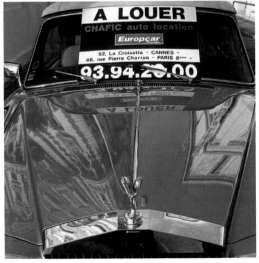

Below
Rolls Royce for hire in Cannes

Option three: Fly-drive or Rail-drive. Whether with a package or booked independently, there are frequent flights to Nice from London and British regional airports. Nice is about 2 hours' flying time from London. Car hire from major international and local companies is available at the airport. It's also possible to travel by rail (Eurostar to Paris, TGV to Marseille and the Riviera, or overnight sleeper to Nice) and hire a car on arrival.

From other regions of France

Autoroute A7 and *route nationale* N7 follow the Rhône from Lyon to Orange. The N7 continues into Provence via Aix-en-Provence to Cannes and Nice. The A7 terminates at Marseille and connects with the A8 and other *autoroutes* for the Riviera.

Motorail and AutoTrain travel to Provence and the Riviera

Travel by train but take your car. Overnight Motorail allows you to travel with your car direct from Calais to Avignon (12½ hours) or Nice (14½ hours). Passengers travel in first- or second-class sleeping compartments, while the cars ride on vehicle transporters at the end of the train. Sleeping accommodation on board in all classes is bunk-bed style.

Note that while Motorail journey times may be longer than driving, especially when the lengthy check-in and collection procedures are taken into account, it still saves time – because most of the travelling is done while you're asleep. Motorail is also much more expensive than driving, but there's a saving on en route hotels, *autoroute* tolls and other driving expenses, and Motorail passengers also benefit from cheaper Channel crossings. The greatest advantage of Motorail is that the rail journey is much less stressful than the long drive. It is especially useful for those with children. Motorail is also available to Provence from Paris and Lille.

AutoTrain is another option from Paris and Lille allowing passenger travel by ordinary rail services (including TGV) during the day while cars travel on a separate train. For information and bookings from Rail Europe, *tel: 08705 848 848*.

From outside Europe

There are seasonal direct charter flights to Nice and Marseille from the US and Canada – any local travel agent can advise what is available during the times you wish to travel. A cheaper and more flexible option could be to fly via Paris. There are frequent direct scheduled flights to Paris from over 30 North American cities, and good internal connections from Paris to Nice and Marseille. From Australia and New Zealand, you'll have to fly to Paris.

Above
Nice and the French Riviera

AUTOROUTE GUIDE: DRIVING FROM THE UK

There are services/stops every 10km; those noted here are some of the best.

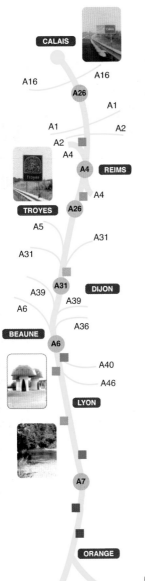

CALAIS

A16

A16

A26

A1

A1

A2

A2

A2

A4

A4

REIMS

A4

TROYES

A26

A5

A31

A31

A31

DIJON

A39

A39

A6

A36

BEAUNE

A6

A40

A46

LYON

A7

ORANGE

AVIGNON

A7

AIX-EN-PROVENCE

A9

A51

A52

A7

MEDITERRANEAN

MARSEILLE

MEDITERRANEAN

Not to scale

Service Station 'Mont de Nizy'
Total petrol service station. LPG. Disabled toilet, flush toilets in shop complex. Vehicle repairs undertaken on site. Restaurant and café bar area. Climbing frames for children. Large area for caravans. Shaded picnic and small BBQ areas.

Service Station 'Sommesous'
Serves both north and southbound routes. Shell petrol services. LPG. Shop sales include hot and cold snacks. Mirabellier restaurant. Café facilities. Pinball games room. Designated TV and rest area. Vehicle repairs and tyre pressure check area. Gendarmerie base.

Service Station 'Langres-Perrogney'
Avia petrol services. LPG. Hot and cold food in service area. Outside snack hut. Restaurant. Large grassed area at back, with shaded picnic areas.

Service Station 'Beaune-Tailly'
Very large Total petrol services. LPG. Large designated areas for cars and caravans. Vehicle repairs on site. Tourist info. No designated play area, but space for children. Hotel, restaurant and café bar. A major stop-over site.

Picnic Area 'Jugy'
Look out for the child-size models of pixies and elves along the autoroute advertising Jugy. Picnic area and large children's play area. Non-flush toilets (except disabled). Large area for caravans.

Picnic Area 'Auberives'
Restful and pretty. Lots of picnic tables and seating under trees. Children's play areas with slides and ropes to climb. Outside mist shower. Non-flush toilets (except disabled). Slow-running stream, shallow enough to walk in, at the back of the area.

Service Station 'St Rambert'd'Albon'
Large Total service station serving both north and southbound routes. LPG. Large selection of hot and cold snacks. Restaurant with outside seating by a small lake. Café bars. Hotel. Mist showers. Basketball practice area. Tourist info centre. A major stop-over area.

APPROXIMATE DISTANCES AND TRAVELLING TIMES

CALAIS TO REIMS
300km – 2hrs 35mins

REIMS TO TROYES
125km – 1hr 15mins

TROYES TO DIJON
150km – 1hr 20mins

DIJON TO BEAUNE
50km – 35mins

BEAUNE TO LYON
200km – 1hr 45mins

LYON TO ORANGE
200km – 2hrs

ORANGE TO NICE
275km – 2hrs 40mins

Picnic Area 'La Coucourde'
Very pleasant shaded picnic area with nice views to east and west. Viewing gallery has been constructed in the shape of a pyramid. Outside mist showers. Non-flush toilets (except disabled). No designated play areas but lots of room.

Service Station 'Montélimar'
Large Elf service station. LPG. Serves both north and southbound routes. Hotel, restaurants and outside snack huts and grills. Tourist info. Good range of children's play areas, including climbing walls for all ages.

AUTOROUTE RADIO 107.7FM

Above
Menton

Setting the scene

The French Riviera

In the 19th century, Britain's aristocrats used to dash to the French Riviera at the drop of a hat. They went in winter rather than summer, and only east of Cannes, later known as the Côte d'Azur, which in those days was part of Italy. The Riviera (an Italian word) is still a favourite haunt of celebrities and the super-rich, and coastal towns such as Nice, Cannes, Monaco and Menton retain a lot of their cachet. It's thrilling to stroll along proms lined with palm and mimosa and admire the lavish 19th-century hotels. There's a good chance of spotting famous – or notorious – personalities. These towns have first-class shops for quality fashions and accessories, and some excellent restaurants. Most also have world-class art museums. But along this classier stretch the beaches are surprisingly poor, or else cordoned off into private areas which you have to pay to use. The beach at Nice, for example, is all stones, yet sunbathers swarm to it. West of Cannes, there's newer money, less grandeur, more sand on the beach. Beaches on the St-Tropez Peninsula attract image-conscious youth, but further west there are popular, down-to-earth family resorts with excellent beaches, good facilities and no pretences. Don't bother to bring your bikini top, by the way – you won't need it.

The cities of Provence

Provence is soaked in history. Medieval conflicts and religious wars have made their mark everywhere. Its cities are mainly Roman in origin, some (such as Marseille) even older. Today, although antiquities and ruins are proudly preserved and form the focal point of much of the tourism, the real appeal has little to do with that long and illustrious past. Instead, it's the civilised *joie de vivre*, the joyous street life, the air of knowing what life's about and how to enjoy it, that are the hallmarks of the city centres of Provence. True, all the big towns have their squalid, disreputable districts, dull commercial zones and off-putting neighbourhoods devoted to cheap apartments whose residents have a different perspective on life in Provence, yet in the heart of each city there is an extraordinary sense of well-being. To enjoy it, all you need to do is sit over a *pastis* or *café* at an outdoor table, in the shade of a leafy tree, relax in the balmy air and watch the world pass by.

Inland Provence

The heartland of Provence remains astonishingly tranquil and unvisited. The wild landscapes, dramatic hills and gorges, terraced hills, vineyards and fields of lavender, copses of parasol pine, ancient silent villages and medieval towns, seem to defy change. The young and the old gather on corners to talk in the open air, as they have always done, in ringing southern accents echoing the past. The church bell rings the time twice, in the southern manner. The flat, wide head of the *chardon* thistle is nailed to doors for luck, and to predict the weather. This year may bring a good harvest, or a bad. Roads have been improved and rivers tamed, and the standard of living raised. Sprinkled across the whole region there are tourist centres and attractions which draw the crowds, but even they usually remain unspoiled by their popularity, and aware of some lingering, enduring quality in the land, something timeless in the air.

Who goes?

To the Côte d'Azur, anyone who is anyone, and everyone else as well. Visitors include not only British, Germans, Americans, Italians and Scandinavians, but also, in high season, millions of French people from all over the country. It's extremely cosmopolitan, appealing to people of all budgets. However, the Riviera west of Cannes, apart from St-Tropez, is not quite so well known around the world and attracts a less flashy crowd, including a lot of Britons, Dutch and Germans. The area west of Toulon is even less visited by foreigners, but is busy with French holiday-makers.

The season

In July and August it's hot, beaches are packed, prices hiked up and traffic is terrible on all roads large and small. But that may be worth putting up with – it's sunny and there's a party atmosphere in all the resorts. Everything is open. Those high summer months are soporifically warm even in the inland hills. In the 19th century, people only came in winter. With air travel to more reliable (and warmer) winter sun destinations, the Riviera has lost its appeal for winter holidays, yet a short out-of-season break on the Côte d'Azur can be delightful, especially in the balmy, flowery springtime. Western Provence suffers most from the *Mistral* wind (*see Climate, page 15*).

The further east you go, the milder and more sheltered the winter climate. Menton, near the Italian border, is especially noted for pleasant winter weather. By contrast, the higher ground in the Provence interior can be cold in winter, and there are chic ski resorts in the Provençal Alps. Best time of all – both on the coast and in the interior – is slightly out of season, in May and June, and then early September, when the weather can be exquisite, there are fewer visitors, and prices are more reasonable.

Artistic Provence

Something in the light, perhaps, something in the air, the landscapes, the colour of Provence, or simply that it was a nice place to live and work, brought many – or even most – of the 20th century's greatest artists to the region. Impressionists, having first associated themselves with the hazy, pearly light of Normandy, moved to Provence. Here Pierre-Auguste Renoir stayed, and Gauguin, Henri Matisse and Dufy, whose images of Nice have become iconic. Vincent van Gogh is particularly associated with Arles and St-Rémy, Pablo Picasso with Vallauris and Vauvenargues, Fernand Léger with Biot, Paul Cézanne (lucky enough to have been brought up here) with Aix-en-Provence. Marc Chagall settled in St-Paul-de-Vence after World War II, and Jean Cocteau came to Menton, on the Côte d'Azur. Part of the complex legacy left to Provence by these painters has been the setting up in this region of several of the world's leading art museums.

Writers of the 19th and 20th centuries, maybe for some of the same reasons, have also gathered in Provence and along the Riviera. They are almost too numerous to list, but include Friedrich Nietzsche, Thomas Mann, Albert Camus, Alphonse Daudet, Marcel Pagnol, Françoise Sagan, Emile Zola, Victor Hugo, Colette and countless English-language authors including Anthony Burgess, Graham Greene, Lawrence Durrell, Ernest Hemingway, Aldous Huxley, D H Lawrence, Scott Fitzgerald and James Baldwin.

The Provençal language

The language of the South, *langue d'oc* or Provençal, started life as Latin – in other words it was one of the Romance languages (the others were Italian, Spanish, Catalan, French, Portuguese, Romanian and Swiss Romansch). It differed from French, but, as with all the Romance group, there were similarities. One difference was in the word for 'yes'. Romans, having no word for 'yes', would say *Hoc Ille* (literally, 'this that'). In the north of France, this became *oïl* or *oui*, while in the South it became *oc*. So it was that the French coined the name *langue d'oc* for the southern language.

From the 11th to 13th centuries, the troubadours – lordly wandering southern entertainers – brought about a great age of fine Provençal literature. They composed elaborate, elegant poems about love and chivalry, and travelled from castle to castle reciting their works. After the Albigensian Crusade, the destruction of the southern nobility and the take-over of the South by the northern French, literary Provençal went into decline. However, even after 1539 when French was made the official language of the South, Provençal remained the everyday speech. Only in the 19th century, when children were prohibited from talking Provençal at school (a law repealed only in 1951), did the southern language die. At the same time, Frédéric Mistral's *Félibrige* movement attempted to revive Provençal as a medium for literature. Although the movement had little lasting impact on the arts, it did lead briefly to some good writing in the southern language, the best of it by Mistral himself. In 1904, Mistral won the Nobel Prize for Literature for his Provençal poem *Miréio*. Mistral failed to save the southern language, although it is taught at Montpellier University and often seen in renamed street signs and regionalist graffiti. Provençal survives now only as a *patois* (which is what its speakers call it) in rural corners of Languedoc but not in Provence. Only the strong *accent du Midi*, the local accent with its distinctive ringing emphasis, is a last reminder of the old language of the South.

Opposite
Juan-les-Pins

Right
Cap de Nice hotels

Where to stay
Provence and the Riviera divides into several areas, each with its own character (which comes largely from the countryside lying just inland). From Cannes eastwards is the true Côte d'Azur, the 'old Riviera', which still has plenty of glamour but is pricey and not ideal for lazing on the sand. It's backed by dramatic mountains that plunge down towards the Mediterranean. West from Cannes are newer resorts, some very fashionable and exclusive, others less so, usually with better beaches. Inland, there are fragrant hills and villages to explore a short distance from the coast. Beyond Toulon, coast and country are more urban, have less charm, and correspondingly lower prices.

Choose your area carefully when it comes to selecting accommodation. In areas with plenty of luxury and highlife, it's the unglitzy middle-range hotels and restaurants which are often slipshod and overpriced, There's plenty of self-catering, but that, too, if near the coast, is usually expensive. Instead, consider staying further inland, where all prices are much lower. For the best value of all, stay on one of the many high-quality campsites. Most are a short distance inland, though a few have their tent-pegs right on the beach. Campsites should also be chosen with care though, as the cheapest have nothing to recommend them.

Snacks, treats, self-catering – and where to buy a picnic

An *alimentation* is a general grocery, for food, wine and all other drinks (there are almost no off-licences/liquor stores). They are often arranged as a 'mini-supermarket' with *libre-service* (self-service).

Supermarché usually means nothing more than a big *alimentation*, but the huge out-of-town *hypermarchés* are open long hours, sell just about everything at good prices and often have a cheap and popular self-service cafeteria as well.

Except in emergencies, buy bread only at a *boulangerie*, where it is freshly baked on the premises twice a day. There will be a selection of white breads and rolls, *pain complet* (wholemeal) and *pain de siègle* (rye). Most have morning croissants and *pain chocolat*. Note that a *dépôt de pain* sells bread but does not bake it; theirs is usually factory-made. A *pâtisserie*, literally a pastry-cook's, has better croissants, a selection of delicious little pastries and ice-cream, everything being made on the premises by a qualified *pâtissier*. Instead of making British or American-style cakes and cream-filled pastries, they make light pastries with delicious fillings or toppings, and rarely if ever use fresh cream.

In all cities, most towns and even villages, skilled speciality confectioners called *chocolatiers* or *confiseurs* make high-quality chocolates on the premises. They also make other sweets, often including some local speciality. Ice-cream shops, called *glaciers*, make delicious fresh ice-cream, but they often only have three flavours (vanilla, chocolate or strawberry).

Boucherie means butcher's, or *boucherie chevaline* if it sells horse meat. A boon for picnics, a *charcuterie* (properly a pork butcher's) , sells a wide variety of cooked meats and other prepared foods, including salads. A *traiteur* is like a delicatessen, again with plenty of prepared meats.

The ordinary town or village *marché*, market, consists mainly of stalls selling fresh fruit and vegetables; traders' vans with dozens of cheeses, big rounds of butter, cold meats and *charcuterie*; other stalls with goats' cheese, cakes, honey, perhaps chickens alive or dead. Larger markets have traders selling work-clothes, fabrics, household goods, excellent kitchenware, freshly gathered herbs, dried fruit and nuts, and much more. You'll rarely see a fishmonger, *poissonnier*, except in markets. Common in rural areas is the travelling general stores van which turns up at the village once or twice a week.

What to expect on a 4-star Riviera campsite

By far the cheapest way to stay on the Riviera is to camp. It's possible to book independently, but almost everyone on a French Med campsite has come on pre-booked packages. Nearly all stay in top-quality family tents with two or three bedrooms, a kitchen area and a big awning to provide shade. Campsites usually set aside a section for mobile homes (despite the name, these are permanently in place), which are a clean, comfortable and efficient, if miniaturised, home-from-home. Park the car adjacent to your tent or mobile home.

Wines

There's no shortage of palatable wines in Provence. Few are made in the backcountry of the Côte d'Azur east of Cannes, because it's all mountains (though one curiosity is vin de Bellet, produced and sold around St-Romain-de-Bellet, near Nice). West of Cannes there's an important wine area, producing inexpensive Côtes de Provence table wines, notably rosé, at its best served chilled with fish dishes. Some good local reds come from west of Toulon, although Cassis, in that area, is known for its white wines. Plenty of high-quality wine comes from further inland and further west, such as the rosé from Tavel, fortified sweet Muscat wines from Beaumes de Venise and Lunel, and first-rank reds such as Côte du Rhône, Gigondas and Châteauneuf du Pape.

Most 4-star sites reach an extremely high standard – though those right beside the beach tend to attract a rowdier late-night crowd. As even the best are not expensive, there's no point in economising. The top sites have a park-like appearance, with trees and greenery; clean, well-equipped toilets, washing and shower blocks; at least one self-service supermarket; a decent snack-bar or restaurant for continental breakfast or a simple three-course meal with wine; and amenities such as tennis courts, laundry, games room and TV room. All the better Riviera campsites have a large well-maintained swimming-pool; many have a children's playground, and almost all provide children's clubs.

Most Riviera sites have *animation* – organised leisure activities and entertainment, including children's shows, excursions to local vineyards, teenage dances, karaoke, night-clubs, *boules* tournaments, etc. These are either free or available for a small fee. Evening entertainment can be noisy, but at many sites is provided only in July and August, which could be factors in choosing a site or a date.

Tents or mobile home emplacements are smaller than elsewhere in France but still adequate. All have electricity and drainage. On arrival at the site a courier will conduct you to your tent or mobile home and explain the site facilities. Several package operators provide a big playbox full of toys for young children, but this must be booked in advance.

Eating and drinking in Provence

Abundant olive oil, garlic and aromatic wild herbs from the Provençal hills – thyme, basil, sage, tarragon, rosemary, fennel – are the hallmarks of cooking in this sunlit southern countryside. Mediterranean vegetables such as aubergines, peppers and big juicy tomatoes are generously used, along with many varieties of river and sea fish. Succulent, highly seasoned stews – meats, fish or vegetable – are the region's favourite dishes. Among vegetable dishes, **ratatouille** (a highly seasoned stew of Provençal vegetables) stands out, while **tian** is any vegetable fried and baked in layers with plenty of oil. Even more commonly seen are the rich and spicy slow-cooked fish stews such as **bouillabaisse** or **bourride** whose ingredients must be fussily correct. The capital of *bouillabaisse* (pronounced 'bweeabaize') is the Marseille area, where it has almost a cult following. **Brandade de morue** is another curious local dish, of salt cod cooked and pounded with oil, cream and garlic. Not just fish, but beef or lamb **en daube** (seasoned and slowly cooked in rich stew) feature often on Provençal menus.

Towards Nice, salads are more popular. **Salad niçoise** has anchovy and tuna in it. Almost alone among French regions, Provence has several traditional snack dishes: look out especially for the Riviera's favourite sandwich, called **pan bagna**. Literally 'soaked bread', it's basically a roll filled with salad niçoise. The area also has its own traditional version of pizza (the area east of Nice was in Italy at one time), called **pissaladière**, a simple pie base with a stewed onion and

Tourist offices

Local tourist offices are called variously *Office de (or du) Tourisme*; *Bureau de (or du) Toursime*; *Syndicat d'Initiative*; or *OTSI* (stands for *Office du Tourisme/Syndicat d'Initiative*). In this book, for clarity, we call them all Tourist Office. Opening hours are generally Mon–Sat 0900–1200, 1400–1800, with longer hours in July and August.

anchovy topping. The Italian influence appears again in *pistou*, which is the same as Italian pesto – a sauce of basil, olive oil, garlic and cheese. The Riviera's *soupe au pistou* is rather like minestrone: noodle soup strongly flavoured with pistou. Provence has other typical piquant sauces, especially *aïoli* (garlic mayonnaise), which are found in numerous dishes, and the delicious *tapenade* (a pâté of black olives, anchovies and capers). Fruits are top quality too – in season, the markets are loaded with the delicious local peaches, green figs, strawberries and cherries. Milk products are not seen so much, except in the ubiquitous home-made ice-creams, though there are a few rustic Provençal cheeses. Small disc-shaped sheep's and goats' cheeses, particularly *Banon* which is wrapped in chestnut leaves, are made by farmers and sold in country markets.

Where and what to buy

Buy from source (at low prices) perfume from Grasse, candied fruit from Apt, olives from Nyons, modern faience from Moustiers and artistic glassware from Biot, olive oil from the Alpilles or lavender from Sénanque abbey. Everywhere look out for bright, colourful Provençal fabrics, table linen, silk scarves and chic summer fashions from Nice, Cannes or any of the well-to-do big towns. In markets find plaited strings of garlic to hang in the kitchen, local olive oil, herbs, truffles and sometimes jars of gourmet conserves such as *rouille* (a spicy pepper paste to accompany soup), nut pâtés, *aïoli*, or the fish dish *brandade de morue*. In *boulangeries* and *confiseries* you'll find local speciality sweets, usually attractively packaged, such as the tasty glazed almond sweets called *calissons* from Aix, or more widely available *marrons glacés*, crystallised chestnuts.

Local crafts include distinctive objects carved from local olive wood. For fine pottery and decorative garden pots (if there's space for them in the car) stop at the many big roadside outlets selling these at low prices. The Provençal speciality of *santons* or *santouns* – traditional carved nativity scenes with figurines of biblical personages and typical Provençal characters assembled round the crib – are of interest both to the serious collector of folk art and to the visitor searching for an interesting present. The best place to buy them is Aubagne, near Marseille.

Provence for less

• Go in May or June – the weather's usually perfect, beaches and sights less crowded, prices lower.
• If you're aiming for a beach holiday, stay 5km inland – it's less hectic, with better value for money.
• Stay west of Cannes – better beaches, more sightseeing, lower prices. Consider making city excursions by train – rail fares are low, and it's a good way to avoid jams.
• A pre-booked camping package in the most economical way to visit Provence.

Next page
Arles cathedral cloister

Touring itineraries

Best routes for

Beaches

Camargue – Plage de l'Espiguette, at the western edge, is best for space, solitude and stripping off.

Cannes to Nice – private beaches at the end of the Cap d'Antibes are sandy, and best for a luxurious waterside meal.

Marseille – best waterfront for watersports.

Nice – stony and backed by traffic, but still beautiful after all these years.

Hyères and the Iles d'Or – cross to the islands for sun, sand and solitude.

L'Esterel – Fréjus beach is supervised, sandy and safe, and one of the best family beaches.

Les Maures – family resorts with good beaches at either end of the Corniches des Maures.

Riviera Corniches – some good beaches, mostly sedate, civilised and best for winter warmth.

St-Tropez Peninsula – sexy, sandy haunt of beautiful people (well, they think they are).

Western Provence Coast – the deep away-from-it-all Calanques coves are best for divers.

Ancient sites

These five routes possess among the most impressive Roman (and some Greek) sites in the world. Other routes also have good Roman sites, such as the Trophée des Alpes at La Turbie (Riviera Corniches) and the ruins at Fréjus (L'Esterel), which are the best on the coast.

Arles – the arena, theatre, Alyscamps necropolis and museums are impressive.

Gard – the Pont du Gard is a phenomenal three-tier Roman aqueduct.

Les Alpilles and Les Baux – don't miss the Glanum site and Les Antiques.

Nîmes – the best surviving Roman arena, the Maison Carrée, and several other exceptional sights.

Upper Vaucluse – at Vaison-la-Romaine, two extensive, extraordinary Roman sites and a perfect Roman bridge, and at Orange, the Roman theatre and Arc de Triomphe are the highlights.

Scenery

Alpes de Haute Provence – dramatic mountain scenery.

Alpilles – *garrigue*, Les Baux.

Camargue – Camargue interior lagoons and flatlands.

Nice to Tende – perched villages.

Les Maures – wild Mediterranean hills.

Nice – Baie des Anges.

Riviera Corniches – coastal views.

Upper Alpes Maritimes – Mercantour peaks.

Var Interior – Grand Canyon du Verdon.

Western Provence Coast – the *calanques*.

Children

Avignon – Pont St-Bénézet and place de l'Hôtel de Ville.

Camargue – white horses, pink flamingos and black bulls.

Cannes to Nice – the Picasso Museum at Antibes, and lots of leisure attractions.

Gard – le Pont du Gard.

L'Esterel, Cannes to Nice and **Les Maures** – sandy beaches.

Les Alpilles – Tarascon Castle.

Monaco, St-Tropez, Cannes – ostentatious wealth.

Nîmes – the arena at Nîmes.

Route Napoléon – the citadel and alleys of Sisteron.

Southern Vaucluse and the Lubéron – the ochre quarries at Roussillon.

Art

These are world class ...

Cannes to Nice – Musée Picasso at Antibes and another at Vallauris, Musée Fernand Léger at Biot, and 20th-century art in the Château Grimaldi and Musée Renoir at Cagnes-sur Mer.
Nice – Musée Chagall, Musée Matisse, Musée d'Art Moderne.
Vence and Loup Valley – Fondation Maeght modern art museum near St-Paul-de-Vence.

The Middle Ages

Avignon – Palais des Papes, Pont St-Bénézet, Ramparts.
Camargue – Les Saintes-Maries-de-la-Mer and Aigues-Mortes.
Cannes to Nice – Vence, Mougins.
Nice to Tende – the perched villages.
Gard – Uzès old town.
Les Alpilles and Les Baux –Les Baux and Tarascon castle.
Route Napoléon – Grasse old quarter, Castellane, Sisteron citadel and *andrones*.

Southern Vaucluse and the Lubéron – Sénanque Abbey.
Upper Vaucluse – Châteauneuf du Pape, wine villages of Montmirail.
Var Interior and the Grand Canyon du Verdon – Le Thoronet Abbey and St-Maximin-la-Sainte-Baume.

Ten unmissable things to do in Provence and the Riviera

- Drive the Grand Canyon du Verdon.
- Eat *bouillabaisse* in Marseille.
- Go to market ... at Aix, Vaison or Nice.
- Pop into the Hotel Carlton in Cannes for coffee on the terrace.
- Saunter the St-Tropez waterfront.
- Step into the arena at Nîmes.
- Try wine-tasting at Châteauneuf du Pape or Gigondas, for example.
- Visit one of the great Riviera art museums.
- Walk across the Pont du Gard.
- Watch the world go by on the Cours Mirabeau, in Aix.

Avignon

Ratings

Street life	●●●●●
Architecture	●●●●○
Art	●●●●○
Museums	●●●●○
Restaurants	●●●●○
Children	●●●○○
Entertainment	●●●○○
Shopping	●●●○○

From the bank of the broad, turbulent River Rhône rise the magnificent ramparts of Avignon, golden stones redolent with medieval grandeur and power. Within the walls, the town seems quintessentially southern; it bursts with energy, yet echoes with history. A crowded central avenue (Jean-Jaurès and République) makes its way from city gate to the looming Papal Palace. The dubious French popes may have proved a blessing to its tourist industry, but while Avignon was their capital it became a corrupt, overblown haven for Europe's outcasts, drifters and rogues ('a sink of vice,' according to the 14th-century poet, Petrarch). Something of that survives, though now it gives Avignon a curious charm: all human life is assembled along this exhilarating street, from bankers to beggars, from chic, fashionable ladies to scrounging New-Agers. The town delights in such contrasts, especially at Festival time, the hectic high point of Avignon's year.

Getting there and getting around

ℹ️ **Main office** *41 cours Jean-Jaurès; tel 04 90 82 65 11. Open Mon–Sat 0900–1300, 1400–1800 (Sat closes at 1700).*

Pont St-Bénézet *No phone. Open Oct–Mar 0900–1300, 1400–1700. Apr–Sep 0900–1830. Closed Mon.*

🚖 **Taxis** *Tel: 04 90 82 20 20 day or night.*

The walled city (signposted 'Avignon Centre') is on the northwestern edge of the city, on the left bank of the Rhône, so is best approached from that side. From the north, the fastest access to the walled area is Exit 23 from *autoroute* A7.

Parking
There are four good central places to park: Parking Palais des Papes, underneath place du Palais (€); Parking Les Halles, at place Pie (€); Parking des Gares, outside Porte de la République, between the bus and train stations (€); and alongside the exterior of the city walls.

Right
Avignon city walls

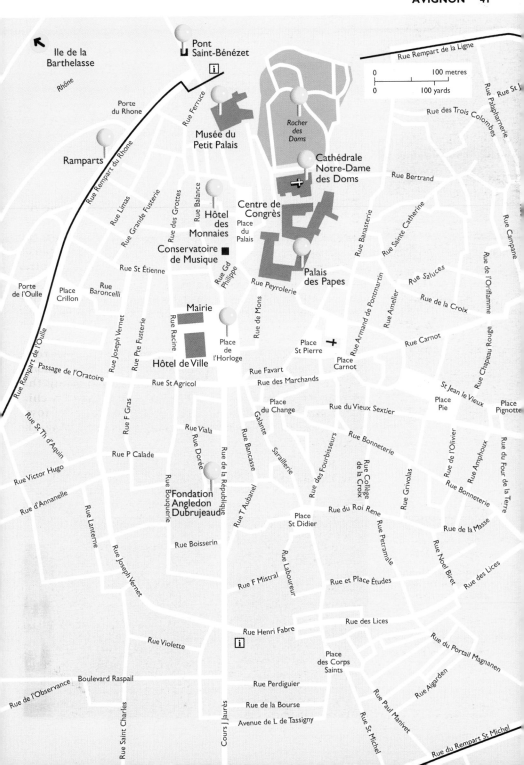

Ile de la
Barthelasse

Rhône

Pont
Saint-Bénézet

Porte
du Rhone

Rue Ferruce

Rampart de la Ligne

Rue Rempart de la Ligne

Rue Palaphamerie

Rue St Je

0   100 metres
0   100 yards

Rue des Trois Colombes

Musée du
Petit Palais

Rocher
des
Doms

Ramparts

Rue Rempart du Rhone

Rue Limas

Rue Grande Fusterie

Rue des Grottes

Rue Balance

Hôtel
des
Monnaies

Cathédrale
Notre-Dame
des Doms

Rue Bertrand

Rue Banasterie

Rue Sainte Catherine

Rue Campane

Centre de
Congrès

Place
du
Palais

Conservatoire
de Musique

Rue St Étienne

Rue Gd Philippe

Rue Peyrolerie

Palais
des Papes

Rue de l'Oriflamme

Rue Saluces

Rue Amelier

Rue de la Croix

Rue Chapeau Rouge

Porte
de l'Oulle

Place
Crillon

Rue
Baroncelli

Mairie

Rue de Mons

Rue Armand de Pontmartin

Rue Carnot

Rue Rempart de l'Oulle

Passage de l'Oratoire

Rue Joseph Vernet

Rue Pte Fusterie

Rue Racine

Place
de
l'Horloge

Place
St Pierre

Place
Carnot

Hôtel de Ville

Rue Favart

Rue des Marchands

St Jean le Vieux

Place
Pie

Place
Pignotte

Rue St Agricol

Rue F Gras

Rue St-Th. d'Aquin

Place
du Change

Galante

Rue du Vieux Sextier

Rue Viala

Rue Dorée

Rue Bancasse

Sarailerie

Rue Bonneterie

Rue de l'Olivier

Rue Amphoux

Rue du Four de la Terre

Rue P Calade

Rue Victor Hugo

Rue d'Annanelle

Rue de la République

Rue T Aubanel

Rue des Fourbisseurs

Rue Collège
de la Croix

Rue Grivolas

Rue Bonneterie

Fondation
Angledon
Dubrujeaud

Rue Bouquerie

Rue Lanterne

Rue du Roi Rene

Place
St Didier

Rue Petramale

Rue de la Masse

Rue Noel Biret

Rue Boisserin

Rue Joseph Vernet

Rue Laboureur

Rue et Place Études

Rue des Lices

Rue F Mistral

Rue des Lices

Rue du Portail Magnanen

Rue Henri Fabre

Rue Violette

Place
des Corps
Saints

Rue Aigarden

Boulevard Raspail

Rue de l'Observance

Rue Saint Charles

Cours J Jaurès

Rue Perdiguier

Rue de la Bourse

Avenue de L de Tassigny

Rue Paul Manivet

Rue St Michel

Rue du Rempart St Michel

Sights

Fondation Angladon Dubrujeaud €€ 5 rue Laboureur; tel: 04 90 82 29 03. Open 1300–1800 (open till 1900 May–Oct). Closed Mon, Tue.

Notre-Dame-des-Doms place du Palais; tel: 04 90 85 62 25. Open daily approximately 0900–1900.

City tours Qualified guides give tours of the city centre to large and small groups, or even individuals, as required. These are available at almost any time and can be arranged by the tourist office.

Fondation Angladon Dubrujeaud✢✢

Once the privately owned Angladon Dubrujeaud collection, this museum contains an interesting selection of 20th-century art including works by Cézanne, Picasso, several Impressionists and a Van Gogh. It is housed in an opulent mansion in a backstreet east of rue de la République.

Hôtel des Monnaies✢✢

Opposite the pope's palace (*see below*), strains of music and song often emanate from the Hôtel des Monnaies, a delight of decoration bordering on the absurd. A balustrade encloses the roof while the Borghese coat of arms, together with handfuls of fruit, plump cherubs, and dragons and eagles – emblems of the Borghese family who originally owned the building – literally come right out of the façade. Cardinal Borghese was one of the papal legates, appointees who ran the city on behalf of the pope. Later, his mansion became Avignon's mint (hence the name), and today houses the Conservatoire de Musique (hence the sounds). It is not open to visitors.

Palais des Papes € place du Palais; tel: 04 90 27 50 74. Open Apr–Oct 0900–1900 (2000 from 21 Aug–30 Sep); rest of year 0900–1245, 1400–1800. No entry if less than 45 minutes before closing.

Petit Palais € place du Palais; tel: 04 90 86 44 58. Open Jul–Aug 1030–1800, closed Tue; rest of year 0930–1200, 1400–1800; closed public holidays.

Ile de la Barthelasse**

The large Barthelasse island which divides the Rhône into two north of Avignon has always been important to the city. Once forested, it was a hunting reserve for the nobility before becoming the haunt of lowlifes, criminals and prostitutes. Gradually cleaned up, it has become a leisure area popular for picnics, walks and sports. There's a swimming-pool on the island, as well as campsites and restaurants.

Notre-Dame-des-Doms*

Standing on the site of an even older church, Avignon's resilient 12th-century cathedral alongside the Papal Palace has been repaired and reconstructed many times during the town's history, incorporating a hotchpotch of styles. The most destructive period was during the Revolution – with Avignon largely on the Royalist side – when the church was pillaged and all but wrecked. Purists argue that even worse damage has been done by misguided restoration work. The cathedral reopened for services in 1822, and in 1859 – continuing the tradition of tasteless restoration – an ostentatious gilded Madonna was placed on the Romanesque bell tower.

Palais des Papes***

Avignon calls itself the Cité des Papes, city of the popes, because in the Middle Ages a line of breakaway popes made it their capital. They were only here for a hundred years, from 1309 to 1403; during that time, Rome remained the Catholic capital and the Avignon papacy was soon marginalised. Yet the city of Avignon and its surrounding countryside remained papal property, and in fact did not become part of France again until 1791. The popes' vast palace – the name is misleading, it's more like a fortress – is still the most prominent landmark in the town, rising high above the ramparts and visible from miles away. Its bleak walls are etched with arches and cautious openings, and topped with castellations and a couple of pointy towers. The grim, imposing edifice is often decorated with fluttering medieval-looking banners. Somehow, it's easy to picture the colourful pomp and ceremonial that used to be enacted here. Inside the palace, you may wander (on your own or with a 1½-hour guided tour in English) through room after room. This now lifeless building is all big, white flagstones, massive halls, gorgeously frescoed walls and decorated timber ceilings. Key sights are the Grand Audience Hall, the Popes' Bedroom with decorated ceiling and walls adorned with birds and golden vines on a blue background, the Grand Tinel Banqueting Hall (with a superb group of Gobelin tapestries), the kitchens, and the view from the Terasses des Grands Dignitaires.

Petit Palais**

The popes acquired this dignified building in 1335 and it was later transformed into a sumptuous residence for the 16th-century Cardinal Giulio della Rovere, who went on to become Pope Julius II. During this

Pont St-Bénézet €
tel: 04 90 85 60 16.
Open Apr–Sep daily
0900–1830; rest of year
Tue–Sun 0900–1300,
1400–1700. Closed public
holidays.

**Musée en Images Pont
d'Avignon** tel: 04 90 82
56 96. Same opening times
as the bridge.

period, and for a long time afterwards, the Petit Palais ('Little Palace') served as a sort of guest-room for the city's visiting royalty and nobility. Cardinal della Rovere took a lively interest in the arts, was a patron of Michelangelo, and began the collection of paintings and sculpture which today has turned the building into a remarkable art museum. It is most acclaimed for its Italian Primitives, but encompasses the Sienese, Venetian, Florentine and Avignon schools, as well as Romanesque and Gothic sculpture, frescos, and other medieval artworks.

Place de l'Horloge***

Much smaller than neighbouring place du Palais, this used to be the forum (public square) of the Roman city, *Avenio*. It is still Avignon's enticing focal point, even in winter surrounded by hundreds of tables under parasols where it is a delight to linger over breakfast or a late lunch. An old-fashioned carousel in the square is usually working, while on one side stands the city's theatre and the grand old 19th-century town hall, which incorporates a 14th-century clock tower (*horloge*).

Pont St-Bénézet***

Projecting somewhat oddly into the Rhône from Avignon's ramparts is the famous bridge of the nursery rhyme. It has surely made the name of the city a household word, this *Pont d'Avignon* on which *on y danse*, its broken arches stepping just halfway across one arm of the river. It is ineffably picturesque. Step down from a rampart walkway to reach the gatehouse which gives access to the narrow cobbled bridge. Originally built in 1177 under the inspiration of a shepherd boy called Bénézet, money for the project was raised by a religious brotherhood called the Frères Pontifes. When complete, the bridge's 22 arches strode across the Rhône to Villeneuve-lès-Avignon via the river island, Ile de la Barthelasse.

In the 1230s, the bridge was enlarged and raised. As a result, the interesting little Chapelle St-Nicolas, standing on one of the bridge supports, had a second chapel built in Gothic style on top of the original Romanesque structure. Today the simple white walls of this elegant little structure are entirely defaced with tourists' graffiti. Most of the bridge was swept away during the catastrophic Rhône floods of 1668. Did people ever dance *sur le pont*? Pedants make much of the fact that it is rather narrow for dancing *en rond* (in a ring), though children prove it can easily be done. In the **Espace St-Bénézet** beside the gatehouse, the **Musée en Images Pont d'Avignon** tells the story of the bridge with a video.

Ramparts**

Avignon's 'honey-coloured, rose-faded walls', as novelist and playwright Lawrence Durrell called them, survive in remarkably intact condition. Built on the orders of the popes at the start of their 14th-century reign, these mighty ramparts still make a complete circle of

The Festival d'Avignon (Avignon International Festival of Theatre) takes place between early Jul and early Aug and features programmed events with top names, plus countless fringe shows, street theatre and a party atmosphere. For official Festival information *tel: 04 90 86 24 43* or see *www.festival-avignon.com*

Buskers and street theatre in the main squares and rue de la République provide entertainment, while in place de l'Horloge, a traditional carousel has been installed. Two little 'land trains' provide a fun way to see the sights on 30-minute tours from place du Palais. Route 1 travels through back streets to Pont St-Bénézet and heads out of the walls. Route 2 goes up on to the Rocher des Doms. For reservations *tel: 04 90 82 64 44*.

Inside the walls, the main shopping street is rue de la République, with a multitude of stores large and small including record and book shops, Galeries Lafayette department store, shoe shops, leather goods shops and jewellers. To find shops (including food stores) used by locals rather than tourists, walk along rue Carnot. Outside the walls are several big hypermarket complexes, about 2km along avenue P Sémard (N7).

the old city, a distance of 4.3km. They stood much higher than today; the lower parts are now hidden by more recent road construction. A deep moat enclosed the town outside the walls, and this too has entirely vanished. Militarily, Avignon's ramparts were largely symbolic; never capable of providing a complete defence of the town, they lack the array of fortifications and machicolations more typical of the period. It is possible either to walk or to drive right around the outside of the ramparts, while inside the walls there are many stretches where it is possible to walk alongside.

Rocher des Doms**
Opening off the place du Palais, the lofty Rocher des Doms' gardens climb to a viewpoint from which most of western Provence can be seen. The view to the north is very striking, showing the curve of the Rhône below, Villeneuve-lès-Avignon to one side and Mont Ventoux to the other. These handsomely laid-out gardens, covering the site of the earliest Ligurian and then Roman settlement of the town, provide a peaceful place to relax away from crowds and noise.

Accommodation and food

Cloître St-Louis €€€ *20 rue du Portail Boquier; tel: 04 90 27 55 55; fax: 04 90 82 24 01.* This unusual hotel, close to the main entrance into the walled town (Porte de la République), oddly combines history and modernity. A former monastery, it still has a chapel inside, where – rather amazingly – the town's Carmelite community hold a service each Sunday evening. The hotel's cool white cloister is open to the street and attracts tourists. Its décor is stylish, luxurious and modern, and part of the hotel is housed in a gratingly modern extension. Ask to stay in the older part, where the bedrooms are former monks' cells.

La Ferme €€ *Chemin des Bois, Ile de la Barthelasse; tel: 04 90 82 57 53; fax: 04 90 27 15 47.* Tucked away on this big island in the Rhône, La Ferme is a simple, pleasing and comfortable family hotel and restaurant and makes an interesting and unusual alternative. It is enclosed by Provençal gardens and greenery and shady plane trees. The cooking is excellent too.

Hôtel de l'Europe €€€ *12 place Crillon; tel: 04 90 14 76 76; fax: 04 90 85 43 66; www.hotel-d-europe.fr.* Avignon's legendary – and still classiest – place to stay is this glorious 16th-century mansion, a haven of good living and elegance tucked away in gardens. Its restaurant, too, is one of the best in town. In the last century, anyone who was anyone stayed here – former guests include writers Charles Dickens and Henry James, philosopher John Stuart Mill, poet Elizabeth Barrett Browning, and most wealthy Victorians on their way to the Riviera. Earlier visitors were Napoleon and Victor Hugo, while more recent names in the visitor's book are Tennessee Williams, Pablo Picasso and Salvador Dalí. Obviously it's good. Car park.

Médiéval € *15 rue Petite Saunerie; tel: 04 90 86 11 06.* An extraordinary find so close to the Palais des Papes, this 17th-century house offers simple, comfortable accommodation and a relaxed atmosphere at a modest price.

Mercure €€€ The up-market Mercure chain has two hotels close to the Palais des Papes – the **Cité des Papes** (*tel: 04 90 86 22 45*) and the pricier **Palais des Papes** (*tel: 04 90 85 91 23*).

Belle Arti € *19 rue des Lices; tel: 04 90 27 30 24.* First-class authentic Italian cooking using fresh seasonal produce, served in a warm, convivial atmosphere at very modest prices.

Les Domaines €€ *28 place de l'Horloge; tel: 04 90 82 58 86.* The table-filled place de l'Horloge offers a wide choice of eating places, but most offer predictable tourist menus and the main attraction is the setting. Here's one that deviates from that formula in one respect – the cooking is a cut above the rest.

Hiely Lucullus €€ *5 rue de la République, tel: 04 90 86 17 07.* This long-established Avignon favourite deserves its success, offering acclaimed

Below
Palais des Papes

and inspired cooking, with excellent fish dishes and exquisite sauces, accompanied by the best of local wines, in a relaxed setting overlooking the main street. One speciality is the unusual 'gateau' of asparagus and tarragon. Prices represent an amazing bargain.

Suggested walk

Total distance: About 2km or 3km including detours.

Time: The main walk will take about 2 hours, allowing for pauses to admire the views, the outsides of buildings, etc, but without entering the museums and monuments. Allow a full day including detours and visits to all the sights.

Route: Start exploring Avignon in busy **PLACE DE L'HORLOGE ❶**. Walk a few paces north into the immense **place du Palais**, the enormous cobbled square dominated in spirit by the memory of Avignon's medieval pomp and splendour, and, physically, by the monumental bulk of its mighty **PALAIS DES PAPES ❷**. Around the square, as around the whole town, there are lavishly ornate buildings, notably the **PETIT PALAIS ❸**, straight ahead, and the **HOTEL DES MONNAIES ❹** on your left.

Detour: The back streets and medieval lanes behind the Palais des Papes are intriguing. Leave the square at the southeast corner, on steeply descending cobbled **rue Peyrollerie**. It clings to the walls of the palace, and the rocks on which it stands. Turn left into rue du Vice-Légat, its name a reminder of the powers-that-were in the papal period. Turn left again into rue Banasterie, 'street of basketmaking' in Provençal. Pause at No 13, a 17th-century mansion called **Hôtel de Madon de Châteaublanc** – its façade is laden with carvings of eagles, masks and fruit. Turn left at rue Ste-Anne (opposite rue Bertrand) to reach the **Escaliers Ste-Anne** steps which climb up directly on to the **ROCHER DES DOMS ❺**. Walk across the gardens towards place du Palais, passing **NOTRE-DAME-DES-DOMS ❻** cathedral as you re-enter the square.

Take the little turn alongside Hôtel des Monnaies into rue de la Balance, the street which gives its name to the whole of this Quartier de la Balance district between the Papal Palace and the river. Follow it down steeply (turning right into rue Ferruce near the bottom) to **PONT ST-BENEZET ❼**. After visiting the bridge, follow the **RAMPARTS ❽** along **rue des Remparts du Rhône** until you reach **place Crillon**. The main landmarks of this attractive square are the old theatre and the legendary **Hôtel de l'Europe**. Rue Baroncelli leads into rue Joseph Vernet. Turn right into this elegant, quiet residential street, following its curve southward. The curve is due to its running along the site of older ramparts which once enclosed a smaller area than today's walled town. Look at a map of Avignon and notice how rue Joseph Vernet, rue des

Villeneuve Tourist Office *I place Charles David; tel: 04 90 25 61 33.*

By bus Catch the Villeneuve bus from the bus stations in rue de la République or place Pie.

By car On the west side of the Avignon ramparts, take Pont Edouard Daladier (D900) – the bridge just south of Pont St-Bénézet – directly into Villeneuve.

Lices and other streets, form an inner circle within the town where these earlier city walls once stood. Numbers 58, 83 and 87 rue Joseph Vernet are good examples of 17th- and 18th-century mansions. On the left, at No 65, the **Musée Calvet** (€ *tel: 04 90 86 33 84*) is an important if eclectic collection of artworks. Next door, **Musée Requien** (€ *tel: 04 90 82 43 51*) is a first-class little natural history museum. Follow the street to its end and turn left into rue de la République, Avignon's main street.

Detour: Take rue Mistral on the right to rue Laboureur, where you will find **FONDATION ANGLATON-DUBRUJEAUD ❾**. The street leads into place St Didier, where you can double back out of the square on rue des Trois Faucons. This street ends at rue des Lices, where you turn left to follow this atmospheric street beside the River Sorgue – *Lices* means an outer protective area, so this formed part of the original defences. Turnings off to the right, across the river, lead into a sleazier quarter around rue de la Grande Monnaie and rue du Portail Mognanen, something of a red-light area after dark, and even during the day. Rue des Teinturiers ('street of dyers'), at the end of rue des Lices, is a pretty cobbled street where the dyers' water-wheels can still be seen. Head left on this street, turning left into rue de la Masse, which in turn leads into rue du Roi-René. Good King René, son of Louis II of Anjou, was the 15th-century King of Naples and Count of Provence, always fondly remembered in Provence as Roi René. On the corner of rue Grivolas, the **Maison du Roi René** is reputed to have been his Avignon residence. There are several other fine mansions in the street, which leads back to place St-Didier and then returns to rue de la République at almost exactly the point you left it.

Continue up rue de la République, which becomes increasingly busy until it reaches place de l'Horloge.

Also worth exploring

There's no better place to view Avignon than the 'New Town by Avignon' on the opposite side of the Rhône. **Villeneuve-lès-Avignon** grew up in the 13th century, partly because of the Pont St-Bénézet linking the two shores. When the popes came to Avignon a hundred years later, the cardinals adopted Villeneuve, constructing great mansions here. This attracted other wealthy people, and gradually the new town grew into an aristocratic haven of high life, high art and high culture. All that was destroyed during the Revolution, but Villeneuve remains a pleasant spot, ideal for a stroll, some gentle sightseeing and a meal at one of the many good restaurants. See the ruins of 13th-century **Fort St André**✶✶, built by John the Good and Charles V (the best view of Avignon is from here); the 14th-century charterhouse **Chartreuse du Val de Bénédiction**✶ and the riverside watchtower **Tour Philippe le Bel**✶.

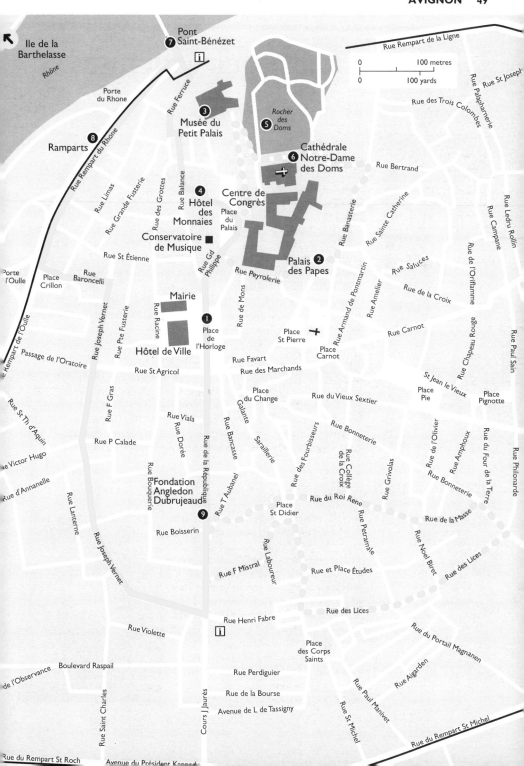

Ile de la Barthelasse

Rhône

Pont Saint-Bénézet
7
ℹ️

Rue Rempart de la Ligne

0   100 metres
0   100 yards

Rue St Joseph

Rue Palapharnerie

Rue des Trois Colombes

Porte du Rhône

Rue Ferruce

Rue des Grottes

Musée du Petit Palais
3

Rocher des Doms
5

Ramparts
8

Rue Rempart du Rhône

Cathédrale Notre-Dame des Doms
6

Rue Bertrand

Rue Ledru Rollin

Rue Campane

Rue Limas

Rue Grande Fusterie

Rue Balance

Hôtel des Monnaies
4

Centre de Congrès

Place du Palais

Rue Banasterie

Rue Sainte Catherine

Rue de l'Oriflamme

Conservatoire de Musique

Rue St Étienne

Rue Gd Philippe

Rue Peyrolerie

Palais des Papes
2

Rue Saluces

Rue Amelier

Rue de la Croix

Rue Chapeau Rouge

Rue Paul Sain

Porte l'Oulle

Place Crillon

Rue Baroncelli

Rue Joseph Vernet

Rue Pte Fusterie

Rue Racine

Mairie

Hôtel de Ville

Place de l'Horloge
1

Rue de Mons

Place St Pierre

Place Carnot

Rue Armand de Pontmartin

Rue Carnot

St Jean le Vieux

Place Pignotte

Rue Philonarde

Rue Rempart de l'Oulle

Passage de l'Oratoire

Rue Favart

Rue des Marchands

Place Pie

Rue de l'Olivier

Rue Amphoux

Rue du Four de la Terre

Rue St Agricol

Rue St-Th d'Aquin

Rue Victor Hugo

Rue F Gras

Rue Viala

Rue Dorée

Place du Change

Galante

Rue du Vieux Sextier

Rue Bonneterie

Rue Grivolas

Rue Bonneterie

Rue d'Annanelle

Rue P Calade

Rue de la République

Rue Bancasse

Saraillerie

Rue des Fourbisseurs

Rue Collège de la Croix

Rue de la Masse

Rue Lanterne

Rue Bouquerie

Fondation Angledon Dubrujeaud
9

Rue T Aubanel

Place St Didier

Rue du Roi Rene

Rue Petramale

Rue Noël Biret

Rue des Lices

Rue Boisserin

Rue Laboureur

Rue F Mistral

Rue et Place Études

Rue Joseph Vernet

Rue des Lices

Rue Henri Fabre
ℹ️

Rue Violette

Boulevard Raspail

de l'Observance

Place des Corps Saints

Rue du Portail Magnanen

Rue Aigarden

Rue Paul Manivet

Cours J Jaurès

Rue Saint Charles

Rue Perdiguier

Rue de la Bourse

Avenue de L de Tassigny

Rue St Michel

Rue du Rempart St Michel

Rue du Rempart St Roch

Avenue du Président Kennedy

The Upper Vaucluse

Ratings

Roman remains	●●●●●
Wine-tasting	●●●●●
Scenery	●●●●●
History	●●●●○
Restaurants	●●●●○
Children	●●○○○
Shopping	●●○○○
Entertainment	●○○○○

The northern half of the Vaucluse *département*, set well back from the coast, is alternately wild and gentle, cultivated and uncultivable, and has a sense of being almost submerged, subdued, beneath millennia of history and sunlight. This tranquil, rustic, often hilly countryside of ancient olive groves, soporific dry-stone villages, farmyards, peach orchards and world-famous vineyards lies between truly majestic physical borders. In the north, it is dominated by the might of Mont Ventoux; the great river highway of the Rhône marks the *département*'s western edge, while to the east rise the Provençal Alps. Despite such awesome topography, this landscape has been conquered and civilised for thousands of years. The Romans left their mark here, as did the medieval Avignon popes (most of the region was part of their Comtat Venaissin). Today the region is packed with first-class hotels and restaurants of character.

LE BARROUX*

You can reach the village on the D78 from the D938.

It is best to park the car at the entrance to the village and visit on foot.

Château € *tel: 04 90 62 35 21. Open Apr–May (weekends only) 1000–1900; Jun and Oct 1430–1900; Jul–Sep 1000–2000; rest of year closed. 45-minute guided tour.*

Steeply pitched on the southeast side of the **Dentelles de Montmirail** (*see page 54*) this curious, picturesque little village is dominated by a massive 16th-century **castle**** with 12th-century towers. Its commanding view of the Vaucluse plain stretched out below shows the military value of the site. Several times destroyed and restored, the castle today retains its chapel, guardroom, Salle d'Audience and other rooms.

Right
Boules player

CARPENTRAS❖❖

ℹ **Carpentras Tourist Office** 170 avenue Jean-Jaurès; tel: 04 90 63 00 78. Guided tours of the town available.

ℹ **Ancienne Cathédrale** place du Général de Gaulle; tel: 04 90 63 04 92. Open approximately 0900–1700.

Synagogue place Maurice Charretier; tel: 04 90 63 39 97. Open 1000–1200, 1500–1700. Closed Fri pm, Sat, Jewish holidays and festivals.

Once capital of the popes' Comtat Venaissin territory (*see page 53*), Carpentras is now just a typical warm Provençal town. The ring of defensive ramparts has been replaced by boulevards around the dense network of lanes in the **old quarter**❖❖❖. Only **Porte d'Orange**❖, on the north side, remains from these 14th-century ramparts. Usually sleepy, on Fridays the old town comes to life for a big street market.

The **synagogue**❖, built in 1367, is believed to be the oldest surviving in France – though thanks to 19th- and 20th-century building work it shows little sign of its true age. The area around the synagogue was a walled ghetto until the Revolution. The central point of the old town is its 15th-century **Ancienne Cathédrale**❖ (St-Suffrein), built on the orders of the Avignon pope, Benedict XIII. The grandest way in is through its flamboyant Porte Juive. The odd name ('Jewish Door') is due to its being the door that Jewish converts to Christianity came through. In the Roman era, too, this was the centre of town, and a

⮂ Approach the old quarter via place Aristide Briand.

🅟 The best place for the old quarter is in Allée des Platanes.

🛈 **Museums** € *tel: 04 90 63 04 92. Open Apr–Oct 1000–1200, 1400–1800; rest of year 1000–1200, 1400–1600.*

🍴 On Fri there is a main market, with smaller markets on other days. The *confiseurs* of Carpentras specialise in stripy triangular boiled sweets called *berlingots*.

🎭 From about 14 Jul to 15 Aug there's an arts festival, with open-air music, dance and drama.

Comtat Venaissin

Before the popes settled at Avignon, the Venaissin countryside to the east had been part of the domain of the cosmopolitan Counts of Toulouse, a centre of trade, foreign ideas and Catharism. To expiate for allowing their possessions to fall under the spell of the Cathar 'heresy', the Counts gave the whole of the Comtat Venaissin – comprising most of today's Vaucluse, though not Orange – to the popes. It was annexed to the Holy See in 1274, and did not become part of France until 1791.

Triumphal Arch✢✢ of the 1st century stands in the rather squalid area behind the cathedral. Today the name of Carpentras is tainted by the anti-semitic episode which occurred here in May 1990 resulting in nationwide anti-racist demonstrations.

Museums in the town include the **Treasury** in the Ancienne Cathédrale (statuary), **Musée Comtadin** (relics of the Comtat Venaissin), **Musée Duplessis** (local artists), **Musée Sobirats** (reconstruction of an 18th-century mansion), **Musée Lapidaire** (relics of Romanesque cloisters) and **Hôtel-Dieu** (18th-century hospital with baroque chapel and original pharmacy).

Accommodation and food in Carpentras

Among the shops under the arcades close to the synagogue are some excellent *traiteurs* and *pâtissiers*, ideal for picnic fare.

Hôtel Fiacre €–€€ *153 rue Vigne; tel: 04 90 63 03 15; fax: 04 90 60 49 73.* Note the fine wrought-iron staircase at this 18th-century town centre mansion transformed into a small hotel with plenty of character. It has its own car parking, but there's no restaurant.

Left
Carpentras

CHATEAUNEUF-DU-PAPE✢✢

🛈 **Châteauneuf-du- Pape Tourist Office** *place Portail; tel: 04 90 83 71 08; fax: 04 90 83 50 34; http://perso.wanadoo.fr/ot- chato9-pape*

North and south from Avignon, the Rhône passes a succession of feudal fortresses, and on its banks are famous vineyards. None is more acclaimed than the exquisitely pretty, if somewhat touristy, village of 'the Pope's New Castle' with its pristine, restored medieval buildings, lovely riverside views and heady rich red wine. All around are the well-kept vineyards, and in a historic wine cellar there is a museum of

Wine Festival on 24–25 April.

winemaking, the **Musée des Outils de Vignerons*** (€ *tel: 04 90 83 70 07. Open 15 Jun–15 Sep 0900–1930; rest of year 0900–1200, 1400–1900*). Only ruins survive of the popes' fortress where they came for summer outings from Avignon.

DENTELLES DE MONTMIRAIL***

Rising between towering Mont Ventoux and the hot flatlands of the Rhône are the strange Dentelles – the name means lacework – forming a line of delicate rocky points resembling the teeth of a saw. From the vine-covered slopes below them come good Côtes du Rhône wines. A country lane joins pretty, sunlit villages and at almost every village there is *dégustation* (wine-tasting). One of the prettiest is **Séguret**, in the northwest. Next on the road come **Gigondas** and **Vacqueyras**. On the south side of the Dentelles at **Beaumes-de-Vénise***, well known for its sweet dessert (or apéritif) wine, there are superb views, especially from the little Romanesque chapel of Notre-Dame-d'Aubune. On the southeast side is **Le Barroux**, and **Malaucène** to the south. **Vaison-la-Romaine** lies beside the River Ouvèze as it skirts the north side of the Dentelles.

Right
Gigondas

Gigondas❖❖

The D7 passes below the village; follow the sign to enter the village.

Park in the little main square. If there's no space, pull in on the approach road.

Resting calmly on the quiet slopes of the Dentelles, this is one of the best of the local red wine names, and also, with its old houses and lovely shaded main square with a fountain, one of the prettiest villages. It has a 14th-century château of the Counts (later Princes) of Orange, and commands a wide view across the vines.

Accommodation and food in Gigondas

Les Florets €€ *route des Dentelles; tel: 04 90 65 85 01; fax: 04 90 65 83 80.* A really pleasant peaceful spot for a quality lunch at moderate prices in full view of the vines whose wine you will probably drink. There are rooms too, but you'll have to book ahead.

Oustalet € *place Portail; tel: 04 90 65 85 30 and 04 90 12 30 03.* With tables laid out of doors in the main square of this tiny village, tasty dishes made from local ingredients and local wines at modest prices, this is a delightful spot.

Malaucene❖

Malaucène Tourist Office *place Mairie; tel: 04 90 65 22 59; fax: 04 90 65 22 59.*

This pleasant crossroads town is squeezed between Mont Ventoux and the Dentelles de Montmirail. Its fortified church, once part of the town ramparts, has fine woodcarving, especially the 18th-century organ loft. Alongside the church, Porte Soubeyran leads into the historic village of tangled lanes where a distinctive, tall belfry rises at the centre.

Mont Ventoux❖❖❖

The D974 skirts the southern flank of Mont Ventoux, and also, with some hair-raising bends, climbs up and over the summit of the mountain.

In the northwest corner of Vaucluse rises a great Provençal landmark, the pale conical mass of Mont Ventoux (1909m), listed as a World Biosphere Reserve by Unesco. The name means windy, and it is, with temperatures substantially lower at the summit than at the foot (usually the drop is about 11°C). The view from the top is quite amazing on a clear day, taking in the Alps, Rhône Valley and Vaucluse Plateau. Though a popular excursion, the drive to the summit should not be undertaken lightly, especially in stormy or windy weather or on cold winter days, when the temperature at the top can fall to -25°C. From Christmas to Easter, the summit is usually snow-capped, making a striking contrast on hot spring days. In early summer, after the snow has vanished, it becomes green and covered with flowers.

ORANGE***

ℹ Orange Tourist Offices Main office: Cours A Briand; tel: 04 90 34 70 88; fax: 04 90 34 99 62; www.provence-orange.com. Summer office: place Frères Mounet. Guided tours available.

⮂ Follow the main boulevard round the town centre to Cours A Briand (west side) or the Théâtre Antique (south side) to park.

P Car parks alongside Cours A Briand and in Cours Pourtoules off avenue G Leclerc, near the Théâtre Antique.

🏛 Théâtre Antique (Roman Theatre) € tel: 04 90 34 70 88. Open Apr–Sep 0900–1830; rest of year 0900–1200, 1330–1700. Closed 1 Jan and 25 Dec.

Musée Municipal € tel: 04 90 51 18 24. Open Apr–Sep 0900–1900. Rest of year 0830 (0900 at weekends) –1200, 1330–1700. Closed 2 Jan and 26 Dec.

🛒 There is a weekly market on Thu.

🎵 Chorégies is the International Music Festival, with opera and choral music, held at the Théâtre Antique and other venues mid-Jul to the beginning of Aug. For information tel: 04 90 34 24 24.

The busy town of Orange, the Catholic principality which came into Dutch hands and whose name subsequently became synonymous with Northern Irish protestantism, formally became part of France as recently as 1713. It possesses some striking antiquities, including an immense wall which Louis XIV described as 'the finest in my kingdom'. The other side of the wall was the original backdrop for performances in the **Théâtre Antique (Roman theatre)***, which still provides the setting for concerts and plays today, including the town's distinguished summer Chorégies festival of choral music. It's the best-preserved Roman theatre surviving anywhere.

In the area around it and on the adjacent hill, **Colline St Eutrope**, several other Roman relics have been uncovered. From the hill, a viewing platform gives an excellent overview of the Roman district. Across the road, the **Musée Municipal*** contains plenty of material excavated here, including the Romans' important Land Survey of Orange inscribed on marble. The museum also has other displays on the town's subsequent history.

The medieval central district, called **Vieil Orange**, is lively and attractive, with little squares, narrow streets and cafés. On the north side of town, standing incongruously on an island encircled by the N7, the **Arc de Triomphe*** is a majestic three-arched monument covered in carvings recalling the defeat of the Gauls, battles, prisoners and naval and military trophies. The north side has survived in remarkably good condition. Dating from about 20 BC, it honours the victories of Augustus and the setting up of *Arausio* (Orange) as a colony. This triumphant display could result from the fact that at their first attempt to conquer the area, the Romans were trounced by the local Gauls.

Accommodation and food in Orange

Hôtel Arène €€ *place Langes; tel: 04 90 11 40 40; fax: 04 90 11 40 45*. Right in the heart of the old town, yet quiet and peaceful, this traditional and comfortable little provincial hotel would be a first choice for an overnight or longer stay. It doesn't have a restaurant, but there are several brasseries in town.

Le Parvis €€ *3 cours Pourtoules; tel: 04 90 34 82 00*. Traditional and reasonably priced, with classic, skilful cooking including *sanglier* (wild boar). Closed Sun pm and Mon.

La Roselière € *4 rue du Renoyer; tel: 04 90 34 50 42*. Tiny restaurant with attractively quirky furnishings, offering a very friendly welcome and delicious food using locally-sourced, organic ingredients. No credit cards. Closed Sun pm and Mon.

SAULT❖

ℹ **Sault Tourist Office** *avenue Promenade; tel: 04 90 64 01 21; fax: 04 90 64 15 03; e-mail: OT-Sault@axit.fr; www.saultenprovence.com/GB/index.asp*

Medieval Sault, in the heart of a lavender-growing area, is high on the edge of a rocky plateau noted for *avens* (potholes). Strikingly situated with views over the Nesque river gorges, the little town has an interesting 12th- to 14th-century church and a small museum of local Gallo-Roman finds. It is a popular spot for walkers, cavers, and for touring Mont Ventoux and the Provençal hills.

Accommodation and food in Sault

Hostellerie du Val de Sault €€–€€€ *Ancien chemin d'Aurel, route de St-Trinité; tel: 04 90 64 01 41; fax: 04 90 64 12 74.* Tucked away in the middle of the countryside, close to Mont Ventoux, this excellent, amiable little hotel and restaurant is a haven of good living. Cooking is full of wild, regional flavours, herbs, lavender, freshly caught fish and local produce.

Above
Roman theatre, Orange

SÉGURET❖❖

 The second and third weekends in Aug feature the Provençal Fair and Winemakers' Festival.

On Christmas Eve Séguret is illuminated by its Pegoulado torchlight procession and folkloric Christmas Eve watch.

Picturebook pretty, this lovely little medieval village, with a 15th-century fountain and 12th-century church, rests on a steep slope just below the rocky teeth of the Dentelles de Montmirail. The village square enjoys an immense view of the Dentelles and the Vaucluse Plain and makes an excellent walking base.

Accommodation and food in Séguret

Domaine de Cabasse €€ *route Sablet; tel: 04 90 46 91 12; fax: 04 90 46 94 01.* A perfect tranquillity reigns at this comfortable rural hotel with its own restaurant in a handsome wine-making *domaine* below the crests of the Dentelles. Open 25 Mar–2 Nov only.

Le Mesclun € *rue des Poternes; tel: 04 90 46 93 43; fax: 04 90 46 93 48.* Good, classic village restaurant with accomplished cooking at moderate prices. Fantastic view across the vines towards the Rhône. Open Apr–Oct only.

Table du Comtat €€ *place du Midi; tel: 04 90 46 91 49; fax: 04 90 46 94 27.* Housed in a 16th-century former hospice, this peaceful, civilised establishment is a relatively simple hotel and a top-quality restaurant with ambitious examples of Provençal classic dishes and a good selection of local wines. Glorious views.

VACQUEYRAS❖

 The village centre lies off the D7.

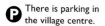 There is parking in the village centre.

Producing a popular, inexpensive red wine, this bustling, pleasant village clusters around its historic centre. It was the birthplace of a famous medieval troubadour, Raimbaud. At the village traffic lights, take the steep little turn (D233) to **Montmirail**❖ that leads high into a peaceful landscape of vineyards and woods threaded with footpaths close to the Dentelles peaks. A spa resort at Montmirail closed down long ago, but the building survives as a luxurious hotel and restaurant.

Accommodation and food in Vacqueyras

Hotel Montmirail €€ *at Montmirail, on the D233 from Vacqueyras; tel: 04 90 65 84 01; fax: 04 90 65 81 50.* In a tranquil spot high among the woods and vines, the Montmirail is a small and comfortable, traditional, family-owned hotel with a reputation for fine cooking. On the immaculate poolside terrace under the big plane tree, tables are smartly laid; a perfect place for lunch. Every evening a marvellous four-course dinner is served.

VAISON-LA-ROMAINE✦✦✦

ℹ Vaison-la-Romaine Tourist Office *place Sautel (between the two Roman sites); tel: 04 90 36 02 11; fax: 04 90 28 76 04; www.vaison-la-romaine.com*

② The D976 (from Orange) arrives on the right bank, the D977 (from Carpentras), and the D938 (from Mont Ventoux) on the left bank. Cross to the right bank to park close to the Roman sites and town centre.

ℙ There's a big parking area at place Burrus, adjacent to the Quartier de la Villasse site.

🏛 Quartier du Puymin, Quartier de la Villasse, Musée Archéologique, cloisters of Notre-Dame-de-Nazareth €€ *tel: 04 90 36 02 11. Open Mar–May and Sep–Oct 0930–1200, 1400–1745; Jun–Aug 0900–1230, 1400–1845; rest of year 1000–1200, 1400–1630. (Roman ruins closed Tue am Nov–Apr.) A single ticket available at any of the sites provides admission to all four of them. The ticket does not have to be used all on one day.*

🛒 There is a weekly market on Tue morning.

Vaison is situated on the River Ouvèze which runs round the northern edges of the Dentelles and Mont Ventoux. This agreeable small town with its big, colourful weekly market is a place for strolling and relaxing at open-air tables, and is a good base for exploring the region. In fact Vaison is three towns, all of them interesting, the newest lying partly on top of the oldest. On the north bank of the Ouvèze was the Gallo-Roman city *Vasio Vocantiorum*. In the Middle Ages the town moved over to the better defended hill south of the river, where in the 12th century the Counts of Toulouse built the castle. During more recent times, up till 1907, life extended back on to the north bank, and many of the Roman ruins were built over. The original Roman bridge or **Pont Romain✦✦✦**, an elegant 2000-year-old single-arch cobbled bridge crossing the Ouvèze, still links the medieval **Ville Haute✦✦** with the north bank and remains in use. Since 1907, in a succession of excavations, the Roman town has been partly uncovered again in two large sites (covering over 15 hectares) with the modern main road running between them. The huge upper site, **Quartier du Puymin✦✦✦**, is the more interesting, with paved streets, walls, frescoes, mosaics, statuary and a complete restored theatre. The best features of the smaller lower site, **Quartier de la Villasse✦✦✦**, are the street of little shops and the mosaic floors of the villas. The **Musée Archéologique (Archaeology Museum)✦✦** has an impressive collection of Roman sculpture. A few paces west of the Villasse site, the interesting Romanesque former cathedral of **Notre-Dame-de-Nazareth✦** has attractive 12th-century cloisters.

Suggested tour

Total distance: About 220km, including the 100-km detour.

Time: Two full days will be needed to do justice to this drive, including the lengthy Nesque and Ventoux detour. There is plenty of accommodation on the route and it could easily be stretched to three days. On the other hand, by leaving out the detour (Mont Ventoux makes quite an impression even if you just admire it from afar) the route could be done as a long one-day drive focused around the Roman sites of Orange and Vaison, and the wine country of the Dentelles de Montmirail.

Links: A detour at Sault links this route with the Alpes de Haute Provence tour (*see page 156*).

Route: From **Avignon** (*see page 40*) take the D942, the fast main road to **CARPENTRAS ❶**. Leave town on the D7 heading towards the Dentelles de Montmirail upland (the jagged shape of the peak is not clear from here). At Aubignan, take the right turn on to the D90 for

Hôtel des Lis €€
*20 cours J Henri-Fabre,
Vaison-la-Romaine; tel: 04
90 36 00 11; fax: 04 90 36
39 05.* Welcoming and
attractive, with pleasant,
comfortable rooms in a
turn-of-the-century house
near a square in the centre
of town, this moderately
priced little hotel
decorates the walls with
paintings by local artists.

Le Moulin à l'Huile €€
*1 quai Maréchal Foch,
Vaison-la-Romaine; tel: 04
90 36 20 67.* There are
several popular
inexpensive brasseries in
the town centre, and some
good restaurants, too, of
which this is certainly one
of the best. The cooking
seems to combine
Provence with every other
part of the world, using
ginger, peppers, soya and
spices to enliven fresh
local ingredients.

The restored Roman
theatre in the
Quartier du Puymin,
Vaison-la-Romaine, is used
throughout the annual
Summer Festival of
drama, music and dance
(early Jul–mid-Aug). There
is a festival of choral music
every summer, generally at
the beginning of Aug.

Above
Vaison-la-Romaine

Beaumes-de-Venise◇. Beautifully situated on the southern slope of the
Dentelles de Montmirail, with wonderful views across the Vaucluse
plain, this village produces a superb rich dessert wine. Turn right on to
the D21, and follow this pretty road eastward towards Mont Ventoux.
Reaching the D938, turn left. After 1km turn off the road to visit the
hillside village and castle of **LE BARROUX** ❷ , on the left. Back on the
D938, continue into the town of **MALAUCENE** ❸ .

Detour: Three kilometres before Malaucène turn right on to the D19
to the pretty, old village of **Bédoin**◇, on the lower slopes of Mont
Ventoux. Leave Bédoin heading east on the D974. After about 2km

take the turn on to the D19, reaching exquisitely picturesque little **Flassan*** after 3km. Stay on the D19 for another 4km through a pretty wooded area to attractive **Villes-sur-Auzon***. The road out of town is the D1, but almost at once take the D942 uphill. The road joins the **Gorge de la Nesque****, the river flowing deep in a narrow valley. Follow the gorge, with dramatic views in places, especially at the belvedere on the right after the fourth tunnel. The road arrives at the pretty village of **Monnieux*** with old houses and a lofty 12th-century tower, then take the D942 into **SAULT ❹**. Northwest of the little town rises the pale conical mass of **MONT VENTOUX ❺**. The D164 (joins the D974) from Sault goes right up to and over the summit. Stay on this road as it runs along the crest of the massif, descending to rejoin the D938 at Malaucène.

From Malaucène continue on the D938 into **VAISON-LA-ROMAINE ❻**. Leave town on the left bank of the Ouvèze on the D977, the main road signposted for Orange and Carpentras. After 5km, take the left turn for **SEGURET ❼**. This delightful lane runs along the side of the **DENTELLES DE MONTMIRAIL ❽**, with wonderful views over the spread of vineyards. Every village is irresistible. Continue to **VACQUEYRAS ❾**, then double back to take the D8 and the D23 to **ORANGE ❿**.

Leave Orange on the south side of town, near the Théâtre Antique: first take avenue Général Leclerc (N7, signposted Avignon), then turn right on to the little road (D68) that goes straight to **CHATEAUNEUF-DU-PAPE ⓫**. Return from there to Avignon.

Lubéron and Southern Vaucluse

Ratings

Scenery ●●●●●

Sightseeing ●●●●●

History ●●●●○

Restaurants ●●●●○

Children ●●○○○

Wine-tasting ●●○○○

Shopping ●●○○○

Entertainment
●○○○○

The southern half of the spacious Vaucluse *département* is quintessential rural Provence, full of sunlight, echoing history and rustic atmosphere. Its exquisite scenery has been half wild, half tamed since time immemorial. Neat terraces of vines climb hillsides, but at their edges bursts out the untamable, scrub-like *garrigue*. Along the southern horizon rise the dark, hazy lines of the Lubéron Massif, a secret world of rocks and ravines, fragrant Provençal woodland trails and remote hamlets. On either side, the Lubéron descends to wide pearly valleys, to the north the Coulon (or Calavon) and its flurry of tributaries, and to the south the unpredictable waters of the broad Durance. The western end of the range is the Petit Lubéron, where the hills descend to the meeting of the two valleys, while the eastern Grand Lubéron rises to more impressive peaks such as Mourre Nègre, and follows the two rivers upstream into the Provence Alps.

BONNIEUX❖

ℹ️ Tourist offices in the region are generally open Mon–Sat 0900–1200, 1400–1900.

Bonnieux Tourist Office *place Carnot; tel: 04 90 75 91 90.*

🏛️ **Musée de la Boulagerie €** *12 rue de la République; tel: 04 90 75 88 34. Open May–Oct 1000–1200, 1500–1830. Closed Tue.*

🛍️ There is a weekly market on Sat.

Poised high on the Petit Lubéron ridge, this delightful hillside village used to be fortified, and still has a fragment of its original ramparts. In one of the old houses is an unusual **museum**❖ devoted to the bakery trade. Take the steep lane up to the 12th-century church, no longer used (services are now held in a large new church on the edge of the village). The terrace beside the old church gives fine views towards Mont Ventoux.

Accommodation and food in Bonnieux

Auberge de l'Aiguebrun €€–€€€ *On the D943; tel: 04 90 04 47 00; fax: 04 90 04 47 01.* The little hotel has a pool, garden, private parking and pretty, well-equipped rooms. The cuisine is dedicatedly Provençal – lovely aubergine gratin, delicious desserts – served in a glorious setting. Hotel closed Dec–Jan; restaurant closed Tue and Wed lunch.

Le Fournil €€ *5 place Carnot; tel: 04 90 75 83 62.* Eat good local cooking out of doors by the fountain, in the heart of the village. Closed Mon.

Pâtisserie Tomas € *9 rue de la République.* Excellent village bakery with tasty sweet and savoury pastries, which you can eat in with a cup of tea or coffee. Closed Tue.

CAVAILLON*

ℹ️ **Cavaillon Tourist Office** *place François Tourel; tel: 04 90 71 32 01; www.cavaillon-luberon.com*

🅿️ Plenty of parking can be found in and near place François Tourel, close to the tourist office and sights.

Cavaillon is synonymous with its pink-fleshed melons and has become a major centre of market gardening. Little survives of the Gallic and Roman settlement of *Cabellio* which stood on the hill of St-Jacques, beside the modern centre. A small **Roman arch***, dating from the 1st century BC, and previously standing a short distance away, has been re-erected in place François Tourel. From the arch, a stepped path leads up the hill, giving sweeping views over town and country. At the top, 12th-century **Chapelle-St Jacques*** stands prettily among the trees. However, to see any remnants of the ancient site you must visit the **Musée Archéologique*** in the lower town. Nearby, in rue Hébraique, is Cavaillon's little **synagogue** of 1772, with a delightful unaltered interior containing a **Musée du Comtat Venaissin Juif (Museum of the Jewish Comtat Venaissin)*** which has relics of the

There is a weekly market on Mon.

Synagogue (Musée du Comtat Venaissin Juif) and **Musée Archéologique** € *tel: 04 90 76 00 34. Open Apr–Sep 0900–1200, 1400–1800; rest of year 1000–1200, 1400–1700. Closed Tue and public holidays. Ticket allows entry to both museums.*

Below
Fontaine-de-Vaucluse

14th-century synagogue on the same site. This quarter was an enclosed *carrière*, or compulsory ghetto. It gives insight into the once considerable Jewish life of the town and of the whole of the Vaucluse, tolerated both by the Avignon popes and the Counts of Toulouse. There is no Jewish community in Cavaillon today.

Accommodation and food in Cavaillon

Le Fin de Siècle € *42 place du Clos, tel: 04 90 71 28 85.* This glorious old brasserie has been open just over a century and is *the* place for a drink or a meal. Closed Sun.

Restaurant Jean-Jacques Prévot €€ *353 avenue Verdun; tel: 04 90 71 32 43; fax: 04 90 71 97 05; www.restaurant-prevot.com.* The colourful, acclaimed chef-proprietor M. Prévot celebrates each season of the year with a crazily indulgent 'festival' of his favourite ingredients – for example, scallops in winter, with gastronomic menus that include them in every course (except dessert). There are classic regional menus, too.

COLORADO DE RUSTREL**

↻ The quarries lie south of the D22 at Rustrel (11km from Apt) and extend towards the D209.

P Off the D22 both before and after Rustrel, roads lead to the car parks for the quarries. The principal one is down the unmarked road opposite the junction of the D30a.

Southern Vaucluse produces around 3000 metric tons of ochre annually and is one of the world's most important sources of this mineral. The two major ochre quarries in the area are in the villages of Roussillon and Rustrel – both names are based on the word *rousse*, redness. The Colorado de Rustrel is a vast area crossed by steep paths where you can wander for hours among the dazzling, luminous, multicoloured earth, which has been cut into bizarre cliffs and pillars by the quarrying. Beware: paths in the quarries are steep and may be slippery.

What is ochre?

A natural mix of sand and clay, iron oxide and minerals produces this distinctive brightly coloured earth. Colours vary according to the exact mix of iron and other metals and minerals. The refining process removes all but the iron oxide and clay, which can then be turned into powder for use in paints and dyes.

FONTAINE-DE-VAUCLUSE**

ℹ Fontaine-de-Vaucluse Tourist Office *Chemin de la Fontaine;* tel: 04 90 20 32 22; e-mail: *officetourisme.vaucluse@ wanadoo.fr*

↻ The D25 leads into Fontaine-de-Vaucluse village, where there is a free car park. The rest of the way is on foot along Chemin de la Fontaine; it takes about 15 minutes to reach the spring.

In springtime up to 12 000m³ of water per minute gush from this astonishing water source at the foot of an impressive cliff, one of the outlets for the complex system of underground rivers beneath the Vaucluse Plateau. When it's pouring like that, the Fontaine-de-Vaucluse is one of the world's most powerful natural sources of fresh water; however, in summer the spectacle is disappointing. The water emerges from a deep pool and flows out of the valley to become (with other sources) the River Sorgue. Along the walk to the spring you will run the gauntlet of tacky souvenir stalls. There's an interesting **Musée d'Histoire 1939–1945****, which deals with the Nazi occupation, the Resistance (very active locally) and the artistic background to the spirit of liberation. Also on the way there's a quirky underground museum of rocks and minerals, called **Le Monde Souterrain de Norbert Casteret (Underground World of Norbert Casteret)***. Close by is a traditional **paper mill** which can be visited.

Apart from seeing the spectacular spring, this is a compulsory stop for lovers of French literature, for it was here that the poet Francesco Petrarca (1304–74), known in English as Petrarch, lived for 16 years in the peaceful but painful isolation described in *De Vita Solitaria*. Here

ⓘ Musée d'Histoire 1939–1945 € *Chemin de la Fontaine; tel: 04 90 20 24 00. Open Jul–Aug 1000–1900; during the Easter school holidays and 15 Apr–30 Jun and 1 Sep–15 Oct 1000–1200, 1400–1800; 1 Mar–14 Apr Sat and Sun only; 16 Oct–31 Dec 1000–1200, 1300–1700. Closed Tue.*

Monde Souterrain de Norbert Casteret €€ *Chemin de la Fontaine; tel: 04 90 20 34 13. Open Jul–Aug 1000–1200, 1400–1830; Apr–Jun closes 1800; Feb–Mar and Sep–10 Nov closes 1700; closed Mon and Tue. Closed 11 Nov–Feb. 45-minute guided tours.*

Musée Pétrarque €€ *Village centre; tel: 04 90 20 37 20. Open Jun–Sep 0930–1200, 1400–1830; Apr–May and 1–15 Oct closes at 1800 (1–14 Apr Sat and Sun only); 15–31 Oct Sat and Sun only and closes at 1700. Rest of year closed. Closed Tue.*

◔ There is a weekly market on Tue (note that museums may be closed on that day).

Above
Fontaine-de-Vaucluse

he wrote about the mysterious and beautiful Laura with whom, after one glimpse in an Avignon church, he had fallen desperately in love. It seems that Laura was no imaginary character: she was a member of the noble de Sade family – and already married. While Petrarch pined in solitude for the mysterious lady, she contracted plague and died. There is a **Musée Pétrarque** in the village.

The Vaucluse *département* originally took its name from the closed valley (*vallis clausa*) in which the Fontaine de Vaucluse emerges.

GORDES**

Gordes Tourist Office *place du Château; tel: 04 90 72 02 75; e-mail: ofice.gordes@wanadoo.fr; www.gordes-village.com*

There is a weekly market on Tue.

Château €€ *tel: 04 90 72 02 89. Open 1000–1200, 1400–1800. Closed Tue.*

The atmospheric old village of Gordes is built in a curious manner – one house almost on top of another – on the sides of a steep hill with a proud **château*** at the summit. Inside the château is a museum dedicated to the work of major op-artist Victor Vasarely (born 1908). The village streets are narrow – sometimes arcaded, sometimes in steps. All around Gordes are settlements of *bories* – primitive stone huts some dating from 200 BC – which were lived in seasonally by poor peasants and labourers up until the 19th century.

Accommodation and food in Gordes

Les Bories €€€ *route de l'Abbaye de Sénanque; tel: 04 90 72 00 51; fax: 04 90 72 01 22.* Not much in common with the surrounding *bories*, this wonderfully situated, tranquil, civilised and comfortable hotel has a pool, tennis and a top-quality restaurant. Pricey.

Mas de la Sénancole €€€ *Hameau Imberts, 4km from Gordes; tel: 04 90 76 76 55; fax: 04 90 76 70 44; e-mail: gordes@mas-de-la-senancole.com; www.mas-de-la-senancole.com/gb/index.html.* Hidden away in greenery near the village, this is a very attractive modern hotel – built in traditional style – with outdoor pool, gardens and comfortable rooms. Its restaurant, Esprit des Ocres, has a cool, airy Provençal atmosphere and luxurious cooking.

Hôtel le Gordois €€ *route du Cavaillon; tel: 04 90 72 00 75; fax: 04 90 72 07 00.* In an area of expensive accommodation, it's a relief to find a decent, sensibly priced, family-run hotel. Pretty garden, pleasant breakfast terrace and pool.

L'ISLE-SUR-LA-SORGUE**

This interesting little town, standing on an island in the Sorgue, is a pleasant place of tree-lined streets and has a 17th-century **church*** with an extremely ornate interior, an 18th-century **Hôtel-Dieu*** (hospital) with its original pharmacy, and several fine old mansions.

Bories

Pointy dry-stone *bories*, strange windowless dwellings or store-places, dot the landscape in parts of the Vaucluse and elsewhere in inland Provence. The village of Gordes in particular has a large restored group called the *village des bories*. On the Lubéron, too, these primeval-looking constructions are numerous. Nearly all have a single opening facing east. From the Iron Age right up to the 19th century, *bories* were used as summer quarters by shepherds and farmers, to sleep, shelter, or store tools and animals.

L'Isle-sur-la-Sorgue Tourist Office place de la Liberté; tel: 04 90 38 04 78; e-mail : contact@ot-islesurlasorgue.fr; www.ot-islesurlasorgue.fr

P Because of the narrow streets and the difficulty of parking, in season it's best to park outside the village. There's a car park off the N100 close to place Gambetta, the main entrance to the village.

Hôtel-Dieu €€ rue J Théophile; tel: 04 90 21 34 00. 30-minute guided tours 0900–1200, 1400–1700. Closed weekends and holidays. Book ahead.

There is a weekly market on Thu, and a larger all-day second-hand market on Sun.

Most striking of all are the large mossy **water-wheels**⁺⁺ on the Sorgue. The town specialises in antiques, hence the busy Sunday market.

Accommodation and food in L'Isle-sur-la-Sorgue

Mas du Cure Bourse €€€ 120 chemin Serre, 3km out of town; tel: 04 90 38 16 58; fax: 04 90 38 52 31. Former 18th-century coaching inn out in the country, now a delightful, comfortable, tranquil place to stay (or eat) with pool, gardens, and rooms in traditional Provençal style. Menus have many regional touches, plus some unusual, cooked cheese dishes (such as brie-de-meaux en tapenade). Restaurant closed Mon and Tue midday.

Le Carré d'Herbes €€ 13 avenue des Quatre-Otages; tel: 04 90 38 62 95. Peaceful green corner of town, furnished with treasures from the local antiques trade. Light, fresh cooking with plenty of spices and herbs and originality brought to local favourites such as beef en daube or lamb with aubergine caviar. Closed Tue, Wed and in Jan.

La Prévôte €€ 4 rue Jean-Jacques Rousseau; tel: 04 90 38 57 29. Salmon cannelloni with goats' cheese, and stuffed courgette flowers are among the delicate dishes at this acclaimed, yet inexpensive, village centre restaurant behind the church. Local wines a speciality.

MENERBES⁺

A Year in Provence Ménerbes' remoteness has been no deterrent to thousands of fans inspired by Peter Mayle's best-selling A Year in Provence, which is set here.

The astonishing and picturesque old village of Ménerbes seems to defy access, perched on a north-facing Lubéron ridge. Indeed, in the 1570s, Ménerbes' fortified **Citadelle**⁺ was held by Calvinists who lived here perfectly freely despite a force of Catholics who tried for 15 months to capture it. Thanks to a seceret underground passage the Calvinists went to and fro undisturbed. Now collapsed, the passageway runs from near place de l'Horloge, the main square. Walk to the church at the end of the village for a wide view over to Mont Ventoux and the Vaucluse Plain.

OPPEDE-LE-VIEUX⁺

Opposite
Ochre quarry, Roussillon

A fortified terraced village of ancient houses, abandoned about a century ago, Oppède was taken up and restored by recent incomers and has since become thoroughly picturesque. The ruined castle, originally built by the powerful southern overlords, the counts of Toulouse, was much altered in later centuries. In 1545, it was the base of Baron Jean Maynier of Oppède, the savage leader of the papal campaign to wipe out the Vaudois sect.

ROUSSILLON✦✦

ⓘ **Roussillon Tourist Office** *place de la Poste; tel: 04 90 05 60 25.*

Ⓟ It is almost impossible to park other than in the large public car parks provided close to the entrance to the quarries.

Poised on a ridge – all that's left of a landscape eaten away over the centuries – this pleasing village stands among brilliant **ochre quarries✦✦✦**. You can walk through tunnels and climb cliffs of dazzling red and yellow sand which clings and stains like water-colours (so dress accordingly). The main footpath through the quarries is part of a long-distance trail, the GR6, which continues to the **Colorado de Rustrel** quarry, 15km away (*see page 65*). After this ochre experience, the everyday colours of nature, when you next see them, are put to shame. All Roussillon's village houses are made of tinted sandstone.

SENANQUE, ABBAYE DE✧✧

Abbaye de Sénanque € tel: 04 90 72 05 72; www.senanque.fr. Open Mar–Oct 1000–1200, 1400–1700; rest of year 1400–1700. Closed Sun and all Christian holidays.

The sturdy, austere 12th-century Sénanque Abbey, hidden in the deep little Sénancole valley close to **Gordes** (*see page 67*), was extensively restored when it was reoccupied by monks of the Cistercian Order in the early 20th century. It has an exquisite simplicity and grace, hallmarks of the Cistercians. Its beauty is enhanced in summer by lines of thick purple lavender growing right up to the building. Inside, linger in the tranquil cloister and church, which lacks any decoration at all, and see the fireplace in the Monks' Hall. Last of the 'Three Cistercian Sisters of Provence' (the other two were Silvacane and Le Thoronet), the original monastic community was dealt a fatal blow by the Vaudois attack in 1544. Fortunately, the surviving buildings were restored, new ones added and Sénanque is once again a monastery. Today the abbey buildings contain a cultural centre and, more surprisingly, an institute (with museum) devoted to the Sahara desert. The monks make excellent oils and other products from their lavender, which are on sale here.

SILVACANE, ABBAYE DE✧

Abbaye de Silvacane € The abbey stands beside the village of la Roque d'Anthéron; tel: 04 42 50 41 69. Open Apr–Sep 0900–1900; rest of year closes at 1700. Closed Tue.

On the south bank of the Durance (therefore not in the Vaucluse), this rustically situated former abbey still has all the simplicity and strength of the Cistercians, despite the damage it has suffered. Frequently attacked, it was abandoned after the Wars of Religion in the 17th century, became the local parish church, was turned into a farm after the Revolution, and was subsequently purchased as a national monument in 1949. Since then, it is gradually being repaired and restored.

Suggested tour

Total distance: 130km, with a detour of 30km. Don't forget to allow at least a couple of hours for a walk in the ochre quarries at Roussillon.

Time: Don't rush. Almost every place deserves a stop and a stroll. The whole tour, including the walks, makes an excellent day out.

Links: The N100 take you to Forcalquier on the Alpes de Haute Provence tour (*see page 159*); and from Cavaillon you can get on to the Les Baux and the Alpilles tour (*see page 90*). At Avignon, this route also links with the Upper Vaucluse (*see page 50*).

Route: From **Avignon** (*see page 40*) take the N100 east out of the city to **L'ISLE-SUR-LA-SORGUE ❶**. Take the D938, then the D175 on the left (good views) through the *garrigue* to reach nearby **FONTAINE-DE-VAUCLUSE ❷**, where you should park and enjoy the 15-minute walk

Left
The Abbaye de Sénanque

Above
Gordes

to the spring. Use the tiny backroads DI00A, D100 and D110 to reach **GORDES** ❸. Further along in the Sénancole valley you will come to the **ABBAYE DE SENANQUE** ❹. Follow the D2, turning right on to the D102 (if you miss it, there are alternative roads) to the amazing village of **ROUSSILLON** ❺. Unmissable at Roussillon is a walk in the brilliant ochre quarries.

Return via the lovely D104 and the D4 to the N100, where you turn left to enter **Apt**, centre for the local ochre-processing industry. It's one of those small attractive old country towns – of which there are so many in Provence – with plane trees, fountains and a square with men playing *boules*. It has a historic church, and a big local market every Saturday.

Detour: Take the N100 east through attractive country up to **Forcalquier.**

From Apt turn south into the Lubéron hills. Take the D943, and turn right on to the D232 or the D36 to enter **BONNIEUX ❻**. You might prefer the D3, a smaller and quieter lane all the way from Apt to Bonnieux.

Detour: Continue on the D943 across the Lubéron range, descending to **Lourmarin**, overlooked by its lofty château which is partly medieval, partly Renaissance. The writer, philosopher (and footballer) Albert Camus (1913–60) is buried in the village cemetery. At the foot of the hill, **Cadenet** lies beside the main D973. Notice the statue of the legendary Tambour d'Arcole ('Arcole drummer'), a heroic local lad who, when Napoleon's forces were trying to capture the Arcole bridge from the Austrians, swam the river and ferociously beat his drum on the Austrian side. Deducing that the French had crossed the river, the Austrians retreated and abandoned the bridge. Ahead on the D943 lies the River Durance and the **ABBAYE DE SILVACANE ❼**. Visit the abbey and retrace your route back to Bonnieux.

Follow the pretty winding lane (D3, D109) to **Lacoste**, where the ruined castle used to belong to the de Sade family, on to **MENERBES ❽** and up to **OPPEDE-LE-VIEUX ❾**. Descend (on the D176) through Maubec and its vineyards to reach the busier D2, where you turn left to reach **CAVAILLON ❿**. From here it's just 10km to join the Les Baux and Alpilles driving tour (*see page 96*). Return from Cavaillon to Avignon on the D973.

Gard

Ratings

Roman remains	●●●●●
Scenery	●●●●●
History	●●●●
Children	●●●
Restaurants	●●●
Wine-tasting	●●●
Shopping	●●
Entertainment	●

W est of the Rhône, the Gard *département* and its border with the Hérault are astonishingly diverse. Since the medieval Albigensian Crusade broke up the old County of Toulouse, the area has belonged more to Languedoc than Provence. Reaching across plain and mountain, it encompasses sun-baked vineyards, lonely Camargue marshes, industry and urbanisation, and cool uninhabited uplands wrapped in chestnut forest. The Gard touches both the Mediterranean and the Rhône, yet also extends inland to the highest peaks of the Cévennes. It seems to possess everything that can be found in southern France, from beaches to the finest remnants of ancient Rome, from country markets to fragrant wild *garrigue*. The wines of the Gard, too, epitome of drinkable, affordable reds, encompass a spectrum of strikingly different *appellations* – Côtes du Rhône, Coteaux du Languedoc and Costières du Gard, with one of the best of inexpensive southern table wines, Costières de Nîmes.

AMBRUSSUM*

ⓘ Tourist Office The nearest is at Lunel.

Spread out on the Hérault side of the border, near Lunel, Ambrussum is the site of a small riverside Roman town on the *Via Domitia* – the Romans' highway from Italy to Spain that existed here from the 3rd century BC to the 1st century AD. It is remarkable not just for the extent of what survives, but also for its quality of preservation, and for its 360-degree panoramic setting, reached by climbing 300m of Roman road. Especially striking are the remnants of a Roman river bridge close by, a great wedge of ancient masonry, a single span standing in the middle of the River Vidourle.

Map of the Gard region showing: allée-Française, Alès, St-Privat-des-Vieux, D6, 23, Bagnols-sur-Cèze, St-Christol-lès-Alès, St-Hilaire-de-Brethmas, Connaux, Laudun, N580, salle, Anduze, Bagard, 15, 30, St-Victor-la-Coste, 19, Roquemaure, Boisset-et-Gaujac, Vézénobres, D981, Uzès, D982, 27, 21, D982, Lézan, 12, 23, 17, Tavel, 14, Puj, Durfort, Lédignan, Moussac, St-Chaptes, 16, Villeneuve-lès-Avignon, Fort, Sauve, N110, 14, S, 17, D999, Gard, Pont du Gard, Remoulins, Les Angles, Avi, Quissac, La Calmette, 214, E15, D986, Aramon, Rognonas, zille-ois, 20, St-Mamert-du-Gard, 16, S, Bézouce, 25, Viv-le-Fesq, 275, Marguerittes, Boulbon, Château, c St-oup, Fontanès, 12, 22, D999, Caveirac, Nîmes, Vallabrègues, 21 Ma, N110, Manduel, Beaucaire, Calvisson, Milhaud, Bouillargues, Tarascon, 2, Sommières, 17, Caissargues, Boisseron, Aubais, Bernis, Garons, Bellegarde, Aigues-Vives, Aubord, A54, Rhône, N570, Alpi, 29, 19, S, Vergèze, D135, E80, Fontvieille, D17, Ambrussum, 10, Vauvert, D42, 29, Fourques, Castries, A9, N113, Aimargues, St-Gilles, Arles, 12, 12, Lunel, D979, N572, St-Martin-de-Crau, ellier, Baillargues, St-Laurent-d'Aigouze, 0, 10 km, n-, Le Crès, Mauguio, 18, Albaron, N568, La Grande-Motte, 29, Aigues-, CAMARGUE, Pérols, 37, 10, 11

ANDUZE❖❖

ⓘ Anduze Tourist Office Plan de Brie; tel: 04 66 61 98 17; e-mail: anduze@ot-anduze.fr; www.ot-anduze.fr. Open daily in season, closed Sun out of season.

🍴 Bambouseraie de Prafrance €€ 2km from Anduze, on the road to Générargues; tel: 04 66 61 70 47; www.bambouseraie.fr. Open Mar–Nov 0900–1200, 1400–1900. No midday closing Jul–Aug.

This picturesque, fortified old village stands at the Porte des Cévennes (Cévennes Gateway), a deep gorge on the River Gardon d'Anduze and a gap in the mountains. Above this point are the profoundly rustic Cévennes mountains. Cross the river to see the **Bambouseraie de Prafrance**❖❖, an amazing privately owned 'woodland' of giant bamboos (*phyllostachys*) through which you can wander on paths. Also in the Bambouseraie are waterways, giant sequoia and many other breathtaking flora. A little further north on the same road, Mas Soubeyran, once home of the legendary Camisard leader Rolland (1675–1704), now contains the **Musée du Désert (Museum of the Desert)**❖❖ – *désert* in this case means lonely, wild country – with displays about his life and the world of the mystical peasant Camisard rebels. Just 2km further on, a side road from the museum brings you to the **Grotte de Trabuc**❖❖, a huge cavern with an underground lake. The cave was lived in during neolithic times and has often been used since as a hiding

Musée du Désert €
Mas Soubeyran, Mialet;
tel: 04 66 85 32 72;
www.museedudesert.com.
Open Mar–Nov 0930–1200,
1430–1800; no midday
closing Jul–Aug.

Grotte de Trabuc €
7km from Anduze on Mialet
road; tel: 04 66 85 03 28.
Open Jun–15 Sep
0930–1800; 15 Mar–15
May and 15 Sep–15 Oct
1030–1230, 1430–1730.

There is a weekly market on Thu.

A religious Protestant gathering takes place at the Musée du Désert for one week in Sep.

place and shelter. The Camisards held many of their clandestine prayer sessions and meetings here.

At Anduze you can climb aboard the funky Transcevenol Train (*summer only; tel: 04 66 85 10 48*), a makeshift-looking old steam train, belching smoke as it chugs up the Gardon valley to St-Jean-du-Gard. Stops on the way include the Bambouseraie de Prafrance.

Accommodation and food near Anduze

Les Demeures du Ranquet €€–€€€ *route de St-Hippolyte-du-Fort, Tornac (6km away); tel: 04 66 77 51 63; fax: 04 66 77 55 62.* Restful comfort at an arty hotel-restaurant in a rural setting, with modern sculpture in the wooded grounds, separate little chalets, good cooking and a refined atmosphere.

Les Trois Barbus €€ *route de Mialet Générargues (5km away); tel: 04 66 61 72 12; fax: 04 66 61 72 74.* Beautifully situated, with good views, this very comfortable and peaceful hotel-restaurant is close to Mas Soubeyran in the heart of Camisard country. Mar–Nov only.

BEAUCAIRE❖

Beaucaire Tourist Office *24 Cours Gambetta; tel: 04 66 59 26 57; fax: 04 66 59 68 51; e-mail: info@ot-beaucaire.fr; www.ot-beaucaire.fr*

There is a weekly Sun market.

Beaucaire was once an important Roman town at a meeting of highways, and an important river port on the Rhône. It later became the site of one of Europe's largest annual trade fairs, where hundreds of thousands of people would gather every July to buy, sell and have fun. The fair died out after the development of the railways. The town was guarded by the mighty **Château de Beaucaire❖**, first built in the 11th century, but largely dismantled in the 17th. Its hilltop ruins are still spectacular, and gaze across the Rhône at its rival in **Tarascon** (*see page 96*). There are demonstrations of birds of prey in flight on afternoons throughout the summer (€€).

LUNEL❖

Lunel Tourist Office *place des Martyrs-de-la-Résistance; tel: 04 67 71 01 37; fax: 04 67 71 26 67; www.lunel.com*

Chodoreille €€ *140 rue Lakanal; tel: 04 67 71 55 77; fax: 04 67 83 19 97.* The regional cooking at this restaurant is the best in town.

Just across the border in the Hérault *département* lies the small and ancient town of Lunel, famous for its rich and delicious sweet wine, Muscat de Lunel. It was once an important Jewish centre dating from Roman times, and had its own Hebrew University and Medical School. While visiting Lunel in 1165, the Jewish traveller and chronicler Benjamin of Tudela reported that he had visited a community with several eminent scholars. The Jews were driven out of the town in a series of expulsions during the 14th century, and today, curiously, there's a large Muslim population. The town's historic **central quarter** is interesting, with impressive old houses, arcaded squares, alleys, lanes

Below
The Pont du Gard

and fortifications, and just outside the old city wall there are remnants of the 12th-century synagogue. This important landmark in the history of the town is now in private hands and being used as a store-room.

PONT DU GARD✦✦✦

Pont du Gard Tourist Office *at Pont du Gard; tel: 04 66 37 00 02. If unattended (out of season) tel: 04 66 21 02 51.*

Pont du Gard is 3km from Remoulins. Follow signs from the D19 north of Remoulins for the north bank, or the D981 from Remoulins for the south bank. If you want to drive across the bridge, traffic is one-way only north–south, so approach from the north bank (road closed in high season – heavy on-the-spot fine for passing through barrier).

This amazing honey-coloured stone bridge was essential to the existence of Roman Nîmes. High and narrow, it strides across the broad, shallow Gard in its deep green valley. It has three tiers of elegant arches, and is a triumph not just of engineering but of design and aesthetics. The lower arches now carry a roadway which provides the main access to the bridge. Along the top runs a small covered waterchannel, the original purpose of the edifice – the rest was built just to hold this channel at the right height and angle. It is awesome to think of all the (slave) labour and mathematical skill that the Romans expended on carrying a water-pipe across a river. Through it flowed 20 000m³ of water daily. Part of a 50-km aqueduct built in around 19 BC to bring fresh stream water from Uzès to Nîmes, it was in use for a thousand years, 500 of which were without any maintenance, yet it survives today in nearly intact condition. The lofty water-channel can be walked through, and daredevils even walk along the unprotected top of the bridge, which is 3.5m wide and has a 50-m drop. The riverbanks at the foot of the bridge are beach-like and popular for sunbathing.

P Parking space is provided on both banks. The north bank car park is 50 per cent more expensive.

Accommodation and food at Pont du Gard

Le Colombier € *Beside Pont du Gard on the right bank; tel: 04 66 37 05 28.* This has been for years the best spot from which to view the aqueduct, the best place to eat nearby, and the best place to be if you'd like to see the bridge after the crowds have gone home. It's an unpretentious, traditional little hotel with an inexpensive terrace restaurant overlooking the river.

La Bégude St Pierre €€ *4km along the D981; tel: 04 66 63 63 63.* In an exquisite rural staging post of the 17th century, enclosed by gardens and near the river, this hotel and restaurant is a good place to enjoy hearty, meaty local dishes, the best of local wines, and a tranquil, civilised atmosphere close to the Roman aqueduct.

SOMMIERES❖❖

i **Sommières Tourist Office** *rue Général Bruyère; tel: 04 66 80 99 30; fax: 04 66 80 06 95; e-mail: ot.sommières@wanadoo.fr; www.ot-sommieres.fr.st. Open Jul and Aug daily.*

Despite a traffic problem, this is an interesting and picturesque town, handsomely sited beside a broad weir on the River Vidourie, where the bridge preserves a Roman arch. Part of the historic town centre is still walled and entered though an impressive old gateway. Within the walls, boutiques, bars and souvenir shops fill the narrow lanes. A big street market takes place in the handsomely arcaded central square every Saturday. Overlooking the place are the ruins of its old château.

The writer Lawrence Durrell (1912–90), although so closely associated with Greece, lived in Sommières at 15 route de Saussines, in a large detached house on the edge of town, from 1957 right up to his death.

Accommodation and food in Sommières

Auberge du Pont Romain €€ *2 rue Emile-Jamais; tel: 04 66 80 00 58; fax: 04 66 80 31 52.* The first impression is of a roadside eyesore topped by a factory chimney. While this former cloth and carpet works on the edge of Sommières looks an unlikely spot to stay or eat, it turns out to be cleverly refurbished as a pleasant hotel with flowery gardens and a decent restaurant. Restaurant closed Wed out of season. Closed 15 Jan–15 Mar and Nov.

UZÈS***

❶ Uzès Tourist Office *avenue Libération; tel: 04 66 22 68 88; fax: 04 66 22 95 19; www.ville-uzes.fr*

❷ The town lies on the D981, the Nîmes–Alès road. Traffic follows the boulevards around the old central quarter.

❸ There are several car parks close to the ring of boulevards and in avenue de la Libération.

❹ Duché (Ducal Castle) €€€ *rue Jacques d'Uzès; tel: 04 66 22 18 96. 45-minute guided tours. Jun–Sep 1000–1830; rest of year 1000–1200, 1400–1800.*

Musée 1900 and Musée du Train et du Jouet €€ *Moulin de Chalier, 4km from Uzès, near Arpaillargues; tel: 04 66 22 58 64. Open 0900–1200, 1400–1900; Jul–Aug no midday closing.*

❺ There is a weekly Sat market.

Known as Uzege in the *langue d'oc* (Provençal), and *Ucetia* to the Romans, the town has an appealing central **Ville Ancienne (Old Quarter)*** of higgledy-piggledy narrow streets and pretty squares with fine old mansions of pale stone. It artfully combines the Middle Ages with the 17th century. All clusters around the impressive, martial-looking **Duché (Ducal Castle)**. Rue Jacques d'Uzès, passing in front of the castle, is the main street through the old centre. It quickly reaches the gorgeous **place aux Herbes**, the main square, with fountain, plane trees and arcades. This old central 'Secteur Sauvegardé' – 'Protected Zone' as the signs proclaim it – is encircled by noisy, lively boulevards of shops and bars, not merely shaded by leafy plane trees but almost dark beneath their masses of heavy foliage. The unusual cylindrical 42m-high Romanesque **Tour Fenestrelle**, on the edge of the old centre, makes a strange but beautiful landmark. Below it, **Promenade Jean-Racine** has a majestic view south. Out of town, the **Musée 1900*** is all about vehicles, technology and daily life a century ago, and the nearby **Musée du Train et du Jouet (Train and Toy Museum)*** has a 400m-long train set and miniature models of local sights, such as the arena at Nîmes.

Accommodation and food in Uzès

Hôtel Général d'Entraigues €€ *8 rue de la Calade; tel: 04 66 22 32 68; fax: 04 66 22 57 01.* This charming 15th-century mansion and other historic buildings within the Old Quarter form a delightful, calm and refined place to stay at a quite moderate price. Its restaurant, **Jardins de Castille**, situated opposite, offers good, imaginative cooking, again at reasonable prices.

VERGEZE*

ℹ **Vergeze Tourist
Office** place de la
Mairie; tel: 04 66 35 45 92;
fax: 04 66 35 45 92;
www.vergeze.fr

🏢 **Source Perrier €**
Near Codognan, 3km
south of Vergèze; tel: 04 66
84 60 27; www.perrier.com/
EN/index2.asp. Open
Mon–Fri for 1-hour guided
tours between 0800–1030,
1300–1530. Additional tours
on summer afternoons.

Three kilometres south of the village in flat, featureless countryside stands the large modern processing and bottling plant of **Source Perrier◆◆◆**. This completely covers the natural spring of what is perhaps now the world's most popular mineral water. Annual sales from this spot exceed an incredible 500 million bottles. The water emerges from an underground lake at a constant 15°C, bubbling with escaping natural gases. Part of the process involves taking the gas out and putting it back in again – to ensure every bottle of Perrier has the same amount of fizz!

Suggested tour

Total distance: 170km; the detour adds on 80km.

Time: The main route will take at least a full day, and includes plenty of sightseeing. The detour to Anduze deserves an overnight stop.

Links: At Beaucaire, you can cross the Rhône to Tarascon, on the Alpilles tour (see page 90). At St-Gilles, this tour links with the Camargue (see page 108).

Route: From **Nîmes** (see page 82) leave town heading northeast on the D979, a picturesque country road, up into the Gard interior. It runs all the way through limestone hills cloaked with mature garrigue to **UZES ❶**. Come down the bigger D981 to the turning (on the right) for **PONT DU GARD ❷**. Take the D19 (or D981, if you want to skip Remoulins) for 3km into **Remoulins**. Cross the main N86 to continue on the D986 to **BEAUCAIRE ❸** on the Rhône, with a view of Tarascon castle across the river. Turn away from the Rhône on the D38. At Bellegarde, the road brushes against the Canal du Rhône, and follows it to **St-Gilles** (see page 112) on the edge of the Camargue. Now run through the flat, reedy terrain and rice paddies of these Camargue fringes (on the N572) to **Vauvert**. From the village centre take the country lane D56 (which changes to the D139) across a rather bleak open plain up to the **Perrier factory** near **VERGEZE ❹**. After visiting the water-bottling plant continue on the busy main Nîmes–Montpellier highway N113 across the départemental border from Gard into Hérault to enter the town of **LUNEL ❺**.

Above
The Tour Fenestrelle in Uzès

Leave Lunel on the D34 (towards Sommières), but after about 3km, take the little lane on the right (D110e) up to Villetelle, and double back down the track to **AMBRUSSUM ❻**. The main site is here on the Hérault side of the River Vidourle, though it can also be seen from the Gard side. Back in Villetelle, cross the Vidourle and turn left on to the D12 all the way into **SOMMIERES ❼**.

Detour: If you have time and would like to reach the foot of the Cévennes hills, take the D35 for 40km into **ANDUZE ❽**. This makes a worthwhile overnight stop or longer stay before returning on the same road to the main route, or returning to Nîmes directly on the D907.

From Sommières turn east on the leisurely country road D40 through vineyards, passing the **Oppidum de Nages** and skirting a succession of Costières de Nîmes wine villages. One worth pausing at is **Langlade**. The D40 passes housing developments and suburbs to re-enter Nîmes.

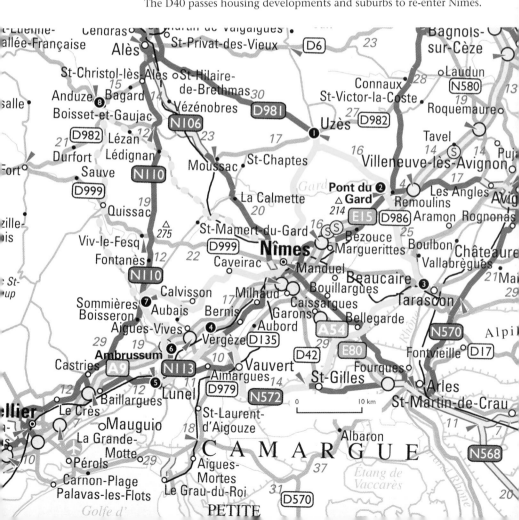

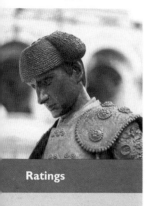

Nîmes

Ratings

History	●●●●●
Roman remains	●●●●●
Architecture	●●●○○
Museums	●●●○○
Shopping	●●●○○
Street life	●●●○○
Children	●●○○○
Entertainment	●●○○○

In Roman times, *Nemausus* was no more than a sleepy town for retired legionnaires. Now, this city west of the Rhône has the most impressive collection of Roman buildings still standing anywhere, including the most complete Roman arena. These marvellous antiquities make a startling contrast with the tall white modern blocks at the city edge and the vibrant sunny up-to-date atmosphere that pervades the Nîmes of today. The city's present character dates not from the Roman era at all, but from booming 19th-century industrialisation, when Nîmes was a leading textile-processing town. Here Lévi Strauss found the cloth he needed to manufacture the first jeans – *de Nîmes*, 'denim'. Bustling shopping streets and busy boulevards trace the line of now demolished ramparts, framing the quieter medieval and Renaissance nucleus. In the 1990s, exciting modern architecture has been integrated into the town, sometimes with imaginative echoes and reflections of the past.

Sights

ⓘ Les Arènes € *place des Arènes (end of boulevard Victor Hugo); tel; 04 66 76 72 77 or 04 66 02 80 80; www.arenesdenimes.com. Open summer 0900–1830; winter 0900–1200, 1400–1700. Closed on days of a show or a bullfight.*

Les Arènes❖❖❖

The most remarkable remnant of Roman *Nemausus* is the amphitheatre, or arena, on the southern edge of the Old Quarter. Constructed early in the 1st century AD with high, robust arches in two storeys, it is much better preserved than, for example, the Colosseum at Rome. A graceful oval in shape (133m by 101m), the interior retains its rows of seats, some still marked with the line showing the space allotted to each person. Patricians sat on the lower seats, for a better view, while plebeians were in the loftier back rows. Then as now, spectators could pay extra to sit in the shade of an awning. All around the arena, beneath the seating, are fascinating vaulted corridors. It is quite astonishingly intact despite the indignities of history. It was converted into a fortress by Visigoths in the 5th century, then seized by Saracens in the 8th. They were driven out by Charles Martel, who himself tried to burn down the structure

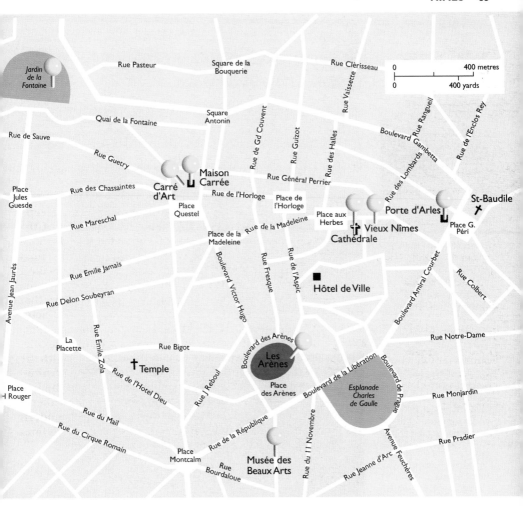

Carré d'Art € *place de la Maison Carrée*; tel: 04 66 76 35 35. Open summer Jun–Aug 1000–1900; winter 1100–1800. Closed Mon, and some holidays.

to prevent it from being taken again by the Saracens. Fortunately it was too sturdy for the fire to do much damage. During the medieval period the arena became entirely filled with houses and squalid dwellings. They were still there when Scottish novelist Tobias Smollett visited in 1766, much to his disgust, but some clearance began soon after and the arena was used again in about 1850.

Carré d'Art*

The architecture of Rome is literally reflected in the glass of British architect Sir Norman Foster's modern art gallery beside the 2000-year-old **Maison Carrée** (*see below*). Primarily an exhibition space for art since the 1960s, it has both permanent and temporary shows of the world's best known contemporary artists as well as avant-garde movements.

ℹ Main office *6 rue Auguste; tel: 04 66 21 80 52 or 04 66 58 38 00; fax: 04 66 58 38 01; e-mail: info@ot-nimes.fr; www.ot-nimes.fr*

Railway station *boulevard Sergent Triaire; tel: 04 66 21 80 52 or 04 66 58 38 00.*

Annexe *3 rue Brousson; tel: 04 66 67 97 40.*

🚲 Nîmes is skirted on the south side by *autoroute* A9 (La Languedocienne) and the major highway N86. All main roads into town eventually lead to the ring of boulevards around Vieux Nîmes (Old Quarter).

ℙ There is no parking within Vieux Nîmes (Old Quarter), but along the boulevards around Vieux Nîmes there are several car parks. Park on the south side of Vieux Nîmes if possible for a shorter walk to the Arena.

🎟 **Opening times for all Roman monuments** *Jun–Sep daily 0830–1930; Oct–May 0900–1200, 1400–1700 (closed Sun mornings, Tue, 1–2 Jan, 1 and 11 Nov, 25–26 Dec).* Entry is cheaper if a combined ticket for all Roman monuments is bought (from the ticket office at any of them).

Markets There are markets on Mon, Fri and Sun.

What went on in the arena?

In its heyday, the Nîmes arena would have been in frequent use, and, judging by the height of the podium wall, was almost certainly primarily given over to contests between human beings rather than animals, although some Christians possibly fought lions here. Slaves and prisoners of war would have been pitted against each other, but the most spectacular and popular of entertainments were the gladiatorial combats, fights to the death between trained men (who although short-lived achieved great fame if they survived several contests). The arena could seat around 20 000 spectators, which makes it only the 20th largest in the Roman world, even though it is now the most complete still in existence. Today it is in frequent use for the citizens' most popular entertainment, *corridas* – traditional Spanish bullfights. They take place frequently throughout the summer (usually every Sunday).

Right
Les Arènes by moonlight

Castellum   *rue de la Lampèze.*

Cathédrale € *place aux Herbes. Open daily.*

Jardin de la Fontaine *Quai de la Fontaine.*

Tour Magne € *Mont Cavalier. Open summer 0900–1900; winter 1000–1230, 1330–1800. Closed holidays.*

Maison Carrée € *place de la Comédie (off rue Perrier); tel: 04 66 36 29 76. Open summer 0900–1900; winter 0900–1200, 1400–1800. Closed holidays.*

Castellum*

The Castellum, overlooking the Old Quarter from the slope to its north, was originally the water tower of Roman Nîmes, supplied by the aqueduct which crossed one of the most magnificently beautiful pieces of civil engineering imaginable, the Pont du Gard (18km northeast of the city). The fortifications over the Castellum were part of a stronghold built to keep watch on the Protestants of Nîmes.

Cathédrale*

At the heart of medieval Nîmes rises its cumbersome and graceless cathedral. Originally built in 1095, but frequently damaged and repaired over the years in this region of religious conflict, it was almost totally rebuilt in Romanesque style in the last century, and remains darkly atmospheric inside, with heavy Roman arches. The region has seen much bitter religious strife, notably during the 13th-century Cathar period, the anti-Jewish violence of the 14th century, and the Camisard Wars (1700–4). Throughout all these troubles the cathedral has stood as a grim monument to the might of Catholicism.

Jardin de la Fontaine**

The spring whose presiding spirit was called Nemausus, after whom the city was named, is now called la Fontaine. Together with ruins of the adjacent Roman baths and a nymphaeum (wrongly known as the Temple of Diana), it was incorporated in the 18th century into these pleasing formal gardens, a few minutes' walk from the town centre. With broad steps, a circuit of waterways between stone embankments and gravelled open areas shaded by leafy plane trees, it is just as American novelist Henry James described it, 'a mixture of Old Rome and 18th-century France'. The Nemausus spring water emerges from the slopes of Mont Cavalier, up the side of which the garden climbs. At the very top a dull Roman watchtower, **Tour Magne***, part of the city defence, has wide views across city and country.

Maison Carrée***

Carrée means 'squared' or 'squared off' rather than simply square, and this beautiful neatly geometrical building is actually twice as long as it is broad, and looks especially pleasing from the front. The small white stone temple (possibly to Youth), standing tranquilly by itself in a little square, is well proportioned and has survived the centuries astonishingly well. Lovely as it is, the extreme praise of other writers for this structure seems puzzling. Even that irascible author Smollett described it as 'ravishingly beautiful'. Henry James, too, not easily impressed, called it 'perfectly felicitous'. The well-travelled writer Arthur Young described it as 'beyond all comparison the most pleasing building I ever beheld'. Stendhal even proposed that an exact copy be built in Paris. Thomas Jefferson also wanted an exact copy built, but in Virginia, and he sent a scale drawing home. French statesman Colbert declared that the Maison

Musée des Beaux-Arts € *rue Cité Foulc;
tel: 04 66 67 38 21. Open
1100–1800. Closed Mon
and holidays.*

Porte d'Arles *boulevard
Amiral Courbet.*

**Musée d'Archéologie et
d'Histoire Naturelle** €
*boulevard Amiral Courbet;
tel: 04 66 67 25 57
(archaeology) and 04 66 21
33 23 (natural history).
Open Jun–Sep 0930–1830;
Oct–May 1100–1800.
Closed Mon and holidays.*

Musée de Vieux Nîmes
€ *place aux Herbes; tel: 04
66 36 00 64. Open
1100–1800. Closed Mon.*

Carrée was so lovely it should be transported stone by stone to Versailles. Fortunately the simple, elegant building remains peacefully where it has stood since AD 5. Inside, a small **Museum of Antiquities** has a collection of Roman marble sculpture and a frieze of Nemausus, spirit of the nearby spring after whom the city was named.

Musée des Beaux-Arts**
A range of high-quality French, Flemish and Italian works spanning five centuries up to the beginnings of modern art are displayed in Nîmes' fine arts museum. Rodin, Watteau and Rubens are represented. There is also a large Roman mosaic on the ground floor, which is worth seeing.

Porte d'Arles (Porte d'Auguste)**
An inscription on this well-preserved Roman gate records that Augustus built the city walls in the year 15 BC and through it the *Via Domitia* entered Nîmes. Since that time, the arms of the city have depicted a crocodile chained to a palm tree, with the words 'Col Nem' (*Colonia Nemausensium*). This ancient logo now appears on everything throughout the city. But what have palms and crocodiles to do with Nîmes? The answer is that this was the crest of the legionnaries who conquered Egypt. Augustus rewarded them with villas, land, money and slaves in Nîmes, where many then retired. The **Musée d'Archéologie et d'Histoire Naturelle***, housed in a 17th-century chapel close to the Roman gate, contains Roman and Greek artefacts found here and provides a useful understanding of Roman Nîmes.

Vieux Nîmes (Old Nîmes)**
The 'Old Quarter' is threaded by narrow backstreets (many of them pedestrianised) along which stand some fine 16th- to 18th-century houses. One native of the medieval town was Jean Nicot, the doctor who, in 1560, introduced tobacco into France (hence *nicotine*). Alphonse Daudet, the writer, was born at 20 boulevard Cambetta in 1840. The **Musée de Vieux Nîmes****, in the 17th-century Bishops' Palace beside the cathedral, has a good collection of Renaissance furnishings (note the six fantastically ornate cupboards), and displays on bullfighting. In square de la Bouquerie, in 1705, towards the end of the Camisard Wars, hundreds of local Protestants were publicly tortured and executed on the gibbet, wheel and stake. Nevertheless, the city remains largely Protestant to this day.

Accommodation and food

Hôtel la Baume €€ *21 rue Nationale; tel: 04 66 76 28 42; fax: 04 66 76 28 45.* A beautifully modernised private mansion on the edge of the Old Quarter, with an attractive, well-equipped, relaxed atmosphere. Nice bathrooms. Own restaurant with good set menus at low prices.

Brandade de Morue, now a great Provençal speciality, has been a local Nîmes dish since Roman times. It's a paste made of cod fillets crushed in olive oil.

Hôtel Clarine-Plazza €€ *10 rue Roussy; tel: 04 66 76 16 20; fax: 04 66 67 65 99.* It's very enjoyable to sit on the little terrace of a top-floor bedroom here and gaze across the chaotic red roof-tiles of the Old Quarter. Decent, modern comforts in this quiet backstreet location, a few minutes' walk from the action. And yes, they really do spell Plazza like that.

Le Cygne and **Le Napoléon** €€ *boulevard Victor Hugo.* These two brasseries near the Maison Carrée are popular places to enjoy a drink or a snack at a pavement table. On the other side of the Old Quarter, there are many others along boulevard de la Libération and boulevard Amiral Courbet near the Arena.

Le Bouchon et l'Assiette €€ *5 bis rue de Sauve; tel/fax: 04 66 62 02 93.* This respected fixture on the Nîmes restaurant scene has a deserved reputation for offering a good, satisfying, imaginative meal at a very reasonable price. Directly opposite the Jardin de la Fontaine. Closed Tue and Wed.

Chez Jacotte € *15 rue Freque; tel: 04 66 21 64 59.* Good, hearty cooking according to the market and the season, with dishes like duck's liver and peppers, *magret* with peaches, and home-made desserts, served in generous portions at this backstreet location in the heart of the Old Quarter. No set menus, but a three-course menu of the day with three choices in each course. Closed Sat midday, Sun, Mon and part of Aug.

Festivals

Ferias focus on bullfights and bull-running. The big three are *Feria de Carnaval* (Winter Festival), February; *Feria de Pentecôte* (4-day Whitsun Festival), May; and *Feria des Vendanges* (Grape Harvest Festival), last weekend in September.

A jazz festival, attracting big names on the jazz scene, takes place in the arena for a week in July.

Suggested walk

Total distance: About 2km; 3km including detours.

Time: The main walk will take about 2 hours, allowing for pauses to admire the façades and sights. Add on another hour for wandering off the route – many turnings and corners invite more exploration. Allow a full day, to include detours and visits to all the sights.

Route: Start from **LES ARENES** ❶, the arena. All around you will see curiously dated-looking posters advertising forthcoming bullfights. Behind the arena in boulevard des Arènes, the **Musée Taurins** (Bull

Provençal bullfights

Bullfighting is a leftover of Roman arena sports that remains popular in Mediterranean France. There are two types. Native to the area is *Course à la Cocarde*, where the lively, half-wild, black bulls from the Camargue are used. The men, called *Razeteurs*, dressed in white, try to remove by hand the *cocarde*, a knot of coloured ribbons which has been fixed to the bull's head. It requires skill and daring. The bull is rarely hurt during the fight, though generally slaughtered afterwards.

Grander and more spectacular is the Spanish-style *Corrida*, performed in the larger arenas, especially Nîmes. On the human side are a skilled *matador* and his *peones*, *banderilleros* and horse-riding *picadores*. The bulls are specially reared adults at the height of their vigour. Before the fight the bull is kept in a *chiquero*, a small dark box, to increase his fear and disorientation when released into the dazzling sunlit arena. At first the *peones* simply tire the animal by encouraging him to run from one man to the other. The *picadores*, from the safety of their horses, then weaken the bull by stabbing the muscles at the back of its neck. The *banderillos* take over, planting colourfully ribboned steel-tipped spikes deep into these muscles. The damage to muscles and the loss of blood generally ensure the bull is flagging by now. For the *faena*, the final episode, the flamboyantly dressed *matador*, concealing his sword under a brilliant cloth, takes command. His elegant movements make a dance in which the bull is his unknowing, doomed partner. At the 'moment of truth', as it is called, the *matador* plants his sword skilfully between the shoulder blades to pass directly into the heart of the animal. Less elegant are *Novilladas* – especially popular at Nîmes – when inexperienced young bullfighters are pitted against young bulls.

Museum) deals with the whole subject. Take rue de l'Aspic. Notice a fragment of frieze set in the wall on the right at the corner of rue Violette. A few paces further, turn left for **place du Marché**, where the corn market used to be held in the Middle Ages. The palm tree and the fountain with a crocodile echo the crest of Nîmes. Leave place du Marché under the vault into rue Fresque and walk up. Turn right into **rue Bernis**: notice the fine 15th- and 16th-century façades. Again reaching rue de l'Aspic with its shops, turn left. Notice the porch of the Renaissance Hôtel Meynier de Salinelles at No 8, with its sarcophagi set in the wall. Turn left again into rue de la Madeleine and walk all the way to busy boulevard Victor Hugo at the end – you come out opposite **St Paul's church**, 19th-century but in Byzantine style, with frescos inside. Turn right and walk up to the ancient **MAISON CARREE ❷** on the right and the modern **CARRE D'ART ❸** on the left (the tourist office is a few paces up the street opposite the Maison Carrée).

Detour: Keep going, into place Antonin, and turn left along quai de la Fontaine, the street divided in two by canalised water from the Nemausus spring flowing down the middle. On the right lies the **JARDIN DE LA FONTAINE ❹**, looking more like a formal French public garden of gravelled paths than a great Roman site, and having much of the relaxed quality of a park.

Return to Maison Carrée and walk past the monument along busy rue Général Perrier. Pass the Halles (covered market) on the left and then turn right into rue des Halles, where, on the corner of rue de la Madeleine, is a house with a fine Romanesque façade known as the **Maison de François I**. The place aux Herbes lies in front of the **CATHEDRALE ❺** and, to its right, the Episcopal Palace which houses the **MUSEE DU VIEUX NIMES ❻**. Walk around the back of the cathedral to **Grand' Rue**.

At rue Curraterie, near the start of Grand' Rue, take a few minutes out to walk up to the **PORTE D'ARLES ❼**, Augustus' gateway to the town, and return the way you came.

Walk down Grand' Rue, where there are good façades to be seen, and take rue du Chapitre on the right. You pass the 17th-century Hôtel de la Prévôte and then the striking 18th-century façade and 16th-century paved courtyard of Hôtel de Régis. At the end turn left into rue des Marchands to get back to rue de l'Aspic and return to the arena.

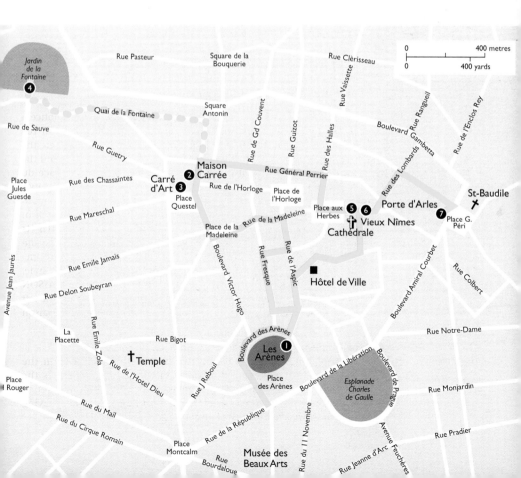

Les Baux and Les Alpilles

Ratings

Restaurants	●●●●●
Scenery	●●●●●
Sightseeing	●●●●○
History	●●●●○
Art	●●●○○
Wine-tasting	●●●○○
Children	●●○○○
Shopping	●●○○○

Although the Alpilles cover a small area, a narrow strip barely 20km by 4km, it is a captivating and enchanted miniature world which feels lost in time and remote from anywhere. The Alpilles form an extraordinary, beautiful landscape of weirdly jagged crests emerging abruptly from flat country between the rivers Durance and Rhône and rising in a series of hills. In places they are weatherworn and barren, sometimes planted with olive groves, almond, cypress, fruit trees and vineyards; elsewhere the slopes are densely cloaked with *garrigue* – wild evergreen Mediterranean vegetation. The air is alive with the creaky soporific scratchings of insects and the aroma of pine and wild herbs. The Alpilles are populated with picturesque, characteristically southern villages, and there are several important Roman and medieval sites in and around the area. Capital of these hills, and one of its most extraordinary spectacles, is the lofty fortified village of les Baux de Provence.

LES ANTIQUES AND GLANUM✦✦✦

ℹ Tourist offices are generally open in summer Mon–Sat 0900–1200, 1400–1900; Sun 0900–1200 only; in winter Mon–Sat 0900–1200, 1400–1800, closed Sun.

Tourist Office *place Jean-Jaurès, St-Rémy-de-Provence; tel: 04 90 92 05 22; fax: 04 90 92 38 52; www.saintremy-de-provence.com*

🏛 **Les Antiques** *Beside the D5. Free unsupervised access.*

The two imposing Roman remnants known as les Antiques, standing at the roadside less than 1km outside St-Rémy-de-Provence, were the last buildings left standing after the destruction of Glanum by Barbarians in the 3rd century. They remain in remarkable condition. Most dramatic is the **Roman mausoleum✦✦✦**. At 18m tall, with a podium and two storeys, decorated with carvings and reliefs, it is the best surviving example anywhere. It dates from around 30 BC, and was built as a memorial according to the inscription, 'Sextius, Lucius, Marcus, sons of Caius of the Julii family, to their parents'. Next to it stands the handsome **Roman arch✦✦**, decorated with carvings, probably by Greek craftsmen, which possibly marked the entrance to the town of Glanum. The tiled roof was added in the 18th century.

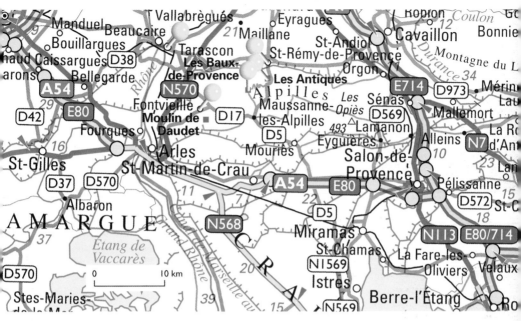

Glanum €€ *Beside the D5; tel: 04 90 92 23 79. Open Apr–Sep 0900 –1900; rest of year 0900–1200, 1400–1700. Closed holidays.*

St-Paul-de-Mausole
Beside the D5; tel: 04 90 92 02 31. Open daily 0800– 1900 (Oct–Apr closes 1700).

The more serious **Glanum archaeological site✦✦✦**, first excavated in 1922 and continuously since 1982, lies across the road. The town of Glanum originally developed out of contact between native Ligurians and the Greek settlers and merchants of *Massilia* (now Marseille). A complex site, sometimes hard to understand, it has a huge number of relics divided into three architectural 'stages' – Greek, early Roman, and late Roman. It is the main site for the study of Hellenisation in southern Gaul. Adjacent to it is the old monastery of **St-Paul-de-Mausole✦✦**, where Van Gogh resided in an asylum from May 1889 to May 1890 after mutilating his ear. His room, and the gardens he painted, may sometimes be seen while visiting the attractive Romanesque church and cloisters.

LES BAUX-DE-PROVENCE✦✦✦

Perched on a dramatic cliff edge among the stony heights at the heart of the Alpilles, the awesome eagle's-nest village of Les Baux has been through many changes. Originally a mountain shelter during 8th-century Arab raids, it became an important and impregnable seigneurial fortress of the Middle Ages, was dismantled in 1483 on the orders of Louis XI of France, fell into ruin, was rebuilt as a 16th-century Protestant stronghold and largely demolished by Richelieu in 1632. Ironically, in view of the site's former inaccessibility, Les Baux this century has become a 'must see' sight, given over entirely to arts and crafts vendors who thrive on the thousands of day visitors

Opposite
Glanum tourists

ⓘ Les Baux-de-Provence Tourist Office 30 Grande Rue; tel: 04 90 54 34 39; fax: 04 90 54 51 15.

🚆 The best route to Les Baux is via the D27. From the village entrance, where you must park, narrow Grande Rue leads up into the village.

Ⓟ Cars must be parked in official car parks at the entrance to the village or foot of the hill. There is a fee for parking.

🏛 Musée Yves Brayer € tel: 04 90 54 36 99. Open 1000–1230, 1400–1730; closed Tue from Oct–Mar. Closed mid-Jan–mid-Feb.

Citadel € tel: 04 90 54 55 56. Open Mar–Nov 0800–1930 (until 2100 Jul–Aug); rest of year 0900–1800.

Cathédrale des Images €€ Beside the D27; tel: 04 90 54 38 65. Open mid-Mar–mid-Nov 1000–1900; rest of year closes 1730. Closed Feb.

meandering the narrow, picturesque streets of restored buildings. The village has hardly any permanent residents.

During its 12th-century heyday, the Lords of Les Baux won control over a considerable area of Provence, and the town preserves as much as it can of that illustrious past. It now consists of a 'modern' village, mainly 16th-century, and the ruins of its spectacular rock-carved medieval stronghold. There is plenty to see, including the **Musée Yves Brayer****, showing the work of this local artist (1907–90), the evocative towers and ruins of the old **Citadel (Ville Morte)*****, lots of pretty corners that catch the eye and lofty views over the surrounding hills. There are more sights at the foot of the village: **Cathédrale des d'Images****, a spectacular former bauxite quarry; **Val d'Enfer***, a wild gorge of chaotic rocks and caves; and **Pavillon de la Reine Jeanne (Queen Jeanne's Pavillion)***, a charming little 16th-century Renaissance structure, built for baroness Jeanne de Quiqueran of les Baux (who was never a queen).

The name Les Baux comes from the Provençal *bau*, 'escarpment'. The village has given its name to bauxite, first discovered in the red rocks of Les Alpilles in 1822.

Accommodation and food in Les Baux

Auberge de la Benvengudo €€€ *Below the village; tel: 04 90 54 32 54; fax: 04 90 54 42 58.* Delicious rustic-luxurious Alpilles farmhouse draped with greenery in a wonderful setting. The air-conditioned bedrooms have genuine old Provençal furniture. Pool, tennis, restaurant.

La Cabro d'Or €€€ *Val d'Enfer; tel: 04 90 54 33 21; fax: 04 90 54 45 98.* An annexe of the legendary L'Oustau de Baumanière (*see below*), this too is a luxurious hotel and restaurant of tremendous character and style, set among extraordinary rocks, trees and flowers. Tennis, riding, pool, first-class restaurant.

L'Oustau de Baumanière €€€ *Val d'Enfer; tel: 04 90 54 33 07; fax: 04 90 54 40 46; e-mail: contact@oustaudebaumaniere.com.* Widely considered one of the best hotels in the world, with a similarly rarefied restaurant. It comprises three buildings of a beautiful 16th-century Provençal farm offering refinement and luxury and every facility, yet with pleasing simplicity and unpretentiousness, buried among lovely gardens and *garrigue*. Fruit, vegetables and herbs for the kitchen are grown on the spot along organic, biodynamic lines, as is a vineyard whose grapes go into Château Romanin, the outstanding local wine. Try sea bream with star anise and orange, or vegetable ragout with sardines and anchovies. If you have something to celebrate, enjoy L'Oustau's famously light, exquisite cooking (the emphasis is on vegetables and fish) on a rose-edged terrace gazing up at the ruins of Les Baux.

La Riboto de Taven €€ *Near Val d'Enfer; tel: 04 90 54 34 23; fax: 04 90 54 38 88.* A fascinating old country house half cut out of the cliff face, hidden among tranquil rocks and flowers and furnished with genuine antiques, this excellent restaurant is noted for simple, fragrant, imaginative local cooking. It also has three bedrooms.

Below
Les Baux

Right
The Moulin de Daudet, Fontvieille

FONTVIEILLE*

Moulin de Daudet
*5 rue Marcel Honorat;
tel: 04 90 54 67 49; fax: 04
90 54 69 82; e-mail:
ot.fontvieille@visitprovence.
com; www.fontvieille-
provence.com. Open Jun–Sep
0900–1200, 1400–1900;
rest of year 1000–1200,
1400–1700. Closed Jan.*

Typically Provençal in appearance and atmosphere (though painfully touristy at times), this village has several good little hotels and restaurants serving thousands of devoted fans of Alphonse Daudet, who stop off before or after a visit to the nearby **Moulin de Daudet (Daudet's Windmill)****, where this popular French author supposedly wrote his best-loved work, *Lettres de mon Moulin* (*Letters from my Mill*). In reality, while Daudet *did* spend time at the mill, most of the writing was done back home in Paris. Even for those who haven't read, or even heard of him, the mill certainly provides a popular excuse for an outing and a picnic.

Accommodation and food in Fontvieille

Hôtel le Daudet €–€€ *7 avenue de Monmajour; tel: 04 90 54 76 06; fax: 04 90 54 76 95.* Modest, peaceful, modern hotel, with pool, terrace, and simple, comfortable rooms. A useful find. Closed Oct–Easter.

Laetitia € *rue Lion; tel: 04 90 54 72 14; fax: 04 90 54 81 75.* Good inexpensive menus in a pleasant restaurant and small simple hotel. Open Mar–Nov only. Closed midday on Thu and Sat.

Hôtel Peiriero €€ *34 avenue des Baux; tel: 04 90 54 76 10; fax: 04 90 54 62 60.* Attractive and pleasing village hotel in a traditional Provençal farmhouse, with pool, spacious air-conditioned rooms, and relaxed atmosphere. Good value. Closed Nov–Mar.

La Régalido €€–€€€ *rue F Mistral; tel: 04 90 54 60 22; fax: 04 90 54 64 29.* Tranquil, fragrant garden setting for this elegant hotel and restaurant full of rural Provençal atmosphere. Reflecting its origins as a turn-of-the-century olive oil mill, in addition to classic regional dishes such as garlicky leg of lamb, the restaurant pays homage to the olive in its crudités with *tapenade*, freshly caught fish simmered in olive oil, olive-filled ravioli and olive omelette. Nice breakfasts on the terrace.

ST-REMY-DE-PROVENCE✥

ⓘ St-Rémy-de-Provence Tourist Office *place Jean-Jaurès; tel: 04 90 92 05 22; fax: 04 90 92 38 52; www.saintremy-de-provence.com. Guided tours can be arranged by the tourist office.*

Ⓟ *Aim for place de la République or place Jean-Jaurès, where there are car parks close to the centre of town.*

ⓘ Centre d'Art Présence Van Gogh € *Hôtel Estrine; tel: 04 90 92 34 72. Open 1030–1230, 1430–1830. Closed Mon and Jan–Mar.*

Archaeological Collection € *Hôtel de Sade; tel: 04 90 92 64 04. Guided tours at 1000, 1100, 1400, 1500, 1600, 1700. In Oct, no 1700 tour; in Jul–Aug, afternoon tours all start 30 minutes later.*

Château de Romanin *Behind Romanin aerodrome, off the D99; tel: 04 90 92 45 87. Open daily, phone ahead.*

ⓔ *There is a daily produce market.*

ⓐ *Around 15 Aug Abrivado: (Provençal bullfight), Carretto Ramado (pompommed horses, chariot laden with flowers, fruit and vegetables) and other traditional events.*

St-Rémy-de-Provence is a delightful, historic yet modest, workaday Provençal country town and market-gardening centre. At its heart it has a picturesque old quarter of lanes, squares and fountains, and avenues shaded by leafy plane trees. The destruction of Roman Glanum, just 1km to the south, led to the creation of St-Rémy, and today tourists visiting Glanum provide much of the town's income. Van Gogh frequented the place as a voluntary inmate of the nursing home at nearby St-Paul-de-Mausole monastery (*see page 91*). Other famous names include cult astrologer Nostradamus (1503–66) who was born here, and Gertrude Stein who stayed a whole year (1922) in the Hôtel de la Ville Verte. A number of fine 16th- to 18th-century mansions can be seen in the old quarter, some housing museums, such as the **Centre d'Art Présence Van Gogh**✥ (about the artist's time here) and the **Archaeological Collection**✥✥ (important finds from Glanum). There are several Appellation Contrôlée Coteaux d'Aix-en-Provence and Les Baux de Provence wine-makers around the area. Four kilometres east on the D99, a side turn leads down to the impressive underground 'cathedral' caverns of **Château de Romanin**, which produce an AC wine, supposedly since the 4th century BC.

Accommodation and food in St-Rémy-de-Provence

Hostellerie du Vallon de Valrugues €€€ *Chemin Canto Cigalo; tel: 04 90 92 04 40; fax: 04 90 92 44 01*. The slightly twee name, not to mention the Provençal street name – lane of the song of cicada – rather portend the self-consciously de-luxe southern style of this bright, colourful, well-equipped hotel and restaurant. Spacious rooms have terraces with views of the gardens and the Alpilles. Closed Feb.

Hôtel Ville Verte € *place de la République; tel: 04 90 92 06 14; fax: 04 90 92 56 54*. This arty place was once frequented by artists and writers, including Charles Gounod, who composed the Provençal opera *Mireille* in room 9 in 1863. Decent, simple, inexpensive rooms, and rooms with kitchenette are available by the week for a very modest price. Pool, terrace; just a few paces from the town centre. Closed Nov–Mar.

Le Bistrot des Alpilles € *15 boulevard Mirabeau; tel: 04 90 92 09 17*. Lively relaxed brasserie-style establishment with good cooking at modest prices, and live piano on Friday nights.

TARASCON❖❖

🛈 Tarascon Tourist Office 59 rue Halles; tel: 04 90 91 03 52; fax: 04 90 91 22 96; e-mail: tourisme@tarascon.org; www.tarascon.org. Guided tours can be arranged by the tourist office.

P There is parking close to the castle.

🏛 Castle € Tel: 04 90 91 01 93. Open Apr–Sep 0900–1900; rest of year 0900–1200, 1400–1700. Closed holidays.

◑ There is a weekly market on Tue.

◐ The folkloric Festival of the Tarasque takes place on the last Sunday in June.

If you ever wanted to see a *real* castle, Tarascon has a fine one. Its spectacular medieval fortress in pale stone, restored to a perfect state, even with water in the moat, gazes with impassive might across the River Rhône as if unaware that the provinces and fiefdoms it protects have faded into forgotten history. First stop are the *Communes* (Commons), working quarters with kitchens, apothecary and workshops. Climb narrow spiral staircases within stone towers; wander through the banqueting hall, hall of audience, king's hall and other stone rooms with great fireplaces; peer through mullioned windows; and discover courtyards, antechambers and 'garderobes' (medieval toilets). For sheer atmosphere it's hard to beat. To cap it all, the castle was home to the popular, party-giving Good King Réné. Fine medieval tapestries hang in the royal rooms, with their simple quarry-tiled floors. The Queen's Apartment is worth seeking out for the beautiful wooden ceiling of tiny decorated panels. Built to defend the western boundary of Provence, the castle was abandoned in the 17th century and became a notorious prison, which it remained until 1926. Look out for graffiti by 18th-century English prisoners of war alongside that of 20th-century English tourists.

Tarascon is famed for two mythical beasts: the Tarasque, which supposedly emerged from the Rhône to eat cattle and children, was subdued by St Martha with the sign of the Cross (*see Les Saintes-Maries-de-Mer, page 114*); and Tartarin of Tarascon, a rotund comic giant invented by Alphonse Daudet in 1872.

Suggested tour

Total distance: 100km, add 10km for the detour.

Time: This is a packed but leisurely day with about 3 hours' driving. Allow 2 hours to explore Les Baux on foot, an hour for Glanum, and if you take the detour, an hour at Tarascon castle. Perhaps allow another hour for wine-tasting at one of Les Alpilles' vineyards along the route.

Links: The eastern end of this tour links, at Orgon, with Lubéron and Southern Vaucluse (*see page 62*); Cavaillon and the Lubéron are under 10km away. Just south of Les Apilles lies Plaine de la Crau, a detour on the Camargue tour (*see page 119)*, while the Gard tour (*see page 74*) can be reached from Tarascon across the Rhône bridge to Beaucaire.

Route: From **Arles** (*see page 100*) leave town on avenue de Stalingrad (on the north side of town centre), initially signed for Avignon and Tarascon, but on reaching the N570, turn right (south) and left on to the D17 for Les Baux. Straight away, the huge, gaunt stone fortifications of the **Abbaye de Montmajour** rise massively on the right. Pause here to admire the lovely cloisters and fine views.

Above
Les Alpilles

Continue to the village of **FONTVIEILLE** ❶ and turn right on to a quiet back road for the **Moulin de Daudet**. A couple of kilometres further down this quiet road (D33), around the junction with the D82/D78e, there are interesting ruins of the twin Gallo-Roman **Barbegal Aqueducts**, one of which brought water to Roman Arles from Eygalières (*see below*) while the other powered a hydraulic flour mill. From the aqueducts, take the D78e (changes to the D27) through Paradou, climbing the rocky landscape at the heart of Les Alpilles in the direction of Les Baux. Pass by **Val d'Enfer**, a curious gorge of caves and strange rock shapes associated with magic and mysteries, and follow the road around on to the D27a to reach the tiny turning on

Garrigue

Garrigue is the dense chest-high jungle of tangled evergreen shrubs, stunted trees, flowers and wild herbs growing wild in the hilly, uncultivated French Mediterranean hinterland. Thorns, thistles and spiky leaves abound. Typical *garrigue* plants are the evergreen kermes oak, with its prickly leaves, cork oak and holm oak, broom and the local gorse *ajonc de Provence* with its bright yellow pea-like flowers. The unkempt, wild form of many garden or indoor plants can be seen, such as pretty rock rose (cistus), juniper and arbutus, and box, as well as flowering viburnum, lentisk and terebinth (turpentine tree), their branches sometimes entangled with vibrant clematis and honeysuckle. Beneath the taller shrubs is an undergrowth of rosemary, myrtle, several varieties of thyme, savory, lavender, and catmint, which releases clouds of scent at every step. Parasol pines are abundant, and the air is fragrant with the warm tang of their resin.

the right for **LES BAUX-DE-PROVENCE ❷**. Les Baux is sometimes so overcrowded that the police refuse to allow any more vehicles into the village. If that happens, park at the foot of the hill and walk up, or return to Les Baux later in the tour after seeing Les Antiques.

Leave Les Baux by descending again to the D27a, turn right, and on reaching the D5 turn right through delightful groves of olive, cherry, apricot and almond trees. The dark red **Rochers d'Entreconque** rocks rising left of the road are remnants of a bauxite quarry. At **Mausanne les Alpilles**, turn left on to the minor road D78 east through olive groves at the foot of the hills. At the Le Destrel junction, turn left on to the D24 to climb again. Descending to a junction with the D25 on the right, take this turn. The road climbs again, then descends, as it skirts the Plaines massif at the eastern end of the Alpilles. After some 9km, reach the junction with the D569, where the ruins of **Castelas de Roquemartine** castle sit on the hillside. Turn right on to the D569, and carry on for 2km to enter **Eyguières**, an appealing and attractive small town. Return along the D569, again passing the Castelas ruins, to reach **Orgon**, where Napoleon, while being taken to exile in Elba, was pursued by a hostile mob. Leave this modest town on the N7 (Avignon direction) but straight away take the D24b to the left to skirt the Plaines massif. On the left, the **Chapelle St-Sixte**, built in the 12th century on the site of a pagan temple dedicated to a local spring, stands on a hill with good views over the Alpilles. Immediately after, the road enters **Eygalières**. This pleasant old town climbs in narrow streets and lanes to its historic castle keep, which offers lovely views. Take the D74a north to reach the busier D99 and turn left. Not far along is the left turn for the distinguished and interesting Château Romanin wine-cellars. Continue on the D99 to reach **ST-REMY-DE-PROVENCE** ❸.

Leave St Rémy-de-Provence on the south side, on the D5. The old monastery and hospital of **St-Paul-de-Mausole** stands left of the road, which quickly reaches **LES ANTIQUES AND GLANUM** ❹. Take time to explore, then return to the southern edge of St-Rémy. On entering the town, where the D5 becomes avenue Durand-Maillane, take the first left on to Chemin de la Combette leading to the Vieux Chemin d'Arles, soon reaching (in 3km) the **Tour du Cardinal**. This is not a tower but a 16th-century country house with a Renaissance balcony and friezes. Stay on this minor road heading due west to reach (after 5km) St-Etienne-du-Grès. Turn left here on to the D32, making a stop after 2km to see the appealing 12th-century **Chapelle St-Gabriel**. The chapel is all that's left to mark the site of the Roman settlement of *Ernaginum*, once a small port for rafts and punts in a marshy area – there is still a meeting of waterways here, linking the Canal des Alpilles and the Canal du Vigueirat. At Chapelle St-Gabriel, the D32 reaches the N570, the main Arles–Avignon road.

Detour: Instead of turning left on to the N570, go directly across on to the D970 for **TARASCON** ❺, 5km away. Return from Tarascon on the same road.

Turn on to the N570 for the 15-km drive back into Arles.

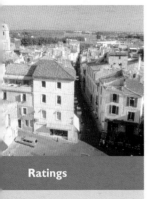

Arles

Ratings

History	●●●●●
Roman remains	●●●●●
Museums	●●●●○
Children	●●●○○
Folklore	●●●○○
Shopping	●●●○○
Street life	●●●○○
Entertainment	●●○○○

Arles, founded by the Greeks as long ago as 600 BC (they called it *Theline*), is today an attractive, pleasing, rather arty provincial market town on the Rhône's left bank, Subsequently, it became a major Roman city and busy trading port, a huge and important city of the Classical world (called *Arelate*). Emperor Constantine – who Christianised the Roman Empire – was born here. The remarkably intact Roman arena where he watched performances is still used for bullfights. Next to it, the Roman theatre, though not so well preserved, continues to be a grand setting for open-air plays. In later centuries, Arles became the greatest city of Provence, and keeps many impressive reminders of its history. It is proud of its Provençal ancestry, and here 19th-century poet Frédéric Mistral struggled to revive the Provençal language. Vincent Van Gogh lived in the town during his most prolific and disturbed period.

Arriving and departing

The town centre and historic quarter lie on the left bank of the Rhône. The east–west expressway, the N113, cuts across the south of town, with an exit directly into the town centre.

From Avignon and the north, the main road is the N570, with a turn on to the D17 (avenue de Stalingrad) leading into the town centre via the railway station.

The old heart of town is enclosed by boulevard Emile Combes and boulevard des Lices (the town's main thoroughfare).

During festivals and on market day (Sat) some roads are closed.

Market and shopping

The town's huge Saturday morning market in boulevard des Lices brings people into town from all over the surrounding area. Other markets are Wednesday morning (boulevard Emile Combes) and the second-hand

P The main car park is Parking des Lices, accessed from boulevard des Lices and rue E Fassin. There is also car parking beside boulevard Georges Clemenceau (an extension of boulevard des Lices), the main road heading towards the Rhône bridge, at the railway station and at place Lamartine, on the north side of the old quarter.

Arles on the web
www.arles.org Good,
clear site put up by the
Mairie (town hall), mainly
for locals, but with some
tourism information. In
French.

market on the first Wednesday of every month (boulevard des Lices).

The main shopping street is boulevard des Lices. Within the old quarter, the main streets are rue de la République and place du Forum.

Global ticket and opening hours

A single ticket covering all the major sights in Arles is good value if you want to see more than three of them. The ticket gives entry to the

ⓘ *www.arles.cci.fr* The website of the Arles Chamber of Commerce, with some tourism information about the town and region, including hotel links. In French. *www.tourisme.ville-arles.fr* The comprehensive tourist office website.

Tourist Offices
Main office: *Esplanade Charles de Gaulle, boulevard des Lices; tel: 04 90 18 41 20; fax: 04 90 18 41 29. Open Mon–Sat 0900–1900, Sun and hols 0900–1300.*
Railway station: *Avenue Paulin Talabot; tel: 04 90 49 36 90. Open 0900–1300, 1400 –1800 (closed Sun and hols).*

🗓 **Festivals and bullfighting**

Easter: *Feria Pascale* (Spanish-style bullfighting).

Last Sun in Apr: *Fêtes des Gardians* (Camargue gardians, processions).

1 May: Election of the Queen of Arles.

Start Jul: *Fête de la Costume* (folkloric displays at which traditional local dress is worn).

1st Mon in Jul: *Course à la Cocarde d'Or* (Provençal-style bullfighting).

Jul: *Festival d'Images des Rencontres de la Photographie* (International Photography Exhibition)

Jul: *Festival d'Arles* (dance festival).

Jul–Sep: frequent Spanish and Provençal bullfights.

Right
Les Arènes, Arles

Alyscamps, Arènes (arena), Cloître St-Trophime, Cryptoporticus, Théâtre Antique (Roman theatre), Thermes de Constantin, Museon Arlaten, Musée de l'Arles Antique and Musée Réattu.

All except the Museon Arlaten and Musée de l'Arles Antiques (*see below*) have the same opening times: Apr–Sep 0900–1900; rest of year: 1000–1630. Closed 1 Jan, 1 Nov, 25 Dec. No entry 30 minutes before closing time.

City tours

Qualified guides give tours of the city centre to large and small groups, or individuals, as required. These are available Mon–Sat Jul–Sep, and can be arranged by the tourist office.

Le Petit Train d'Arles (The Little Arles Train) does a jolly little tour of the town, pausing at all the sights (*tel: 04 90 18 41 20. Open Easter to 1 Nov only*).

Sights

Les Alyscamps✤✤
The Alyscamps cemetery at Arles, painted by Van Gogh, was for over 1200 years among the grandest of final resting places, the most famous burial ground in the western world. By the 4th century, there were already thousands of graves here, and a second level was begun on top. Finally, a third level of tombs was stacked on top of those, while at the same time, the site was associated with miracles and holiness. Eventually there were 19 chapels here. Suddenly there was a change in attitude. The grandest sarcophagi were stolen for their fine stonework, given away to honoured guests, or removed as decorations for churches. Largely dismantled and destroyed in the 15th century, it is today a graceful, heavily atmospheric avenue lined with poplars and tombs.

Arènes (Arena or Amphitheatre)✤✤✤
Magnificent, vast, overbearing, this amphitheatre within the old heart of Arles is one of the finest surviving examples. Here men and animals were set against one another for the amusement of the crowds of up to 20000, as they are today. Although slaves do not grapple with lions any more, and gladiators do not fight to the death, the sand in Arles Arena is still regularly soaked with blood during the popular bullfights throughout the summer, both *mise-à-mort* (Spanish-style *corrida*) and *course à la cocarde* (Provençal bullfighting in which the bull is not mutilated, and generally survives

2nd week Sep: *Fête des Prémices du Riz* (celebrating Camargue rice, processions with floats).

All Dec: *Salon des Santonniers* (Trade Fair of *santons* and *santon*-making)

Les Alyscamps €
Follow avenue des Alyscamps from boulevard des Lices.

Les Arènes €€ *Rond Point des Arènes.*

Cathédrale St-Trophime € *place de la République.*

Cryptoporticus€ *rue Balze.*

Espace Van Gogh €
place Félix Rey; tel: 04 90 49 39 39; fax: 04 90 93 80 85. Open daily 0730–1930.

Fondation Van Gogh €
26 rond-point des Arènes; tel/fax: 04 90 49 94 04; www.fondationvangogh-arles.org. Open summer 1000–1900; winter 1000–1230, 1400–1730.

the fight to be slaughtered afterwards). The incongruous towers at each end of the structure are not Roman but 12th-century, a relic of the time when the whole arena became a fortified village. At that time, there were 200 houses, and even a church, within the amphitheatre. The towers give an excellent overview of the arena and surrounding rooftops.

Cathédrale et Cloître St-Trophime✦✦✦

The medieval cathedral of St-Trophime was one of the first Romanesque churches to be constructed in France (6th century), though the present building is largely 12th century. It's a good example of what became the Provençal style, though the **west front✦✦✦**, with its highly decorative doorway facing place de la République, is untypical, and regarded as one of the best examples of Provençal medieval stonework. The elaborate frieze shows the damned descending naked into the flames of Hell, while the saved, smirking self-righteously and fully dressed in rather smart robes, ascend to Heaven. Inside, the church is lofty and simple. Through the Bishops' Palace, the lovely, airy **cloisters✦✦✦** mix Gothic and Romanesque styles. There's fine carving on the columns. The sunlit upper gallery is sometimes used for exhibitions.

Cryptoporticus✦

This weird, gloomy, musty space – two large parallel curved galleries – constructed by the Romans beneath the town's Forum was most likely used as a storage area for grain and other goods and slaves. During excavations, a number of sculptures were found here. However, the primary purpose of this underground structure was to give stability and strength to the Forum and its buildings. It found a use during World War II as a shelter during Allied bombing raids.

Espace Van Gogh✦

The former Hôtel Dieu hospital where Van Gogh was treated following the self-mutilation of his ear has now become a 'Médiathèque' (so much more up to date than a Bibliothèque) with a rather twee academic study and exhibition centre on the theme of Vincent van Gogh. The artist was confined here for several months before admitting himself to the St-Paul-de-Mausole asylum, and during his stay he painted the *Jardin de l'Hôpital à Arles* which has been used as the basis for the restoration of the arcaded courtyard and gardens.

Fondation Van Gogh✦

This old-quarter art museum facing the arena contains a variety of modern works by distinguished artists, writers and even musicians, all of them apparently created in honour of Vincent van Gogh. Exhibits include work by Francis Bacon, Jasper Johns, Olivier Dubré and many others.

Musée de l'Arles Antique € *presqu'île du Cirque Romain, avenue de la 1ére DFL; tel: 04 90 18 88 88 (access via Chemin de Barriol). Open Mar–Oct 0900–1900; Nov–Feb 1000–1700. Closed Tue.*

Musée Réattu € *rue du Grand Prieuré; tel: 04 90 49 37 58. Open Jan, Feb, Nov, Dec 1300–1730; Mar, Apr, Oct 1000–1230, 1400–1730; May–Sep: 1000–1230, 1400–1900.*

Museon Arlaten € *rue de la République; tel: 04 90 93 58 11. Open 0900–1200, 1400–1700 (1830 in Jun, 1800 in Apr, May and Sep, 1900 in Jul–Aug, 1730 in Oct). Closed Mon and holidays (excluding Jul–Sep).*

Théâtre Antique € *rue de la Calade; tel: 04 90 96 93 30; open Nov–Feb 1000–1130, 1400–1630; Mar, Apr and Oct 0900–1130, 1400–1730; May–Sep 0900–1830.*

Musée de l'Arles Antique**

An important museum constructed in the mid-1990s, this startling modern triangular building with enamel walls stands on the Rhône riverbank beside a large **Roman circus** (a racetrack), where a hoard of gold coins has been found. The Roman circus is now crossed by the N113 flyover. Set a little away from the centre of things, the Museum of Ancient Arles puts on view the finest of the numerous antiquities found in the town's various Classical sites. It's airy, light and open, a pleasure to walk around, and an intriguing setting for the antiquities, which are effectively and imaginatively displayed. They include rich mosaics and several large sculptures of exceptional artistry, notably of Augustus, the Venus of Arles, a bust of Aphrodite, a torso of Mithras and others, together with many everyday objects of the period. The museum possesses an exceptional range of carved marble **sarcophagi**, some Christian, others pre-Christian, considered the best collection after the one in Rome.

Musée Réattu**

Near the bank of the Rhône, opposite the Thermes de Constantin, a 15th-century Templar priory houses the town's arts museum, created from the private collection of Jacques Réattu (1760–1833). Least interesting are the works of Réattu himself. Most interesting is a surprising collection of 57 rough sketches (each one dated but not signed or named) by **Picasso**, a frequent visitor to the town. These are strange little works done between 31 December, 1970 and 4 February, 1971, some hardly more than doodles, really of interest for the hand that drew them. Yet even these possess the Picasso magic. The museum's other galleries contain many minor treasures from the 16th century to the present day, with a considerable number of good modern works. Among a wide range of artists, Dufy, Gauguin, Léger, Vlaminck and Rousseau are represented.

Museon Arlaten**

The Provençal name is deliberate, for the Museum of Art is the region's premier showcase for local history and folk culture. It was set up by Provençal poet Frédéric Mistral, financed by his 1904 Nobel Prize for Literature, and was one of his practical projects for the preservation of the threatened language, literature and culture of Provence. There are all sorts of everyday household items, *santons*, photos, an exhaustive display on local costume (the museum attendants themselves wear traditional local dress), and a curious collection of Mistral's own possessions. Also here are documents about the Félibrige, who held meetings in this building.

Théâtre Antique**

Vandalised by early Christians and then used as a quarry to build the town's churches and ramparts, the large Roman theatre now preserves just a couple of columns from the original stage wall, and 20 rows of

Thermes de Constantin €€ *rue D Maisto. Open Apr–Sep 0900–1200, 1400–1900; Oct–Mar 1000–1200, 1400–1630.*

On the menu While in town, try *Saucisson d'Arles*, grilled *sandre* fish from the Camargue, or *brouffado* (beef cooked in strips layered with garlic and onion, capers and anchovies).

seats. Even so, it is atmospheric, and enough survives for the theatre to be used for concerts. It is also the setting for the town's colourful folklore and local dress bonanza in July.

Thermes de Constantin*

The 4th-century Roman baths close to the river may have been the largest in Provence. Part of the now vanished waterside palace of Emperor Constantine, only ruins of the *tepidarium, caldarium*, two pools and a steam room survive. Even these sections – a fragment of the total area – are impressive.

Accommodation and food

There are scores of town-centre restaurants and brasseries offering value-for-money set menus. Look along boulevard des Lices and in place Forum.

Hôtel d'Arlatan €€€ *26 rue Sauvage; tel: 04 90 93 56 66; fax: 04 90 49 68 45.* Pricier and more luxurious than the average, this hotel is a beautifully furnished 15th-century house, centrally located.

Hôtel Calendal €€ *22 place Pomme; tel: 04 90 96 11 89; fax: 04 90 96 05 84.* This simple, inexpensive hotel is quiet and central, with a shady courtyard.

Hôtel Nord Pinus €€€ *place Forum; tel: 04 90 93 44 44; fax: 04 90 93 34 00.* Grandiose, atmospheric old hotel replete with history and character and old-fashioned luxury. Go in for a meal at least, at the distinguished **Brasserie Nord Pinus**.

Suggested walk

Total distance: About 2km, or 3km including detour.

Time: The walking itself will take less than an hour, with an extra 30 minutes for the detour. Allow a full day to visit the sights en route.

Route: Start from the tourist office off boulevard des Lices, armed with their map and leaflets. Cross the boulevard to walk along rue Jean-Jaurès. This straight away comes to place de la République, where ahead you can see the 17th-century Hôtel de Ville (town hall), which includes the clock tower of a previous building. The granite obelisk in the square comes from the Roman circus (*see Musée de l'Arles Antique*). To one side stands the west front and entrance of **CATHEDRALE ST-TROPHIME** ❶. Take pedestrianised rue de la République away from the square, soon reaching the **MUSEON ARLATEN** ❷.

Above
The Théâtre Antique

Van Gogh in Arles

'All the future of the new art is in the Midi!' cried Van Gogh when he reached the town on the Paris train, on 20 February, 1888.

In some ways almost nothing remains of Van Gogh's visit to Arles, setting for many of his greatest works. None of his paintings can be seen here. Instead, you must be content to stand in place Lamartine where he lodged and dined, but where there is no trace of his 'yellow house' (destroyed by American bombs in 1944). Or you can find bars with tables on the pavement, under a night sky, looking just like his famous *Café Terrace at Night* – several fit the bill. It was from the bar in place du Forum that Van Gogh painted one of his most dazzling starlit nights.

At first, Van Gogh was happy here. 'In the Midi, all the senses are enhanced, the hand is swifter, the eye livelier, the mind clearer,' he wrote. But after a disastrous row with his friend, fellow artist Paul Gauguin, his intensity and passion got the better of him. He slashed off part of his ear and gave it to a prostitute. At first he was cared for in a hospital which has become L'Espace Van Gogh, close to the Roman arena. The garden is almost exactly as in Van Gogh's painting, *Le Jardin de la Maison de Santé*.

Deteriorating, in May 1889 he went to the asylum at nearby St-Paul-de-Mausole (*see page 91*). Unable to drive away his depression, sadly Van Gogh abandoned the South in which he had had such hopes. On 16 May, 1890, he returned north, to the clinic at Auvers-sur-Oise, near Paris. Thirty months later, after a wildly creative period, 37-year-old Vincent shot himself dead in a cornfield at Auvers.

Detour: Opposite is rue du Président Wilson: a few steps along here is rue P F Rey and the **ESPACE VAN GOGH ❸**. Via rue Molière and rue Gambetta, reach busy boulevard Georges Clémenceau. A 10-minute walk (follow signs) brings you to the **MUSEE DE L'ARLES ANTIQUE ❹**. Because of the traffic, you may prefer to leave this till later and drive to the museum.

Round the back of the Museon Arlaten in rue Balze is the 17th-century Jesuit chapel which provides access to the **CRYPTOPORTICUS ❺**. Carry on along rue Balze, and turn right to reach the central square, **place du Forum**. Part of the site of the ancient Forum, it's still a popular meeting place for tourists, beggars and local youth. On one corner, Van Gogh's famous *Café at Arles* still thrives. Overlooking the square, the oddly named Hôtel Nord Pinus, stayed in by Stendhal, Merimée and Henry James, has two Corinthian columns in one wall, remnants of a 2nd-century temple. In the centre, a statue of Mistral is surrounded by a railing of Camargue pitchforks. It was unveiled in his presence in 1909, and he then made a speech to the assembled dignitaries which, legend records, reduced many to tears of emotion. Carry on via rue de la Place and rue Sauvage to rue du Grand Prieuré and place Constantin where the **THERMES DE CONSTANTIN ❻** and **MUSEE REATTU** ❼ almost face each other. Walk back along rue de l'Hôtel de Ville and take almost any left turn – for example, rue des Arènes – to walk up to the **LES ARENES** ❽.

The arena deserves to be thoroughly explored, so allow time to wander its galleries. Behind the arena on its east side, **Notre-Dame-la-Major** is a Romanesque church standing on the site of a Roman temple. From the terrace beside it, there are magnificent views far to the north. Across place H Bornier is the **THEATRE ANTIQUE** ❾. Descend via rue Porte de Loure (behind the Roman theatre) and Montée Vauban to Carrefour de la Croisière, where you can cross boulevard des Lices for avenue des Alyscamps. Walk along here to the **ALYSCAMPS** ❿. Return to the tourist office by walking along boulevard des Lices.

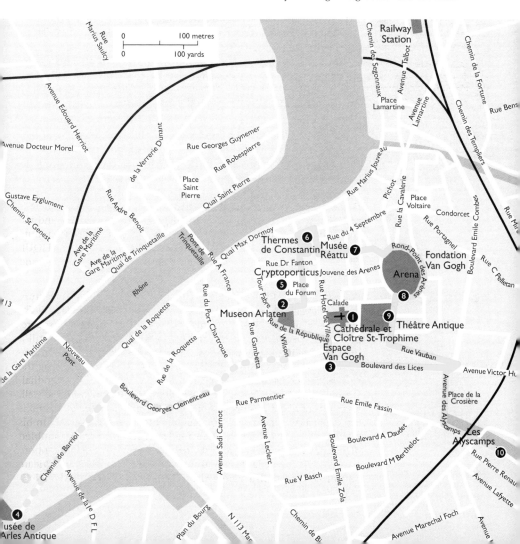

The Camargue

Ratings

Folklore	●●●●●
National parks	●●●●●
Wildlife	●●●●●
Beaches	●●●●○
Children	●●●○○
Museums	●●●○○
Architecture	●●○○○
Entertainment	●●○○○

The Rhône does not simply pour into the sea, but fans into a huge delta where river water and sea water merge, creating this fascinating wetland, the largest in Europe. It is a vast, flat, awesome wilderness of air and water and light covering 72000 hectares. Everything is veiled by curtains of tall, bamboo-like reeds. A multitude of water channels and *étangs* – shallow salty lakes – break up the land, providing refuge for vast numbers of birds. Roaming herds of *bouvines*, the black bulls of the Camargue, wander in the distance. Groups of half-wild white ponies graze closer at hand. Most of the area falls within the Parc Régional de Camargue, part of which is an enclosed wildlife sanctuary not open to the public. Within the Park, look-outs have been erected so that you can watch the wildlife or just gaze at the scenery. It's a place for binoculars and telephoto lenses.

AIGUES-MORTES✢✢✢

ⓘ Aigues-Mortes Tourist Office *Porte de la Gardette; tel. 04 66 53 73 00; fax: 04 66 53 65 94; www.ot-aiguesmortes.fr*

🚉 On reaching the town, the D979 and D58 arrive at Porte de la Gardette.

🅿 There are car parks outside the walls on both sides of Porte de la Gardette.

🏰 Tour Carbonnière *On the D46, near the D58.*

No Camargue town is more fascinating, nor more perfectly preserved, than the Crusaders' fortified seaport of Aigues-Mortes. The name means 'dead waters' (in Provençal), and dead they are, for the town, within an imposing square of medieval ramparts, stands among weird salt flats where nothing can live. Despite its impressive appearance, the town's charm is diminished by the adjacent housing estate and the Salins du Midi industrial area which extracts and refines the salt.

The town was constructed as a seaport by Louis IX (St Louis) in the 13th century specifically for use by Crusaders. Constant efforts to control the silting-up of its ship channels, together with ceaseless battles to defend it from invaders, exhausted the various factions who at different times seized and held the town. At last the silt beat them all. The harbour and the waterways to the sea became unusable, and now – even though new water channels have been opened up to feed the Canal du Sète à Rhône – Aigues-Mortes stands like a bizarre stone

Tour de Constance (and visitor centre at foot of tower) € *place A France; tel: 04 66 53 61 55. Open Apr–Sept 0930–1900; Oct–Mar 0930–1200, 1400–1630.*

sculpture among a featureless landscape. Within the walls, the enticing but touristy old streets lead to the central main square, now full of restaurant tables. The streets are in the grid pattern typical of the many fortified 'new towns' or *bastides* of the Middle Ages. Principal landmark and essential sight is the **Tour de Constance*****, part of the ramparts, used as a prison for Camisard women during the 18th century. Starting from this tower, a walk around the ramparts takes about 30 minutes. Three kilometres out of town on the main road, Aigues-Mortes' advance barbican, **La Tour Carbonnière*****, survives as a magnificent fortification with portcullises, battlements and (66 steps up) a viewing platform with a panoramic view of the town and the surrounding landscape.

Accommodation and food in Aigues-Mortes

Les Arcades €€ *23 boulevard Gambetta; 04 66 53 81 13; fax: 04 66 53 75 46.* Within the handsome walls of this town, there are far too many coach parties and unappealing tourist eateries. One exception which can be recommended is this *restaurant avec chambres* in a 16th-century house.

St Louis €€ *10 rue l'Amiral-Courbet; tel: 04 66 53 72 68; fax: 04 66 53 75 92.* Much-liked, unpretentious little hotel in a quiet backstreet. Open 15 Mar–15 Nov only.

Café de Bouzigues € *7 rue Pasteur; tel: 04 66 53 93* 95. A warm, relaxed, informal place with plenty of atmosphere and appeal. A blackboard menu lists an eclectic choice of tasty dishes.

Right
Aigues-Mortes

La Digue de la Mer*

Avenue Gilbert Leroy heading east from town takes you to the start of the sea wall walk.

There is roadside parking beside avenue Gilbert Leroy.

A 10-km wall of stones topped with a path extends across the watery mouth of the Camargue. It winds through the marshland from the vast sand dunes and glistening white salt-pans of Plage de Piémanson and the eastern Camargue coast, to the beaches beside Les Saintes-Maries-de-la-Mer. The section from Les Saintes-Maries to La Gacholle lighthouse, running between the beach and the *étangs* makes an excellent walk or bike ride.

Le Grau-du-Roi and Port Camargue*

Le Grau-du-Roi 30 rue Michel Rédarès; tel; 04 66 51 67 70.

The D979 runs straight into the resorts from Aigues-Mortes; the D62b skirts the perimeter.

The road around the Port Camargue marina has more than a dozen parking areas.

Port Camargue Carrefour 2000; tel: 04 66 51 71 68.

The old resort of Le Grau-du-Roi and the imaginative, purpose-built marina resort of Port Camargue, constructed in the late 1960s as part of a (fairly successful) plan to develop the Languedoc coast, lie at the mouth of the Chenal Maritime linking Aigues-Mortes to the sea. A *grau* is an opening from an *étang* to the sea, so this was the King's Channel. The town stands at the point where once Louis IX's crusaders set sail for Palestine. South of the two resorts stretch the vast sands of **l'Espiguette**, which can be reached along the rough road to Phare de l'Espiguette (Espiguette Lighthouse). Behind the dunes stretch the salt marshes of La Petite Camargue – the area west of La Petite Rhône.

Accommodation and food in Port Camargue

Relais de l'Oustau Camarguen €€ *3 route Marines; tel: 04 66 51 51 65; fax: 04 66 53 06 65.* A genuine old farmhouse on the edge of this modern resort. Attractive comfortable rooms, gardens, and close to the *étangs*.

Le Spinaker €€ *Pointe Môle; tel: 04 66 53 36 37; fax: 04 66 53 17 47.* An extraordinary, delightful hotel improbably located on the very point of the verdant peninsula which winds around the marina, this is a comfortable, leisurely spot in a thoroughly touristy setting. Its amiable restaurant is open in summer only, serving acclaimed high-quality cooking.

Musee Camarguais*

Musée Camarguais € Le Mas du Pont de Rousty; tel: 04 90 97 10 82. Open 1015–1645 (Oct–Mar closed Tue).

Located in a traditional old Camargue ranch and sheep farm beside the main D570 at Pont de Rousty, the museum tells the whole story of the Camargue. Both the natural and the human history is covered, starting with the gradual formation of the Rhône delta, which came into being as recently as around 7000 years ago. Despite its inhospitality, the region was inhabited and developed from earliest times. The museum's emphasis, however, is on 19th-century farm life.

There's an enjoyable one-hour marked walk through the grounds to the edges of the Marée de la Grand Mar marshes. The administration offices of the National Park are also located here.

Le Parc Naturel Regional de Camargue (et la Reserve Nationale)✦✦✦

La Capelière €
On east shore of Etang de Vaccarès (for directions see page 116); tel: 04 90 97 00 97. Open Apr–Sep Mon–Fri 0900–1800, Sat 1000–1300, 1400–1700; rest of year closed. Times liable to alteration.

Centre d'Information de Ginès Pont de Gau, 4km from Les Saintes-Maries-de-la-Mer on the D570; tel: 04 90 97 86 32. Open Apr–Sep 0900–1800; Oct–Mar 0930–1700. Closed Fri. Times liable to alteration.

Created in 1970, the 85 000-hectare Camargue Regional Nature Park encompasses most of the Camargue region and offshore waters. Its objective is to control development and safeguard the environment and traditional local culture. These goals have been strained by the growth of tourism, and the Parc's activities now include trying to teach visitors to respect the Camargue's flora and fauna. The **Musée Camarguais**✦ (see above) and the **Centre d'Information de Ginès**✦, just outside Les Saintes-Maries, are two places to see and learn about the Parc. The heart of the region is the Réserve Nationale de la Camargue. Not open to casual visitors (though permission is granted for any researcher or academic making a written application in advance), the Réserve consists mainly of the large Etang de Vaccarès and the watery terrain between there and the sea. Within these borders, it attempts to offer total protection to the terrain and wildlife. Visitors do get a look in: hides and viewing platforms have been erected at various points around the edge of the Réserve, and there are permanent exhibitions and short walks at the Parc information centre at **La Capelière**✦✦, on the *étang*'s eastern shore.

Parc Ornithologique (bird sanctuary)✦✦

Parc Ornithologique € Pont de Gau, on the D570, 4km from Les Saintes-Maries-de-la-Mer; tel: 04 90 97 82 62. Open 0900–sunset (opens 0930 Oct–Mar).

The main attraction of this 60-hectare bird sanctuary, next to the Ginès Parc information centre, is its marked trail through marshland. An extraordinary variety of birds live here, including flamingos, herons, marsh harriers and other birds of prey, avocets and oyster-catchers and other waders, and a multitude of ducks. Panels explain everything. In the distance, black bulls can often be seen.

St-Gilles✦

Originally the site of the hermitage of this half-mythical, 8th-century mystic, the town kept its religious importance over the centuries, and is now best known for the beautiful and unusual surviving west front of its 12th-century **abbey church**✦✦✦; the rest has been destroyed. The former **chancel** and **crypt** and a spiral stone staircase called the **Vis de St-Gilles** can also be seen. The town was a favourite place of the counts of Languedoc, especially Count Raymond IV of Toulouse, who preferred to call himself Raymond of St-Gilles. At the time of the

**i St-Gilles Tourist
Office** place Frédéric
Mistral; tel: 04 66 87 33 75.
Guided tours arranged by the
tourist office.

**i Abbey chancel,
crypt, Vis de St
Gilles** € tel: 04 66 87 41
31. Generally open
0900–1700 (longer in
summer).

Crusades, perhaps partly because of the fervent piety of Raymond IV, St-Gilles became the object of a fanatical devotion, inspiring huge bequests and pilgrimages. Today it is a modest little country town.

Count Raymond

An incident at St-Gilles sparked the 13th-century Albigensian Crusade that was to devastate Languedoc. Catharism had taken hold in the County of Toulouse. The pope instructed Count Raymond VI of Toulouse to eradicate the creed, which had been adopted by nobility, peasants and even clergymen, and had become an anti-Catholic, anti-French movement throughout Languedoc. The papal legate sent to meet Count Raymond at St-Gilles was murdered on arriving in the town. The pope responded by ordering the savage Crusade which finally destroyed the independence of Languedoc.

Below
Carmargue white horses

LES SAINTES-MARIES-DE-LA-MER✦✦✦

ⓘ **Les Saintes-Maries-de-la-Mer Tourist Office** *avenue Van Gogh; tel: 04 90 97 82 55; e-mail: info@saintesmaries.com; www.saintesmaries.com. Open summer daily 0900–1200, 1400–1900; winter Mon–Sat 0900–1200, 1400–1700, Sun 0900–1200.*

⇄ Follow the D570 straight through town to the seafront, where the tourist office and parking areas are located.

Ⓟ The coast road east from the town centre is lined with parking areas.

Ⓣ **Church** *place de l'Eglise. Open May–Sep 0800–1200, 1400–1900; in Mar, Apr and Oct, no midday closing; rest of year 0800–1800.*

Musée Baroncelli € *place Lamartine; tel: 04 90 97 87 60. Open 1000–1200, 1400–1800. Closed Tue and Oct–May.*

This small, picturesque town with its medieval fortified harbour on the Mediterranean seashore has become a busy focal point for visitors to the Camargue, whether they have come for the birdlife or the beaches. Shows, nightclubs and discos join with bullfights and rodeos to provide entertainment. Even in the last century, it was a favourite spot for outings: Van Gogh, living in Arles at the time, made frequent visits to its bright and busy waterfront. The massive walls and strange open bell tower of the fortified Romanesque **church✦✦✦** are the most attractive feature. Known as Les-Saintes-Maries, 'the Holy Maries', for short, the town takes its name from an improbable Catholic legend. It claims that a boat carrying Mary Magdalene, a sister of the Virgin Mary who was also called Mary, the mother of the apostles John and James whose name was also Mary, and their Ethiopian maidservant Sarah, together with Martha, Lazarus, Maximinus and Sidonius, put to sea from the shores of the Land of Israel after Christ's crucifixion and landed at this spot on the Camargue coast. On landing, the group separated, Mary Magdalene and Maximinus going to St-Maximin in Provence (*see page 170*) where, according to the legend, they are buried in the church. Martha went to Tarascon to kill a mythical dragon, while the other Maries and their servant Sarah stayed at Les-Saintes-Maries. If you're here around 24 May, try not to miss the dramatic gypsy gathering at their Festival of Saint Sarah and Saints Mary (*see page 117*). Worth a visit is the **Musée Baroncelli✦**. Located in a tall tower near the church, it houses an interesting collection of local bygones and has a good view from the top. East of town there are campsites and beaches of fine sand backed by *étangs* and the Camargue **seawall** (*La Digue de la Mer, see page 111*). The immense curve of sand reaches for over 20km.

Accommodation and food in Les Saintes-Maries-de-la-Mer

Le Mas de la Fouque €€€ *Route du Bac du Sauvage, 4km out of town on D38; tel: 04 90 97 81 02; fax: 04 90 97 96 84.* Despite the rustic sounding name, this is an extremely luxurious and pricey little country hotel of character standing in its own 4-hectare chunk of Camargue wilderness. There's a pool, sports facilities and every amenity, and each room has a terrace looking out over the *étangs*.

Hostellerie du Pont de Gau €€ *On the main D570, about 4km out of town; tel: 04 90 97 81 53; fax: 04 90 97 98 54.* Right beside an *étang*, the Parc Ornithologique and a Parc Régional information office is a small, traditional hotel-restaurant with excellent cheap menus. Quiet, comfortable and satisfying.

Suggested tour

Total distance: About 125km, or 205km including detours.

Time: Allow a long day to linger over the whole route including detours. Better still, spend the night en route and continue the next morning. For a quicker drive, the basic journey without detours and only brief stops could be done in about 3 or 4 hours.

Links: This route connects with Les Alpilles at Arles (*see page 100*) and with the Gard (*see page 74*) at St Gilles.

Route: Start from **Arles**, on the northern fringes of the wetland region. Leave town on the D570, signposted Les Saintes-Maries-de-la-Mer. Tourist traffic pours down this main road from Arles to the Camargue coast, but turn off into the cat's-cradle of narrow lanes which run beside watery channels through the heart of the delta. Here you will see few other visitors. Drive slowly with the windows wide open, sometimes coming to a stop to look and listen. After the junction with the D36, look out for a minor turn on the left signposted to Mas d'Agon. Take this deserted minor road across the Marais de la Grand Mar in the heart of the Camargue: through minute hamlet **Mas Ste-**

Cecile, to tiny **Mas d'Agon.** This is pure essence of Camargue; flat, lonely, populated mainly by birdlife. Continue until you reach the D37. The main route then turns right.

Detour: Turn left instead to take the D37 in an easterly direction. This road runs beside the Camargue's largest *étang*, Le Vaccarès, on the edge of the prohibited area of the Nature Reserve, home of thousands of flamingos, herons, ducks and other water-birds. It veers away from the waterside to approach a small crossroads at a location called Villeneuve. Here turn right for la Capelière. This lonely road returns to the Vaccarès *étang*, on the way giving fantastic views over the water, and at last reaching the Nature Reserve's information centre at **La Capelière**, on the *étang's* eastern shore. This definitely deserves a stop – and a walk. Press on along this little-used road

Below
Aigues-Mortes

Gypsy festival

Gitans, or gypsies, have strong connections with the region. The 'Holy Maries' who give their name to Les Saintes-Maries-de-la-Mer were accompanied, according to the story, by their Ethiopian maidservant Sarah. Gypsies long ago decided that the servant Sarah wasn't Ethiopian but Egyptian, and that she was their patron saint. Sarah is reputedly buried here and a revered silk-clothed statue of her, together with those of the Saints Mary, stands in the town's atmospheric, fortified medieval church. Sarah has become known to the gitans as La Vierge Noire, the black Virgin. Every year on 24 and 25 May, gypsies gather here in thousands to feast, play guitar, have fun and honour their saint. After a crowded, fervent service in the old fortress church, the statue of their saint is carried at the head of a huge procession to the seashore and into the waves.

through the eastern Camargue, which is developed for salt-extraction. **Salin-de-Badon** is a former royal salt marsh, where now there are footpaths and explanatory plaques. At **Le Paradis**, a side turn leads 6km to Etang de Galabert and Etang de Fangassier, an important breeding and nesting area for the Camargue flamingos. This side road runs partly on the **DIGUE DE LA MER ❶** (seawall) at its eastern end. Return on the same road, past la Capelière, back to the D37 and to the Mas d'Agon junction, making a detour altogether of around 60km.

Stay on the D37 until it rejoins the main D570, then turn left. Along the road here the Camargue seems to become almost tawdry, with unappealing stables where tourists can ride miserable-looking white horses. The better attractions include the **PARC ORNITHOLOGIQUE ❷**. Continue into **LES SAINTES-MARIES-DE-LA-MER ❸**. After visiting the town, return along the Arles road, the D570, as far as the Aigues-Mortes turning, the D38, on the left. After crossing the Petite Rhône – the western arm of the divided Rhône – the road number changes to D58. Continue to **AIGUES-MORTES ❹**, pausing before you reach the town at **La Tour Carbonnière**.

Detour: Take the D979 beside a canal to reach the coast again at the marina resorts of **LE GRAU-DU-ROI ❺** and **PORT CAMARGUE ❻**, a round trip of about 20km.

Return from Aigues-Mortes along the D58 as far as the D179 on the left. Take this very unfrequented back route across the marshes, via Mas des Iscles, all the way to **ST-GILLES ❼**. Return to Arles on the N572.

Life in the Camargue

As well as the flamingos, herons and an abundance of other bird life in the salt meadows and marshes, the half-wild black bulls of the Camargue have long been bred here and used in the bullfights of Provence and Languedoc. More often seen are the famous white horses, which frequently graze close to the bigger roads. The bulls are herded, and the horses tamed and ridden, by *gardians*, Camargue herdsmen who bear an uncanny resemblance to Wild West cowboys, or perhaps 'dudes', in their dark jackets, leather leggings and wide-brimmed hats. The animals are owned by *manadiers*, who live in spacious old farmhouses built around a large yard. *Gardians* make their homes in low whitewashed cottages called *cabanes*, which may be isolated or in primitive villages. One other resident of this watery terrain deserves a mention: the mosquito is horribly prolific all summer long. To avoid its attentions, visit the Camargue in spring or autumn.

Also worth exploring

A landscape even stranger than the Camargue lies on the other side of the Grande Rhône. La Crau is certainly not a pretty sight, just an extraordinary one, and should appeal to those who want to hear silence and see emptiness. It consists only of pebbles, a vast flat expanse of them in a bleak, waterless landscape, yet there is life here. The margins of the plain have been cultivated, while even in the stony heart of the region there are species of birds for whom nothing could be nicer than this. The lesser kestrel is found nowhere else in France. Stone curlews and little bustards nest here, larks can be heard, and blue-headed rollers pick over the stones. Tough thorny plants grow in places, and the occasional wild rose gives a flash of colour. Look more closely and there are lizards and crickets, locusts and other insects. There is a village here, St-Martin-de-Crau, about 15km from Arles and easily reached on the N113.

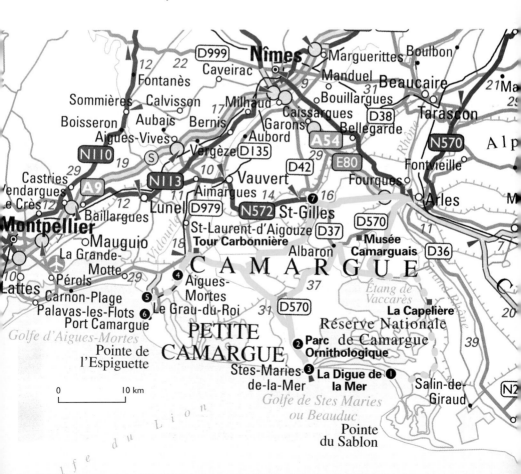

Marseille

Ratings

Restaurants	●●●●●
Shopping	●●●●●
Sightseeing	●●●●●
Entertainment	●●●●○
Museums	●●●●○
Street life	●●●●○
Children	●●●○○
Architecture	●●○○○

F rance's second city is thrilling, a sprawling, squalid, teeming, energetic and visually stunning Mediterranean metropolis which encloses a major industrial harbour. Founded by Ancient Greeks as *Massalia* 2500 years ago, Marseille is also ultra-modern. Sightseeing spans the centuries, from museums of those early beginnings and remnants of medieval defences right up to the horrible concrete tower block – La Cité Radieuse – designed by architect Le Corbusier. The Vieux Port area, with its boat-filled harbour and narrow streets, is lively and picturesque, and is *the* place to stroll, relax and enjoy a meal of classic Marseille fish dishes. Of course, the city has another side. It is notorious for crime, corruption, violence and racial strife and is considered one of Europe's capitals of drug trafficking – the French side of *The French Connection* was set here. Central avenue La Canebière is synonymous with decadence and presents a stark, exhilarating contrast between opulence and low life. Though Marseille is traditionally considered France's second city, and Lyon the third, the two conurbations are running neck and neck with population size around a million.

Arriving and departing

ⓘ **Main office** *4 La Canebière tel: 04 91 13 89 00; fax: 04 91 13 89 20; e-mail: info@marseille-tourisme.com; www.marseille-tourisme.com. Mon–Sat 0900–1900, Sun 1000–1700. Longer hours in peak season.*

Le Panier office *Opposite la Vieille Charité, place des Pistoles; tel: 04 91 90 53 39. Open Mon–Sat, hours variable.*

Use *autoroute* A50 and the D559 to approach Marseille from the Riviera and the east, the A51 from Aix and the north, the A55 and N568 from the Camargue and the west.

Unless you have accommodation in another quarter of the city, follow signs for Vieux Port, the main centre for both residents and visitors, from whichever direction you enter Marseille.

Parking

As with most Provençal cities, it is difficult to find street parking in the city centre and Vieux Port area. Use the big, well-signed car parks and be prepared to pay. The most convenient is Parking Hôtel de Ville behind the Hôtel de Ville (town hall) on quai du Port. Other car parks close by are Parking de Gaulle, Parking Bourse, Parking Monthyon and Parking Vieux Port. Charges are reasonable at all of them.

Palais Longchamp

Rue Villeneuve

Rue Lafayette

Boulevard d'Athénes

Allée L Gambetta

Rue Senac

Rue des 3 Mages

Cours Julien

Cours Julien

Gare
Saint Charles

Bd Dugommier

La Canebière

Cours Lieutaud

Place
P Cezanne

Cours Lieutaud

Boulevard C Nédélec

Rue Longue des Capucins

Rue Nationale

Rue Tapis Vert

Rue Thubaneau

Rue d'Aubagne

Rue Fongate

Rue Fr de Pressence

Rue du Baignoir

Rue de Rome

Place
F Baret

Rue d'Aix

Cours Belsunce

Rue Pavillon

Rue St Ferreol

Rue Sylvabelle

Musée d'Histoire
de Marseille

Rue Corbet

Centre
Bourse

Rue Haxo

Rue Paradis

Rue Grignan

Rue Montgrand

Rue Armeny

Boulevard des Dames

Jardin des
Vestiges

Rue Sainte

ℹ

Place
J Ballard

Rue Breteuil

Rue E Delanglade

Rue de la République

Rue St Saens

Cours Pierre Puget

Pl
Sadi
Carnot

Rue Mary

Grande Rue

Rue de la République

Rue Sainte

Rue Grignan

La Vieille
Charité

Rue des P Puits

Rue du Panier

Quai du Port

Vieux Port

Quai de Rive Neuve

Rue Fort Notre Dame

Place
de la
Corderie

Boulevard Notre Dame

Boulevard Andre Aune

Le Panier

Rue de la Loge

Rue Rigord

Jardin
Puget

Rue Schuman

Rue Nve Sainte Catherine

Rue de la Croix

Boulevard de la Corderie

Basilique N D
de la Garde

Cathédrale

Avenue St-Jean

Rue Sainte

Quai de la Tourette

Avenue Vaudoyer

Rue St Laurent

Avenue de la Tourette

Rue Robert

Place
St Victor

Rue d'Endoume

Blvd Tellene

Fort St-Jean

Fort
Saint Nicolas

Boulevard Charles Livon

St Maurice

Avenue de la Corse

Rue Sauveur Tobelem

Rue d'Endoume

South
Marseille

Rue E Duchesne

Rue J Recher

Château d'If
& Iles de Frioul

Rue Crinas

| 0 | 100 metres |
| 0 | 100 yards |

Public transport

Station office *Gare St-Charles, square Narvik; tel: 04 91 50 59 18. Open Mon–Sat, very varied hours.*

Local weather *Tel: 08 36 68 01 01.*

Visiting museums Municipal museums are closed Mon, national museums closed Tue. The tourist office sells a discount 'city-card' giving entry to most Marseille museums.

Beaches There are sandy beaches and bays a short distance along the coast east of the city, and on the Frioul islands.

Markets Several food markets take place every day in the city, except Sun and holidays.

The Festival de Marseille during most of July is a brilliant, exuberant, multifaceted arts festival with dance, lectures, music, shows, flamenco, tango, cinema, etc. *www.festivaldemarseille.com*

City transport authority RTM runs a comprehensive bus and tram network, and two metro lines. The main hub is Réformés Canebière, at the end of La Canebière. A limited bus service runs all night (called Fluobus). There's a useful go-as-you-please discount pass valid for one day (*Carte Journée*). Information from Espace Infos, *6 rue des Fabres (off La Canebière, near Centre Bourse), tel; 04 91 91 92 10.*

Security

The main tourist areas are generally safe, though caution is advised at night. Avoid the section of the city centre north of La Canebière, except for Le Panier. Keep all valuables hidden from view anywhere in the city.

Tours

- **Guided tours on foot** A wide variety of options with Ministry-approved guides can be arranged through the tourist office. Most tours are available in English.
- **Taxi tours** Four set options from 1½–4 hours. Commentary in English on cassette. Arranged through the tourist office.
- **Histobus** Bus tour taking in 26 monuments and a ride around the city with an interpreter on board. Every Sunday at 1430 from Vieux Port. Run by Marseille transport authority RTM; *tel: 04 91 10 54 71.*
- **Petit Train** (Little Train) tours trundle through the traffic to Notre-Dame-de-la-Garde (50-minute round trip; Apr–Sep every 30 minutes from 1000–1230, 1400–1830; rest of year less frequently, but always with departures at 1415 and 1515). There's also a tour of Vieux Marseille (40-minute trip; Apr–Oct departures start at 1015; daily in season; variable out of season). Both from quai des Belges; *tel: 04 91 40 17 75.*

- **Boat** departures daily from Vieux Port to the islands **Château d'If** (15 minutes) and **Frioul** (30 minutes), tours of the new **docks**, excursions along the *calanques* sometimes including glass-bottomed boats (*see West Provence Coast, page 130*). All leave from quai des Belges; *tel: 04 91 55 50 09; fax: 04 91 55 60 23.*

Right
Vieux Port

Sights

Château d'If € *Open for guided tours only while ferries or excursions are visiting.*

Jardin des Vestiges *Beside Centre Bourse; tel: 04 91 90 42 22. Open Mon–Sat 1200–1900 (Dec–Feb closes at 1800).*

Musée d'Histoire de Marseille *Entrance inside Centre Bourse. Tel: 04 91 90 42 22. Same opening times as Jardin des Vestiges.*

Iles de Frioul**

The small archipelago of the Frioul islands lies a few minutes offshore. The harbour village of **Frioul** is on the island of Ratonneau, which is linked to Pomègues island by a 17th-century dike. These two islands are especially popular for diving; you can also pass a pleasant half-day at shingle-and-sand beaches and rocky *calanques*, and there are several eating places. The island of If, usually a separate excursion, is the setting for the notorious **Château d'If**, the 16th-century fortress long used as a ghastly prison, described by Alexandre Dumas in *The Count of Monte Cristo*. Dumas' hero, Edmond Dantès, escapes and rises to great heights of daring and vengeance, but few real prisoners ever survived their time here. Aristocratic inmates had 'better' quarters in the upper cells. On the visit you'll see the cells occupied by the mysterious 'Man in the Iron Mask', Mirabeau, Prince Casimir of Poland and the unfortunate Glandèves de Niozelles, imprisoned here for six years for failing to doff his hat to Louis XIV.

Jardin des Vestiges and Musée d'Histoire de Marseille***

Large fragments of half-buried stonework in the well-tended **Jardin des Vestiges*** (Garden of Remnants) are the best archaeological finds yet dating back to the city's origins. Uncovered in 1967, they consist of ruins of the original Greek ramparts (3rd and 2nd century BC), traces of a white limestone roadway and parts of the Greek dock after it had been restructured by the Romans (1st century AD). Either enter the gardens or follow the Centre Bourse walkway which looks down on them. Among the finds here was a 3rd-century Roman ship, displayed in the adjacent **Musée d'Histoire de Marseille*** (Museum of the History of Marseille), which traces the whole history of the city from those origins to recent times. The latest additions include wrecks of Greek ships (6th century BC).

La Canebière***

The name derives from *canabé*, the hemp plant that yields both rope and cannabis, which seems appropriate enough for this raw, assertive avenue driven right through the centre of Marseille, skirting fetid ancient neighbourhoods and reaching down to the port. Built in the 17th century, it soon became a byword for all the entertainments sailors sought on reaching a big port, as well as a veritable hub of the everyday life of the city. Nowadays, it's mainly the reputation that has survived – La Canebière isn't even a major shopping street any more – though it's still a majestic sight.

Le Panier**

North of the Old Port rises the Le Panier district, a neighbourhood of scruffy, sometimes slummy steep back streets and stairways and narrow lanes lined by tall narrow houses with peeling façades and washing

ⓘ Cathédrale de la Major place de la Major; tel: 04 91 90 53 57. Open 15 Jun–31 Aug 0900–1830; rest of year 0900–1200, 1400–1730. Closed Mon.

Musée du Vieux Marseille € La Maison Diamanté, 2 rue de la Prison; tel: 04 91 55 28 68. Open Jul–Sep 1100–1800; rest of year 1000–1700. Closed Mon and holidays.

Musée des Beaux-Arts € Palais Longchamp, 142 boulevard Longchamp; tel: 04 91 14 59 30. Open Jun–Sep 1100–1800; rest of year 1000–1700. Closed Mon.

Musée d'Histoire Naturelle Palais Longchamp, 142 boulevard Longchamp; tel: 04 91 14 59 50. Open 1000–1700. Closed Mon and holidays.

Basilique Notre-Dame-de-la-Garde rue Fort de Sanctuaire. Usually open all day. There's a big pilgrimage to the basilica on 15 Aug.

hanging on makeshift lines. Here stood the original Marseille, the *Massalia* of the Greek settlers of 600 BC, the *Massilia* of their Roman successors. Bordered by quai du Port, place de la Major and rue de la République, it remained the atmospheric, famously seedy and densely populated working-class Old Quarter of Marseille right up to 1945. High on the hill stands **La Vieille Charité** (*see opposite*). Go a few paces down towards the new port area to reach the large 19th-century **Cathédrale de la Major*** in a striking Byzantine style with harmonious domes and striped light and dark façade. The church is surrounded on three sides by never-ending traffic. The odd mutilated fragment of the fine 12th-century Romanesque **Ancienne Cathédrale de la Major***, so much smaller, so much less pretentious, stands right next to it.

An ungovernable hotbed of radical politics and resistance, Le Panier was a thorn in the side of the occupying Nazis. In February 1943, they removed 25000 residents and blew up 1924 of the buildings. One of the few to survive is **Hôtel de Cabre***, on Grand' Rue, a lovely sight – a substantial stone house of 1535 in a homely jumble of Gothic and Renaissance styles. After the war, it was taken apart and reconstructed in a different location: that's why it says rue de la Bonneterie on the side facing Grand' Rue. The **Musée du Vieux Marseille*** (Museum of Old Marseille) occupies one of the few buildings which survived, a wealthy 16th-century merchant's mansion, called La Maison Diamanté because of its façade of stones carved into diamond-like points. Inside, it has a large collection of 18th-century Provençal furnishings, *santons*, and information about the esoteric playing cards called the Tarot Marseillaise.

Palais Longchamp*

The wonderfully ornate fountain in the central courtyard of this grandiose 19th-century building was the destination of an aqueduct constructed to bring water from the River Durance. Today the aqueduct is no longer in use, but the Palais houses two important museums. The **Musée des Beaux-Arts*** contains an extensive collection of 16th- and 17th-century French and Italian paintings; a room devoted to architect, sculptor and painter Pierre Puget, a Marseille native; and another to the satirical cartoons of Honoré Daumier, also a local boy. Across the courtyard, there's a **Musée d'Histoire Naturelle***, with a zoo behind.

South Marseille**

The southern districts rise to a peak on which stands the **Basilique Notre-Dame-de-la-Garde***. Pious locals believe (rather optimistically) that the conspicuous golden Virgin atop this lofty 19th-century edifice gives divine protection to the city. Running around the foot of the southern section of the city, Promenade de la Corniche Président Kennedy hugs the shoreline, giving some great sea views. The road passes right over the exquisite old-fashioned fishing harbour at **Anse des Auffes****; pause on the road to see it from above, or take any side

Opposite
Vieux Port

① Centre Polyculturel de la Vieille Charité and **Musée de l'Archéologie Méditeranéenne** € *2 rue de la Vieille Charité; tel: 04 91 14 58 80. The museums are open 1100–1800 daily, but the courtyard and galleries open earlier. In the courtyard there's a bookshop and a pleasing bar-restaurant with tables under the arcades.*

Musée d'Art Contemporain € *69 boulevard de Haifa; tel: 04 91 25 01 07. Open Jun–Sep 1100–1800; rest of year 1000–1700. Closed Mon.*

Musée Cantini € *19 rue Grignan; tel: 04 91 54 77 75; fax: 04 91 55 03 01. Open Jun–Sep 1100–1800; rest of year 1000–1700. Closed Mon.*

turn to reach the harbour, where rowing boats are pulled up on the steeply sloping sides. Below the corniche road as it swings round Plage du Prado bay are beaches popular with locals. Close to the bay, the **Musée d'Art Contemporain⁕** displays interesting, resolutely modern artworks mainly by Marseille artists, including some examples of graffiti. Just north of here, in a locality now called Lecorbusier, stands the uninspiring **Cité Radieuse⁕** tower block (*280 boulevard Michelet*), built in 1952 by the pioneer of concrete architecture, Le Corbusier, so much admired and imitated by modern architects. Closer to the city centre, in the main shopping area off rue St-Ferréol, the **Musée Cantini⁕⁕⁕** is a good modern art museum with famous works on southern themes by Matisse, Derain, Dufy, Max Ernst, Miró and Paul Signac as well as Kandinsky, Chagall and Picasso.

La Vieille Charité⁕⁕

The one-time Hospice de la Charité, at the top of the Le Panier quarter, was built between 1671 and 1745 as a sort of lock-up, soup kitchen and place of overnight shelter for the city's numerous homeless vagrants. Under restoration since 1963, it has become the beautiful setting for the Centre Polyculturel de la Vieille Charité. It's a rectangle of fine three-storey arcaded galleries in pale stone enclosing a large gravelled courtyard with a little baroque chapel in the centre. Walk around the galleries to find art exhibitions and an extensive, easy to follow **Musée de l'Archéologie Meditéranéenne⁕⁕** (Museum of Mediterranean Archaeology).

Vieux Port⁕⁕⁕

The best (and best known) of all the sights in this ancient maritime city is its historic port. The original Phocaean (Ancient Greek) harbour, called *Lacydon*, was constructed here in 600 BC, and Marseille

Quai des Belges is the Vieux Port's shorter waterfront at the end of La Canebière. The other two sides are **quai du Port** (north side) and **quai du Rive Neuve** (south side).

Musée des Docks Romains € *28 place Vivaux; tel: 04 91 91 24 62. Open Jun–Sep 1100–1800; rest of year 1000–1700. Closed Mon.*

Basilique St-Victor *place St-Victor; tel: 04 91 33 25 86.*

Marseille's new port

Today Marseille is Europe's third largest port. The Vieux Port has been abandoned to tourism and pleasure craft, while the city's maritime activities occupy the 30km of quays and warehouses from la Joliette (next to Vieux Port) to Fos-sur-Mer.

is proud of its antiquity. Today's long, wide, neatly rectlinear fortified harbour with its handsome Italianate quays is mainly 17th-century. Facing west, under Marseille's typically clear blue skies, it is full of space and light. Thousands of boats are berthed here, their masts resembling a curious forest of reeds growing in the sparkling water. The main quay is the short **quai des Belges**, at the end of **La Canebière**. The quayside and the whole area around is deliciously alive, scruffy and hectic. Hillside districts slope down to the waterside, russet and ochre roofs and façades piled up to left and right of the harbour. Set a few paces back from the north quay, **quai du Port**, close to the Hôtel de Ville, is the **Musée des Docks Romains** (Museum of the Roman Docks), displaying a good collection of 1st- to 3rd-century Roman objects discovered here during work on the site in 1947. On the opposite side, behind **quai de Rive Neuve**, are the squared-off streets and buildings of the **Quartier de l'Arsenal**, former site of the historic shipyards where thousands of galley slaves were housed: it's now an area full of restaurants. Overlooking one end of Vieux Port rises the daunting **Fort St Nicolas** citadel. Behind it, **Basilique St-Victor** is a remarkably heavily fortified Romanesque church with an interesting 5th-century crypt. On the other side of the port entrance, the **Fort St-Jean** stands guard. To the south rises **Notre-Dame-de-la-Garde**, standing high and alone with its vast gilded statue. Illuminated at night, these grand landmarks help give the Vieux Port an unexpected touch of romance after dark.

Accommodation and food

Rue St-Saens, parallel to Vieux Port a block south, is lined with restaurants all serving *fruits de mer, marmite du pêcheur* and other fish specialities, including several different overpriced versions of *bouillabaisse*. **Quai du Port**, on the other side of the harbour, has less interesting pizzerias, brasseries, etc. In the **Centre Bourse** shopping mall, **Le Grand Café**, **Bel Oustau** and **L'Oliveraie** are enjoyable places for lunch.

Hôtel Alizé € *35 quai des Belges; tel: 04 91 33 66 97; fax: 04 91 54 80 06.* A little place with rooms above the bars and pavements of the Vieux Port, the Alizé has decent, comfortable rooms with great street life outside, brilliant Vieux Port views and modest prices.

Mercure Beauvau Vieux Port €€€ *4 rue Beauvau; tel: 04 91 54 91 00; fax: 04 91 54 15 76.* Hotels around Vieux Port include several members of big chains, such as Climat de France, Frantour, Mercure, Sofitel. Wherever you chose in this part of town, you'll need *insonorisation* – soundproofing. Especially notable is the Beauvau Vieux Port, an unusual and characterful historic hotel skilfully modernised and backing on to the quai des Belges and La Canebière. Ask for a Port view.

Opposite
Marseille street scene

On the menu
Bouillabaisse, that classic Provençal fish stew which originates in Marseille and – so gastronomes claim – can only be made correctly here, features on most menus. Marseille fish restaurants generally offer several versions of this dish.

Entertainment and nightlife The official free quarterly *L'Agenda*, from the tourist office lists hundreds of events, theatres, jazz, street theatre, puppet shows, concerts and more. The monthly *Marseille Poche* from news stands and tourist offices deals more fully with what's on, from opera to disco, cinema to cabaret. *Taktik*, a weekly current affairs and events paper, has details of happening and forthcoming shows, and reviews.

Hôtel Petit Nice and **Restaurant Passédat** €€€ *Anse de Maldormé, Promenade de la Corniche Président Kennedy; tel: 04 91 59 25 92; fax: 04 91 59 28 08.* The best restaurant in the best hotel in Marseille, vastly expensive and housed in a beautiful villa overlooking the water at Anse de Maldormé off the corniche road. The restaurant, with its toes almost in the sea, concentrates on the highest standard of fish cuisine. The hotel will arrange to take you on a boat trip to the *calanques*.

L'Art des Thés € *Centre de la Vieille Charité; tel: 04 91 14 58 71.* In one corner of the Vieille Charité's peaceful courtyards is a bookshop and this pleasing, simple bar-restaurant with tables under the arcades. Main courses such as *tabouleh* and savoury tarts are very good value.

Miramar €€ *12 quai du Port; tel: 04 91 91 10 40; fax: 04 91 56 64 31.* You want to eat *bouillabaisse* alongside the Vieux Port? This is the place. Michelin-rosetted, it's more than a cut above most of the other quayside eateries. Other fish dishes too, and decent local wines.

Suggested walk

Total distance: About 6km, including detour.

Time: The main walk will take about 3–4 hours allowing for pauses to admire the views and the outsides of buildings, but without entering the museums and monuments. Allow a full day, including detour and visits to all the sights.

Route: Start from the city's hub, quai des Belges at the **VIEUX PORT ❶**.

The main shopping streets off La Canebière are **rue Paradis** and parallel, pedestrianised **rue St-Ferréol**, both with fashions, accessories and gourmet foods. Across La Canebière, **Centre Bourse** (Mon–Fri 0930–1900 or 1930, Sat 0930–1930), a large pleasant mall with over 60 stores, includes a major FNAC book and record store which hosts frequent 'encounters' with writers and artists; Loisirs et Créations for children; a fascinating Nature et Découverte eco-store; Nouvelles Galeries and Le Fleuron for quality leather goods and accessories.

Turn along quai du Port on the north side of the port and walk beside the water to the very end. Walk right around Fort St-Jean at the harbour entrance, the pale peach-coloured stone castle with a round tower and wonderful views out to sea. From here you get an odd perspective on Cathédrale de la Major standing amid teeming traffic (do not continue to the cathedral yet – there is no pedestrian access). Ahead lies the Gare Maritime, with ferries to Algeria, Tunisia and Corsica. Coming back past the Fort, notice the **Memorial des Camps de Mort (Death Camps Memorial)**, a sombre museum of the Nazi death camps, with a display of stark photographs (closed Mon and Tue). Return along the quai du Port to any left turn into the steep lanes of **LE PANIER** district ❷. Wander through Le Panier up to **LA VIEILLE CHARITE** ❸.

Detour: Take rue Antoine Becker past the police HQ to reach **Cathédrale de la Major** and the **Ancienne Cathédrale**.

Walk down through Le Panier to rue de la Loge at the bottom. Along here, turn off for the **Musée des Docks Romains** and carry on to **Musée du Vieux Marseille**. Grande Rue is nearby, so turn right into it to find **Hôtel de Cabre**. Reaching rue de la République, turn right and, near the end of the street, turn left for the **JARDIN DE VESTIGES** ❹, the **MUSEE D'HISTOIRE DE MARSEILLE** ❺ and the **Centre Bourse** shopping mall. Head into adjacent **LA CANEBIERE** ❻, and take a stroll up and down the avenue before turning into the busy shopping street rue St-Ferréol. Follow this to its end in place Félix Baret where café tables are laid out under trees opposite the large ornate Préfecture. Return along the parallel street, rue Paradis, the city's main shopping thoroughfare. On the way, pause at the **Musée Cantini** in rue Grignan. Turn left into rue du Anarcharsis and follow it as it becomes rue St-Saens and continues through the **Quartier de l'Arsenal** with its many restaurants. Keep going all the way to **Basilique St-Victor**. It's a couple of blocks to the quai de Rive Neuve at the Vieux Port. Walk along here back to quai des Belges.

La Marseillaise

Despite its present name, the French national anthem was composed in Alsace in April 1792 to honour the war declared by France against Austria, and originally had the title *Chant de Guerre pour l'Armée du Rhin* (*War Song for the Army of the Rhine*). In June, it was sung in Marseille for the first time by a visitor, and proved a hit. National Guardsmen from Marseille, ordered north to defend the French capital, dubbed the song *Chant de Guerre aux Armées des Frontières* (*War Song for the Border Armies*) and sang it rousingly all the way to Paris. The Revolutionary fervour of Marseille was already legendary, and when Parisians saw and heard the new troops singing as they marched into the city, they called the song *Chant des Marseillais* (*Song of the Men of Marseille*).

Palais Longchamp

Rue Villeneuve
Rue Senac
Rue Lafayette
Allée L Gambetta
Rue des 3 Mages
Boulevard d'Athènes
Bd Dugommier
Cours Julien
Cours Julien
Gare
Saint Charles
La Canebière
Cours Lieutaud
Place
P Cezanne
Cours Lieutaud
Boulevard C Nedelec
Rue Longue des Capucins
Rue Nationale
Rue Tapis Vert
Rue Thubaneau
Rue Fongate
Rue d'Aubagne
Rue Fr de Pressence
Rue du Baignoir
Rue de Rome
Place
F Baret
Rue d'Aix
Cours Belsunce
Rue St Ferreol
Rue Sylvabelle
Rue Pavillon
Rue Armeny
Boulevard des Dames
Musée d'Histoire
de Marseille
Rue Haxo
Rue Montgrand
6
5 Centre
Bourse
Rue Paradis
Rue Corbet
Rue Grignan
Jardin des
Vestiges
4
Place
J Ballard
Rue Breteuil
Rue de la République
Rue St Saens
Rue Sainte
Cours Pierre Puget
Rue E Delanglade
Pl
Sadi
Carnot
Rue de la République
Rue Mary
Grande Rue
Rue Sainte
Rue Grignan
Place
de la
Corderie
Boulevard Notre Dame
3
La Vieille
Charité
Rue des P Puits
Rue du Panier
Quai du Port
Vieux Port
1
Rue Fort Notre Dame
Rue Rigord
Boulevard Andre Aune
Jardin
Puget
Rue Schuman
2 Le Panier
Rue de la Loge
Quai de Rive Neuve
Rue Nve Sainte Catherine
Rue de la Croix
Boulevard de la Corderie
Basilique N D
de la Garde
Cathédrale
Rue Sainte
Quai de la Tourette
Avenue St Jean
Rue St Laurent
Avenue Vaudoyer
Avenue de la Tourette
Rue Robert
Place
St Victor
Rue d'Endoume
Blvd Tellene
Rue Sauveur Tobelem
Rue d'Endoume
Fort
Saint Nicolas
St Maurice
Rue J Recher
South
Marseille
Fort St-Jean
Boulevard Charles Livon
Avenue de la Corse
Rue E Duchesne

0   100 metres
0   100 yards

Château d'If
& Iles de Frioul

Rue Crinas

The West Provence Coast

Ratings

Scenery	●●●●●
Beaches	●●●○○
Children	●●●○○
Entertainment	●●●○○
History	●●●○○
Restaurants	●●●○○
Wine-tasting	●●●○○
Shopping	●●○○○

This is by far the least stylish stretch of the Riviera, though some people wouldn't care to class it as the Riviera at all. Most tourists along this stretch of Mediterranean coast have come no further than from their homes in Marseille and Toulon, which sprawl towards one another along the seashore. Yet in between the urban areas there's beautiful coastal scenery, vineyards and attractive small towns with picturesque ports and fishing harbours. Bandol and Sanary are the highlights. Visit, but don't linger long in the big urban areas, especially Toulon. Look carefully, though, and this will prove a good area for cheaper, simpler hotels and moderately priced campsites. Appealingly, there's a more French family atmosphere than in the big resorts further east. The beaches here are close to some of the greatest Provençal sights. An hour or two inland, there are towns such as Aix, as well as Roman remains and picturesque scenery.

BANDOL❖❖

Dégustation

The Bandol wine area of the Côtes de Provence extends most of the way from Toulon to Les Lecques. Roadside signs – *dégustation* – invite passers-by to sample the reds, whites and rosés of this popular wine district.

A pretty working town with a large, crowded marina, Bandol attracts a wealthier clientele than other resorts along this coast. It's more stylish, more old-fashioned, yet there's less to see and do – apart from sunbathing, eating and drinking. Some of the waterfront fish restaurants are of a high standard, and you can spend an enjoyable few hours visiting and sampling the well-known local Côtes de Provence wines at vineyards just behind the town. A little offshore, the touristy little **Ile de Bendor❖** (*ferries €, taking 7 minutes, leave every 30 minutes throughout the day from Bandol harbour; tel 04 94 29 44 34*) has beaches, restaurants and craft shops, while inland the **Jardin Exotique et Zoo❖** (Exotic Gardens and Zoo) (*€ 2km from Bandol, on access road on other side of autoroute A50; tel: 04 94 29 40 38. Open 0800–1200, 1400–1800. Closed Sun am Oct–Mar*), where monkeys and other animals wander among lush tropical greenery, makes an interesting and enjoyable outing.

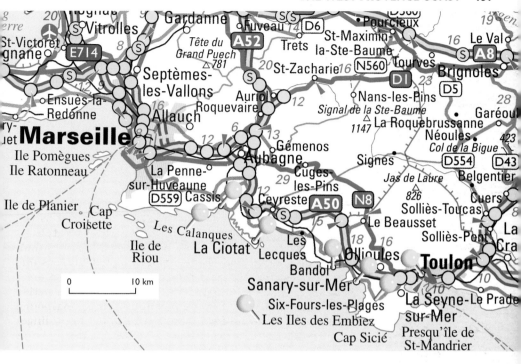

Bandol Tourist Office *Allées Vivien;* tel: 04 94 29 41 35; fax: 04 94 32 50 39; e-mail: otbandol@bandol.fr; www.bandol.fr

The D559 passes right through the middle of town, running beside the sea.

There is parking on the waterfront.

Accommodation and food in Bandol

There are dozens of touristy restaurants and cafés with tables set out under awnings, one after another along the main street beside the sea.

L'Ile Rousse €€€ *boulevard Lumière; tel: 04 94 29 33 00; fax: 04 94 29 49 49.* There are several pricey little hotels in and around town, but this one is Bandol's best. Ideally located by beach, port and town, the hotel has lovely views, amply equipped rooms in rather varied styles and good fitness facilities. Its three restaurants are also among the best in town.

LES CALANQUES❖❖❖

Boat trips from Cassis and Marseille Vieux Port take about 4 hours. Check whether swimming stops will be made at the *calanques*. Access to most of the beaches is by boat only.

The most striking part of this western end of the Riviera is the coastline east of Marseille, where the land fragments into imposing *calanques*, fiord-like bays between high cliffs. These are best seen on foot from the coast path which runs from Cassis to Marseille. Rough, thorny scrub and pine grows on the cliffs, where lizards thrive and where Europe's longest snake, the 2-m long Montpellier grass snake, can be seen. Sea birds cluster on and around the cliff faces. An easy section of path gives access to three of the bays, and keen walkers can

There are car parks in Cassis, at Calanque de Callelongue and at the end of Chemin de Sormiou.

From Marseille, drive out to Calanque de Callelongue via les Goudes or drive to Cassis for access to the footpath. Calanque de Sormiou and Calanque de Morgiou can be accessed directly on footpaths from Chemin de Sormiou, near Baumette prison, in Marseille.

continue past another eight before reaching Cap Croisette near the edges of Marseille. Cutting as much as 1.5km into the land from the sea, the *calanques* continue out to sea beneath the water. Before the rise in sea level after the Ice Age, now-flooded caves at the foot of the cliffs were inhabited. One of these, named for the diver Henri Cosquer, contains 27 000-year-old wallpaintings (no access). Highlights are **Cap Morgiou***, for great views, and **Calanque de Morgiou***, where there is a small port and restaurant.

Getting around in Les Calanques

The footpath along the clifftop is part of long-distance coastal path GR98. WARNING: sometimes, due to fire hazard, no walking is allowed on the clifftop in Jul, Aug and Sep. Note, temperatures can be high and there is no shade and no facilities on the coastal path. It is illegal to pick any plant or light a fire.

CASSIS**

Cassis Tourist Office *Oustau Calendal, quai des Moulins; tel: 04 42 01 71 17; fax: 04 42 01 28 31.*

Parking is difficult. It is best to park away from the centre and walk in.

This jaunty little town backed by pale cliffs is known throughout France for its wines; it is one of the oldest vineyard regions in the country. Its white wine is the most famous, though local growers also make reds and rosés. Cassis also made a name for itself in the 1900s as the regular summer meeting place of the artists Matisse, Dufy, Derain and Vlaminck. It's still easy to see what drew them here. Only about 16km from the edge of Marseille, it's a world away in atmosphere. The attractive port is busy with yachts, there's a little museum of local history, an old castle, a small crowded sand-and-pebble beach and woods of fragrant *garrigue* and parasol pine rise up behind the town. Cassis is the best starting point for a visit to the *calanques* (*see above*).

Accommodation and food in Cassis

Le Jardin d'Emile €€ *La Plage du Bestouan; tel: 04 42 01 80 55; fax: 04 42 01 80 70.* A delightful ochre-washed traditional Provençal house close to the Port-Miou *calanque* at the western edge of town, this is a most attractive hotel and restaurant. There's a lovely garden and terrace, small and attractive hotel bedrooms, and good Provençal dishes such as fish soup and stuffed vegetables.

LA CIOTAT✥

La Ciotat Tourist Office boulevard A France; tel: 04 42 08 61 32; fax: 04 42 08 17 88.

No village, this, but a good-sized town with a working industrial harbour, yet it's very appealing, with houses stacked steeply on the descent to the harbour. La Ciotat used to be a shipbuilding port, but though the cranes still loom over the docks it has become a pleasant resort with accommodation at moderate prices. There are also well-equipped campsites for an even cheaper option. Its delightful little **Vieux Port**✥✥ has been a small trading and fishing harbour ever since it was built by the Greeks of Marseille to serve their colony at present-day Ceyreste, a couple of kilometres inland. One charming landmark is the pink baroque church overlooking the port. Somewhat separate from the rest of La Ciotat is the resort-style part of town called **Clos des Plages**, which curves away from the port along boulevard Beau Rivage, with a marina and a promenade beside small sandy beaches.

A curious distinction was conferred on La Ciotat with the world's first showing of a 'moving picture' in September 1895. The Lumières brothers, inventors of cinema, tested their new idea by filming a train arriving at La Ciotat station and then showing the results to local people. The film was then shown to astonished audiences in Paris.

Accommodation and food in La Ciotat

La Fresque €€ 18 rue des Combattants; tel: 04 42 08 00 60; fax: 04 42 71 40 34. Good views and great local fish and game dishes at the best restaurant in town.

Auberge le Revestol € Le Liouquet; tel: 04 42 83 11 06; fax: 04 42 83 29 50. This quiet, classic, little Provençal hotel and restaurant, 6km out of town along the coast, has a sea-facing terrace where you can enjoy the view and good traditional local cooking. Closed Wed and Sun pm out of season.

LES ILES DES EMBIEZ (EMBIEZ ISLANDS)✥✥

Tourist Office At Le Brusc, on the waterfront; tel: 04 94 34 15 06.

There are about 20 return crossings daily from Le Brusc, taking 12 minutes. Inexpensive.

Three small islands lie just offshore from the village of Le Brusc, near **Six-Fours-les-Plages**. The largest, at only 95 hectares, is **L'Ile d'Embiez**✥✥ (also called l'Ile de la Tour Fondue or l'Ile Principale), with a marina, beaches, rocky bays, marshes, a ruined medieval castle, houses, forest and productive vineyards. A little train makes a tour of the island. The waters all around are crystal clear and full of fish, some exotic. It's a popular place with anglers and divers – there's a diving centre on the island. At the northern tip, the **Institut Océanographique Paul Ricard**✥ € (tel: 04 94 34 02 49. Open 1000–1230,

1330–1730), at a former navy site, is both a serious place of marine research, and an interesting maritime museum and sealife centre. The smaller islands are called **Grand Gaou** and **Grand Rouveau**.

SANARY-SUR-MER*

ⓘ Plage de Bonnegrâce *(beach east of town)*; tel: 04 94 07 02 21; fax: 04 94 25 13 36.

This sedate resort retains its fishing harbour feeling, as well as having a beach, attractive little port and plenty of waterside places for a relaxing meal or drink. It also offers some low-key sightseeing: a Saracen tower, Roman remains, and picturesque pink and white houses in the old upper part of the town.

SIX-FOURS-LES-PLAGES*

ⓘ The nearest tourist offices are at Bonnegrâce beach, between Six-Fours and Sanary; tel: 04 94 07 02 21; fax: 04 94 25 13 36; and at Le Brusc, on the waterfront; tel: 04 94 34 15 06; e-mail: tourisme@six-fours-les-plages.com; www.six-fours-les-plages.com

The local name means 'six ovens' – adding *les plages* or *la plage* on to the name was a later innovation. The village spreads out, with no centre, and the *commune* (parish) encompasses not just the ribbon development along the D16 but the whole of the peninsula on which it stands, including no fewer than 125 separate districts or hamlets. The only village really named Six-Fours is now abandoned, and lies at the foot of the **Fort de Six-Fours***, which stands at the site of the original fortified Greek settlement here. Climb up to the fortress, via avenue du Maréchal-Juin, for superb coastal views. The area is growing in popularity, with development spreading along the coast at Le Brusc.

Accommodation and food in Six-Fours

Clos des Pins € *101bis rue République; tel: 04 94 25 43 68; fax: 04 94 07 63 07.* Exceptional value for money at this decent modern hotel and restaurant (closed Sun pm and Sat).

Hôtel Parc € *112 rue Bondil, Le Brusc; tel: 04 94 34 00 15; fax: 04 94 34 16 94.* Out at Le Brusc, this tranquil little place offers traditional, modest bed and board. Very good value. Apr–Sep only.

TOULON**

One look (from the heights of Mont Faron) at Toulon's extensive and beautiful **harbour*** makes it clear why the city, now capital of the Var *département*, developed at this spot. An important naval base since Roman times, and at one point held by the British (who were seen off by a young Napoleon), the **waterfront** and **naval port** is most impressive and the town remains one of the principal bases of the

ℹ Tourist offices:
Main office place J
Raimu; tel: 04 94 18 53 00;
fax: 04 94 18 53 09; e-mail:
toulon.tourisme@wanadoo.fr;
www.toulontourisme.com
Dockside office quai
Cronstadt; tel: 04 94 36 31
80; fax: 04 94 18 53 09.

🚗 The busy D559, partly
an expressway, runs
right through the town.
Autoroute A50 terminates
on the west side of the
city centre, the A57 on the
east side.

🅿 The town centre
underground car park
is at place de la Liberté.

**⚓ Boat excursions
around the harbour**
Tours lasting 50 minutes
depart from quai
Cronstadt. Summer
morning and afternoon;
winter afternoon only.

🛒 There is a daily
market from
0600–1300 in Cours
Lafayette.

French navy. The rather ornate **Musée de la Marine (Naval Museum)**✶✶ houses an eclectic collection of Toulon's memorabilia, artwork and models all on a naval theme. Nearby **quai Cronstadt** is an ugly but popular waterfront gathering place with bars and shops, next to the Darse Vieille, the old town centre ferry dock which had to be completely rebuilt after wartime destruction in 1943–4. Behind it, the tangled streets of the **Vieille Ville (Old Quarter)**✶ managed to preserve many 18th-century façades which have undergone renovation. However, most signs of Toulon's long history have been swept away, leaving an unsightly industrial town with extensive suburbs which are inching along the seashore. In the town's favour is the feeling of being an oasis of ordinary French life in the midst of holidayland. Along the tree-shaded **Cours Lafayette**✶✶ in the restored Old Town, there's a large, colourful local market and good shops and restaurants at prices which are low by Riviera standards.

Imposing **Mont Faron**✶✶✶ dominates the town and makes an enjoyable excursion. On the hilltop there's a zoo, a museum of the Allied Landings in Provence, remnants of fortifications, a play area, picnic tables, walks through trees and truly magnificent views.

Accommodation and food in Toulon

Savoury, flat cakes called *Cade* and *Pompe à l'huile*, and doughnuts called *chichifrei*, made and sold in the street, are Toulon specialities.

La Corniche €€ *17 Littoral F Mistral; tel: 04 94 41 35 12; fax: 04 94 41 24 58.* Down by the sea, this hotel-restaurant has several eating places, including a bistro and oyster bar. Some of the pretty rooms in the hotel have a balcony with good views out to the Iles d'Hyères.

La Chamade €€ *25 rue Denfert-Rochereau; tel: 04 94 92 28 58.* Gourmets probably already know about this place, while the rest of us should stop, learn and enjoy. The fixed menu offers remarkably good value. The rich, meaty cuisine is conservative, cautious and skilful. Closed 1–20 Aug, Sat midday and Sun.

Suggested tour

Total distance: 100km, plus a visit to an island and a coastal walk.

Time: The main route could be driven in 2 hours. Allow 2 hours for sightseeing. A 20-minute (return) boat trip is included as a detour, and there's a suggested walk that could take 2 hours.

Links: This tour connects in the west with Marseille (*see page 120*) and in the east with Hyères and the Iles d'Or (*see page 138*).

Jazz est Toulon every July – free open-air concerts.

Musée de la Marine
€ On waterfront, off avenue de la République; tel: 04 94 02 02 01. Open 1000–1200, 1330–1800 (1900 in Jul and Aug). Closed Tue.

Mont Faron Téléphérique (cablecar) €€ 10-minute trip from boulevard Amiral-Vence (signposted Téléphérique du Mont Faron) to the summit of the hill; tel: 04 94 92 68 25. Services from 0930–1945. Stops earlier in winter. Closed Mon am except in Jul and Aug.

Start at **TOULON** ❶. You have to get well away from Toulon to enjoy the coast, so the best route out of town could be *autoroute* A50. Leave the *autoroute* at Exit 14 on to the D559 for **La Seyne**, an industrial harbour with naval shipyards facing into the immense Toulon anchorage. Follow the coast road around a little bay, with **Fort Balaguier** poised on its tip. The sturdy fortress which guarded Toulon harbour on this side now contains a small naval museum recalling Napoleon's capture of the fortress from the English in 1793. There's a marvellous coastal view from the fort's terrace. Stay on the shore road into **Tamaris**, where George Sand stayed and did much of her writing. Pass mussel beds to reach **Les Sablettes**, rebuilt after World War II. Here at last is a proper sandy beach, facing away from Toulon and out to sea. Continue on the little road round the coast of the Six-Fours or Cap Sicié peninsula. The road skirts the Janas pine forest, heading to the peninsula's southern tip, Cap Sicié. Turn right before reaching the *cap* to climb towards the lofty chapel of **Notre-Dame-du-Mai**✶✶, on the left. Park next to the radio installation and walk up to the chapel, which is much revered locally as a place bringing divine protection. If it happens to be open (it's usually closed), you'll find votive offerings inside from those who believe Our Lady of the May Tree has helped them. There is a pilgrimage here on 14 Sep. Follow the road around the peninsula to **Le Brusc**, a surprisingly unspoiled fishing village.

Detour: From Le Brusc, catch a boat to **ILE D'EMBIEZ** ❷. There are about 20 crossings daily to the island and the trip only takes 10 minutes.

From Le Brusc, follow the D616 up the coast. A right turn leads away from the sea to the rather unfocused district of **SIX-FOURS-LES-PLAGES** ❸. Turn back to the sea taking the D559 to **SANARY** ❹. Next door is **BANDOL** ❺, the other main resort, just 4km away. A better bargain, and one of the most enjoyable places for a peaceful stay along this stretch of coast is a little further west at **Les Lecques***. This unpretentious little resort has 3km of sandy beach, backed by attractive woods. Along the waterfront there's a family atmosphere and lots of decent eating places at modest prices. At La Madragues, on the eastern edge of the resort, the **Musée de Tauroentum** is an interesting museum built over the ruins of a Roman villa. Continuing west through pine forest, 5km beyond Les Lecques you reach **LA CIOTAT** ❻. Leave town on the very steep little road (the D141) up to the **Grande Tête** heights, and along the high and winding clifftop road through amazing rock formations, via the **Cap Canaille**, and round the bay into **CASSIS** ❼.

Getting out of the car: An enjoyable and spectacular 2-hour return walk along the coastal path gives access to three of **LES CALANQUES** ❽. Start by parking in the car park in Cassis at the start of the coastal path GR98. At first the track runs alongside **Calanque Port-Miou**, the longest, but also certainly the least interesting or beautiful of the *calanques*. After 30 minutes, the path reaches **Calanque de Port-Pin**, which has a sandy beach at the bottom of wooded slopes. Then comes narrower **Calanque d'En-Vau**, with its steep pale cliffs, one of the most beautiful of the *calanques*. Return the way you came.

From Cassis, continue on the scenic road (the D559) over the white rocky hills of the **Massif des Calanques** into **Marseille** (*see page 120*) or take *autoroute* A50 back to Toulon.

Hyères and the Iles d'Or

Ratings

Scenery	●●●●●
Walking	●●●●●
Beaches	●●●○○
Children	●●●○○
Restaurants	●●●○○
Shopping	●●○○○
Sightseeing	●●○○○
Entertainment	●○○○○

From Le Lavandou to Hyères, the coastline first juts into the sea then follows a huge bay. Some is sandy, and there are holiday developments, but much is industrialised, while other parts are used by the army. You can find, but have to search for, Provençal charm here. Around the town of Hyères, cheaper-quality campsites are numerous. If you're tempted, beware: several are right beside the perimeter fence of busy Toulon airport. On the other hand, this area has a warm, sultry, intriguing air. This seems more like Africa than France. Somehow the palm trees appear to thrive better, and massive flowering bushes luxuriate. The great treasure of Hyères bay is its islands, truly the best of the western Riviera. Locally, the Iles d'Hyères are never called by that name – they are always the Iles d'Or, the Golden Islands, though in fact they are intense green on brilliant blue.

GIENS PENINSULA❖

Giens Peninsula
The western *tombolo*, as it is called, is open to vehicles from Easter to All Saints (1 Nov), but no parking is allowed except in the car parks at either end. The eastern *tombolo* carries the main road between Hyères and Giens island. La Tour Fondue on the eastern end of Giens island is the main port for ferries between the mainland and Porquerolles.

Giens, at the end of a curiously long and narrow spit of land, used to be one of the Iles d'Or. That was thousands of years ago. Since then, two parallel sandbars – a rare natural phenomenon – have formed, and are still forming, between the island and the mainland. In between the two 4-km ribbons of sand lies a shallow, salty lagoon. This has become a veritable paradise for wading birds, including flamingos, as well as a wide variety of marsh plants. It is also being worked as a rather malodorous saltpan. Each autumn and winter the western sandbar is almost destroyed by the weather, but after some uncertainty as to the correct ecological approach, it has been decided that the site should be protected to ensure its survival. Meanwhile, the eastern bar is not under threat, and has a sandy beach resort called Hyères Plage, backed by parasol pine. Giens itself, the village on its tranquil former island, is a pleasant small resort with a ruined castle and pinewoods.

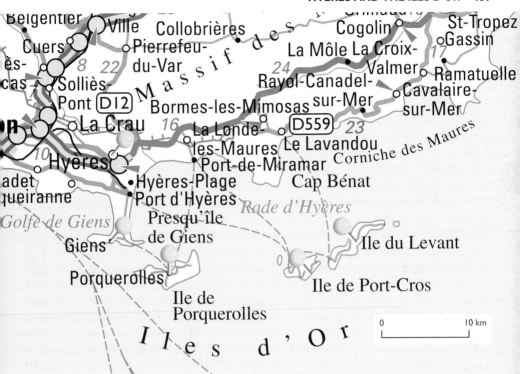

Accommodation and food in Giens

L'Eau Salée € *Port du Niel; tel: 04 94 58 92 33*. Great value at this unpretentious little place where seafood is the strong point, and you can eat it on a terrace with sea views.

Hôtel Provençal €€ *place St-Pierre; tel: 04 98 04 54 54; fax: 04 98 04 54 40*. If you want to be near the islands, but still on the mainland, here's a comfortable haven where you can swim in the pool, play tennis, enjoy the sea view and tuck into a generous breakfast. Apr–Oct only.

HYERES**

🛈 Hyères Tourist Office *Forum du Casino, 3 avenue Ambroise Thomas; tel: 04 94 01 84 50; fax: 04 94 01 84 51; e-mail: info@ot-hyeres.fr; www.ot-hyeres.fr*

Sometimes the name of this sedate, pleasant coastal town uses the suffix les Palmiers, and indeed there are hundreds of palms around the centre. That, the heat, the exuberant flowering bushes and the ethnic make-up of the population, give the impression you have drifted away from the coast of Provence to some point much further south. In fact, Hyères is the most southerly of the Riviera resorts, and also one of the oldest. A Greek town established well over 2000 years ago, it prospered through the centuries until Toulon overtook it in the 17th century. By

Getting to the islands

From La Tour Fondue (Giens Peninsula)

- **Operator: TVM-TLV** *tel: 04 94 58 21 81; fax: 04 94 58 91 73; www.tlv-tvm.com*
- **Direct to Porquerolles** Frequent departures all day, every day from about 0730 to 1800. Journey time 20 minutes.
- **Three Island tour** All-day trip with 1–2 hours on each island. *1 Jul–10 Sep only Mon–Fri.*

From Port d'Hyères

- **Operator: TVM-TLV** *tel: 04 94 57 44 07; fax: 04 94 38 30 58; www.tlv-tvm.com*
- **Port-Cros and Le Levant** *Daily except 11 Oct–31 Dec.* Journey time 1 hour to Port-Cros; 1½ hours to Le Levant. Outbound at 0930, 1030 and 1415, with one or two additional morning departures in season. Last return from Le Levant usually at 1700, last from Port-Cros usually 1730.

From Le Lavandou

- **Operator: Vedettes Iles d'Or (CTM)** *tel: 04 94 71 01 02; fax: 04 94 71 78 95; www.vedettesilesdor.fr*
- **To Port-Cros and Le Levant** There are 4–7 crossings daily. Journey time 30 minutes to Le Levant; 30 or 55 minutes to Port-Cros depending on crossing. Last return from Le Levant or Port-Cros around 1815.
- **To Porquerolles** *Apr–Oct only. 1 Jul–8 Sep daily; rest of time Mon, Wed and Sat only.* One departure (either 0945 or 1010). Journey time: 40–50 minutes. Last return 1700 or 1715 (1630 in Oct).

From other points

There are ferries to the Iles d'Or in season from Port de Miramar (*tel: 04 94 71 01 02*), Toulon (Batelier de la Rade; *tel: 04 94 46 24 65* and Transmed 2000; *tel: 04 94 92 96 82*), Cavalaire (*tel: 04 94 71 01 02*) and La Croix Valmer (*tel: 04 94 79 53 06*).

By taxi-boat

Call Bateau Taxi Pélican for travel to or from Porquerolles day or night; *tel: 04 94 58 31 19; fax: 04 94 71 78 95.*

Autoroute A570, a spur from the A57, leads on to the main through road N98, which skirts the south side of the centre of town.

the 18th century, it was already being discovered as a resort. It was here that the expression Côte d'Azur was coined in 1887. However, today's Hyères has a resolutely modern look, with broad, light, palm-lined boulevards. Take a stroll along **Avenue Godillot**✳, one of the most beautiful streets, where the Anglican church is a reminder that the place found favour with English visitors. Nineteenth-century winters brought illustrious tourists, including Queen Victoria. Many successful writers stayed regularly in its luxury hotels, including Robert Louis Stevenson, Guy de Maupassant and Victor Hugo.

🅿 In the centre there is parking off avenue A Denis and avenue J Jaurès, close to the Vieille Ville.

🏛 **Jardins Olbius-Riquier** *Open 0800 –1900 (1700 in winter).*

Parc St-Bernard. *rue Barruc. Open 0800–1900 (1700 in winter).*

Villa de Noailles € *Montée de Noailles. Open mid-Jun–mid-Sep for a 2-hour guided tour every Thur at 0900, by arrangement with the tourist office.*

🕐 There are markets every morning in place Massillon, Sun morning at the port, Tue and Thu in place de la République and Saturday in avenue Gambetta. On the third Thu of every month is a cattle market in place Lefebvre.

🔺 Mar/Apr: *Corso (flower procession).*

In the southeast section of town, the magnificent **Jardins Olbius-Riquier✣✣** are amazing tropical gardens with numerous varieties of palm and cactus thriving in the open air. At the heart of the new avenues and modern districts is the **Vieille Ville✣✣**. Enclosed by a defensive wall of dwellings, it is entered through an impressive little fortified Gothic gateway. Inside, tall Italianate buildings, shabby but attractive, line steep paved streets and lanes. Many have fine Renaissance doorways. Triangular place Massillon is filled either with market stalls or restaurant tables, watched over by the pale 12th-century Templar tower of St-Blaise. Rising above Hyères north of the Vieille Ville, the **Parc St-Bernard✣** contains the considerable ruins of the town's medieval fortifications, with dramatic views. Also here is the legendary **Villa de Noailles✣**, the 1920s home of the Noailles family whose parties made headlines and whose house guests included Picasso, Salvador Dalì and Man Ray. Luis Buñuel's film *L'Age d'Or* was set in the villa.

ILE DU LEVANT✣

ℹ **Ile du Levant Tourist Office** *At Heliopolis; tel: 04 94 05 93 52.*

Unprepared ferry passengers putting into the tiny harbour of the Ile du Levant are sometimes more than a little taken aback by their first sight of people coming and going on the quayside. Most of them are completely naked, for this most easterly of the Iles d'Or is devoted to naturism. The houses stacked up the steep, wooded slopes climbing away from the dock are the holiday homes that make up the little naturist resort village of Heliopolis. With a school, church, town hall, police station, restaurants and shops, there is a real community of about 100 permanent residents at Heliopolis, which was set up in 1931, though there is little to see or do here except sunbathe. The naturist village and other accessible areas make up just 20 per cent of this steep-sided, rocky little island, only about 1km by 8km in size. The other 80 per cent, closed to the public, is under the control of the military.

Accommodation and food in Heliopolis

Simple, but comfortable and well-equipped naturist hotel-restaurants (all €€) at Heliopolis include pretty **La Brise Marine** (*tel: 04 94 05 91 15; fax: 04 94 05 93 21*), **L'Esquinade** (*tel: 04 94 05 91 39*), **Hôtel le Ponant** (*tel: 04 94 05 90 41; fax: 04 94 05 93 41*), **Héliotel** (*tel: 04 94 00 44 88*), **La Source** (*tel: 04 94 05 91 36; fax: 04 94 05 93 47*) – with one of the better restaurants – and **Hôtel Gaetan** (*tel: 04 94 05 91 78; fax: 04 94 36 77 17*). Most close Nov–Mar.

PORQUEROLLES✦✦

Porquerolles Tourist Office *On waterfront by harbour; tel: 04 94 58 33 76; fax: 04 94 58 36 39; www.porquerolles.net. Open Jun–Sep only; rest of year apply to Hyères tourist office.*

Nature Reserve *www.see.it/cbn/cbn2.html*

Fort Ste-Agathe €€ *No phone. Open May–Sep only, 1000–1200, 1400–1730.*

Lighthouse € *Tel: 04 94 58 30 78. 30-minute guided tour morning and afternoon.*

Most accessible and largest of the Iles d'Or, Porquerolles is also the most popular and most developed. The island measures 7km by 3km, is lower and less rocky than the others, though it, too, is largely wooded with an exquisite mix of Provençal trees and shrubs. Most of Porquerolles is under protection as a Nature Reserve affiliated to the Port-Cros National Park. Tracks and paths weave all over the island. The best option for touring is by bicycle, and bike hire is available at many outlets in Porquerolles village – look out for signs (*Location de Bicyclettes*, or for mountain bikes, *VTT*).

The focal point of the village is the bustling, attractive quayside itself, where shops, post office and restaurants stand by the water. A few paces away is the village proper, originally built for the military but now given over entirely to tourists. In the dusty main square, place d'Armes, locals and visitors play *boules* in front of the tiny church. Porquerolles' north coast is low and sandy, with two good beaches – Plage Notre Dame to the east and smaller Plage d'Argent to the west. Both are about 40 minutes' walk from the village. Another enjoyable walk, with a bit of a climb, is up to **Fort Ste-Agathe**✦. This well-designed and pleasingly compact fortress, standing on a high point overlooking the harbour approaches, is mainly 19th-century, though the sturdy corner tower survives from the earlier fort on the site. The fortress is now used for exhibitions about the islands. The south coast of the island is more rugged, with rocky cliffs and a **lighthouse** open to visitors. The 45-minute walk to the lighthouse is the most popular on the island.

WARNING

Smoking is prohibited everywhere on the island of Porquerolles except in the village.

Accommodation and food in Porquerolles

Auberge des Glycines €€€ *place d'Armes; tel: 04 94 58 30 36; fax: 04 94 58 35 22; e-mail: auberge.glycines@wanadoo.fr* Adorable Provençal hotel-restaurant with style, delightful patio, pretty bedrooms and its own restaurant specialising in fish.

Le Mas de Langoustier €€€ *tel: 04 94 58 30 09; fax: 04 94 58 36 02.* In the wilds at the far west of the island, close to the Grand Langoustier peninsula and the Plage du Grand Langoustier, this sumptuous mansion offers perfect peace and the luxurious simple life. Above all, the restaurant is outstanding, with the most accomplished and astonishing cooking, gorgeous desserts, tasty home-made bread and interesting Porquerolles wines. Closed mid-Oct–May.

L'Oustaou de Porquerolles €€€ *place d'Armes; tel: 04 94 58 30 13; fax: 04 94 58 34 93.* Overpriced but pleasant hotel and restaurant well placed on the large main square of the village.

Le Relais de la Poste €€€ *place d'Armes; tel: 04 94 04 62 62; fax: 04 94 58 33 57; e-mail: relaispost@aol.com* This convivial, rather overpriced 2-star hotel and popular bar looking over the dusty main square is one of the oldest on the island. Surprisingly, it has its own Website at *www.relais-de-la-poste.com/*

Il Pescatore € *On quayside; tel: 04 94 58 30 61; fax: 04 94 58 35 53.* The main place on the quayside is this large red restaurant and brasserie with a wide range of dishes and snacks, with the emphasis on Provençal fish specialities.

PORT-CROS✦✦✦

ⓘ Port-Cros Tourist Office *On the quayside; tel: 04 94 05 90 17. Summer only. Otherwise use tourist office in Hyères.*

National Park Information *Parc National de Port-Cros, Castel Ste Claire, Hyères; tel: 04 94 12 82 30.*

Port-Cros National Park *www.see.it/cbn/index.html*

Port-Cros, the most southerly point of the French Riviera, on a line with Corsica, is a special place. The whole island and its surrounding waters are a National Park, so it is utterly tranquil, magnificently unspoiled – a marvellous remnant of native Provençal vegetation, albeit almost too lush. Arrive at a pretty little harbour village with unpaved quays, where restaurants and bars look across the water. There are no vehicles – not even bikes. To get anywhere you must walk on lovely flowery rocky tracks and paths by the sea or in the steep, forested interior. The scent of pine in the hot air is intense. Two hilltop forts, Fort de l'Estissac and Fort du Moulin, rise above the village. Follow the sign 'Route des Forts' which leads to three other little fortresses (they can only be visited by special arrangement).

Porquerolles, Port-Cros and Ile du Levant are not the full total of Iles d'Or. Among smaller islets in the group, Ile de Bagaud lies just offshore from Port-Cros (no ferry).

Accommodation and food on Port-Cros

Hostellerie Provençale €€ *on the quayside; tel: 04 94 05 90 43.* Of the few eating places on the quayside, this is the most appealing, with grilled fresh fish, langoustes and *bouillabaisse*. In summer, it can sometimes provide simple accommodation.

WARNING

No smoking is allowed anywhere on Port-Cros outside the village. Also forbidden: camping, lighting a match, picking any plant, killing any animal, bird or fish.

Le Manoir €€€ *tel: 04 94 05 90 52; fax: 04 94 05 90 89.* One of the best places to stay in Provence. From the ferry, walk to the right for 10 minutes – the sign first reads Plage de Sud, then Le Manoir. Alternatively, get collected by the little mini-moke which can at least take the luggage. How is this possible on an island where even bicycles are banned? Maybe it's because this superb little mansion shaded by eucalyptus used to be the lordly manor which ruled Port-Cros, or maybe it's because this is the only hotel on the island. Inside, it's deliciously elegant in a colonial style, with luxurious simplicity. The restaurant rings a bell when the food is ready and serves a set three-course, *prix-fixe* dinner, vastly overpriced by French standards, such as lovely *petits farcis Provençaux*, grilled *loup* (bass) with fennel and raspberry *mille feuille*.

Suggested tour

Total distance: Just 10km driving at most, and 2 hours' walking.

Time: 1 day.

Links: The route connects with the Massif des Maures (*see page 186*) via the ferry from Le Larandou, and the visits to Port-Cros and Ile du Levant could be done from there.

Set out from **HYERES ❶** in good time to catch an early ferry to Port-Cros from **Port d'Hyères**, making your way to the port on the D97, avenue de l'Aéroport. Park the car and, depending on the time of year, either buy a round trip ticket to Port-Cros or (best in Jul–Aug) a *Circuit des Deux Iles* ticket for both islands. Catch the ferry to Port-Cros. The crossing takes an hour.

Arriving at **PORT-CROS ❷**, check the times of ferries to Ile du Levant. If you do not have a *Circuit des Deux Iles* ticket, you could use a different operator, but be sure that timings will permit you to return to Port-Cros in time for the ferry back to Hyères.

Here begins a two-hour walk, the classic Port-Cros walk to the Vallon de Solitude. Turn right on to the unpaved Port-Cros quayside, passing

'Plan Alarme'

The Iles d'Or operate a fire prevention Alarm Plan, put into action at times of higher-than-average fire risk or strong winds. You will be told before boarding your ferry to the islands if 'Plan Alarme' is in force. The main consequence for visitors is that access to the interior is very restricted. Most paths are closed. Both walking and cycling are discouraged. However, the beaches are generally accessible.

the restaurants and souvenir shop to follow a path initially marked Plage du Sud. Passing the turn for Le Manoir hotel, fork left for the Vallon de Solitude. For most of the distance you are walking in deep shade. The **Vallon de Solitude❋❋**, its air cool and refreshing, continues between dense holm oak, shrubs and bushes until it meets another marked path, the **Route des Crêtes❋❋**. The Fort de la Vigie is in view. Follow the Route des Crêtes, which gives some wonderful vistas over the rugged southern shore and out to sea. The path skirts Mont Vinaigre (194m), the high point of Port-Cros. The path now turns on to the Vallon de la Fausse Monnaie, which leads back to the north coast. Turn back (bearing right) towards the village and harbour of Port-Cros.

Detour: So long as ferry times permit (most likely in Jul–Aug) make the short hop to **ILE DU LEVANT ❸**, first ensuring you can get back to Port-Cros before the last boat back to Hyères.

On returning to Hyères, drive along the **GIENS PENINSULA ❹** to **Giens** and **La Tour Fondue**.

Detour: If time permits – or you could return the next day – park the car in one of the harbourside car parks and catch a ferry for the 20-minute crossing to **PORQUEROLLES ❺**. At Porquerolles, relax on the quayside and stroll through the village to place des Armes, perhaps following the path up to **Fort Ste-Agathe** or to one of the beaches if there is plenty of time before the last ferry back to Hyères.

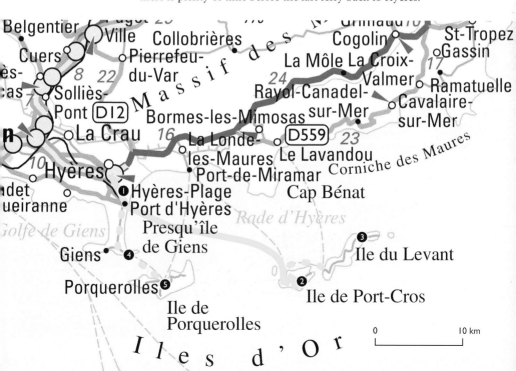

Ratings

Street life	●●●●●
Architecture	●●●●○
Art	●●●●○
Restaurants	●●●●○
Entertainment	●●●○○
Museums	●●●○○
Children	●●○○○
Shopping	●●○○○

Aix-en-Provence and Cézanne Country

No wonder it's the capital of Provence. Aix exudes joy, yet has an air of dignity. It revels in the simple pleasures of life, yet epitomises civilisation and refinement. Much of that mood is due to a wonderful central avenue, Cours Mirabeau. Under the Romans, the town was already a capital, and a prosperous spa, *Aquae Sextiae*. A thousand years later, Good King René built it up as a place of elegance, festivities, art and culture, which it has remained. The creation of the Parlement de Provence (*see feature, page 155*) brought gentry, pomp, officials and churchmen and their wealth, and streets of Renaissance mansions were built. Today that lavish architecture also adds to the appeal of the town. Though so near to Marseille, it couldn't be more different. Aix rewards a quick visit, or a long stay, and makes a perfect base for touring the Provençal backcountry.

Arriving and departing

Aix lies at the meeting of the east–west *autoroute* A8 'La Provençale' and north–south *autoroute* A51. Follow signs to Centre Ville/Mirabeau. Aim for place Général de Gaulle. (Avoid the difficult Vieil Aix quarter north of Cours Mirabeau.)

ⓘ Aix Tourist Office 2 *place Général de Gaulle; tel: 04 42 16 11 61; e-mail: infos@aixenprovencetourism. com; www.aixenprovencetourism. com. Open Mon–Sat 0830–1900 (Apr–Sep, open until 2000), Sun 1000–1300, 1400–1800.*

ⓦ Local bus information *Tel: 04 42 27 17 91.*

Right
Stone dolphin

Parking

The nearest car park to Cours Mirabeau is place Général de Gaulle (La Rotonde). Other car parks are at the train station and in place de Verdun. Parking is difficult on market days.

Markets

A huge, colourful market (often visited by coach parties, which detracts from its charm) takes place in Le Vieil Aix north of Cours Mirabeau every Tuesday, Thursday and especially Saturday. The general market stalls are in and around place des Prêcheurs, and flowers in and around place de l'Hôtel de Ville, with a second-hand market in place de Verdun. There's a fresh produce market daily in place Richelme. On the first Sunday in the month you can buy antiquarian and second-hand books in place de l'Hôtel de Ville, 0900–1800.

Fairs and festivals

Aix holds frequent festivals, exhibitions and events, including seven annual festivals.

The annual **Festival d'Aix** (Festival International d'Art Lyrique et de la Musique) is a world-class opera festival, lasting about three weeks from around mid-Jul to early Aug. For information *tel: 04 42 17 34 00.*

Sights in Aix-en-Provence

Atelier Paul Cézanne*

Cézanne fans rather than art connoisseurs will be interested in the studio and garden Cézanne acquired in 1897, just north of the city centre, after his mother died. He was in his 50s, and had achieved a measure of success. Following his father's death in 1886, Cézanne had married Hortense Fiquet, and they lived at 23 rue Boulegon. After creating the studio, he worked on the first floor of the house. The

Atelier Paul Cézanne € *9 avenue Paul Cézanne; tel: 04 42 21 06 53; fax: 04 42 21 90 34; e-mail: atelier.cezanne@ wanadoo.fr; www.atelier-cezanne.com. Open 1000–1200, 1430–1800 (Oct–May closes 1700). Closed Tue and holidays.*

main attraction is the glimpse into turn-of-the-century life; everything has been left just as it was when he died nine years later. Some memorabilia, including his easel, pipe and beret, and a bottle of wine he had just finished are on view, but none of his original work can be seen, though some reproductions are on display.

Paul Cézanne

Born in Aix at 28 rue de l'Opéra, Paul Cézanne (1839–1906) – now one of the world's most popular artists – was unsuccessful in the Paris salons until late in life and also unappreciated in his own land. Aix makes much of Cézanne now (sometimes too much: hotels, restaurants, even garages are named after him), though not until 1984 did the city buy one of his works. Cézanne frequently wandered in the rustic country to the east of Aix, attempting to capture images of the Provençal light itself, which so fascinated him. 'The great Classical landscapes, our Provence, and Greece, and Italy,' he said, 'are those where light is spiritualised.' Every day he studied the massive shape of Mont Ste-Victoire, which dominates the Aix countryside and was often at the centre of Cézanne's canvas.

Cathédrale St-Sauveur Tel: 04 42 21 10 51. Open 0930–1200, 1400–1630. Closed Sun.

Musée de Tapisserie € 28 place des martyrs de la Rèsistance; tel: 04 42 23 09 91. Open 1000–1200, 1400–1745. Closed Tue.

Cathédrale St-Sauveur**

Aix cathedral, an odd mix of styles ranging from a 5th-century baptistery to a 16th-century Gothic tower and façade, possesses excellent craftsmanship and many outstanding artworks. Most celebrated is Nicolas Froment's strange iconic triptych of the **Burning Bush***, displayed in the central nave. Depicting the Madonna and Child in flames being seen by Moses, it became an important image during the Middle Ages. The painting was originally commissioned by King René in 1476, and he appears in it (accompanied by saints), on the left wing. His wife Jeanne de Laval is shown (with similarly illustrious companions) on the right. The fine 16th-century **Flemish tapestries**** in the chancel were the property of Canterbury Cathedral, stolen during the Civil War, and eventually sold in Aix. The ancient baptistery opens off the south aisle, and stands on the site of a Roman forum. Roman columns have been used to hold up the Renaissance dome. The Archbishop's Palace next door to the cathedral houses, on the first floor, an important **Musée de Tapisserie (Tapestry Museum)*** with some beautiful and priceless 17th-century work.

Right
Hats in Aix market

Cours Mirabeau◊◊◊

This is the perfect southern street, its pavement tables, shaded by leafy plane trees, the ideal place to watch the passing crowd, strolling on surely one of the grandest, most beautiful avenues ever built. On the leisurely north side is the legendary *Les Deux Garçons* which dates from the 1790s. Also on this side are a handful of bookstores and other shops. Across the road on the south side there is a sombre, commercial air of banks and offices housed in grandiose 17th- and 18th-century *hôtels* (private mansions), some with massive façades and doorways adorned with wrought-iron balconies and supported by monumental caryatids. Four fountains along the middle of the avenue include the moss-covered Fontaine d'Eau Thermale, a natural hot spring with water pouring out at 34°C, and the Fontaine du Roi René, showing the Good King holding a bunch of Muscat grapes, a strain that he personally introduced into Provence.

Fondation Vasarely
€€ 1 avenue Marcel
Pagnol; tel: 04 42 20 01 09;
fax: 04 42 59 14 65; e-mail:
fondation.vasarely@wanadoo.
fr; www.fondationvasarely.com.
Open Mon–Fri 1000–1300,
1400–1900, Sat–Sun
1000–1900.

Fondation Vasarely*

To the untrained eye the geometric patterns of Hungarian-born op-artist Victor Vasarely (b 1908) don't have much in common with Cézanne's work. Yet Vasarely thinks they do, and so admired the Aix artist that he selected this site for his art foundation because Cézanne had lived here. The huge foundation building, designed by Vasarely, consists of glass, marble and metal hexagons decorated with circles and squares. Inside are large, brilliant collections of Vasarely's fascinating works, not just paintings but intriguing multi-material constructions and astonishing kinetic works. The Fondation also puts on exhibitions of modern artists.

Musée Granet €
place St-Jean-de-Malte;
tel: 04 42 38 14 70. Open
1000–1200, 1400–1800.
Closed Tue.

Eglise St-Jean-de-Malte
place St-Jean-de-Malte; tel:
04 42 38 25 70. Open
Mon–Sat 0800–1300,
1500–1930, Sun
0830–1230, 1800–1930.

Musée Granet**

Here, the extensive collection of important European paintings and other works assembled by local artist François Granet (1775–1849) has been combined with archaeological finds illustrating the Roman life and art of *Aquae Sextiae* and the Celtic-Lugurian hilltop settlement of nearby Entremont. The pictures cover a wide range of European art from Flemish up to 19th-century French paintings. The **Cézanne gallery** displays eight paintings and three watercolours acquired by the town in 1984, but these include early, minor works that don't do justice to the artist. The museum occupies the former priory of the 13th-century Knights of Malta. Next door is their chapel, **Eglise St-Jean-de-Malte***, the oldest Gothic building in Aix.

Opposite
Pavillion Vendôme fountain

Right
Aix hôtel

Musée du Vieil Aix
€ 17 rue Gaston-de-Saporta; tel: 04 42 21 43 55. Open Apr–Sep 1000–1200, 1430–1800; Nov–Mar 1000–1200, 1400–1700. Closed Mon, holidays and Oct.

Le Vieil Aix✦✦✦

Cours Mirabeau marks the southern edge of the old quarter of Aix, a peaceful tangle of narrow streets and lanes opening suddenly into elegant little squares enclosed by fine mansions. Much of the area is traffic-free, and a delight to explore. A 16th-century belfry overlooks the quarter's charming main square, place de l'Hôtel de Ville with its attractive town hall. There are fine Renaissance mansions in place d'Albertas, rue Aude and rue Gaston de Saporta, where the **Musée du Vieil Aix✦** gives an overview of local social history and folklore. There's a large display of exquisite *santons*, the traditional Provençal Christmas crib figurines.

Accommodation and food

Hôtel des Augustins €€€ *3 rue Masse; tel: 04 42 27 28 59; fax: 04 42 26 74 87.* Superb accommodation in a grand former 12th- to 15th-century monastery, and in an unbeatable location beside Cours Mirabeau. Only 29 rooms, so book well ahead for this one.

Hôtel Paul € *10 avenue Pasteur; tel: 04 42 23 23 89; fax: 04 42 63 17 80.* A simple, traditional little hotel just a few paces beyond the northern edge of Vieil Aix. Clean and welcoming.

Hôtel Quatre Dauphins €€ *54 rue Roux Alpheran; tel: 04 42 38 16 39; fax: 04 42 38 60 19.* This small, simple and friendly hotel redolent with discreet charm and polished antiquity is in an 18th-century mansion in the less touristy area just south of Cours Mirabeau. A good base.

Relais Ste-Victoire €€€ *at Beaurecueil, 10km east of Aix; tel: 04 42 66 94 98; fax: 04 42 66 85 96.* Follow the D17 out of Aix along the south side of Montagne Ste-Victoire, then turn right on to the D46 into the village to find this enticing and tranquil family-run *restaurant avec chambres,* specialising in accomplished, imaginative Provençal cooking, served with the best of local wines and a view of the gardens.

L'Amphitryon €€ *2–4 rue Paul Doumer; tel: 04 42 26 54 10; fax: 04 42 38 36 15.* Picture-book Provence where you can eat out of doors just off Cours Mirabeau, with high-quality fresh-from-the-market menus of regional dishes and local wines. Closed Sun, Mon midday.

Le Bistro Latin € *18 rue de la Couronne; tel: 04 42 38 22 88, fax; 04 42 38 22 88.* In a narrow Vieil Aix street, enjoy simple, excellent Provençal menus with dishes such as lamb *en daube* in an intimate art deco setting. Closed Sun, Mon midday.

Café des Deux Garçons € *Cours Mirabeau; tel: 04 42 26 00 51.* Under the Cours Mirabeau trees is one of the most famous bars in France with a convivial atmosphere, traditional service and its original late 18th-century interior.

Sights of Mont Ste-Victoire

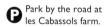
Park by the road at les Cabassols farm.

La Croix-de-Provence**

A track, part of the long-distance footpath GR9, climbs the north side of Mont Ste-Victoire from the D10 to La Croix-de-Provence (969m). At first steep and through pines, the gradient eases off and the path arrives at the restored 17th-century priory of Notre-Dame-de-Ste-Victoire. It's a little further uphill to reach the crucifix on the summit. Visible from a vast distance, the cross is 17m tall and stands on a 36-m high plinth. Walk east from La Croix-de-Provence along the path on

Above
Mont Ste-Victoire

the crest of Mont Ste-Victoire and you come to a 'bottomless' chasm (in fact about 150m deep) which long fascinated and frightened local people and appears in ancient myths and legends.

The GR9 continues along the crest of the Montagne to its highest point, and descends on the south slope to the village of Puyloubier.

Vauvenargues*

The imposing 16th- to 17th-century hilltop château where Pablo Picasso lived for the last 15 years of his life survives as an enigmatic shrine to an enigmatic man. The interior walls are said to have frescos which he painted, but there is no admission to the public. Picasso died here in 1973 and is buried in the grounds.

Suggested tour

Total distance: 60km, with a 3-hour walk on Mont Ste-Victoire.

Time: Aix requires at least a whole day to itself. The driving tour around Mont Ste-Victoire takes half a day.

Route: From **AIX** ❶ the peaceful D17 runs along the southern edge of the mountain through exquisite country. After **Le Tholonet**, the first village on the way, with its Roman quarries and 18th-century château, a number of footpaths climb up Mont Ste-Victoire on one side of the road and Montagne du Cengle on the other. Travelling through gentle greenery, roadside flowers and strongly scented firs, continue on the D17 through **Puyloubier**, whose modern touches do not destroy its charm, and take the D57d to curiously named **Pourrières** (literally 'rottenness' – apparently the Romans left great numbers of corpses to rot after a battle here with the Celts in 102 BC). Turn north on the D25 through wild but pretty country. Take the D223 on the left (direction Vauvenargues, changes to the D10), to drive along the northern edge of the mountain. The road clambers up quite steeply then down to the wooded valley of the Infemet and reaches **VAUVENARGUES** ❷ .

Getting out of the car: A footpath (part of the GR9) heads steeply up from **les Cabassols**, just after Vauvenargues, to **LA CROIX-DE-**

Below
Mont Ste-Victoire

PROVENCE ❸, which has a panoramic view. The walk takes about 1½ hours each way. If you're fit and have more time, another longer and more difficult path from Vauvenargues climbs to **Pic des Mouches**, highest point of the Ste-Victoire massif (1011m), which has even better views.

Continuing on the D10, a little turning on the left (the D10f) leads to the **Bimont Dam** at the head of a large picturesque lake on the Infernet. The view of Mont Ste-Victoire from here is impressive. Return to Aix on the D10.

The Three Scourges of Provence

The River Durance was once considered one of the 'Three Scourges of Provence' because of its unpredictable flooding. Now properly controlled, it has been turned from scourge into blessing, and provides much of the irrigation which has made the region more prosperous.

The other two scourges were the *Mistral* and the *Aix Parlement*. The *Mistral*, still a nuisance, is the dry north wind that in summer holds its temper and keeps skies clear, but in winter howls down the Rhône valley for days, bringing ice-cold air.

The *Parlement de Provence*, or *Aix Parlement*, has been forgotten altogether. Already the capital city of Provence when French kings inherited the region, in 1501 Aix became the seat of the *Parlement de Provence*. Set up to govern Provence on the king's behalf, it was in fact the worst and most powerful of the three scourges. It disappeared after the Revolution.

The Alpes de Haute Provence

Ratings

Scenery	●●●●●
Walking	●●●●○
History	●●●○○
Prehistory	●●●○○
Sightseeing	●●●○○
Children	●●○○○
Restaurants	●●○○○
Shopping	●●○○○

Approaching western Provence, the Alps step down in a series of high limestone ranges separated by deeply carved valleys. The region is wild, open and airy, and enjoys a Mediterranean climate, but is always several degrees cooler than on the lower altitudes. Resilient *garrigue*, typically Provençal, thrives on the lower slopes, gradually thinning out to become green and fresh mountain pasture as altitudes rise, still with a mat of wild herbs and flowers. On the upper slopes and peaks, forests of beech, oak and pine alternate with austere, barren ridges. Towns and villages have a jaunty, contented quality, enjoying the tranquillity and the cool, clean air and clear light. As for centuries past, almost all roads and modern influences follow the rivers, leaving the large upland areas in peace and solitude. For this reason the tour does not attempt to explore the whole region.

BANON❖

🛈 **Tourist offices** in the region are generally open Mon–Sat 0900–1200, 1400–1900.

Banon Tourist Office
rue Peyron; tel: 04 92 73 36 37.

🛈 **Gouffre du Caladaire** *Ask at the tourist office for details.*

Right
Bougainvillaea

This pleasing hill village, with its old fortified centre and arcaded pavements, stands high on a rock. Banon gives its name to a distinctive goats' cheese wrapped in chestnut leaves for which it has long been renowned. This whole high undulating terrain is tunnelled with scores of strange natural caves, underground rivers and pot-holes. The **Gouffre du Caladaire**, for example, close to Banon, is nearly 500m in depth and contains a system of prehistoric 'canals'.

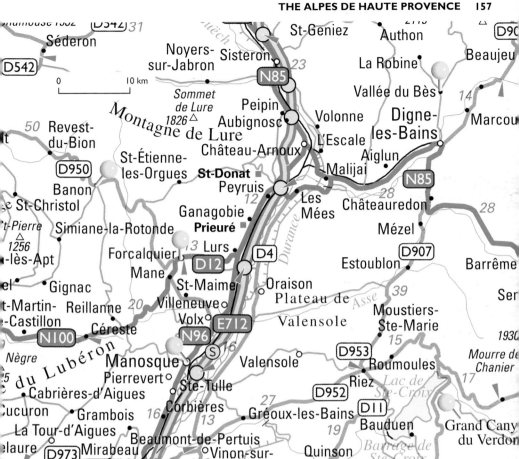

Vallee du Bes**

ℹ The nearest tourist office is in Digne at *place du Tampinet*; tel: 04 92 36 62 62; fax: 04 92 32 27 24; e-mail: info@ ot.digneslesbains.fr; www.ot-dignelesbains.fr

🏛 **Dalle à Ammonites Géantes** *1km from Digne beside the D900A (Route de Barles).*

The Bès flows into the River Bléone just outside **Digne** (*see page 177*). The hills here, called the Pre-Alpes de Digne, are wild, empty and unpopulated. The once bare limestone hills have been planted with pine and larch, but apart from a few fertile basins, they remain stark and uncultivable. Here, streams and rivers carve dramatic gorges. Most curious of all, the area is sprinkled with fossils from around 200 million years ago when it was all underwater. The Bès valley in particular has intriguing examples of this type. Among them are the remarkable **Dalle à Ammonites Géantes**, a slab of stone marked with the print of giant ammonites from that era; the fossilised footprints of wading birds (signposted **Empreintes de Pattes d'Oiseau****); and the so-called **Musée de Site de l'Ichtyosaure***** (Museum of the Ichtyosaurus Site). This is actually the skeleton of a

Empreintes de Pattes d'Oiseau €
10km from Digne beside the D900A (Route de Barles).

Musée de Site de l'Ichtyosaure *From la Robine, 7km north of Digne; take signposted footpath for an hour.*

For accommodation and restaurants, see Digne (*page 178*).

4.5-m long ichtyosaurus (a prehistoric sea reptile) found here and displayed *in situ*, under glass. To see it you have to walk an hour each way (clearly marked) through an amazing landscape of waterfalls, ravines, woods and pasture.

FORCALQUIER**

ⓘ Forcalquier Region Tourist Office 8 place du Bourguet; tel: 04 92 75 10 02; fax: 04 92 75 06 41; e-mail: oti@forcalquier.com

Web sites:
www.forcalquier.com
Official tourist office site.
http://forcalquier.enfrance.org
All about Forcalquier and its region.

ⓘ Couvent des Cordeliers €
boulevard des Martyres; tel: 04 92 75 02 38. 1-hour guided tours Jul–mid Sep at 1000, 1430, 1530, 1630, 1730, closed Tue; May, Jun, mid-Sep–Oct Sun and holidays only, at 1430, 1600.

⬤ There is a weekly market on Mon.

A modest little place which nowadays appears to be in the middle of nowhere, yet once this quiet town was a great political and cultural centre, the capital of Haute Provence. It's still the capital of its little region, still has a cathedral, built over a 500-year period from the 12th to 17th centuries, and is adorned with numerous medieval buildings in its narrow and picturesque old lanes. There's a former Jewish quarter and a few traces of the town's once-powerful castle. A lane leads from the cathedral to the town gate, Porte des Cordeliers, and on to the **Couvent des Cordeliers***, a handsome 12th-century monastery much altered in the 1960s. Today, Forcalquier is just a peaceful agricultural centre deep in lavender country, with important monthly trading fairs and big weekly markets. Its location gives magnificent views over the surrounding hills and valleys.

Accommodation and food in Forcalquier

Auberge Charembeau €€ *route de Nizelles; tel: 04 92 70 91 70; fax: 04 92 70 91 82*. In the midst of the countryside, this 18th-century farmhouse with views of the Lure mountains has become an enticing hotel with spacious rooms, a pool, good facilities and plenty of character.

Hostellerie des Deux Lions €€ *11 place Bourguet; tel: 04 92 75 25 30*. In the heart of town here's a very good, rather simple hotel and restaurant with delicious inexpensive menus.

Real lavender

This is lavender country, but the lavender becomes different as the road climbs. *Lavandus vera officinalis augustifolia* is the true, noble lavender found mainly in the higher altitudes of these uplands of Provence. It is renowned for its brilliant colour, strong scent and medicinal qualities. The lavender of lower altitudes is actually *lavandin*, a more commercially viable hybrid, which, despite its beauty, does not reach the quality of true lavender.

MANOSQUE*

**ⓘ Manosque Tourist
Office** *place Dr P
Joubert; tel: 04 92 72 16 00;
fax: 04 92 72 58 98;
www.ville-manosque.fr. Open
mornings only Mon–Sat.*

◓ There is a weekly
market on Sat.

◓ *Fête Médiévales* is a
colourful folkloric
festival which takes place
at the end of Jun.

Right
Manosque

Manosque is the model of a busy, thriving Provençal country town. It is
the biggest town in the *département* and the most industrial, lying close
to the Durance as it flows out of the Provençal Alps to skirt the
Lubéron. On hills behind the town, olive groves enhance the southern
scene. The siting nearby of a nuclear power station has diminished its
charms, but the tiny central old quarter still has plenty of character.
Enter it on the south side through **Porte Saunerie***, a splendidly

Centre Jean Giono
*1 boulevard Elémir
Bourges; tel: 04 92 70 54
54.*

Chaste Manosque

'*La pudique*' ('the modest') has long been Manosque's soubriquet. The name comes from a rather gruesome local tale. When François I visited Manosque, he made a pass at the Consul's daughter, Péronne de Voland, who had greeted him at Porte Saunerie as part of the welcome ceremony. Prevented by protocol from refusing him, she burned her face with sulphur fumes. Thus disfigured, she succeeded in deterring his advances.

fortified 12th-century gateway, or more altered **Porte Soubeyran*** on the north side. The ramparts through which these gateways once passed have become a ring road taking traffic round the edge of the old heart of town. Inside, narrow streets and handsome old houses are connected by covered passageways and alleys known in this part of Provence as *andrones*. There are many attractive buildings and features along rue Grande, the main street of the old quarter, which runs into the appealing main square and market-place, place de l'Hôtel de Ville. Much of the architecture is 17th century. On the encircling boulevard is **Fondation Carzou****, a museum devoted mainly to the extraordinary modern artworks of Jean Carzou (b 1907), a surprise in this provincial setting. The **Centre Jean Giono***, close by, is devoted to the writings and the life of the lyrical and poetic local novelist Giono (1895–1970), who described the town as 'like a tortoiseshell in the grass'. The Centre also organises excursions and tours in Giono country.

Accommodation and food in Manosque

Hostellerie de la Fuste €€€ *route Oraison; tel: 04 92 72 05 95; fax: 04 92 72 92 93.* About 6km from town, across the Durance, is the hamlet known as La Fuste, where this handsome and tranquil country house hotel-restaurant offers luxurious and charming accommodation and distinguished (Michelin-starred) cooking.

Hôtel-Restaurant Sud € *boulevard Général de Gaulle; tel: 04 92 87 78 58; fax: 04 92 72 66 60.* A 2-star *Logis de France* hotel with a restaurant offering great local dishes. Satisfyingly good value.

La Source € *route de Dauphin; tel/fax: 04 92 72 12 79.* This modern out-of-town restaurant (about 2km north) offers skilful Provençal cooking based on what's fresh, local and in season. It is roomy, pleasant, nicely laid out and prices are amazingly good value.

Upper Verdon Valley**

ℹ **Tourist Office** place
M Pastorelli, St-André-
les-Alpes; tel: 04 92 89 02
39; fax: 04 92 89 19 23;
e-mail: info@ot-st-andre-les-
alpes.fr; www.ot-st-andre-les-
alpes.fr

🍴 **Auberge du Parc €**
place Charles Bron, St-
Andre-les-Alpes; tel: 04 92
89 00 03; fax: 04 92 89 17
38. Well placed in the
heart of the Upper
Verdon, this appealing
'restaurant with rooms'
offers excellent value for
money.

The **Grand Canyon du Verdon** (*see page 168*) lies a short distance downriver from Castellane, while upriver are the attractive waters of the **Lac de Castillon** (*see page 184*). Above this point, the Upper Valley is rarely visited. Its grandiose hills and valleys are ideal for lovers of walking, rafting and canoeing. The main centre is the town of **St-André-les-Alpes***, a pleasant little resort prettily set among lavender fields and fruit orchards.

Suggested tour

Total distance: 235km, and a detour of 52km with a 2-hour walk.

Time: 1 day, or 2 if you decide to do the detour and walk. The roads can sometimes be slow, steep and winding. Several places invite a stroll, or a pause to admire fine views, so allow time. Much of the drive is in lavender country.

Links: At Sisteron and Château-Arnoux the route connects with the Route Napoléon (*see page 174*). At Sault it links with Upper Vaucluse (*see page 50*).

Route: From **MANOSQUE** ❶, travel on the D5, climbing up and over the scenic **Col de la Mort d'Imbert**, and passing through attractive country up to **FORCALQUIER** ❷. Take the D950 on to the Vaucluse Plateau to **BANON** ❸. Stay on this road all the way into **Sault** (*see page 57*). Turning north – with Mont Ventoux rising on the left – take the D942 (it becomes the D542). Stay on this road all the way into **Sisteron** (*see page 181*). From Sisteron travel back south on the N85. At **Château-Arnoux** (*see page 177*), cross the River Bléone and carry on (in the Digne direction) to the **Château of Malijai**, where Napoleon spent the night on 4 March, 1815.

Detour: Go all the way to **Digne** (*see page 177*) and leave town to the north on the D900A (Route de Barles). A remarkable sight after just 1km, on the left side of the road, is the **Dalle à Ammonites Géantes**, a black stone slab bearing the fossilised marks of 1553 large ammonites, 200 million years old. The road climbs into the **VALLEE DU BES** ❹. In the Vallée du Bès, take the turn to la Robine and make the one-hour walk through the amazing scenery of ravines, woods and pasture to see the **Ichtyosaurus skeleton**. Return the way you came, via Digne, and rejoin the main route at Malijai.

At Malijai turn right on to the D4, doubling back on the other side of the river to reach the tall rocks called the **Rochers des Mées**, which loom over the village of Mées. Unaccountably, legend has it that these rocks are monks that were turned into stone for feeling lust towards

Arab slave girls belonging to a local lord. On the D4A, head down to the N96, but simply cross over on the D101. This runs up a lovely wooded valley to **Eglise St-Donat**, a beautful, simple 11th-century basilica in early Romanesque style. Why is such a large church in such an out-of-the-way spot? At one time pilgrimages were made to this place where the mystical hermit Donat once lived. Return to the N96 and turn right. Pass through old **Peyruis** village and 6km later turn right on to the D30 to climb up to the 12th-century **Monastère de Ganagobie (Ganagobie Monastery)**, high among the lavender and broom on the Ganagobie plateau. There are fantastic viewpoints round about. Inside the church, note especially the fine 12th-century mosaics in the chancel and transept.

Returning towards the N96, instead of joining the main road, take the little right turn up to **Lurs**.

The Var Interior and the Grand Canyon du Verdon

Ratings

Scenery	●●●●●
History	●●●○○
Restaurants	●●●○○
Shopping	●●●○○
Sightseeing	●●●○○
Wine-tasting	●●●○○
Children	●●○○○
Entertainment	●○○○○

The Var Interior must certainly be one of the most pleasing, satisfying and, in places, most spectacular regions in the south of France. Probably no other French *département* is quite so endowed with a sense of physical well-being, nor so perfectly designed for leisurely, unhurried enjoyment of life. It rises away from the beautiful *corniches* of the Mediterranean into a quiet, warming, rustic hinterland of peaceful, basking villages with their shaded squares, while all around are terraced hills, vineyards, great tracts of scented, unkempt *garrigue* and woods of parasol pine. There are modest sights to see, agreeable enough, but the further inland, the more dramatic and wild the scenery becomes, culminating with the gorges along the River Verdon, which make a dramatic border with the Alpes-de-Haute-Provence. Grand Canyon is a fitting name for this astonishing ravine, though anyone who has seen the American version should resist the temptation to make comparisons.

BARJOLS❖❖

ℹ️ **Barjols Tourist Office** *boulevard Grisolle; tel: 04 94 77 20 01; fax: 04 94 77 08 41; e-mail: ot.barjols@free.fr; www.ville-barjols.fr*

🛒 There are markets on Tue, Thu and Sat.

🎉 The Fête de St-Marcel takes place on the closest Sun to 17 Jan.

Right
Flute player

Barjols is quintessential South of France, a well-located, pleasing town with its shady squares, numerous old fountains and warm, relaxed atmosphere. In addition to some 30 fountains, of which the grandest and most encrusted is dubbed the 'champignon' (mushroom), there are a dozen wash-houses. The plane tree shading the main square, 12m around, is said to be the biggest in all Provence. Many traditional customs have survived, including the making of tambourines and *galoubets* (3-holed flutes) to play at ancient festivals such as the three-day Fête des Tripettes (every four years in January:

next 2005), when an ox heads a procession of butchers through the town, only (of course) to be slaughtered, roasted on a spit and distributed to the townspeople amid much revelry. On the other three years, the Fête de St-Marcel involves carrying a bust of this 5th-century saint through the town. Round about, there are many other little country towns and villages of great charm and sunny atmosphere – such as faience-making Varages, la Verdière and Tavernes.

DRAGUIGNAN**

Draguignan Tourist Office 2 avenue Carnot; tel: 04 98 10 51 05; fax: 04 98 10 51 10; e-mail: Contact@ot-draguignan.fr; www.ot-draguignan.fr

Musée du Cannon et des Artilleurs €
At the artillery school 3km east; tel: 04 94 60 23 85/86. Open Mon–Fri 0815–1100, 1415–1700. Closed 15 Dec–15 Jan and holidays.

Tour de l'Horloge
Access only on guided tours organised by the tourist office.

Musée Municipal rue de la République; tel: 04 94 47 28 80. Open 0900–1200, 1600–1800. Closed Sun.

Musée des Arts et Traditions Populaires €
15 rue Roumanille; tel: 04 94 47 05 72. Open 0900–1400, 1400–1800. Closed Sun and Mon am and holidays.

A quietly busy market town with an extensive medieval **old quarter****, Draguignan is refreshingly authentic and not dependent on tourism – one of the nearest such towns to the Var coast. It has an artillery school (with its own museum of weaponry, the **Musée du Cannon et des Artilleurs***), and there has always been a military edge to the town. The strange 17th-century **Tour de l'Horloge (clocktower)**** with its incongruous turrets and wrought-iron campanile, standing alone on a little hill in the heart of the old quarter, marks the spot where Draguignan came into existence as a Roman fort. In the Middle Ages, when the town began to grow, it had a defensive ring of ramparts put around it and became a prosperous regional centre. Remnants of the fortifications, especially the **Porte de Portaiguières*** (end of Grand' Rue) and **Porte de Romaine*** (rue de l'Observance), and the façade of a **13th-century synagogue*** (rue de la Juiverie), recall that period. For a while, from 1797 to 1974, Draguignan was the capital of the Var. There are a couple of good rainy-day museums in the city centre: the **Musée Municipal***, with artworks, faience and local archaeological finds; and the **Musée des Arts et Traditions Populaires****, with collections relating to farming techniques and rural domestic life in the past. In August 1944 there was massive fighting close to Draguignan when 9000 British and American soldiers were parachuted in above nearby Le Muy. There's an American military cemetery on the edge of town.

Accommodation and food in Draguignan

L'Oustaou €€ 5 place Brémond, Flayosc; tel: 04 94 70 42 69. In the main square of Flayosc, 7km west of Draguignan, this little country restaurant is typically Provençal, reaching a high standard, and is amazingly good value for money. The daube provençal is exceptional, and there's a selection of local wines.

Hostellerie du Moulin de la Foux and **Restaurant La Truite Dorée** €€ quartier de la Foux; tel: 04 94 68 55 33; fax: 04 94 68 70 10. A pleasant, modest little Logis de France hotel in a green setting, with a moderately priced restaurant serving some local specialities.

FAYENCE**

Fayence (nothing to do with faience) is an atmospheric, lively country town. In the historic heart of town, old houses line steep streets, and precipitous alleys run between. It has a picturesque market, several reasonable restaurants (see page 172), good views south and remnants of its old defences against Saracen raiders. It's also a great centre for

ℹ Tourist offices
Fayence *place L Roux; tel: 04 94 76 20 08; fax: 04 94 39 15 96; e-mail: ot.fayence@wanadoo.fr; www.mairie-fayence.com*
Callian *3 place Bourguignon (across road from church); tel: 04 94 47 75 77.*

Fayence has a market on Tue and a bigger one on Thu. Callian's market takes place on Fri morning.

An Aïoli fair is held on 26–28 Aug.

Above
Fayence

arts and crafts, and there's a glider airfield just below the town.

All around is attractive country and appealing old villages, such as its neighbour **Tourettes**, and especially **Seillans**** and **Callian****. Seillans, a gem of a medieval village 8km west of Fayence on the D19, clings to the southern slopes of the Canjuers upland. Its delightful fountains and pink pastel houses cascade prettily down through the town, while cobbled walkways climb to the attractive Romanesque parish church and a daunting 12th-century fortress that once held out against the Saracens. At Callian, 8 km east of Fayence, café tables stand in the tiny tree-shaded square next to a strange old 'fountain' and a church with a spire of patterned, glazed tiles. Art exhibitions are held in the old Chapelle des Pénitents in the heart of the village. Narrow, steep, flowery lanes twist around the hilltop château (now private homes), which is impressively floodlit at night.

GRAND CANYON DU VERDON✦✦✦

ℹ See Moustiers-Ste-Marie or Castellane for tourist office.

⇄ The north and south sides of the canyon are readily accessible from Moustiers-Ste-Marie. From Castellane, the north side only is readily accessible. Parking is only at designated viewpoints.

Grand indeed, for along the canyon of the Verdon river, sheer rock face plunges sometimes 700m on both sides of the valley down to the twisting ribbon of water below. This precipitous ravine is an astonishing sight. On the sinuous clifftop road a succession of *Points Sublime* offer amazing views into and across the deepest and most impressive river gorge in Europe. On the north side of the Grand Canyon, a circular drive of 23km gives a succession of breathtaking vistas. The south side – the *Corniche Sublime* – is even more grandiose, though it involves a longer drive. It is possible to make a round trip, seeing the gorge from both the north and south sides; however, driving the tortuous roads on the canyon edge is long and slow – some 75km – and, magnificent as it is, the ravine's appeal can be readily grasped in a shorter visit, especially on the more striking south side. The Verdon canyon ends at **Moustiers-Ste-Marie**.

Right
The Grand Canyon du Verdon

MOUSTIERS-STE-MARIE✦✦✦

ℹ **Moustiers-Ste-Marie Tourist Office** *Hôtel-Dieu; tel: 04 92 74 67 84; fax: 04 92 74 60 65; e-mail: moustiers@ wanadoo.fr; www.ville-moustiers-sainte-marie.fr*

🏛 **Musée de la Faïence** € *Hôtel de Ville; tel: 04 92 74 61 64. Open Apr–Oct 0900–1200, 1400–1800 (till 1900 in Jul and Aug). Closed Tue.*

🕐 There is a weekly Fri market.

It is no surprise that visitors are attracted to Moustiers, a marvellously picturesque medieval village of narrow streets and stairways, and attractive old houses, built precariously on the slopes of a spectacular ravine. Most curious of all the 'sights' is the gilded star on a chain hanging right across the ravine. Exactly who put it there and why has almost been forgotten – but it's said to be a votive offering made by a Crusader after he was freed from captivity. The town's **church**✦ is a fine Romanesque building of the 12th and 14th centuries, with an unusual Gothic choir. The name of Moustiers is synonymous with a certain style of faience ware of the very highest quality made here from the 17th to the 19th centuries. At its peak, a dozen small manufactories were producing the town's fine earthenware, and examples of the work of the leading makers can be seen in the **Musée de la Faïence**✦. These originals are valuable collectors' items, but for a modest price you can buy some Moustiers ware of your own: the

⊘ The Fête de Diane, during the first week in Sep, is a whole week of festivity and partying, reaching its peak for the Fête de la Nativité de Notre-Dame, 8 Sep.

town's faience-making was revived in the 1920s, and again is highly regarded; it's on sale at many stores in town.

Accommodation and food in Moustiers-Ste-Marie

Hôtel Le Colombier €€ *route de Castellane; tel: 04 92 74 66 02; fax: 04 92 74 66 70.* This decent, well-equipped hotel in the Quartier St-Michel is a peaceful place to stay. No restaurant.

Les Santons €€€ *place Eglise; tel: 04 92 74 66 48; fax: 04 92 74 63 67.* An excellent little restaurant, much loved by local gourmets, with the emphasis on everything fresh and local. Offers lavish dishes such as fresh noodles with *foie gras* and truffles, as well as Sisteron lamb, wonderful cheeses and local wines.

Faience

The town of Faenza in Italy lies at the origin of this ornate, glazed and delicately decorated fine earthenware. Its manufacturing secrets were brought into Provence in the 17th century, and seized upon in Moustiers-Ste-Marie, where skilled potters already worked in local clay. Moustiers faience soon became the benchmark for high-quality earthenware. After flourishing in the 17th and 18th centuries, then declining in the 19th, faience-making died out altogether. In the 1920s it was revived at Moustiers and has again become important. Close by, the village of Varages (near Barjols) was also once renowned for its faience, and here, too, the industry has been revived. In Varages' local church the altar of St Claude, patron of faience-makers, is adorned with their work, and the village has a faience fair each summer. Both Varages and Moustiers have a Musée de la Faïence highlighting the makers, history and techniques of local earthenware.

MASSIF DE LA SAINTE-BAUME❖❖❖

❷ Several small roads and footpaths give access to the Massif, from the villages of Gémenos and Auriol in the west, St-Zacharie and Rougiers in the north, and la Roquebrussanne in the east. The main route into the heart of the hills and to the Sainte-Baume is the D80, off the N560.

Sainte Baume means 'holy cavern', and these majestic forested hills and cliffs hold at their heart a place of worship venerated through the ages. This is the highest of the ranges of hills behind the Riviera, reaching 1147m at its summit, the Signal de la Sainte-Baume. Where the dense, cool, curiously northern-looking forest cover of lime, beech, holly and maple gives way to rock, the landscape is bare, pale limestone. The revered **Saint-Baume❖❖** itself is close to the central crest of the massif, 994m **Saint-Pilon❖❖**. It was long worshipped as the magical site of a water and fertility deity, and there are menhirs nearby. The awesome rock cavern, cool and damp, reached after a climb and mounting a stairway of 150 steps, is arranged inside as a chapel. Beside the altar a shrine holds bones believed to be those of

The main pilgrimage to the Sainte-Baume cave is on Whit Mon.

Festival of St Mary Magdalene, a religious entertainment, takes place in the cave on 21 Jul, with Mass on 22 Jul.

At Christmas, crowds gather for Midnight Mass in the cave.

Mary Magdalene (her skull is in St-Maximin-la-Sainte-Baume). Since the discovery of these bones at St-Maximin in 1279, and their removal to this cave, millions of pilgrims have made their way here, including several popes and French kings. They say Mary Magdalene lived her last years here, being transported seven times daily by angels to the summit of Saint-Pilon.

Accommodation and food near Sainte-Baume

Hostellerie de la Sainte-Baume € *On the D80; tel: 04 42 04 54 84.* Standing at an altitude of 675m in the Massif, the former convent has become a spiritual and cultural centre but is still a guesthouse for pilgrims visiting the Holy Cave.

Is this really Mary Magdalene?

Cult objects were vital to create pilgrimage centres in the Middle Ages. They gave regional power and influence, especially if high-ranking figures visited. That the skull at St-Maximin is Mary Magdalene's follows local legend claiming several of Jesus' companions reached the Camargue (*page 114*). Among them were Mary Magdalene, who resided in Ste-Baume cave, a pagan site, and Maximinus, who lived at Gallo-Roman Villa Latta. Monks at Ste-Baume cave were scattered by Saracens in the 8th century. In the 11th century, Benedictines at Vézelay in Burgundy claimed to have Mary Magdalene's bones. Pilgrims flocked there, and the 2nd and 3rd Crusades (1146 and 1190) started from Vézelay. In 1279, Charles of Anjou, having inherited Provence, ordered Provençal Benedictines to find the 'true' relics, and they discovered the two saints' sarcophagi. St-Maximin's church was built over them and so replaced Vézelay as a centre of pilgrimage.

ST-MAXIMIN-LA-SAINTE-BAUME✧✧

St-Maximin-la-Sainte-Baume Tourist Office *Hôtel de Ville; tel: 04 94 59 84 59; fax: 04 94 59 82 92.*

Basilique € *Open 0830–1200, 1400–1900 (closes 1800 in winter).*

There is a weekly Wed market.

Leading off the handsome tree-shaded esplanade on the main road, narrow lanes and streets redolent of the Middle Ages, lined with curious 14th- and 15th-century houses, make their way up to a strange **Basilique✧✧✧**, a former abbey church, which dominates the town. It is the most complete example of a Northern Gothic building in Provence. Its exterior doors are superb, rough and huge. Inside, there's a wealth of artwork, traces of frescos and a massive ornate organ. Note especially the 16th-century painted wooden statue of St John the Baptist and a fascinating 16th-century retable, in a gold-painted frame, of the crucifixion. There's also some appalling 17th-century and later decoration. Down below is the basilica's 4th-century Roman **crypt✧✧✧**,

A pilgrimage and festival takes place on 21–22 Jul. There is also a music festival from mid-Jul to the end of Aug *(for details, tel: 04 94 78 01 93)*.

originally the funerary vault of a Roman villa. Here, a skull said to be that of Mary Magdalene is set into a gold statue (you look at it through a metal grille, and press a button to get five minutes of light). Other sarcophagi displayed here are said to be those of saints Maximinus, Cedonius, Marcella and Susan. All the bones and sarcophagi here were found in the Roman funerary vault and date to the 4th century. Much myth and medieval political manoeuvring surrounds the creation of the cult of Mary Magdalene, whose bones were said to have been found here in 1279.

Accommodation and food in St-Maximin

Hotellerie du Couvent Royal €€ *place Jean Salusse; tel: 04 94 86 55 66; fax: 04 94 59 82 82.* Excellent restaurant set in the chapterhouse beside the basilica. In fine weather, dine in the cloisters. A bar and lounge serve snacks all day.

Hôtel de France €€ *3 avenue Albert-1er; tel: 04 94 78 00 14; fax: 04 94 59 83 80.* Traditional, provincial hotel and restaurant in the town centre with comfortable and adequately equipped rooms, a pool, terrace and restaurant.

ABBAYE DE THORONET**

Abbaye de Thoronet € *The abbey is 11km from Carcès. It lies off the D79 between the D13 and the D84; tel: 04 94 60 43 90. Open Apr–Sep 0900–1900 (closed 1200–1400 on Sun); Oct–Mar 1000–1300, 1400–1700. Closed holidays.*

Buried in peaceful seclusion in the midst of the woods, this church, mainly in 12th-century Provençal Romanesque style, together with three-level cloisters, a chapter house, a tithe barn and outbuildings, has survived remarkably unscathed. The church, sturdy and austere in keeping with Cistercian principles, is beautifully simple and unadorned inside. The monks' polygonal communal bathroom is also delightful. Together with Silvacane and Sénanque *(see page 71)*, Thoronet was one of the 'Three Cistercian Sisters of Provence'.

Suggested tour

Total distance: 235km, and a detour of 50km.

Time: It would be best to allow a couple of days for this tour, though concentrating only on highlights could make it manageable in one day. The Grand Canyon du Verdon itself takes several hours because of the narrow, winding road and slow traffic.

Route: Start at **DRAGUIGNAN ❶**. Travel west out of town on the route de Lorgues (the D567; it changes to the D562) through delightful, rough, hilly country of Mediterranean pines, wild flowers, abandoned terraces and tiny vineyards. **Lorgues** itself is an old, unpretentious town

① Moulin de la Camandoule €€
2km west of Fayence via route de Seillans; tel: 04 94 76 00 84; fax: 04 94 76 10 40. This tranquil and rustic hotel and restaurant used to be an oil mill, and preserves a tremendous traditional atmosphere. Hearty, classic cooking of *foie gras,* duck and fish in delicious sauces, plus local wines to choose from.

Castellaras €€€ *4km west of Fayence via route de Seillans; tel: 04 94 76 13 80; fax: 04 94 76 17 50.* Here's an acclaimed Provençal gastronomic halt, serving stuffed vegetables, fish terrines, *bouillabaisse,* oysters and *foie gras.*

Restaurant La France
€€ 1 Grand' Rue du Château, Fayence; tel/fax: 04 94 76 00 14. It's really enjoyable to eat on the gallery of this stylish yet relaxed first-floor restaurant in the centre of Fayence. The imaginative chef makes good use of local sauces and seasonings – *tapenade, pistou,* etc – and the wine list includes organic Domaine de Thuerry.

① Hôtel de France €€
place du Thouron, Seillans; tel: 04 94 76 96 10; fax: 04 94 76 89 20. A comfortable and satisfying little family-run hotel with plane trees, a pool and a fountain nearby.

with many pretty corners. Travelling between masses of roadside flowers and pine woods, stay on the D562, shortly turning left on to the D17 to reach the village of **Le Thoronet** (where you turn right on to the D84) and its **ABBEY ②**. Continue on the D84 to rejoin the D562, where you turn left to enter **Carcès**, a small medieval town attractively bordered with vineyards and vegetable gardens. Follow the D562 (and the D554) to **Brignoles**, a small, but once rather important town on the ancient Provençal highway, the N7. This was the *Via Aurelia,* which went from Rome, through Nice, Fréjus and Aix, to Arles; one of the busiest roads in the Roman Empire. Some local country people still know it as *lou camin aurelien* (Provençal for 'the Aurelian Way'). Travel west on this road to **ST-MAXIMIN-LA-SAINTE-BAUME ③**.

Detour: From St-Maximin-la-Sainte-Baume, turn away from the main route into the dark druidic forests of the **MASSIF DE LA SAINTE-BAUME ④**, perhaps including the hour's walk to visit the **Sainte-Baume** itself. To get there, head south from St-Maximin on the N560. After 9km, soon after the junction with the D1, take the left turn (the D80) via Nans-les-Pins up to the heights of the Massif. Follow the D80 beyond the Hôtellerie (guesthouse) and turn right on the steep, winding little road down to St-Zacharie. From here take the N560 back to St-Maximin.

From St-Maximin, take the D560 north through attractive country to **BARJOLS ⑤**. The D71 (changing to the D13, then the D11) continues from Barjols in rich farmland through **Tavernes** and **Montmeyan**, where you turn right on to the D30 and left on to the D71 to **Baudinard**. Alternatively, for a nice, quiet hotel with restaurant, in a lovely village overlooking the pines of the valley of the Aups, go 10km further to Moissac-Bellevue, where **Le Calalou** (€ *tel: 04 94 70 17 91*) has pretty, simple rooms. Carry on through Baudinard down to the Ste-Croix dam, which has created the beautiful **Lac de Ste-Croix** on the Verdon river. Here, cross the river on to the D111 and travel beside the lake, passing by the village of Ste-Croix de Verdon and continuing all the way beside brilliant lavender fields in places. Continue into **MOUSTIERS-STE-MARIE ⑥**, which is so crowded and popular that it may come as quite a shock after such a tranquil drive.

Leave Moustiers heading towards the **GRAND CANYON DU VERDON ⑦**, and take the turn (the D957) across the river next to the lake. This gets you to the Canyon's south bank road (the D19) called – and signposted – the *Corniche Sublime.* Stay on this magnificent road, though to enjoy it you'll have to make frequent stops at the designated viewpoints with parking space as it is impossible to admire the scenery while driving on this road. In particular, to get a sense of the depth of the gorge, it's essential to stop somewhere and just take a look. The road number changes to the D71 and eventually leaves the Canyon behind. Follow this road all the way to Comps-sur-Artuby, where you meet up with the D955. Turn right (south) here and return across the wild hills to Draguignan.

Also worth exploring

There is fine country of hills and woods, half-wild, half-terraced and cultivated, east of Draguignan and out towards **St-Vallier-de-Thiey** (*see page 184*). From Draguignan, drive to **Callas** and **Bargemon** (on the D25), over to **Seillans**, **Fayence** (on the D19) and attractive **Callian**.

The Route Napoléon

Ratings

Scenery	●●●●●
History	●●●●○
Restaurants	●●●●○
Sightseeing	●●●○○
Architecture	●●○○○
Children	●●○○○
Shopping	●●○○○
Entertainment	●○○○○

In 1815, Napoleon Bonaparte escaped from exile on the island of Elba and made his way overnight to the French coast, landing on 1 March at Golfe-Juan. With a band of a thousand armed supporters he made his way inland, meeting no resistance from local authorities and gathering ever more support from the population. The sign of the eagle, seen along the road, marks his route along the ancient Alpine highway. Today it has mainly become the N85. The symbol reflects Napoleon's ambitious (and elegantly expressed) declaration, 'L'aigle avec les couleurs nationales volera de clocher en clocher jusqu'aux tours de Notre Dame' ('The nation's eagle will fly from steeple to steeple as far as the towers of Notre Dame'). Towns and villages along this road are much too dependent on tourism to be exactly rural, but this makes a glorious drive through the mountainous backcountry of Provence.

CABRIS*

ⓘ Cabris Tourist Office 4 rue Porte Haute; tel: 04 93 60 55 63; fax: 04 93 60 55 94.

⮂ Cabris is 6km from Grasse. The D11 passes through the village.

🍴 Chèvre d'Or € In the village; tel: 04 93 60 54 22. This decent village eatery in place Puits has good food at moderate prices.

Cabris has castle ruins and an interesting 17th-century church, but the great appeal of this attractive village is its stunning location. Poised on the edge of a high plateau ridge, it commands a view south reaching across beautiful countryside and down to the Mediterranean coast. On clear days, even the island of Corsica can be made out on the horizon. The village is no typical Provençal community, and has long been a favourite of second-homers and arty types.

CASTELLANE***

Castellane Tourist Office *34 rue Nationale; tel: 04 92 83 61 14; fax: 04 92 83 76 89; e-mail: office@castellane.org; www.castellane.org*

Opposite
Wrought-iron Napoleon sign

Compellingly attractive and in a superb location, this modest mountain town has become tragically overcrowded. In the main square, where local men play *boules* oblivious to the rest of the world, there are parked cars from everywhere in Europe. Castellane is probably the most popular point on the Route Napoléon, standing across the banks of the Verdon just 12km from the start of the river's spectacular canyon, one of the most dramatic drives in France (*see Var*

There is parking in place Sauvaire.

Markets are held on Wed and Sat.

Interior and Grand Canyon du Verdon, page 164). The town is surrounded by campsites, and is a popular base for hikers.

On 3 March, 1815, at the invitation of the local authorities, Napoleon rested here at what is now the tourist office. There's a good deal left of the old part of town together with some stretches of its original 14th-century ramparts. The centre of the old quarter is the main square, place Marcel Sauvaire. Most striking of all, though, is a soaring limestone cliff adjacent to Castellane which physically dominates the town. High on this pillar of rock stands a small chapel, **Notre-Dame-du-Roc****. At first sight it looks completely inaccessible, but there's a path all the way from the town and it's only a half-hour walk to the top.

Accommodation and food in Castellane

Hôtel du Commerce €€ *place de l'Eglise; tel: 04 92 83 61 00; fax: 04 92 83 72 82.* A traditional little family-run hotel-restaurant, in the main square, the Commerce is unpretentious, comfortable and moderately priced. Its restaurant serves good classic dishes.

Below
Notre-Dame-du-Roc, Castellane

CHATEAU-ARNOUX*

ⓘ Château-Arnoux Tourist Office *La Ferme de Font Robert; tel: 04 92 64 02 64; fax: 04 92 62 60 67.*

A quiet, civilised river resort on the Lac de l'Escale (part of the Durance river), with a Renaissance château, the town makes a good stopover. Seven kilometres south is the **Château de Malijai***, where Napoleon spent the night. Across the river at Volonne, the Emperor and his men took a break in their march. About 2km outside Château-Arnoux, on the N85, a sign directs you up the lane to **Chapelle St-Jean***. Walk the last 15 minutes to the picnic spot and viewing platform, which gives a phenomenal panorama across the peaks and valleys of the western Alpes de Haute Provence.

Accommodation and food in Château-Arnoux

La Bonne Etape €€€ *Chemin du Lac; tel: 04 92 64 00 09; fax: 04 92 64 37 36.* This *Relais et Châteaux* establishment, a pretty, charming 18th-century inn among its olive and cypress trees, is one of the best places to stay on the Route Napoléon. Its main restaurant is exceptional, using the best of local ingredients seasoned with wild herbs. Its less expensive bistro-style restaurant **Au Goût du Jour** doesn't aim for such gastronomic heights, but here, too, the menu uses all local, fresh produce depending on what's in season. Lamb is the speciality in both restaurants, and there's a good choice of Provençal wines.

L'Oustaou de la Foun €€ *On the N85, about 2km north of the village; tel: 04 92 62 65 30; fax: 04 92 62 65 32.* The Provençal name and pretty, rustic setting give a clue to the elegant traditional style of this restaurant and its imaginative interpretation of classic regional dishes served with good regional wines.

DIGNE***

ⓘ Digne Tourist Office *place du Tampinet; tel: 04 92 36 62 62; fax: 04 92 32 27 24; e-mail: info@ot.digneslesbains.fr; www.ot-dignelesbains.fr*

Ⓟ You can park in place du Tampinet, next to bus station; alongside boulevard Thiers; and in place Charles-de-Gaulle.

Digne is an important place to pause or spend the night on the Route Napoléon (the Emperor stopped here for lunch). It is a bright, clean, prosperous and very appealing town, refreshing and airy, dominated by the surrounding green hills, and is a great centre for lavender. Modern sculptures decorate the town centre. Many visitors to Digne come to take the waters at the town's thriving **Etablissement Thermal***, or spa baths. The spa dates back to Roman times, and officially the full name of the town is Digne-les-Bains (Digne Baths). Its much acclaimed mineral-rich spa waters are used in the treatment of rheumatism. There are eight hot springs (and one cold), the hottest rising from the ground at a steamy 42°C. The town's quasi-Classical **Great Fountain***, in boulevard Gassendi, shows clearly enough how much calcium there is in the spring water: barely a century and a half old, the fountain is already choked by an amorphous mass of 'fur' deposits. Further along the road, **Notre-Dame-du-Bourg*** is a fine Romanesque former cathedral.

There are markets on Wed and Sat.

Etablissement Thermal € *3km out of town on the D20 tel: 04 92 32 32 92. Open Oct–Apr Mon–Sat 0845–1200, 1400–1800 (Sun and national holidays 1000–1200); May–Sep Mon–Sat 0845–1230, 1400–1900 (Sun and national holidays 1000–1200, 1500–1900).*

Along with spa enthusiasts, Digne also attracts keen hikers so, unlike other towns on the Route Napoléon, many of its visitors have little interest in the Emperor and are not following his route. It's pleasant enough staying within the confines of the town, enjoying the cool, fresh air, eating, drinking, admiring the views and strolling the long main street, boulevard Gassendi, heavily shaded by plane trees. In the attractive main square there are frequent outdoor events on summer evenings. Digne is ancient, but almost disappeared some 300 years ago when the 16th-century religious wars all but destroyed the town, and a generation later, most of the population was wiped out by an outbreak of plague. The narrow streets and tall houses of the interesting *vieille ville* cluster around a hill with the distinctive **Cathédrale St Jérôme**◦ poised on the summit – the episode of the bishop's candlesticks in Victor Hugo's *Les Misérables* is set here.

Accommodation and food in Digne

Le Grand Paris €€ *19 boulevard Thiers; tel: 04 92 31 11 15; fax: 04 92 32 32 82.* The best hotel and restaurant in town stands close to the centre, near the river. A former monastic building, it is now a rather grand mansion with a lot of Provençal character, offering spacious,

Fairs and festivals
The Fête de la Lavande (Lavender Festival) is held on the first Sunday in August and is marked by a delightful Corso Fleuri (flower parade). At the end of the month comes the big Foire Lavande (Lavender Fair).

Le Train des Pignes. Chemins de Fer de la Provence, 4bis rue Alfred-Binet, Nice; tel: 04 93 82 10 17; www.trainprovence.com

comfortable rooms and a broad terrace shaded by plane trees. The cooking is substantial, thoroughly based in fresh regional ingredients and rich in local flavour. You'll have to book ahead.

L'Origan € 6 rue Pied-de-Ville; tel/fax: 04 92 31 62 13. This convivial little restaurant with rooms is well located and offers excellent, imaginative cooking with plenty of dishes au romarin, à la sauge, or à la tapenade (with rosemary, sage, or olive paste) to remind you that you are in Provence. All at very moderate prices.

Le Train des Pignes

One terrific way to reach Digne is on the endearing little Train des Pignes (literally, train of the pine-cones), which climbs on a narrow gauge track through the Provençal hills in a great curve from the Mediterranean. The 3-hour journey from Nice to Digne takes in extraordinary, thrilling scenery, and pauses in tiny old-fashioned stations. Here and there along the way are some remarkable feats of engineering, where the track spirals up inside a mountain, or crosses plunging valleys. The train can be taken the other way, from Digne. There are several departures daily. It is popular with hikers, who walk from one station to another, then catch the train back to base.

GRASSE**

Grasse Tourist Office Palais de Congrès, 22 cours Honoré Cresp; tel: 04 93 36 66 66; fax: 04 93 36 86 36.

There is parking in place du Cours (near the tourist office). The Parfumeries have their own car parks.

Parfumerie Molinard 60 boulevard Victor-Hugo, tel: 04 93 36 01 62; fax: 04 93 36 03 91; www.molinard.com

Opposite
Digne-les-Bains

Although Grasse, the world's 'Capital of Perfume', is industrial and largely unattractive, it still repays a visit. Its old town is full of atmosphere, there are good views on to the plain below, and then, there's the perfume. An incredible 75 per cent of all the world's bottles of perfume use Grasse essences. Amazingly, it all started with a strange 16th-century fad for perfumed gloves. At the time, Grasse was a typical glove-making town, but quickly became acclaimed as having the most exquisitely scented perfumes. The next century was devoted to building up the perfume industry and the development of processes for extracting essences from flowers. With similar foresight, in the 20th century, these processes were developed to make natural food flavourings. The town's three great parfumeries*** are Molinard, Galimard and – the largest – Fragonard. All three, combining factory with elegant house and gardens, put on interesting and enjoyable guided visits. You will learn about perfume-making, discover how the smell (or 'essence') is extracted from flowers and other fragrant plants, and be given a chance to buy at a discount. Fragonard is a great name locally, as the distinguished 18th-century artist Fragonard was a native of the town. The **Villa-Musée Fragonard***, where he lived, is now an

Parfumerie Galimard 73 route de Cannes (3km south of the town centre); tel: 04 93 09 20 00; fax: 04 93 70 36 22. www.galimard.com

Parfumerie Fragonard
20 boulevard Fragonard; tel: 04 93 36 44 65; fax: 04 93 36 57 32 and Les 4 Chemins, route de Cannes; tel: 04 93 77 94 30; www.fragonard.com

Villa-Musée Fragonard
€ 23 boulevard Fragonard; tel: 04 93 36 01 61. Open Jun–Sep 1000–1900; Oct–May 1000–1200, 1400–1700 (closed Mon and Tue). Closed whole of Nov.

Musée d'Art et d'Histoire de Provence
2 rue Mirabeau; tel: 04 93 36 01 61. Opening times as for Villa-Musée Fragonard.

Musée de la Parfumerie
8 place du Cours; tel: 04 93 36 80 20. Opening times as for Villa-Musée Fragonard.

A colourful flower and produce market takes place every morning in place aux Aires, in the Vieille Ville.

There is a Rose festival during the second or third weekend in May and a Jasmine festival on the first Sun in Aug.

Right
Grasse

art museum, as is the more interesting **Musée d'Art et d'Histoire de Provence**✦✦, which has a local emphasis. The **Musée de la Parfumerie**✦✦ deals with perfume's 3000-year history, as well as showing Marie-Antoinette's travelling 'essentials'.

The **Vieille Ville**✦✦✦ is a medieval district of narrow alleys, steep stairways and tall, narrow houses. Main points of interest are the cathedral, the 12th-century watchtower Tour de Guet, and the squares, place du 24-août and place aux Aires. And Napoleon? On 2 March, 1815, he and his men rested briefly at dawn on the outskirts of Grasse at what is now called the Plateau Napoléon before continuing their march.

Accommodation and food in Grasse

La Bastide St Antoine €€€ *48 rue Henri Dunant; tel: 04 93 70 94 94; fax: 04 93 70 94 95.* About 2km south of the town centre, this 18th-century mansion, set among olive groves, houses an outstanding hotel-restaurant, famous for its skilful, imaginative approach to local ingredients. Desserts are fantastic. There are just a dozen bedrooms, very pricey.

Hôtel du Patti €€ *place du Patti; tel: 04 93 36 01 00; fax: 04 93 36 36 40.* Modern, and perhaps a little characterless, but this unpretentious hotel and restaurant in the Vieille Ville is affordable, comfortable and well placed near the market-place, place aux Aires.

Le Préjoly € *place Fabre, St-Vallier-de-Thiey; tel: 04 93 42 60 86; fax: 04 93 42 67 80.* About 12km further along the N85 at this village where Napoleon halted is an excellent, inexpensive little hotel-restaurant. It stands opposite the *pré jolie* (pretty meadow) which gives it its name. Facilities include a sauna and turkish bath.

SISTERON✦✦✦

ℹ Sisteron Tourist Office *place de la République; tel: 04 92 61 12 03; fax: 04 92 61 19 57; www.sisteron.com*

🅿 There is parking in place du Dr Robert, at the edge of Vieille Ville; and place de la République, close to tourist office.

⊖ There are markets on Wed and Sat.

Just below the confluence of the Durance and the Buëch rivers, the valley narrows, the mountains closing in as if to stem the river altogether. It flows between two sheer and monumental faces of rock, each scored with the lines of vertical strata, and seeming to stand guard between Provence to the south and Dauphiné to the north. Indeed Sisteron was long known, in Occitan, as La Clau de Provenço – the Key to Provence. The town, standing dramatically above the river, today has only the five sturdy towers of its former ramparts which enclosed the *vieille ville*✦✦✦. A walk in the old quarter – a maze of narrow streets, stairways and curious covered alleys (known locally as *androns*) – is fascinating. The 12th-century church of **Notre-Dame-des-Pommiers**✦ is a satisfying, unsophisticated Romanesque building; its few (mostly later) attempts at frivolity are subdued by the massive simplicity of the structure. Little survives of the town's

Fairs and festivals include Nuits de la Citadelle, a summer music, dance and drama festival in the Citadel's 70-year-old open-air theatre.

Citadelle € Tel: 04 92 61 27 57. Open 15 Mar–15 Nov 0800–1900 (closes an hour earlier out of season).

daunting medieval **Citadelle*** except the angular and intricate outer walls, perched eagle-like on a crag of rock high above the river valley. It is well worth a visit if only for the view. The Nazis were the last to make use of the Citadelle, as a military base and prison. The Resistance liberated the prison, then on 15 August, 1944, allied bombers destroyed the ancient Citadelle – a move much opposed by locals to this day.

Accommodation and food in Sisteron

Grand Hôtel du Cours €€ *place de l'Eglise; tel: 04 92 61 04 51; fax: 04 92 61 41 73*. In an old cloister opposite the cathedral, this atmospheric, family-run hotel offers decent accommodation (sometimes rooms are a little cramped) in a central location. Open Mar–Nov only.

Suggested tour

Total distance: About 175km, or 205km including detours.

Time: The famous journey from Cannes to Sisteron can easily be done in a day, but a more leisurely approach, taking time to see the sights,

Napoleon's return from Elba

For many French people, their national glory reached its height under the Corsican 'Little Emperor'. Ironically, he was born to militant Corsican separatists in 1769, the year that France bought the island from Italy, and as a young soldier Napoleon vowed to follow in their footsteps and oppose French rule.

He went on instead to make France the most powerful country in Europe, destroyed the detested French Revolutionary junta known as the Directory, crowned himself Emperor and stepped comfortably into the shoes of France's recently beheaded monarchy. Along the way, he eliminated the old French regions, centralised all administration in Paris, imposed a new legal system, and also found time to invent the kilometre. By 1809 he controlled most of the Continent and was prepared to tackle Russia.

It took the combined might of Prussia, England, Austria and Russia to check the growing power of France under Napoleon's leadership. By 1814, these ill-assorted allies were able to conquer France and banish Napoleon to 'house arrest' on the island of Elba, so close to his native Corsica.

No wonder the Emperor was met with enthusiasm as he made the return journey along the Alpine highway. All this triumph was of course temporary – Napoleon was to meet his Waterloo a matter of weeks later. Even today, though, anything to do with Napoleon allows the French an opportunity for colourful pomp and ceremony. For example, at Golfe-Juan each year (unaccountably in September) a half-fun, half-serious re-enactment of Napoleon's return from Elba involves a group of men in full Napoleonic military outfits (rather hot in the sunshine) arriving dramatically from the sea. One of them, suitably short, middle-aged and pugnacious looking, plays the role of Bonaparte, to much cheering of 'Vive l'Empereur!' and the blaring of an improbable popular song about Napoleon.

Above
The Villa Fragonard, Grasse

Horizon € 100
*Promenade St Jean,
Cabris; tel: 04 93 60 51 69;
fax: 04 93 60 56 29.*
Excellent, classic little
village hotel with
marvellous views. Open in
summer only Apr–Oct.

visit the towns and explore the detours, requires at least one overnight stop.

Links: At Castellane this route connects with the Var Interior and the Grand Canyon du Verdon (*see page 164*). From Digne to Sisteron, it can be linked to the Alpes de Haute Provence (*see page 156*). Napoleon himself carried on to Grenoble. Taking the same itinerary as the Emperor, the Route Napoléon could be considered as a scenic through-route between the Rhône Valley and the Côte d'Azur. At Cannes (*see page 212*), the route links to the Cannes–Nice (*see page 220*) and Esterel (*see page 204*) tours.

Route: From **Cannes** take the N85, following signs to Grasse. Soon after the road has left the town and passed the *autoroute*, high on the right rises **Mougins** (*see page 226*). Skirting **Mouans-Sartoux**, overlooked by its 16th-century château, the N85 continues towards **GRASSE ❶**, climbing steeply to enter the town.

Detour: Abandon the Route Napoléon briefly to explore the pretty Pays de Grasse countryside. Leave Grasse on boulevard Georges-Clémenceau and turn left on to the D11, signposted Cabris. The road

March 1815 – Napoleon's Route

March 1 – 0500: Napoleon and around a thousand supporters land at **Golfe-Juan**. A plaque marks the spot today. The men set up camp but later march beside the sea to **Cannes** and rest briefly on the beach. They turn inland and walk through the night.

March 2 – 0500: rest stop at **GRASSE**. Lunch break at St-Vallier-de-Thiey. 1700: rest stop at Escragnolles.

They stop for the night at Séranon. Napoleon is invited by the Mayor of Grasse to spend the night in the Château de Brondet.

March 3 – 0700: the men move off again. At the small town of **Logis du Pin**: refreshments are offered (Napoleon is given a bowl of broth). Noon: Lunch at **CASTELLANE**. Napoleon is invited to eat and rest in the Sous-Préfect's office. 2000: stop for the night at Barrême. Napoleon spends the night at the home of Judge Tartanson.

March 4 – after an early start the group marches along a difficult mountain trail through the barren Pré-Alpes de Digne (now mainly the D20). The men pause in **DIGNE**. Napoleon lunches and rests at Hôtel de Petit-Paris. 1500: the group moves off again. Overnight stop beside the River Bléone at **Malijai**, where Napoleon spends the night at the château.

March 5 – 0600: move off. Napoleon continues on the left bank of the Durance. At Volonne: a rest stop. Braced for resistance, the men enter **SISTERON**, but are not challenged. They take a break there. Napoleon lunches at the Hôtel du Bras d'Or. 1500: the men continue the journey and march until 2200, when they arrive at Gap and set up camp. Napoleon spends the night at Hôtel Marchand.

On the Alpes de Haute-Provence route, a detour runs through Digne into the Vallée du Bès – see page 157).

climbs, with spectacular views, to the village of **CABRIS** ❷. Although it is possible to work back to the N85 on different roads, this takes time and the simplest route is to return on the same road.

Shortly after leaving Grasse, the N85 reaches one of its most spectacular points, the **Col du Pilon** (786m). A few kilometres further on, after **St-Vallier-de-Thiey** – a pleasant little hill town with a lofty bust of Napoleon (*see Grasse, Accommodation and food, page 181*) – the road climbs in great sweeps up to the **Pas de la Faye** (981m). All the way up, and down the other side, there are marvellous views. The next little town is **CASTELLANE** ❸.

Detour: The most popular excursion from Castellane is to the Grand Canyon on the River Verdon (*see page 168*). Less usual is this detour to the dramatic scenery of the Verdon lakes, a short distance upriver. Turn right from the N85 on to the D955 and climb up to the Col de Blache. There are good views from here. The road descends to the Barrage de Castillon (Castillon Dam) and actually runs along the top of the dam. Take the right towards Demandolx, pausing to admire the views of the **Lac de Castillon**✲ and **Lac de Chaudanne**✲. Take the D102 down to the shore of the lake and river. The N85 returns into Castellane. The detour distance is about 14km.

The N85 rises circuitously to **Col des Leques** and **Clue de Taulanne**, then falls away to follow the valley of the Asse between the rocky massifs, their slopes covered with acacia, Mediterranean pine and wild *garrigue*. Most of the road has been considerably improved since Napoleon passed this way, but even so some of the bends are hair-raising. After Barrême, the N85 does not follow Napoleon's route. Instead, take the N85 to Chaudon-Norante, the D2c to Chaudon and the D20 to **DIGNE** ❹, passing the spa baths and entering the town, as Napoleon did, on rue Mère de Dieu. Just before Digne, the **Alexandra David Neel Foundation**✲ is a Tibetan Centre created in the home of this remarkable traveller who during her long life (1868–1969) 'always chose the longest route and the slowest means of locomotion'.

From Digne to Sisteron the route is flatter and straighter, running first along the valley of the Bléone, and passing the **Château of Malijai**, where Napoleon spent the night. The road then meets the broad island-filled River Durance. The confluence of Bléone and Durance is also the meeting point of the N85 with the N96, which heads back down through lavender fields towards Aix-en-Provence. At this convergence of ways stands the village of **CHATEAU-ARNOUX** ❺. At l'Escale, the N85 today crosses to the right bank of the Durance, but to follow in Napoleon's footsteps continue on the left bank, on what is now the D4. Continue into **SISTERON** ❻.

Les Maures

Ratings

Beaches	●●●●●
Scenery	●●●●●
Children	●●●●
Restaurants	●●●●
Entertainment	●●●
Shopping	●●●
Sightseeing	●●●
Walking	●●●

With its sandy bays, high rocky cliffs and bijou resorts, as well as some less appealing recent developments, the Maures coast is varied. It's more totally devoted to tourism than the older towns further east. Few resorts along here are expensive or exclusive, yet along its whole length this shore is visually breathtaking. Most of the beaches are clean, sandy and accessible. Inland rise dry, intense hills, sparsely populated, darkly wooded with parasol pine and Mediterranean pine, holm oak and cork oak, ivy clinging to the bark. Grasshoppers, crickets and cicadas clatter among dense undergrowth of ferns, flowers and thistles. The Maures hills have country roads ideal for touring by car, and many paths for walking. They're not high, they are warm, wild, quiet and untouristy, and the atmosphere in their tiny vineyards and villages, cork oak plantations and fragrant scrubland is haunting and remote.

ⓘ Tourist office for Massif des Maures
Maison du Golfe de St-Tropez et du Pays de Maures, Carrefour de la Foux, Gassin; tel: 04 94 55 22 00; fax: 04 94 55 22 01; www.golfe-infos.com Local tourist offices in the region are generally open Mon–Sat 0900–1200, 1400–1900; some also open Sun morning.

Why Massif des Maures?

Maures, moors, were the Arabs of Spain, notorious for piratical raids on the Provençal coast. Together with other Muslim raiders from North Africa and Turkey, they were known as Saracens. In the 8th and 9th centuries, they established several settlements on the slopes of what is now called the Massif des Maures. Strange then that the name has nothing to do with them. It comes from the Provençal *maouro*, a dark, dense pinewood.

BORMES-LES-MIMOSAS✲✲

In the heights behind the coast at Le Lavandou is the flowery medieval village of Bormes. Its suffix was added in honour of the wonderful mimosas growing on the hills all around. The village has an

D957

Montmeyan Aups Bargemon Seillans Callian
D71 Montferrat Fayence
D557 D562
Sillans-la- Villecroze Ampus Callas
Cascade Salernes Figaniéres St-Paul-en-Forêt
Gros Bessillon D560 Flayosc Bagnols-en-Forêt D4
813 Cotignac Draguignan
E s t e
Lorgues Trans-en- Le Muy r e l
Carcès Provence
Le Val Taradeau
Cabasse Vidauban Roquebrune- Fréjus
A8 sur-Argens
E80 S Golfe de Fréjus
Flassans- Le Luc Le Cannet-des-Maures D25
sur-Issole St-Aygulf
Besse-sur-Issole D558 Col de Gratteloup
N97 Plan-de-la-Tour N98 Les Issambres
Garéoult Gonfaron
Carnoules La Garde Freinet M Ste-Maxime
A57 La Sauvette Golfe de St-Tropez
D43 Puget- 779 Grimaud Port Grimaud Cap de
Ville Collobrières Cogolin St-Tropez St-Tropez
Pierrefeu- La Môle La Croix- Gassin
D12 du-Var Valmer Ramatuelle
Bormes-les- Rayol-Canadel- Cavalaire- Cap Cartaya
La Crau Mimosas sur-Mer sur-Mer
Hyères D559
Carqueiranne La Londe- Le Lavandou Corniche des Maures
Hyères-Plage les-Maures Cap Bénat
Port d'Hyères Rade d'Hyères
Presqu'île
de Giens Ile du Levant
Giens

0   10 km

Place Gambetta; tel: 04 94 71 15 17; fax: 04 94 01 38 39. Boulevard de la Plage, La Favière; tel: 04 94 64 82 57; fax: 04 94 64 79 61; e-mail: mail@ bormeslesmimosas.com; www.bormeslesmimosas.com

abundance of oleander, too, and other colourful flora. Near the church a marked walk among flowers (signposted *Parcours Fleuri*) climbs up and round an old castle. The oldest part of the village, below the church, is a delicious tangle of lanes and alleys, archways, covered passageways and steep slopes. By contrast, down on the coast, Bormes also possesses a good stretch of beachfront at **La Favière** and a new marina, **Port de Bormes**.

There's a weekly Wed market on place St-François.

Corso (a mimosa procession) takes place every third Sun in Feb.

Accommodation and food in Bormes-les-Mimosas

L'Escoundudo €€ *2 ruelle du Moulin; tel/ fax: 04 94 71 15 53.* The Provençal name suggests a hidden treasure, and sure enough this wonderful little gem with its exquisite terrace is reached by climbing enticing lanes and alleys. You'll find good Provençal cooking – *bourride*, stuffed vegetables, delicious pastries – and quality local wines at modest prices.

La Cassole €€ *1 ruelle du Moulin; tel: 04 94 71 14 86.* Neighbour to l'Escoundudo, this delightful, convivial little restaurant offers excellent, classic Provençal cooking such as *bouillabaisse*, delicious salads, superb fish and imaginative meat dishes, all generously seasoned with herbs. Don't miss the chocolate and mint dessert.

Le Mirage €€€ *38 rue de la Vue des Iles; tel: 04 94 05 32 60; fax: 04 94 64 93 03.* The name of the road explains one of the great attractions at this hotel, the lovely view of the Lavandou bay and the Iles d'Or from the terrace. Everything else about the place is equally satisfying: the beautiful gardens, luxurious bedrooms, amiable but efficient service.

CAVALAIRE-SUR-MER✤

Cavalaire-sur-Mer Tourist Office *Maison de la Mer, square de Lattre-de-Tassigny; tel: 04 94 01 92 10; fax: 04 94 05 49 89; e-mail: ot-cavalaire@golfe-infos.com; www.golfe-infos.com/cavalaire*

Full- and half-day boat excursions are offered all year by Vedettes Iles d'Or; *tel: 04 94 64 08 04,* and Bâteaux Verts; *tel: 04 94 64 48 38.*

There is a Wed morning market in place de la Mairie.

15 Aug: Pilgrimage to Notre-Dame de la Queste, 2km east.

Early Sep: *Fête des Vendanges* (Grape Harvest Festival).

Right
Pizza van

Not a pretty place but refreshingly 'normal' compared with the charged atmosphere of nearby St-Tropez, Cavalaire caters to families, has decent facilities, budget-priced eateries and bars, useful shops, a busy marina and miles of (extremely crowded) sandy beach. It merges into neighbouring **La Croix Valmer** (*see page 196*) and the combined resort makes an excellent, less expensive base for touring the St-Tropez Peninsula and Corniche des Maures. There is a wide choice of enjoyable **boat excursions** to the **Iles d'Or** (*see page 138*) and along the coast.

LA GARDE FREINET✢✢✢

ⓘ La Garde Freinet Tourist Office *place Neuve; tel: 04 94 43 67 41 www.lagarde-freinet.com/index.html*

◐ Markets take place on Wed and Sun.

The main village on the Maures Massif, an atmospheric cluster of stone houses among the rocky hills, was once a stronghold of the Arab brigands who terrorised this coast in centuries past. A ruined fortress survives from those days. Though full of tourists today, La Garde Freinet keeps its rustic aspect, with crumbling façades, quiet backstreets and a community of locals (called Fraxinois) indifferent to the comings and goings of outsiders.

GRIMAUD✢✢

ⓘ Grimaud Tourist Office *boulevard des Aliziers; tel: 04 94 43 26 98; fax: 04 94 43 32 40; e-mail: bureau.du.tourisme.grimaud @wanadoo.fr; www.grimaud-provence.com*

◐ There is a Thu morning market in place Neuve.

Proud to have been selected as a 'Ville Fleurie' (a national scheme for pretty, flower-decked villages), Grimaud is an appealing and picturesque old village. It is overlooked by the imposing ruins of a castle standing on a high peak, which gives tremendous views over the dark blue St-Tropez bay speckled with white yachts. However, the village is a favourite outing for coach parties from the coast, which can detract from its charm.

Accommodation and food in Grimaud

Hostellerie du Coteau Fleurie €€€ *place des Pénitents; tel: 04 94 43 20 17; fax: 04 94 43 33 42.* In a village where tourism is steadily driving standards down and prices up, the long-established little Coteau Fleurie remains a haven of good Provençal cooking, comfortable accommodation of great character in a former medieval monastic church, and an exquisite setting on the edge of the village.

LE LAVANDOU✢

ⓘ Le Lavandou Tourist Office *quai Gabriel Péri (opposite ferry port); tel: 04 94 00 40 50; fax: 04 94 00 40 59; www.lelavandou.com*

Next page Yachts

Le Lavandou is a bigger, livelier resort town than most on this quiet coast, combining a modern waterfront development with a pedestrianised old centre and busy port. It's not smart or fashionable, but this family resort offers good facilities, quality entertainment and places to stay at affordable prices, plus a constant round of fêtes and festivals, and a choice of beaches of coarse golden sand. The main town beach can get horrendously crowded. There's precious little sightseeing to be done, and until a century ago the place was a tiny,

P Parking is difficult in town, and free car parks by the beach are often full.

☺ Ferries to Iles d'Or (or Iles d'Hyères): several daily, all year. Vedettes Iles d'Or, *15 quai Gabriel Péri; tel: 04 94 71 01 02; fax: 04 94 71 78 95.*

⚓ There are several local parades, *festins* and fêtes throughout the summer.

On the menu

Marrons glacés and *pigeonneau* (young pigeon) are local specialities. There's a also a Massif des Maures rosé wine.

unimportant fishing hamlet. Then some 19th-century artists, writers and musicians happened upon it, and it grew into a place for quiet holidays. For a day-trip, take one of the coastal boat excursions or catch a ferry from Le Lavandou to the offshore islands, the car-free **Iles d'Or**, also called Iles d'Hyères (*see page 138*).

Accommodation and food in Le Lavandou

The main beach is backed by snack-bars, ice-cream places and budget restaurants. At the far west end, a wooden walkway follows the beach and gives access to several good beach restaurants and bars.

Auberge de la Calanque €€€ and **Restaurant l'Algue Bleue €€** *62 avenue Général de Gaulle; tel: 04 94 71 05 96; fax: 04 94 71 20 12.* The poshest hotel in town, and one of the best restaurants; gaze across the harbour to the Iles d'Or.

Belle Vue €€ *Plage de St Clair; tel: 04 94 00 45 00; fax: 04 94 00 45 25.* This most appealing traditional Provençal house is aptly named, looking across the St-Clair beach (2km from town) to the blue bay and the islands. It's a straightforward and unpretentious family-run hotel and restaurant with a perfectly lovely, flowery garden. Hotel open Apr–Oct only. Restaurant open Jun–Sep only.

There is a weekly Thu morning market in avenue V Auriol.

Les Tamaris €€ *Plage de St-Clair; tel: 04 94 71 79 19; fax: 04 94 71 88 64.* St-Clair beach also provides the relatively quiet location for this decent, mid-range hotel and excellent fish restaurant.

PORT GRIMAUD***

ⓘ Tourist Information *By the car park close to the resort's main gate. Summer only. Tel: 04 94 56 02 01; www.grimaud-provence.com*

⊜ The resort can only be reached via a side turn off the N98. The whole resort is privately owned and can be entered only on foot through designated gates.

Ⓟ No cars are allowed within the resort (except residents). Parking is available in the car parks opposite the main entrance to the resort (expensive), or in the access road from the N98 (free).

ⓠ Coche d'Eau *From main square for 20-minute tours.*

Ferries to St-Tropez *run approximately every hour daily from 0915–2015, with fewer services in winter; tel: 04 94 96 51 00.*

There are markets on Thu and Sun mornings.

Set into the shore of the Golfe de St-Tropez, Port Grimaud is a modern, purpose-built marina resort which has proved a great success. The village was constructed and the canals dug in the late 1960s on a former swamp. Now it comprises nearly 3000 buildings and 7km of canals, with moorings for 3000 boats. Truth is though, the resort lacks all authenticity, and seems undecided between self-images of Provence or Venice. Not everyone likes its architecture, which imitates local traditional styles, but one appealing feature is that it's totally car-free, the original plan being that residents would go everywhere by boat! While that hasn't quite happened, boats are important here. Even though it's perfectly possible to see the whole of Port Grimaud on foot, the preferred way is on a *Coche d'Eau* (waterbus)***. Or you can do it yourself by hiring a small motorised punt. Despite the unhelpfulness of the residents (some rich and famous) and their local governing body, within its walls, the marina resort is always teeming. St-Tropez is under 10km away by road, just a few minutes by boat, and there's holiday accommodation adjacent to Port Grimaud to fit all budgets, including a campsite and hotel right on the resort's (pebbly) beach.

Accommodation and food in Port Grimaud

Hôtel Giraglia €€–€€€ *place de 14 juin; tel: 04 94 56 31 33; fax: 04 94 56 33 77.* Most of the tourists in Port Grimaud are staying on the good-quality campsites nearby, or have come across the bay from St-Tropez, but there is also accommodation at the resort itself, at this calm and civilised hotel facing on to the beach beside the marina, looking across the bay. The restaurant offers good food at moderate prices. Open 15 Apr–15 Oct only.

ROQUEBRUNE-SUR-ARGENS*

ⓘ Roquebrune-sur-Argens Tourist Office *I rue Jean Alcard/square J Moulin; tel: 04 94 45 72 70; fax: 04 94 45 38 04; www.ville-roquebrune-argens.fr*

Up the River Argens, some 11km from the sea, is Roquebrune. At its centre is a historic village with a 16th-century gateway and medieval streets, some of them arcaded. Modern districts have extended it, and the area has cottages and camps featured in package-holiday brochures, though there's little for the independent traveller. The village has an impressive location close to the Rocher de Roquebrune, a jagged, isolated massif rising next to the Maures hills. Its striking red

ⓘ Musée de Préhistoire et Histoire Locales €
rue de l'Hospice; tel: 04 94 45 75 51. Open 1000–1200, 1400–1800 (Jun–Sep closed Sun and Mon; Oct–May open Thu and Fri only).

◒ Markets on Tue and Fri in place Germain Olivier, and a big one on 8 Jun, the Foire de la St Médard.

sandstone crests soar above lower slopes covered with cork oak and pines. Once occupied by Saracens, the village was conquered in about the 11th century. Several houses in the village date from the 16th century (look especially along rue des Portiques), and there's a **Musée de Préhistoire et Histoire Locales**✢ (Museum of Local Prehistory and History) devoted to archaeological finds from the nearby Bouverie caves, an important site occupied from 30000–8000 BC by members of a culture unique to Provence.

For walkers who enjoy a challenge, there's a marked walk from Roquebrune to the summit of the Rocher de Roquebrune (372m). It takes about an hour each way.

ST AYGULF✢

ⓘ St-Aygulf Tourist Office *place Poste; tel: 04 94 81 22 09; fax: 04 94 81 23 04.*

ⓒ Chante Mer €€ *In place Ottaviani, Village Provençal, Les Issambres; tel: 04 94 96 93 23. This delightful little restaurant, 4km from St-Aygulf, is phenomenally good value, and offers excellent mouclade, fish soups, beef and morilles mushrooms.*

Of the string of touristy modern resorts along the Maures coast, the largest is St-Aygulf, not a pretty place. Beyond the eastern edge of town, there's a sandy beach on the edge of the Argens estuary, with half a dozen well-equipped campsites close by (in town, there are only small, pebbly bays). These include some of the Riviera's best sites – though you probably won't spot any film stars here! Nearby there are good viewpoints looking either across the sea or towards the Rocher de Roquebrune.

Accommodation and food in St-Aygulf

Le Catalogne €€ *avenue de la Corniche d'Azur; tel: 04 94 81 01 44; fax: 04 94 81 32 42; e-mail: hotel.catalogne@wanadoo.fr.* This sensible modern establishment offers acceptable and friendly accommodation about 100m from the beach. Open Easter–end Oct only.

Villa St-Elme €€€ *Les Issambres; tel: 04 94 49 52 52; fax: 04 94 49 63 18.* In an elegant pink mansion overlooking the sea at Les Issambres, this is a solid, even staid, gastronomic highspot of the region, offering delectable dishes such as lasagne of lobster *au pistou*, roast pigeon and fresh fish, prepared with skill.

STE-MAXIME-SUR-MER✢

ⓘ Ste-Maxime-sur-Mer Tourist Office
promenade Simon Lorière; tel: 04 94 55 75 55; fax: 04 94 55 75 56; e-mail: office@sainte-maxime.com; www.sainte-maxime.com

At this civilised, agreeable family resort, in reality little more than a village, gardens separate the hectic main road from a palm-lined promenade and sandy beach, enticing visitors with its parasols and waterside cafés. There's a lack of showiness, yet an air of prosperity, with smart yachts in the harbour and some good fish restaurants. The little waterside town stands at one tip of the Golfe de St-Tropez, a big blue bay fringed with sand, and looks straight across the water at St-

Ferries to St-Tropez leave approximately every hour daily from 0800–0100, with fewer services in winter; *tel: 04 94 96 51 00.*

Musée du Phonographie et de la Musique Mécanique € *Parc de St-Donat (between le Muy and Ste-Maxime); tel: 04 94 96 50 52. Open Easter–Oct Wed–Sun 1000–1200, 1500–1800.*

Musée des Traditions (Museum of Local Traditions) € *In Tour Carrée des Dames, facing port; tel: 04 94 96 70 30. Open daily except Tue Apr–Jun 1000–1200, 1500–1830; Jul–Sep 1000–1200, 1600–1900; Oct–Mar 1500–1800.*

Hôtel de la Poste €€–€€€ *7 boulevard F Mistral; tel: 04 94 96 18 33.* Modern, centrally located, this well-equipped little hotel is bright and comfortable, with attractive rooms, and a pool, restaurant and other facilities. *Open May–Oct only.*

Hostellerie La Croisette €€ *2 boulevard des Romarins; tel: 04 94 96 17 75; fax: 04 94 96 52 40.* Pleasant, modernised hotel with some Provençal decor, attractive garden and sea views. *Open Mar–Oct only.*

Tropez. One difference between this side of the bay and the other is that the *Mistral* can hardly be felt here, even when it's lashing through St-Tropez. The central area of old Ste-Maxime, pedestrianised in summer, provides some pleasant strolling, and there's a little **Musée des Traditions***, all about local history and culture, housed in a 16th-century watchtower. An enjoyable excursion is into the interior up the D25 to the Parc de St-Donat leisure park, where the main attraction is the quite extraordinary **Musée du Phonographie et de la Musique Mécanique**** (Museum of Sound Recording and Mechanical Music). Here you'll find weird and wonderful musical instrument ideas whose time has passed or never made it at all, as well as the first recording machines (1878) and other astonishing devices.

Accommodation and food in Ste-Maxime-sur-Mer

Hostellerie de la Belle Aurore €€–€€€ *4 boulevard Jean-Moulin; tel: 04 94 96 02 45; fax: 04 94 96 63 87; e-mail: info@belleaurore.com.* The smartest hotel in town; rather pricey but worth it, with the best restaurant, where the accomplished, ambitious cooking (sometimes criticised by the more serious gourmets) represents excellent value.

Hôtel Calidianus €€€ *boulevard Jean-Moulin; tel: 04 94 96 23 21; fax: 04 94 49 12 10.* Set back from the sea west of town, this hotel offers comfortable modern accommodation, with spacious rooms (some with terrace) and a pool, but no restaurant.

Suggested tour

Total distance: 125 km, and a detour of 85km.

Time: 1 day, or 2 if you decide to see the sights and do the detour.

Links: At Fréjus the route connects with the Massif de l'Esterel (*see page 204*). At Le Lavandou it links (by ferry) with Hyères and the Iles d'Or (*see page 138*). For St-Tropez, on the Maures coast, see the St-Tropez Peninsula (*see page 196*).

Route: From **Fréjus** (*see page 206*), take the N98 across the Argens river (passing **Aquatica** leisure park) to the Massif des Maures coast road, which straight away reaches **ST-AYGULF** ❶. After this resort, the coast becomes rocky, but lined with villas. In places the coast in cut by rocky *calanques*, with lovely wooded hills rising inland. You pass through the expanding tourist resort of **Les Issambres** and a succession of other coastal developments, more or less pleasant. The road follows the shore out to Cap des Sardinaux, after which comes the long sandy beach (Plage de la Nartelle) east of busier **STE-MAXIME** ❷. There can be a lot of traffic after this point, and the

There is a Fri morning market in place Mermoz, Ste-Maxime-sur-Mer. There's also a morning fish market (quai des Plaisanciers) and a touristy market most days in the pedestrian zone (summer only).

influence of St Tropez will be felt. The road continues along the edge of the Golfe de St-Tropez, reaching a turn-off for **PORT GRIMAUD ❸**.

Detour: From Port Grimaud cross over the main road to take the smaller route to **GRIMAUD ❹**. The D558 winds up through scenic hills, densely wooded in places, with some good views, to **LA GARDE FREINET ❺**. Return on the same road, or, to explore the heartland of the Maures Massif, continue on the D558 for 7km to the turn on the left (D75). After about 13km is the delightful, rustic **Village des Tortues** (*tel: 04 94 78 26 41; open 0900–1900*), a favourite children's outing. Properly called the Centre de Repeuplement des Tortues des Maures, it protects and conserves the only French variety of tortoise, Hermann's Tortoise, native to the Massif des Maures but under threat from environmental changes. Continue through the vines and across the *autoroute* to take a break at **Gonfaron**, a pleasant village on the main road, before turning back on the D39 for a scenic drive on the high, winding, narrow road to **Collobrières**, a pretty, rustic old village among cork oak and vineyards in the middle of the Maures. From here take the steep, twisting and narrow D14 through exquisite *garrigue* and forest 20km back to Grimaud.

Beyond Port Grimaud, follow the N98 (direction St-Tropez) to a large giratory called Carrefour de la Foux where most traffic is going to **St-Tropez** (*see page 198*) or along the N98 to **Hyères** (*see page 139*). Instead, keep your eyes open for the D559 exit to **La Croix Valmer** (*see page 196*). On the other side of the Cap sprawls **CAVALAIRE-SUR-MER ❻**. From Cavalaire, the high jutting hills of the **Corniche des Maures**, with woods of parasol pine and chestnut and cork oak, are a delight, though they're gradually getting covered in housing estates. Where the slopes plunge into the blue sea, there's a string of small modern resorts with pebble-and-sand beaches, holiday flats, small beachside hotels and campsites. The best of them are at **Le Rayol** (with beautiful gardens at the Domaine du Rayol; *tel: 04 94 05 32 50*) and the more down-market **Cavalière**, Mediterranean pine casting islands of shade at the back of its popular beach. Between these two, as the road passes over rocky Pointe de Layet, hundreds of cars are passed: these belong to naturists who come to this attractive wooded headland to walk on the paths, or sunbathe or swim on the rocky coves and secluded beaches. Nearby, a monument beside the road at the headland of Pramousquier recalls that the Allied invasion of 14 August, 1944, included French North African volunteers. **Aiguebelle** beach is a pleasant quiet little resort in a pretty bay, with villas in the steep woods behind. The corniche ends at **LE LAVANDOU ❼**. The D559 works its way through the centre of the resort town, turning away from the waterfront developments of **Plage de la Favière** beach and the marina **Port de Bormes**. Take the turn on the right (D41) for **BORMES-LES-MIMOSAS ❽**. Staying on this little road, continue through Bormes and uphill through wooded country to the N98 again.

Coastal paths

A string of coastal paths edges along the Maures, though they do not necessarily link up (only half the coastline is covered). Waymarked on rough wooden boards which give expected journey times, they vary from 1km to over 20km in length. They were originally created by Napoleon to allow Customs officers to intercept smugglers, and on most the walking is relatively easy. Walkers are asked to respect the fragile coastal environment and beware of fire.

You might want to head 5km west to see the **Jardin des Oiseaux Tropicaux (Tropical Bird Garden)** just off the road near la Londe (*summer 0930–1930, winter 1400–1800; tel: 04 94 35 02 15*), but our route now turns back east on the N98, climbing up and over Col de Gratteloup (199m). Just past the *col* (pass), there's a 3-hectare **Arboretum**. As you head back to St-Tropez bay on this road, the countryside – at first wooded, then more open – is quiet, beautiful and unpeopled. Continue all the way to **Cogolin**, past its coastal development **Port Cogolin**, and on to Port Grimaud, Ste-Maxime and back to Fréjus.

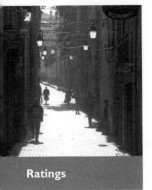

The St-Tropez Peninsula

Ratings

Beaches	●●●●●
Children	●●●●○
Entertainment	●●●●○
Restaurants	●●●●○
Shopping	●●●●○
Walking	●●●●○
Scenery	●●●○○
Sightseeing	●●●○○

St-Tropez comes as a surprise. It's neither a slick resort for the super-rich, nor yet has it been cheapened by popularity. True, there are long traffic queues just to get into the place, palatial yachts in the harbour, a pounding nightlife, chic boutiques and thousands of self-conscious visitors wandering about, but St-Tropez somehow retains an unpretentious charm in spite of its fame. It's beautiful. It has style. It has flair. What it doesn't have are beaches – for those you must head out of town on to the glorious sand-fringed Cap de St-Tropez, which has among the best on the Riviera, though you may have to pay to use some of them. Tour the hilly interior of the rest of St-Tropez Peninsula to discover – another surprise – that just minutes away from this crowded, intense little film-set are ordinary Provençal villages, deliciously picturesque, with wonderful views.

LA CROIX VALMER❖

ℹ️ **Tourist Office**
esplanade de la Gare;
tel: 04 94 55 12 12; fax: 04 94 55 12 10.

📞 There are hydrofoils, boat excursions and ferries to Iles d'Or. A ticket desk for these excursions is by the beach. *Tel: 04 94 79 53 06.*

🛒 There is a Sun morning market.

This pleasant little town near the coast gives its name to one of the Côtes de Provence appellation wines. Below the town is the Plage de Débarquement, a strip of beach where on 15 August, 1944, the American army invaded occupied France. Today it's part of a long, popular sandy beach resort area which curves gently around Baie de Cavalaire from Cavalaire-sur-Mer (*see page 188*) to Plage de Gigaro. The dark hills of the Massif des Maures rise behind.

Accommodation and food in La Croix Valmer

Souleias €€€ *plage de Gigaro; tel: 04 94 55 10 55; fax: 04 94 54 36 23; e-mail: infos@hotel-souleias.com.* A veritable institution of gastronomy, style and luxury, with highly accomplished and imaginative cooking in the restaurant; the hotel rooms are rather sombre but faultlessly equipped and with views of the gardens or the sea.

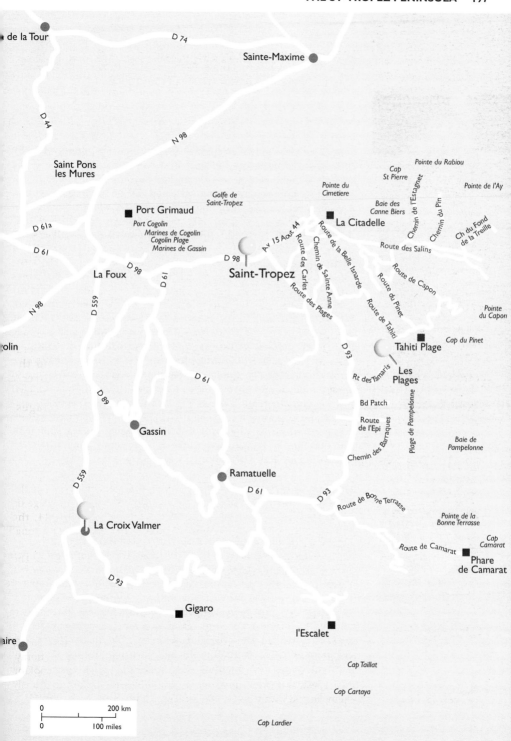

de la Tour

D 74

Sainte-Maxime

D 44

N 98

Saint Pons
les Mures

Golfe de
Saint-Tropez

Pointe du Rabiou

Cap
St Pierre

Pointe de l'Ay

Port Grimaud

Port Cogolin

Marines de Cogolin
Cogolin Plage
Marines de Gassin

D 61a

D 61

La Foux

D 98

D 91

D 98

D 559

N 98

Saint-Tropez

Av 15 Août 44

Route des Carles

Chemin de Sainte Anne

Route des Plages

Pointe du
Cimetiere

Baie des
Canne Biers

La Citadelle

Route de la Belle Isnarde

Route des Salins

Chemin de l'Estagnet

Chemin du Pin

Ch du Fond
de la Treille

Route de Capon

Route du Pinet

Route de Tahiti

Pointe
du Capon

Tahiti Plage

Cap du Pinet

olin

D 61

D 93

Les
Plages

Rt des Tamaris

Bd Patch

Route
de l'Epi

Chemin des Barraques

Plage de Pampelonne

Baie de
Pampelonne

D 89

Gassin

D 559

Ramatuelle

D 61

D 93

Route de Bonne Terrasse

Pointe de la
Bonne Terrasse

La Croix Valmer

Route de Camarat

Cap
Camarat

Phare
de Camarat

D 93

Gigaro

l'Escalet

aire

Cap Taillat

Cap Cartaya

0   200 km

0   100 miles

Cap Lardier

Les Moulins des Paillas €€€ *plage de Gigaro; tel: 04 94 79 71 11; fax: 04 94 54 37 05*. Wonderful, amply equipped place to stay, with attractive rooms overlooking a private section of the Gigaro beach.

ST-TROPEZ***

ℹ *Quai Jean-Jaurès (main part of harbourfront); tel: 04 94 97 45 21; fax: 04 94 97 82 66; e-mail: tourism@saint-tropez.st; www.saint-tropez.st*

🚗 Jams and queues on the D98A, the only main road into town, can be frustrating. Sometimes the road is closed and no more vehicles are allowed into St-Tropez. The D98A loops round place des Lices and leads back out of town again. In the old centre of town, most roads are one-way. This part of town is pedestrianised during the summer.

An ideal alternative is to park at Ste-Maxime or Port Grimaud and catch the passenger ferry from there – it's faster than driving, more enjoyable, and brings you to the quays at the heart of St-Tropez.

🅿 The town centre is difficult. Use the big car park at the entrance to the town.

St-Trop' (as it's known to *aficionados*) is still a nice, pretty, friendly little town with a busy port and attractive houses. However, if the surging harbourfront crowds during the daytime don't make it clear that this is no ordinary fishing port, wait till the evening, when bars and clubs belt out dance rhythms, champagne dinner parties are held on board the gigantic luxury yachts, and sauntering tourists parade designer clothes. Nightlife – discos, floorshows, bars – continues until dawn, and doesn't get into its swing until long after midnight. Day or night, the magic of St Trop' exerts a powerful pull. What's the attraction? Most of it is image and hype. If all you want are pretty villages, there are others just as picturesque.

If you want to bump into film stars, be assured that they do not normally hang around the harbour with the tourists. Yet the sheer party atmosphere, the sense that this is a *paparazzi* capital, together with its manicured backstreets and coloured shutters and façades, make St-Trop' a delight, a visual treat and a brush with the highlife. Stroll the **harbour***, lined with boutiques and bars. The centre of things is the statue of the 18th-century Bailli (judge) de Suffren. At one end of the quay, **L'Annonciade Musée de St-Tropez***, in a bright and airy former 16th-century chapel, displays an excellent art collection with works by many Impressionists and Fauvists and some line drawings by Picasso. The works on view amply demonstrate the fascination St-Tropez held for many modern painters, notably the key figure Paul Signac (*see Who Invented St-Tropez?*). Down a side turn nearby is **La Maison des Papillons*** (Butterfly Museum), where 25 000 (dead) butterflies are displayed. At the other end of the quay stand Tour Vieille, Tour Suffren and Tour de Portalet, remnants of old fortifications, guarding the **Môle** (jetty) **Jean Réveille*** – walk to the end for a stunning view of the town and its waterfront.

The walk along the shore leads into the little **La Ponche*** former fishermen's quarter, protected by Porche de la Ponche. Tour Jarlier, close by, is another part of the old defences against pirates and raiders. On a hilltop rising at the east end of town, the imposing **Citadelle*** is a large, attractively unkempt area of pines and oleander within 16th- to 17th-century defences, giving wonderful views over town and sea. Inside its handsome hexagonal fortress, the **Musée Naval*** tells the story of St-Tropez through its long maritime history. By far the most interesting and important room is devoted to the Allied invasion of 16 August, 1944. Explore away from the harbour, too, in the little squares and narrow paved streets of the **Vieille Ville (Old Quarter)***,

Right
Hôtel de Ville, St-Tropez

which lead to **Place des Lices****, the perfect French town square with *boules*-players under leafy plane trees.

For tours of the town on foot or by boat, consult the tourist office. On the quayside, check for boat excursions such as the Villas des Stars, which points out millionaire homes from the water, or call Transport Maritime MMG; *tel: 04 94 96 51 00 (www.nova.fr/mmg)*, or Transport Maritime Vasse; *tel: 04 94 54 40 61.*

L'Annonciade Musée de St-Tropez € *place Georges Grammont; tel: 04 94 97 04 01; fax: 04 94 97 87 24. Open Jun–Sep 1000– 1200, 1400–1800; Oct–May 1000–1200, 1500–1900. Closed Tue, all of Nov, and holidays.*

La Maison des Papillons (Butterfly Museum) € *9 rue Etienne Berny; tel: 04 94 97 63 45. Open Apr–Sep 1000–1200, 1400–1900; Oct–Mar 1500–1800. Closed Tue.*

Musée Naval *In the Citadel; tel: 04 94 97 49 53. Open 16 Jun–Oct 1000–1800; Dec–15 Jun 1000–1700. Closed Tue and all Nov.*

On the menu

Tarte Tropézienne is a sweet, biscuity tart served in slices from *pâtissiers* or sometimes as dessert in restaurants.

Tue market and a larger summer market on Sat on place des Lices. A fish market takes place every morning, except Mon in winter on place aux Herbes.

The two annual *Bravades* are colourful, picturesque festivals, one honouring the saint after whom the town is named, the other celebrating the defence of the town against a Spanish attack on 15 June, 1637.

16–18 May: *Bravade*
Around 15 Jun: *Bravade*
29 Jun: Fishermen's festival
Jul–Aug: music festival.

Accommodation and food in St-Tropez

Hôtel Sube €€€ *quai Suffren; tel: 04 94 97 30 04; fax: 04 94 54 89 08.* This characterful hotel with old-fashioned service has the very best quayside position by the Suffren statue. Décor is on a nautical theme. The first-floor bar with old wooden counter and deep armchairs has a balcony overlooking the harbour.

Touristy restaurants and brasseries cluster around the port. Famous but overpriced brasseries include Bar Tea Room **Senequier €€€** (*tel: 04 94 97 00 90*), next to the tourist office (Patissier-Chocolatier Senequier, next door, is one of the best in town). In the La Ponche area of the harbour, there are places with more local character beside the sea. Place des Lices is the 'ordinary' end of St-Tropez, with some less expensive restaurants, though **Brasserie La Renaissance €€€** (*tel: 04 94 54 83 78*) and **Le Café des Arts €€€** (*tel: 04 94 97 44 69*) on the north side of the square are classy and fashionable.

The 'big five' hotel-restaurants at St-Tropez, offering the highest standard of luxury and haute-cuisine, with rooms costing around 2000–3000F per night are:

Hôtel Byblos, Restaurant Les Arcades and **Relais des Caves** *avenue Paul Signac; tel: 04 94 56 68 00; fax: 04 94 56 68 01.*

Wine-tasting

Ask the tourist office about wine-tasting at the Peninsula's vineyards and *caves*. They have a leaflet, and a map showing wine-tasting locations. You can taste and buy local wines in St-Tropez at SCAV du Golfe de St-Tropez, *avenue Paul Roussel; tel: 04 94 97 01 60; fax: 04 94 97 70 24.*

Domaine de l'Astragale *route de Gassin; tel: 04 94 97 48 98; fax: 04 94 97 16 01.*

Résidence de la Pinède *Plage de la Bouillabaisse; tel: 04 94 55 91 00; fax: 04 94 97 73 64.*

Bastide de St-Tropez *route de Carles; tel: 04 94 55 82 55; fax: 04 94 97 21 71; www.bastide-saint-tropez.com*

Château de la Messardière *route de Tahiti; tel: 04 94 56 76 00; fax: 04 94 56 76 01; www.messardiere.com*

Beaches of St-Tropez Peninsula (Les Plages)

Clockwise round the Peninsula. Access to beaches is via the D93 except where stated.

Bouillabaisse – beside the D98A traffic, 1km west of St-Tropez. Faces across St-Tropez gulf.

Graniers and **Salins** – reached from St-Tropez, small bays of gritty sand.

Tahiti and **Pampelonne** – north and south parts of Pampelonne Bay, east side of the Peninsula. Wide strip of fine-to-grainy golden sand taken up in places with beach bars, lounger rentals, jetskis, etc. Beware broken glass on the sand near bars.

Below
Vieux Port, St-Tropez

L'Escalet – south side of the Peninsula, well off the road, but still attracts a crowd. Pleasant little beach of grainy sand with rocks.

La Douane and Gigaro – southwest corner of the Peninsula facing across Cavalaire Bay, adjacent to the protected area of the wild *garrigue*-covered Lardier headland. Quiet, relaxed resort area with gravelly sand and rocks.

Débarquement/Cavalaire/La Croix Valmer – big popular family beach off the D559 with good facilities and golden sand.

Suggested tour

Total distance: 30km, and a detour of 25km.

Time: An unhurried 3–4-hour trip, with only about an hour's driving.

Links: The route can be connected with Les Maures (*see page 186*).

Route: From ST-TROPEZ ❶, take the D98A (direction Grimaud) for 3km to the D61 junction on the left. Turn here and take the fork which climbs up to Gassin, a little village utterly picturesque, on a peak in the heart of the St-Tropez Peninsula's extraordinary beauty. Place de Barri is its big, high square full of café tables with glorious views over the rolling wooded hills and the azure sea beyond. Take the road which climbs to Col de Paillas, and perhaps also take the path up to the Moulins de Paillas to see these three ruined olive oil mills, before descending into Ramatuelle, a small picture-postcard Provençal town surrounded by its vineyards and woods. Almost everything here was rebuilt in 1620, the older village – occupied by Saracens for a time – having been destroyed during the religious wars. Descend on the D61 to the D93.

Detour: Take the D93 along a winding, attractive route into LA CROIX VALMER ❷. Continue from the town down to the main beach area on Cavalaire bay (signposted Plage de Débarquement). If you prefer a wilder, less manicured beach, take the coast road through pinewoods to the dunes of Plage de Gigaro.

Take the D93 back to St-Tropez. Narrow roads or tracks on the right along this road lead to the Pampelonne Bay beaches.

Getting out of the car: The St-Tropez Peninsula *Sentier Littoral* (coastal footpath) is part of the 19th-century *Chemin des Douaniers* (Customs Officers' Way). The path, waymarked with yellow signs, runs round the coast from Gigaro to St-Tropez, and only serious walkers should attempt the whole 35-km route, taking note that the old path has collapsed in places. Several sections are fairly easy and worth attempting, though you should have a head for heights. Try Plage de Gigaro to Cap Taillat (3 hours), Plage de l'Escalet to Cap Camarat (1½ hours), and St-Tropez to Plage de Tahiti (3 hours).

Who Invented St-Tropez?

'Sex kitten' Brigitte Bardot – now a venerable campaigner for animal rights – and her director-husband Roger Vadim drew the world's eyes towards St-Tropez in the 1950s, and helped give this part of the French Mediterranean a wilder, less formal, more bohemian glamour. Today it's synonymous with exoticism and extravagance, a place in the mind – a symbol – more than a real place, and the name of this little fishing port has become known all over the world. However, Bardot's St-Tropez was already a haunt of the film world, having been frequented by unconventional but successful pre-War writers and artists. Colette (1873–1954), for example, was a fan of the place. It had become known in such circles through artists such as post-Impressionist Paul Signac (1863–1935), who, enthralled by St-Tropez, came to live here in 1892. The writer Guy de Maupassant (1850–93) had chanced upon it just before and praised it among friends.

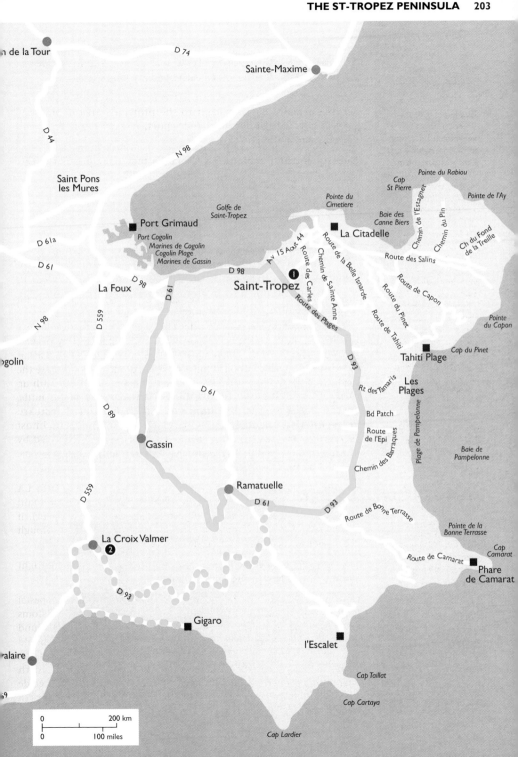

n de la Tour

D 74

Sainte-Maxime

D 44

N 98

Saint Pons
les Mures

Golfe de
Saint-Tropez

Pointe du Rabiou

Cap
St Pierre

Pointe du
Cimetiere

Pointe de l'Ay

Port Grimaud

Baie des
Canne Biers

Chemin de l'Estagnet

Chemin du Pin

Ch du Fond
de la Treille

D 61a

Port Cogolin
Marines de Cogolin
Cogolin Plage
Marines de Gassin

La Citadelle

Route des Salins

D 61

D 98

D 98

D 161

Ay 15 Aot 44

Route des Carles

Route des Plages

Chemin de Sainte Anne

Route de la Belle Isnarde

Route du Pinet

Route de Capon

La Foux

D 98

Saint-Tropez

Route de Tahiti

Pointe
du Capon

N 98

D 559

D 93

Tahiti Plage

Cap du Pinet

ogolin

Les
Plages

D 61

Rt des Tamaris

Bd Patch

Route
de l'Epi

Chemin des Barraques

Plage de Pampelonne

Baie de
Pampelonne

D 89

Gassin

Ramatuelle

D 61

D 93

Route de Bonne Terrasse

Pointe de la
Bonne Terrasse

D 559

Route de Camarat

Cap
Camarat

La Croix Valmer

Phare
de Camarat

D 93

Gigaro

l'Escalet

alaire

Cap Taillat

Cap Cartaya

0   200 km

0   100 miles

Cap Lardier

Esterel

Ratings

Children	●●●●●
Scenery	●●●●●
Beaches	●●●●○
Restaurants	●●●●○
Entertainment	●●●○○
History	●●●○○
Roman remains	●●●○○
Shopping	●●●○○

Victorian aristocrats never wintered here. The Esterel coast west of Cannes has only been developed since the growth of mass tourism in the 1960s. Its sandy bays, soaring red cliffs and bijou resorts almost guarantee satisfaction. The small rocky hill range called the Massif de L'Esterel reaches from the Argens river plain nearly to the suburbs of Cannes. Unlike the softer, more rustic Maures hills across the Argens, the Esterel is wild and rugged, with dense forest and a spectacular coastline. The easy way to see the Massif de l'Esterel is to drive from Fréjus to Cannes on the main inland road, N7, which passes across the hills. The massif is bordered on the north by the A8 *autoroute*, which lies like a frontier between the coastal region and the rural heartland of Provence. But roads give only a tantalising hint of this untamed, secretive little region, crisscrossed with footpaths.

CORNICHE DE L'ESTEREL✦✦✦

🛈 **Théoule-sur-Mer Tourist Office** /–2 *avenue de la Corniche d'Or; tel: 04 93 49 28 28; fax: 04 93 19 00 04; e-mail: ot@theoule-sur-mer.org; www.theoule-sur-mer.org*

WARNING: there is no camping in the Esterel Massif, and no driving on fire roads. For the latest Esterel fire risk information, *tel: 04 94 47 35 45.*

The Esterel meets the sea in great style, its jagged, jumbled red crests of rock plunging to the shore. This stretch of coast is very beautiful, though some of its modern resorts don't do it justice. These little developments have small beaches, beachside bars, and on the hillside behind, hundreds of villas. Also along here are many relatively inexpensive places to stay. **Théoule-sur-Mer** is small, low-budget and unchic but has some reasonable hotels and is located in a *calanque* backed by pine-covered hills. It has a narrow sandy beach with a couple of well-placed bars. **La Galère**, soon after, is an uninspiring development with villas on the cliffs but in a lovely location with magnificent views. **Miramar** is a big hillside estate of identical villas facing one of the few stony beaches along this stretch. **Le Trayas** is an unassuming development on a bay, where the Esterel railway line cuts through the rock behind the resort. Although there are other headlands and cliffs, the 8km between Le Trayas and Anthéor is

ⓘ Agay Tourist Office *place Charles Gianetti, boulevard de la Plage; tel: 04 94 82 01 85; fax: 04 94 82 74 20.*

ⓜ Musée-aquarium des Roches Rouges € *1387 avenue du Gratadis, Agay; tel: 04 94 82 77 94. Open Jul–Aug 1100–2000 daily; rest of year Mon–Fri 1400–1800, Sat, Sun and holidays 1100–1900.*

special – a wilder clifftop, almost no development, red rock, blue sea and wonderful views. The road passes dramatically between **Pic du Cap Roux** (453m) and **Point du Cap Roux** – *roux* meaning red, or russet. **Anthéor** is little more than a small bay beneath a railway viaduct, though, viaduct apart, it's an attractive setting. The corniche road follows the edge of a deep, protected bay with Pointe de Baumette at one side and Cap du Dramont at the other. Hidden at its end, **Agay** is a small seaside resort with beaches and a ribbon of villas along the corniche, and some delightful coves overlooked by the Esterel's strange red-tinted rockface. It was once a Greek and Roman anchorage. There's a popular **Musée-aquarium** at the back of the town. **Boat excursions** (*tel: 04 94 95 17 46*) from Agay include tours of the Calanques, trips to St-Tropez and to the offshore Iles de Lérins.

Accommodation and food in the Corniche l'Esterel

Auberge d'Anthéor €€ *On the N98 at Anthéor; tel: 04 94 44 83 38; fax: 04 94 44 84 20.* This modern little hotel has a beautiful clifftop setting. There's a pool, and a nearby harbour, but no beach.

Miramar Beach Hotel et Restaurant l'Etoile des Mers €€€ *47 avenue de Miramar; tel: 04 93 75 05 05; fax: 04 93 75 44 83; e-mail: reception@mbhriviera.com.* The most elegant place either to stay or to eat on this beautiful coastline, with a private beach.

FREJUS❖❖

ℹ *325 rue Jean-Jaurès; tel: 04 94 51 83 83; fax: 04 94 51 00 26; e-mail: frejus.tourisme@wanadoo.fr*

Ⓟ Easy at the beach, with parking along the length of the coast road. Difficult in the town centre, where it's best to use the main car parks indicated along the ring road.

🏛 Cathédrale *place Formigé. Open daily 0900–1200, 1600–1800.*

Cloisters and Baptistery € *rue de Fleury; tel: 04 94 51 26 30. Open Apr–Sep daily 0900–1900; Oct–Mar Tue–Sun 0900–1200, 1400–1700. Closed holidays.*

Arènes (amphitheatre) *rue H Vadon. Open 0900–1200, 1400–1830 (1630 Oct–Mar). Closed Tue.*

Parc Zoologique (zoo) €€ *Le Capitou (near autoroute A8 junction 38); tel: 04 94 40 70 65. Open May–Sep 0930–1830; rest of year 1000–1700.*

Aquatica €€ *On the N98 (St-Tropez direction); tel: 04 94 51 82 51. Open Jun–15 Sep 1000–1800 (later in Jul–Aug).*

On the western edge of the Esterel Massif, looking across at the neighbouring Massif des Maures (*see page 186*), this ancient town encompasses a lively and authentic inland old quarter and town centre and a somewhat characterless modern coastal development of cafés and bars beside a wide beach of rather gritty pale sand. **Fréjus-Port**❖ is a new and developing marina, vibrant and appealing in season. Fréjus lacks any trace of Riviera glamour, and aims mainly for middle-income family holiday-makers, but has a congenial atmosphere and leisurely squares such as place de la Liberté with its shaded tables. Sightseeing includes a strange and attractive medieval **cathédrale**❖❖ at the heart of town, part of a small 'Cité Episcopale' (Cathedral Close) including charming **cloisters**❖❖ and a **baptistery**❖❖ dating to the 5th century, one of the oldest in France.

Close by are impressive Roman ruins, including the Roman **amphitheatre**❖❖, the city gates, a few pillars and the arches of an aqueduct, traces of the theatre, remnants of a *praetorium* (army base) and the fortified quay. In the town centre, walk along rue Siéyes to see some fine 17th- and 18th-century mansions. Out of town, leave Fréjus on the N7 in the direction of Le Muy, and soon after leaving the edge of town turn right on the D4 to see the astounding African **Mosque**❖, a perfect replica of a red mosque in Mali, and a bizarre legacy of the presence in the 1920s of African troops in the naval base at Fréjus. There's a **Parc Zoologique**❖ nearby. Among several other family attractions around town, **Aquatica**❖❖, on the way to St-Aygulf, is a popular waterpark with waterslides, water toboggans and a big wave pool.

The first air crossing of the Mediterranean took off from Fréjus on 23 September, 1913. The pilot was Roland Garros and the flight to North Africa took over eight hours.

Accommodation and food in Fréjus

L'Aréna €€ *139 rue du Général de Gaulle; tel: 04 94 17 09 40; fax: 04 94 52 01 52; e-mail: a.r.e.n.a.@wanadoo.fr.* Not particularly well placed on one of the avenues taking traffic around the town centre, this little hotel and restaurant is still one of the most appealing in the area. The hotel has an interior patio, pool and garden, and pleasant comfortable rooms. Everything is in classic Provençal style. The restaurant serves elegant, ambitious cuisine that's winning a reputation locally.

Les Potiers €€ *135 rue des Potiers; tel: 04 94 51 33 74.* For those who like a classic, tasty and skilful set meal without fuss, at a really affordable price, this small restaurant in a quiet traffic-free backstreet is a great find – but you'll have to book.

Right
Roman amphitheatre, Fréjus

Rise and fall of a Roman city

Forum Julii, a small trading post on the new *Via Aurelia*, came into being in 49 BC. With an excellent harbour, it developed gradually into a fortified naval base, and also became a retirement town for legionnaires, who were given a pension and a plot of land to build on. By the 1st century AD, Fréjus had become a substantial city of over 40 000 inhabitants, with a theatre, arena, baths and fine buildings. The port was enlarged and had fortified quays. Canals linked the town harbour with the sea. The final touch was a large wall to provide shelter from the *Mistral*. In the 2nd century, the Roman navy, for military considerations, stopped using Fréjus, and in the 3rd century the harbour began silting up. Full Roman withdrawal in the 4th and 5th centuries saw the decline of the city, which Saracen raiders all but destroyed in the 10th century. The medieval town grew amongst its ruins.

MANDELIEU/LA NAPOULE*

ⓘ Tourist Offices *340 rue Jean Monnet; tel: 04 93 93 64 65; fax: 04 93 93 64 66; e-mail: ota@ ot-mandelieu.fr; www.ot-mandelieu.fr*

Summer annexes
274 boulevard H Clews; tel: 04 93 49 95 31.

Autoroute exit; tel: 04 92 97 99 27.

ⓘ Château-Musée €
Tel: 04 93 49 22 93. Open Mar–Oct. One-hour guided tours only, at 1500 and 1600. Jul–Aug additional tour at 1700.

Mandelieu is the inland part of this *commune*, given over to villa rentals and budget holidays, and is capital of the Tanneron mimosa country just north. La Napoule is its large, busy resort facing Cannes across the Golfe de Napoule. This is no new creation, though. La Napoule has been here since ancient times and preserves two towers and a gateway from its medieval coastal fortification known as the **Château-Musée*** (restored by the eccentric Henry Clews, an American sculptor, whose work is on display inside, and his wife Marie). It also has a lovely marina filled with craft big and small, including some grandiose yachts. There's a casino, plenty of little restaurants, some green and shady public gardens and pleasant seafront shopping streets shaded by parasol pine.

Accommodation and food in La Napoule

L'Oasis €€€ *rue J H Carle; tel: 04 93 49 95 52; fax: 04 93 49 64 13.* High-quality fine dining is offered here on a shady, flowery terrace in La Napoule, probably the best restaurant in the Esterel, with polished service and stylish cooking. The acclaimed chef, Stéphane Raimbault, has a leaning to marry flavours, and combine the Provençal with other influences, as in the squid ravioli with ratatouille, or clam daurade risotto.

L'Armorial €€ *boulevard Clews; tel: 04 93 49 91 80; fax: 04 93 93 28 50.* Here you can enjoy classic, traditional French dining right on the La Napoule seafront avenue. The menu is mainly freshly caught fish, and you can sample *bouillabaisse* and *bourride*, as well as other dishes such as capon stuffed with crab. Wines, too, have a strong local emphasis (lots of half bottles).

ST-RAPHAËL✥✥

ℹ️ **St-Raphaël Tourist Office** *rue W Rousseau; tel: 04 94 19 52 52; fax: 04 94 83 85 40; e-mail: information@saint-raphael.com; www.saint-raphael.com*

�- The N98 runs through the town. From the A8, take exits 37 or 38.

🅿️ Parking is difficult. Best is the car park along the waterfront at place Kennedy or along the coast road beside the beach.

🏛️ **Musée Archéologique (Archaeological Museum)** *Parvis de l'Eglise. Open 1000–1200, 1500–1800. Closed Tue.*

🛒 There is a daily market except Mon, with a bigger one on Thu morning.

Don't worry about tourists spoiling the place – St-Raphaël was purpose-built as a resort by the Romans, two thousand years ago. The Roman town, about 350m from the port, was essentially the old quarter of today, clustered around the church of St-Raphaël. Fragments of their ramparts can be seen. The **Musée Archéologique**✥ (Archaeological Museum), beside the church, displays local finds dating back to the 5th century BC. St-Raphaël may lack Riviera style (though it does put on a few airs) but this small resort has a pleasantly bustling harbour, as well as decent affordable restaurants and down-to-earth shops. The modern town is right next to the sea. It has a big, busy, sandy beach of its own, and is close to Fréjus. Despite historic origins, the town is mainly 19th-century. It sprang into life when a journalist, Alphonse Karr, came here in 1864 to keep his head down after writing inflammatory pieces against Napoleon III. He invited friends to visit and keep him company, and they did. Among them were Berlioz, Maupassant, Alexandre Dumas and other leading writers, musicians and artists of the day. Others followed. Gounod composed *Romeo et Juliette* in St-Raphaël, and Scott Fitzgerald wrote *Tender is the Night* here. The mayor seized the opportunity to engage an architect and develop the resort. Fine seafront villas survive from the period. Fifty paces from the beach rises the imposing Byzantine dome and decorated towers of the town's 19th-century church; and right next to it stands the casino.

Accommodation and food in St-Raphaël

Excelsior €€€ *Promenade rue Coty; tel: 04 94 95 02 42; fax: 04 94 95 33 82; e-mail: info@excelsior-hotel.com.* This white *belle-époque* confection is the place to stay in St-Raphaël, at the heart of the resort, on the seafront, and right next to the equally splendid casino. It's luxurious, family-run, not terribly expensive and has a good restaurant.

Pastorel €€ *54 rue Liberté; tel: 04 94 95 02 36; fax: 04 94 95 64 07.* Long-standing favourite of locals and regulars, offering good, sensible local cooking, an amiable welcome and a pleasant setting.

MASSIF DU TANNERON✥

ℹ️ **Tourist offices** *see Mandelieu/La Napoule.*

The Massif de l'Esterel extends north into the Massif du Tanneron, the two uplands separated by the Argentière valley. Though partly bare, partly cloaked with a range of trees and shrubs, the Tanneron – like the Massif de l'Esterel – has been much cleared by fire in the 20th century. Still, these hills are especially renowned for dazzling mimosa of several varieties, flowering in winter. Many cut flowers sold in

The coastal forest

The Esterel Massif was the last section of the Provence coast to keep its original forest cover of cork oak and maritime pine. Until the beginning of the 20th century, this almost impenetrable native woodland extended over the whole Massif. The more mixed scrub of *maquis* or *garrigue* flora – low trees and bushes, holm oak, wild flowers and herbs – so typical elsewhere in the region had not penetrated here. Since then, more than 60 per cent of the original forest has disappeared. The main cause has been fire, with several exceptional disasters during the century. Replanting has been only partially successful, and pine re-growth has been hindered by disease. The Esterel forest is now less than 20 per cent cork oak, about 13 per cent pine, and the rest largely covered by a dense, beautiful mixture of lentisk, arbutus, wild rock rose, thyme, gorse and lavender. Fire roads now give fire-fighters access to the whole range.

Provence and further afield have been cultivated on the Tanneron. Near Tanneron village, the Romanesque chapel of Notre-Dame-de-Peygros gives broad views over the Esterel and Lac de St-Cassien.

Suggested tour

Total distance: 80km, with an inland detour of 30km and a mountain walk.

Time: To do the drive without stopping would take only 2 hours. The whole tour, with time to see the sights, including the walk and detour, makes a full day.

Links: At Cannes, this tour links with the Route Napoléon (*see page 174*) and the Cannes to Nice tour (*see page 220*). To the west it connects with the Maures tour (*see page 186*).

Route: Start from **Cannes** (*see page 212*). At first, the main coast road out of Cannes (the N98) makes a poor start, passing an unsightly ribbon of development round the Golfe de Napoule. After the resort of **LA NAPOULE ❶** the **CORNICHE DE L'ESTEREL ❷** begins, and the coast starts to become beautiful. The corniche road runs through a string of small resorts and holiday developments following one another, many having possession of a little sandy cove or bay. First is cheap and cheerful **Théoule**, then a succession of others. Pass **Point de l'Esquillon**, a beautiful cape with steep cliffs and lovely views to Cannes and the islands, to reach **Miramar, Le Trayas, Anthéor** and **Agay**.

At the other end of the Esterel corniche, the road suddenly straightens out for a run into **ST-RAPHAËL ❸**. The N98 works its way through town along the waterfront, competing with a lot of local traffic, crossing into **Fréjus-Plage** and eventually entering **FREJUS ❹**.

From Fréjus, take the N7 in the direction of Cannes. Leaving town, it passes the remains of the Roman aqueduct, then a surprising **pagoda**, a memorial to Indo-Chinese soldiers who died in the Great War. About 5km out of Fréjus, notice the chapel of **Notre-Dame-de-Jerusalem** on the right. This tiny structure was designed by Jean Cocteau, though not built until after his death in 1963. The road keeps climbing, and passes below the peak of **Mont Vinaigre**, highest point of the Esterel (618m).

Getting out of the car: A signposted track on the right leads up to the Mont Vinaigre summit. It's a steep but clear path and on reaching the top there's a superb vista across the wild hills, extending along the azure coast and in the other direction to the Alps rising in the north. The whole walk takes around half an hour return.

Just past Mont Vinaigre, as the road starts to descend, the historic staging post **Auberge des Adrets**, now a smart *restaurant avec chambres* (*tel: 04 94 40 36 24*) is a reminder of the times when this road was notorious and the Esterel synonymous with highwaymen: this inn was a legendary haunt of robbers.

Detour: About 14km out of Fréjus, just past Mont Vinaigre, turn left for Les Adret de l'Esterel. Follow this (fairly busy) road through the countryside on the edge of the Montauroux forest to **Lac de St-Cassien**. This large, utterly tranquil lake, enclosed by steep forested slopes, has green, wooded banks, some beachy edges, and attracts anglers and sportsmen, though no motor boats are allowed. In high season, it's a popular picnic area. Reaching the Pont de Pré Claou, instead of turning on to the bridge (though it's worth doing so just for the view), turn right on to the steep, narrow and winding D38 through pine forest. The road struggles up, down and up again (road changes to the D138) into the **MASSIF DU TANNERON** ❺. Descend on the precipitous D92 into Mandelieu to rejoin the N7.

The N7 continues into Cannes.

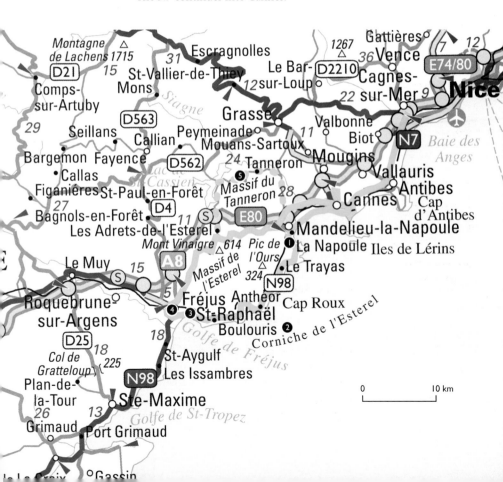

Cannes

Ratings

Entertainment	●●●●●
Restaurants	●●●●●
Shopping	●●●●●
Street life	●●●●●
Architecture	●●●●○
Children	●●●○○
Museums	●●○○○
Sightseeing	●●○○○

Slick, stylish and money-conscious, Cannes is synonymous with *nouveau-riche* high life, frivolity, stardom and glamour. There are sumptuous villas, palatial Edwardian hotels grandly luxurious in the old-fashioned way and a central Gold-Card shopping area. There's an old quarter on the hill, and a wonderful flower market, but today the whole life of the place focuses on La Croisette, the waterfront. This majestic, vivacious curve of palm-lined promenade around a bay of dazzling blue is the greatest of the town's sights. There you'll find the remnant of the original fishing harbour, as well as two yacht-crammed marinas and a long sandy beach. The hilly backcountry behind the town is beautiful and, despite the crowds, the steep villages (many with top-quality restaurants) have a lot of character. For a different perspective on things, visit the offshore Lérins islands and see Cannes from the sea.

Arriving and departing

Main office *Palais des Festivals, 1 boulevard de la Croisette; tel 04 93 39 24 53; fax: 04 93 99 37 06; e-mail: tourisme@semec.com*

Station office *Gare SNCF, rue Jean-Jaurès; tel: 04 93 99 19 77; fax: 04 92 99 84 23.*

La Bocca office *tel: 04 93 47 04 12; fax: 04 93 90 99 85.*

Web site
www.cannes.fr

The N7 and the coastal N98 run right through Cannes (the N98 becomes boulevard de la Croisette). Three exits from *autoroute* A8 lead into Cannes. To get to the heart of the city follow signs for Palais des Festivals.

Parking

The best located car park is beneath the Palais des Festivals at the west end of boulevard de la Croisette. If it's full there are several other car parks around the adjacent main port (Cannes I) area and another by the Noga Hilton, about 1km along the boulevard.

Festivals

Cannes sees itself as a city of festivals, but these are really trade fairs.

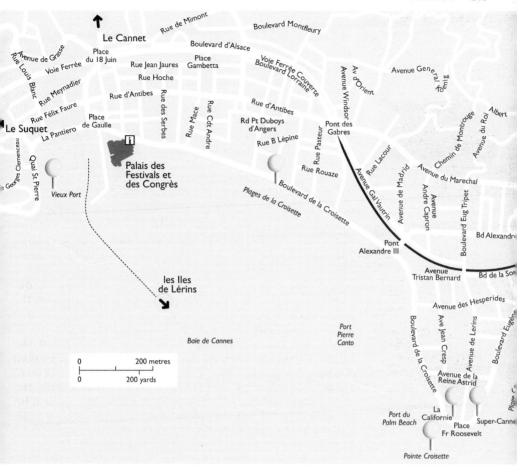

Le Cannet
Rue de Mimont
Boulevard Montfleury
Place du 18 Juin
Boulevard d'Alsace
Avenue de Grasse
Rue Louis Blanc
Voie Ferrée
Place Gambetta
Rue Jean Jaures
Rue Hoche
Voie Ferrée Couverte
Boulevard Lorraine
Av. d'Orient
Avenue Windsor
Avenue General Foch
Rue Meynadier
Rue d'Antibes
Rue d'Antibes
Avenue du Roi Albert
Rue Félix Faure
Le Suquet
La Pantiero
Place de Gaulle
Rue des Serbes
Rue Mace
Rue Cdt Andre
Rd Pt Duboys d'Angers
Pont des Gabres
Chemin de Montrouge
Avenue du Marechal
Georges Clemenceau
Quai St Pierre
Vieux Port
Rue B Lépine
Rue Pasteur
Rue Rouaze
Palais des Festivals et des Congrès
Plages de la Croisette
Boulevard de la Croisette
Avenue Gal Vaurin
Rue Lacour
Avenue de Madrid
Avenue Andre Capron
Boulevard Eug Tripet
Bd Alexandre
les Iles de Lérins
Pont Alexandre III
Avenue Tristan Bernard
Bd de la So
Avenue des Hesperides
Baie de Cannes
Port Pierre Canto
Boulevard de la Croisette
Ave Jean Cresp
Avenue de Lerins
Boulevard Eugène
0   200 metres
0   200 yards
Avenue de la Reine Astrid
Port du Palm Beach
La Californie
Place Fr Roosevelt
Super-Cann
Pointe Croisette

Prices and seasons Hotel prices in Cannes, and some other prices, are at their highest during the Film Festival in May and for some other festivals, at their lowest from November to March.

Boulevard de la Croisette – or simply 'La Croisette' – is especially magical when floodlit, at night.

The glitzy two-week Cannes Film Festival every May, for example, is a high point in the Cannes year, the most prestigious film festival in the world, but is strictly for film people – the public may merely stargaze, though occasional film showings are open to the public.

Sights

Boulevard de la Croisette✦✦✦
It's worth driving through Cannes just to see this. The wide, palmy, flowery, beachside boulevard that curves round the azure Golfe de la Napoule to the Pointe de la Croisette is one of the most luxurious, prosperous and beautiful avenues in Europe. Along with the wealthy older strollers with permed poodles and the equally wealthy younger ones flaunting this summer's promenade-wear chic, there's a whole mass of ordinary tourists. The lavish *belle-époque* hotels are spectacular,

ℹ **St-Michel-Archange** Open only by request; tel: 04 93 43 00 28.

Fort Royal € Ile Ste Marguerite; tel: 04 93 43 18 17. Open 1030–1215, 1415–1830 (1730 Oct–Jun). Closed Tue and whole of Jan.

ℹ **Le Cannet Tourist Office** on autoroute; tel: 04 93 45 34 27; fax: 04 93 45 28 06; www.Mairie-Le-Cannet.fr

↦ Rue Jean de Riouffe, opposite the Palais des Festivals, leads into boulevard Carnot, which runs straight into Le Cannet.

the setting magnificent. Key sight is the playfully domed, richly stuccoed **Carlton** hotel, the film stars' favourite, though the **Majestic**, the **Noga-Hilton** and the art-deco **Martinez** cut a dash as well. At the western end of the boulevard is the modern **Palais des Festivals et des Congrès**, the ugliest building on la Croisette, site of prestigious events; it also houses the main Casino. Outside it, film personalities have preserved their handprints in the concrete of the **Allee des Stars**. The sandy beach is mostly out of bounds except for diners at the beach restaurants and guests of the grand hotels, and the different beach sections with their themed coloured awnings, loungers and parasols add to the air of happy frivolity. Why hold back? Pay up and join in. Alternatively, there are public areas of beach at both ends. At the eastern end, la Croisette turns past a harbour to reach **Pointe Croisette**.

La Californie and Super-Cannes*

For a glimpse into the extravagant money-no-object lifestyle of *fin de siècle* devotees of Cannes, the La Californie and Super-Cannes neighbourhoods behind **Pointe Croisette** are fascinating. Scattered among newer, duller homes are huge elaborate villas, adorned with minarets and pagodas, porches and mock fortifications. All are private homes, hidden in lush gardens, and they can only be viewed from outside. The Russian Orthodox church of **St-Michel-Archange** in this area was constructed by Tsar Alexandre III especially for the Tsarina and her court on their winter visits to Cannes. Inside are several icons.

Le Cannet*

Until recently a separate village, Le Cannet was taken up as a winter resort by an artier crowd than Cannes. Impressionists Renoir and Bonnard both had holiday homes here. There are several grand turn-of-the-century villas. The old quarter climbs picturesquely with shaded squares and narrow lanes, place Bellevue – aptly named – giving a dramatic overview of the town and coast.

Iles de Lérins**

Once upon a time Cannes was an insignificant place owned by the Iles de Lérins. Now the situation is reversed. Historic, unworldly, tranquil and traffic-free, the islands make an almost too-sharp contrast with the rest of the city. Closest to the mainland is **Ile Sainte-Marguerite**. Thickly covered with pine and eucalyptus woods threaded by paths, it's also the biggest of the islands and the most developed, with a few bars and restaurants by the harbour. Walk up to its **Fort Royal*** (or Fort Vauban), where the unidentified 'Man in the Iron Mask' was kept prisoner. You can see his cell, and among other sights inside is a marine museum with interesting relics of historic ships and cargo. A footpath encircles the whole island in about two hours. A little further from the mainland, **Ile Saint-Honorat** is similar, but smaller and

**ⓘ Ancienne
Monastère
Fortifiée (fortified
abbey) €** in summer,
(free in winter) *Ile St-
Honorat; tel: 04 93 48 68
68. Open Jul–Aug
1000–1200, 1430–1630;
Sep–Jun 0900–1600. Closed
Sun am and holidays.*

largely taken up by the old **fortified abbey***, now part of a new abbey, still occupied by Cistercians. The channel between the two islands, known as the Plateau du Milieu, offers protected anchorage to hundreds of yachts and small boats in summer. There are two other tiny islands in the group, Tradelière and St-Féréol.

There are frequent daily ferry crossings to the islands all year. Journey times from Cannes Vieux Port: 15 minutes to St-Honorat, 30 minutes to Ste-Marguerite. In season, other ferries to the islands leave from Antibes, Golfe-Juan, La Napoule and Nice. *Tel: 04 93 39 11 82.*

Le Suquet and the Port***

At the western end of boulevard de la Croisette is the appealing marina and old port area. The more homely, laid-back mood here contrasts with the charged atmosphere of the promenade and beach. On the pleasantly busy road behind, there are quite ordinary shops, good restaurants and a delightful flower market in allées de la Liberté, adorned with a statue of Cannes' 'discoverer', Lord Brougham (*see feature*). The city's Hôtel de Ville (town hall), overlooking the scene, is a rather fine old building. The historic quarter of Cannes is little Le Suquet, rising west of the port. Once a Roman fortress called Canois Castrum, it was again fortified in the Middle Ages by the Lérins island monks. Narrow medieval lanes and stairways winding around the hill lead to place de la Castre with its ramparts and 16th-century Provençal

Gothic church of Notre-Dame-d'Espérance. The lovely tree-lined terrace from here to the 11th- and 14th-century Tour du Suquet gives a wonderful view over the city, port and bay. Inside the old fortifications, **Musée de la Castre⁕** contains diverse antiquities and archaeological and ethnographic collections (the best are the musical instruments) and temporary exhibitions.

Pointe Croisette⁕

The rocky headland marks the eastern end of the beachfront, and gave its name to Cannes' spectacular promenade. With attractive gardens, Palm Beach casino (summer only), Mouré Rouge marina and the creation of sandy beaches, the 'Pointe' has become a little seafront resort area in its own right, especially on its east side.

La Croisette means The Little Cross, for the crucifix that used to stand at the end of the Pointe.

Accommodation and food

You'll find hundreds of places to eat on and off boulevard de la Croisette. Most set a high standard and are pricey. For lower-priced places look along rue Meynadier, quai St-Pierre on the west side of the port, and along rue Suquet and rue St-Antoine which climb into Le Suquet. For quality picnic fare, go to the food shops in rue Meynadier. Finding a modestly priced hotel isn't easy. Prices, already high, shoot up according to the season and depending on what's on at the Palais des Festivals.

Above
Vieux Port restaurants

Lord Brougham of Cannes

Cannes' days as a fishing community ended abruptly in 1834. At that time, many English aristocrats enjoyed wintering on the Italian Riviera. Most went to Nice, part of Italy in those days. In November 1834, Lord Brougham, charismatic politician, Lord Chancellor of England and inventor of the popular *brougham* carriage, accompanied by his sick daughter Eleonore, found the Italian border closed because of a cholera outbreak on the French side. Pausing at Cannes to consider his situation, Brougham (pronounced Broom, but called Broog-am by the French) was so taken with the place that he bought land west of the village and had a luxurious villa built. His daughter died and he called it Villa Eleonore in her honour. Every winter, until his own death there in 1868, Lord Brougham visited his villa at Cannes. Thanks to his huge influence, scores of leading figures followed his example, rapidly transforming the village into a high-class resort.

Hôtel Beau Séjour €€ *5 rue des Fauvettes; tel: 04 93 39 63 00; fax: 04 92 98 64 66*. On the wrong side of the busy central ring road, this modern comfortable place, set away from the heart of things, offers excellent value for money.

Hôtel de Paris €€€ *34 boulevard Alsace; tel: 04 93 38 30 89; fax: 04 93 39 04 61*. This charming, classic old Riviera house, with a garden, palm trees, balconies, pool and good facilities is on the wrong side of the boulevard that encloses the town centre, but even from here it's only about 500m to la Croisette. For Cannes, it's excellent value.

Restaurant La Magnanerie €€ *avenue Georges Pompidou, Le Cannet; tel: 04 93 46 44 22; fax: 04 93 45 38 93*. Enjoy good cooking with local wines, served either indoors at this atmospheric 18th-century house or on the flowery terrace.

Restaurant l'Armenien €€ *82 boulevard de la Croisette; tel: 04 93 94 00 58; fax: 04 93 94 56 12*. Claims to be the only Armenian restaurant on the Riviera, and the first to be recommended in a French food guide. Your choice of Middle-Eastern-style dishes is laid out on your table – vegetarians have plenty to choose from. Flavours are delicate and tasty.

Restaurant Pacific Express € *8 rue du Suquet; tel: 04 93 39 43 43*. Robust cooking using whatever is available from the fishing boats, served in a convivial setting popular with locals.

Le Relais des Semailles €€–€€€ *9 rue St-Antoine; tel: 04 93 39 22 32; fax: 04 93 39 84 73*. For the gastronomes and connoisseurs among the army of tourists who march up and down this street into Le Suquet, here's a superb, satisfying spot dedicated to the very best of Provençal cuisine and at affordable prices.

La Croisette's big four

If you care how much they cost, you probably can't afford to stay here...

Carlton €€€ *58 boulevard de la Croisette; tel: 04 93 06 40 06; fax: 04 93 06 40 25; www.cannes.interconti.com*. The most luxurious accommodation on the Côte d'Azur can be found at this sumptuous *belle-époque* masterpiece which dominates la Croisette with flair and *joie de vivre* (the domes are said to be modelled on the breasts of a dancer who took the architect's fancy). Interiors combine every modern convenience with 19th-century elegance. Its restaurants are the **Belle Otero**, considered the best in Cannes; **La Côte**, whose terrace is one of the sights and institutions of Cannes and acclaimed for fine Provençal cooking; and the **Brasserie Carlton**.

Noga-Hilton €€€ *50 boulevard de la Croisette; tel: 04 92 99 70 00; fax: 04 92 99 70 11; www.hiltoncannes.com*. The most modern of the top four, mid-way along la Croisette and with its own casino. Its restaurants are **La Scala**, offering excellent, less rarefied Provençal cooking; and the **Grand Bleu** brasserie.

Majestic €€€ *14 boulevard de la Croisette; tel: 04 92 98 77 00; fax: 04 93 38 97 90.* Highest standards of modern comforts and amenities together with exquisite Edwardian refinement and elegance. Wonderful swimming-pool. The hotel's restaurant, **Villa des Lys**, is among the best in Cannes.

Martinez €€€ *73 boulevard de la Croisette; tel: 04 92 98 73 00; fax: 04 93 39 67 82; www.hotel-martinez.com.* At the 'other' end of la Croisette, this art deco palace went out of fashion but is now back in force. Its restaurants are the top-flight gastronomic **Palme d'Or** and the excellent, less expensive **Relais Martinez.**

Shopping

The main shopping street, rue d'Antibes, runs the full length of Cannes city centre, two or three blocks inland, parallel to the beach. Here you'll find top-name designers, jewellery, perfumes, expensive fashions and luxurious accessories. There's more high-class browsing for artworks, jewellery and designer fashion on and off boulevard de la Croisette. Good-quality but less grand shopping can be found in busy, pedestrianised rue Meynadier, just inland from the port.

The principal daily market is Marché Forville, inside the market-place a couple of blocks back from the port. At one end it's a colourful flower market. Every Monday there's a second-hand market here, too. Another daily market takes place under cover in place Gambetta market-place off rue Chabaud, just east of the rail station. Tree-shaded allées de la Liberté beside the port has a flower market every morning. There's a second-hand market here every Saturday (and Sunday, at the start of the month).

Suggested walk

Total distance: About 3km; 4km including detours.

Time: The main walk will take about 2 hours, allowing for pauses to admire the views and the outsides of buildings, but without entering the museums and monuments. Allow a long day including visits to the islands and all the sights.

Route: Start at the Tourist Office, Palais des Festivals, on **BOULEVARD DE LA CROISETTE ❶**. Turn right out of the building. Walk – either beside the sea or across the central gardens on the livelier inland side of the street – for the full length of the boulevard.

The districts of La Californie, Super-Cannes and Le Cannet are better explored by car.

Detour: If you don't mind a longer walk, follow the promenade all the way round to **POINTE CROISETTE ❷**. Then return.

Turn inland beside the Hôtel Martinez and turn left on to rue d'Antibes. Walk the full length of this de-luxe high street, Cannes' main shopping thoroughfare (partly pedestrianised). At the end, continue on rue Félix Faure and then turn right to join bustling, pedestrianised rue **Meynadier**, heading towards the hill of Le Suquet. Cross rue Georges Clemenceau and climb pedestrianised rue St-Antoine and rue Suquet up to **LE SUQUET ❸**. Explore this old quarter, and descend again to the port area. Stroll through the area of the **port** and **allées de la Liberté**. Perhaps follow the port's west side round to the start of the sandy public beach called **Plage du Midi**.

Detour: Catch a ferry to the **ILES DE LERINS ❹**, then return at leisure. Allow a minimum of 2 hours.

From the port it's a few paces back to the Palais des Festivals.

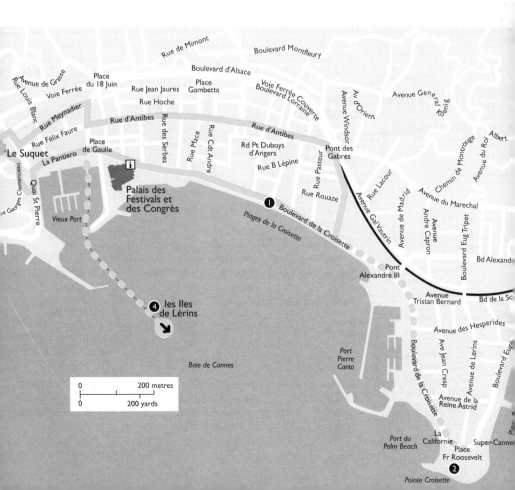

Cannes to Nice

Ratings

Art	●●●●●
Children	●●●●●
Entertainment	●●●●●
Museums	●●●●●
Restaurants	●●●●●
Scenery	●●●●●
Shopping	●●●●●
Architecture	●●●○○

This little corner of Provence has everything. Here is the whole region in microcosm, the high point of all that's best on the Riviera and inland Provence, with plenty of what's worst, too. Palms, lentisk, mimosa; azure sea and sky; mild winters, sunwashed summers; the best beaches, spectacular inland towns and medieval villages; thrilling rocky, *garrigue*-cloaked Mediterranean landscapes; impeccable restaurants offering the heights of gastronomic elegance; outstanding, world-class art museums and entertainment for everyone in the family – it's all here. Here, too, are the highest prices and the worst *nouveau-riche* élitism, the nastiest ribbon developments and a countryside peppered with ugly housing, and above all, the most horrendous traffic. So here's how to enjoy it to the full: come early in the season, or late. Avoid driving in towns. Be prepared to spend a little extra. Take it slowly. Explore on the little roads.

ANTIBES✦✦✦

ℹ️ **Antibes Tourist Office** *11 place Général de Gaulle; tel: 04 92 90 53 00; fax: 04 92 90 53 01; e-mail: accueil@antibes-juanlespins.com; www.antibes-juanlespins.com*

Ferries

Summer ferry excursions depart from Juan-les-Pins and Golfe-Juan to the Iles de Lérins (see page 214).

Gleaming luxury yachts pack Port Vauban harbour, and there's a crowded little sunbathing beach close by. Though it's right on the waterfront and full of tourists, Antibes doesn't have the air of a resort. It's an ancient town of tremendous character and appeal, with a lively working centre. Historic 17th-century ramparts built by Vauban, with a daunting fortress wall plunging into the sea, edge its authentic old quarter, **Vieil Antibes✦✦**, where streets are lined with attractive, Italianate old houses. Narrow rue G Clemenceau is lined with boutiques, place Nationale encircled by trees and filled with café tables. Head through to place des Martyrs de la Résistance to find more shops, café tables, public gardens, a playground and carousel. In part of the ramparts, the **Musée Archéologique✦** displays numerous valuable finds made here dating back to the foundation of the town by the Greeks in the 4th century BC.

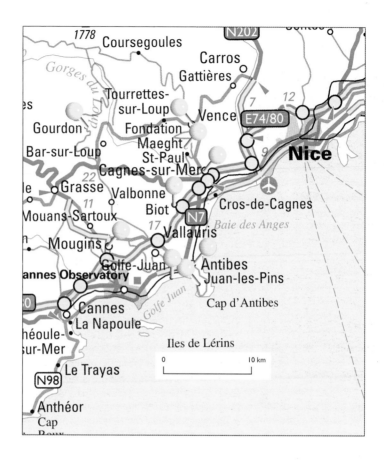

ⓘ Musée Archéologique €

Bastion St-André; tel: 04 92 90 54 35. Open 1000–1200, 1400–1800. Closed Mon, holidays and all Nov.

Musée Picasso-Château Grimaldi € *place Mariéjol; tel: 04 92 90 54 20; fax: 04 92 90 54 21. Open Tue–Sun 1000–1200, 1400–1800. In summer, no midday closing. Closed Nov.*

They called it Antipolis, or 'facing the city', because it looked across the Baie des Anges to Nice.

The small Greek town expanded under Roman rule. A heavily fortified possession of the Grimaldi family in the Middle Ages, for centuries it stood on the frontier of France. The 12th- and 16th-century **Château Grimaldi✱✱**, standing on the site of the original Greek town, now contains the Riviera's leading **Musée Picasso✱✱✱**, with an extraordinary collection of ceramics and pottery, as well as lithographs and works using cement, together with paintings. Much of the work is strange, geometric and obscure, using elemental and mythological themes; most was produced at nearby **Vallauris**, though some was done here in the château where Picasso had a studio in 1946. His former studio is used to display paintings by Antibes-born Nicholas de Staël. The stairs and first floor have works by other modern artists, including Léger, Max Ernst, Modigliani and Miró. For many, the less highbrow **Musée Peynet✱**, with over 200 of the

Musée Peynet €
(free on Valentine's Day) *place Nationale; tel: 04 92 90 54 30. Open 1000–1200, 1400–1800. Closed holidays.*

Marineland €€ *On the N7 east of town; tel: 04 93 33 49 49. Open daily at 1000. Entertainments and shows at 1030, 1430, 1630, 1800. Closing time according to time of year. Night opening Jul–Aug.*

There is a local market at Cours Masséna every morning (except Mon); craftwork in the afternoon, Tue, Thu, Fri and Sun.

endearing, sweetly romantic works by the successful commercial cartoonist and designer Raymond Peynet (a Valentine's card favourite), will be more enjoyable. For others, **Marineland◆◆◆**, the huge out-of-town sea life centre with sharks, dolphins, sealions and, for landlubbers, a nearby children's farm and a butterfly jungle, beats anything else on offer.

Accommodation and food in Antibes

Mas Djoliba €€–€€€ *29 avenue Provence; tel: 04 93 34 02 48; fax: 04 93 34 05 81.* Most appealing of the several good, unpretentious little hotels (no restaurant) in Antibes, this is a handsome mansion in extensive grounds, well equipped and beautifully located between town and beach.

Les Vieux Murs €€€ *Promenade Amiral de Grasse; tel: 04 93 34 06 73; fax: 04 93 34 81 08.* This first-class restaurant on the fortified clifftop promenade was English novelist Graham Greene's favourite, close to the block of flats where he used to live. In atmospheric vaulted rooms and with an outdoor terrace, it serves classic gastronomic dishes with flair and with Provençal touches. Closed 31 Oct–31 Mar.

BIOT◆◆◆

Biot Tourist Office
46 rue Saint Sébastien; tel: 04 93 65 78 00; fax: 04 93 65 78 04; e-mail: tourisme@biot-coteazur.com; www.biot-coteazur.com

The town and attractions are best approached from the N7. If approaching from *autoroute* A8, take exit 44 (Antibes Est, Sophia Antipolis) and direction 'Les Trois Moulins' and follow the D504 into Biot.

For the glassworks, the Arboretum and the Léger museum, there is plenty of parking space. For the old village, cars must be left in the compulsory car parks.

First a Ligurian settlement, then a Greek colony, taken over by the Romans and subsequently a fortress of the Knights Templar, this pretty hilltop village has two handsome 16th-century gateways and a lovely arcaded main square, place des Arcades. Its astonishing pedigree has depended largely on its pottery and ceramics industry, important since ancient times. The **Musée de Biot◆** devotes attention to the role of ceramics in local history. The village **church◆** contains two fine altarpieces. Today, Biot (the 't' is sounded) is better known for its **Musée National Fernand Léger◆◆◆**, a short distance from the village. The building is suitably modern, decorated with Léger's own mosaic designs, and houses some 350 works by the artist (1881–1955). These are among the best of his big, bright, colourful works, including his astonishing vivid and chunky ceramic 'paintings'. The place is a delight. Right next door, the **Bonsaï Arboretum◆◆** is an extraordinary collection of a thousand miniaturised trees, some a hundred years old. At the **Verrerie de Biot◆◆** – one of several glassworks at the foot of the village – you can watch skilled glass-workers quickly turning out inexpensive popular items using traditional glassblowing, which you can then buy in the glassworks' shop. Also on sale in a separate gallery are glass artworks costing thousands.

Musée de Biot €
*place de la Chapelle;
tel: 04 93 65 54 54. Open
Wed–Sun 1430–1830
(1400–1800 out of season).
Closed holidays.*

**Musée National
Fernand Léger €** *Chemin
du Val de Pome; tel: 04 92
91 50 30; fax: 04 92 91 50
31. Open daily except Tue;
Jul–Sep 1100–1800;
Oct–Jun 1000–1230,
1400–1730.*

Bonsaï Arboretum €
*Chemin du Val de Pome; tel:
04 93 65 63 99. Open
May–Sep 1000–1200,
1500–1830, closed Tue;
Oct–Apr 1000–1200,
1400–1730.*

Verrerie de Biot *Chemin
des Combes; tel: 04 93 65
03 00; fax: 04 93 65 00 56;
www.biotverre.fr. Open
Mon–Sat 0900–1800, Sun
1030–1300, 1430–1830.
Extended in season. Several
other small commercial
glassworks have sprung up
nearby. The original has
large pink signs.*

Accommodation and food in Biot

Domaine du Jas €€€ *625 route de la Mer; tel: 04 93 65 50 50; fax: 04 93 65 02 01.* Good modern place to stay, well equipped and efficiently run.

Auberge du Jarrier €€ *30 passage Bourgade; tel: 04 93 65 11 68; fax: 04 93 65 50 03.* An outstanding restaurant with surprisingly modest prices, specialising in herbs, vegetables and fish, cooked with the utmost flair and skill. Excellent wine list, too.

Les Terrailleurs €€€ *11 route du Chemin Neuf (the foot of the village on the D4); tel: 04 93 65 01 59; fax: 04 93 65 13 78.* Housed in a former 16th-century pottery works with simple elegance and a good old-fashioned rustic feel, this exceptional restaurant offers brilliant, imaginative and attractive dishes served with the best of local wines.

CAGNES-SUR-MER❖❖

Tourist Office
*Cagnes Ville 6
boulevard Maréchal Juin; tel:
04 93 20 61 64; fax: 04 93
20 52 63; e-mail:
info@cagnes-tourisme.com;
www.cagnes-tourisme.com*

*Cros-de-Cagnes avenue des
Oliviers; tel: 04 93 07 67 08.*

The part of Cagnes that is really 'sur mer' is properly known as Cros-de-Cagnes. A tacky resort beside a stony beach, it's not the most appealing section of town. Inland from here lies the modern town centre called Cagnes-Ville. Above, further inland, rises the original fortified medieval village of picturesque old streets and alleys and 15th- to 17th-century houses, now called **Haut-de-Cagnes❖❖**. Highlight of this attractive upper village is its large well-defended **Château❖❖**. Once a frontier fortress owned by the Grimaldis, it now contains the **Musée de l'Olivier❖** (Olive Tree Museum), which is all about olive cultivation, and, on the first and second floors, the **Donation Suzy Solidor** art collection and the **Musée d'Art Moderne Méditerranéenne❖**. Notice, too, the wonderful, first-floor, 17th-

Above
Biot

Château (including **Musée de l'Olivier, Donation Suzy Solidor** and **Musée d'Art Moderne Mediterranéenne**) € *place Grimaldi; tel: 04 93 20 85 57. Open 1030–1230, 1330–1800 (1700 Oct–Apr); closed Tue, 20 Oct–21 Nov and some holidays.*

Musée Renoir € *Chemin des Collettes; tel: 04 93 20 61 07. Open 1000–1230, 1400–1800 (1700 Oct–Apr); closed Tue, 20 Oct–9 Nov and some holidays.*

The **Festival International de la Peinture** (International Art Festival) takes place every summer.

century ceiling painted by G-B Carlone. Heading to Cagnes-Ville, it's clear that much has changed here since Renoir (1841–1919) decided to make Cagnes his home. Villa des Collettes, his house for the last 16 agonising years of his life (he was crippled by arthritis from the age of 48, and had to work with a brush taped to his hand), has become the **Musée Renoir** – a memorial to the artist rather than an art gallery, with interiors partly preserved just as they were on the day he died. There are pictures by others depicting Renoir himself, as well as ten sensual works of his own. In front of the house stands his large bronze *Venus Victrix*, like some sumptuous giantess, symbol of Renoir's greatest preoccupation.

Accommodation and food in Cagnes-sur-Mer

Hôtel-Restaurant Le Cagnard €€€ *1 rue Sous Bari; tel: 04 93 20 73 21; fax: 04 93 22 06 39*. A grand, charming, romantic and thoroughly civilised little 14th-century mansion in an exquisite setting by the ramparts in the upper village, this *Relais et Château* is one of the most appealing hotels in this part of the Riviera, and with one of the best restaurants. Wines include the rarely seen Bellet from Nice. Prices are only a little higher than usual for the area.

Above
Bougainvillaea in
Cagnes-sur-Mer

Josy-Jo €€€ *4 place Panastel; tel: 04 93 20 68 76.* Madame Josy Bandecchi's acclaimed Haute-de-Cagnes restaurant is straightforward, unpretentious and offers accomplished Provençal cooking with generosity and flair. Here, too, Bellet wines are featured.

Restaurant des Peintres €€–€€€ *71 Montée de la Bourgade; tel: 04 93 20 83 08; fax: 04 93 20 61 01.* A great local favourite, lively and convivial, with brilliant seafood, strongly Provençal seasoning and sumptuous desserts.

GOURDON**

ℹ️ **Gourdon Tourist Office** *place Victoria; tel: 04 93 09 68 25; fax: 04 93 09 68 25, e-mail: gourdon@wanadoo.fr; www.Gourdon-France.com*

🏛️ **Château-Musée €** *Village; tel: 04 93 09 68 02. Open Jun–Sep Wed–Mon 1100–1300, 1400–1900; Oct–May 1400–1800. Visit is by 20-minute guided tour.*

This arty, much-restored old *village perché* stands strikingly on a spur of rock. There's a fine 13th-century castle, altered over the centuries, built on Saracen foundations. The carefully preserved interior contains original 17th-century armour, decor and furnishings and an

Right
Gourdon

interesting, eclectic **museum***, with sections devoted to history and modern naïve painting. From in front of the village church there's a truly spectacular panorama extending some 50km.

JUAN-LES-PINS*

ⓘ Juan-les-Pins Tourist Office *51 boulevard Guillaumont; tel: 04 92 90 53 05; www.antibes-juanlespins.com*

ⓖ Ferries and boat excursions leave from Ponton Courbet, Juan-les-Pins to the Iles de Lérins from Apr to Sep, six times daily. *Tel: 04 92 93 02 36.*

Also to Cap d'Antibes by glass-bottomed boat. *Tel: 04 93 67 02 11.*

ⓐ *Jazz à Juan*, the renowned Riviera jazz festival with top international names, takes place during the second half of July.

Situated where the **Cap d'Antibes** coast road returns to the western edge of **Antibes**, Juan-les-Pins is a rather hectic, brash modern resort. Its crowded but clean sandy beach has been largely divided up into pay-to-use sections by restaurants with sunlounger and parasol hire, and the sea seems rather obscured by all their unsightly signs, roofs and awnings. The resort has a lovely promenade and lots of touristy shops and eateries. It's one of the few Riviera towns featured in package holiday brochures. Frequent music events attract a young clientele, and there are plenty of discos, night-clubs, cabarets and shows.

Accommodation and food in Juan-les-Pins

Belles Rives €€€ *33 boulevard Baudoin; tel: 04 93 61 02 79; fax: 04 93 67 43 51; e-mail: info@bellesrives.com.* Above the beach just south of La Pinède, at the east end of town, this wonderful art deco hotel and its luxurious beach-terrace restaurant offer the most accomplished of Provençal cooking, together with a superb sea view. Apr–Oct only.

Hôtel Juana and **Restaurant La Terrasse €€€** *avenue Gallice, La Pinède, tel: 04 93 61 08 70; fax: 04 93 61 76 60; e-mail: info@hotel-juana.com.* If there's a posh end to Juan-les-Pins, this is it – east and south of the pines with sea views of La Pinède, where the summer Jazz Festival is held. This is the smartest hotel in town, offering civilised art deco style and unabashed luxury. It has a private section of beach about 150m away, and its restaurant is outstanding, with elegant, modern cooking using only the finest ingredients. One of the best in France. Easter–Oct only.

Hôtel Juan Beach €€ *5 rue Oratoire; tel: 04 93 61 02 89; fax: 04 93 61 16 63; e-mail: juan.beach@atsat.com.* Yes, it can be found. An inexpensive, comfortable little family-run hotel close to a Riviera beach. This one's near La Pinède and only about 100 paces from the sea. Half-board is particularly good value.

MOUGINS**

ⓘ Mougins Tourist Office *avenue J C Mallet; tel: 04 93 75 87 67; www.mougins-coteazur.org. Open Tue –Sat only except Jun–Sep.*

When Lord Brougham built his villa at the fishing village of Cannes, he unwittingly sealed the fate of this beautiful little town nearby with a fortified medieval perched village at its centre. Now almost part of Cannes, it has given itself over entirely to day-trippers from the city in search of lunch. There's more to Mougins than restaurants, though. Its

P There are car parks at the edge of the village and these must be used. Sometimes the town is 'full', and so are the car parks, so there's no alternative but to try again another day.

Church tower *Tel:* 04 93 75 85 67. *Open 1300–1800 (2000 in Jul–Aug).*

Musée Municipal *place de la Mairie; tel: 04 92 92 50 42. Open 1000–1200, 1400–1800; summer daily; winter Mon–Fri. Closed Nov.*

Musée de la Photographie € *Porte Sarassine; tel: 04 93 75 85 67. Daily except Mon and Tue. Jul–Aug 1400–2300; rest of year 1300–1800. Closed Nov and holidays.*

Musée de l'Automobile Beside autoroute A8 5km away and easily visited from Mougins *(see page 231 for details).*

lofty old centre of steep cobbled lanes and alleys and old houses clustered tightly together remains delightful. The **Musée Municipal***, in the town hall, tells the history of the town. A 12th-century gateway, the Porte Sarassine (Saracen Gate), survives, with an unusual little church beside it. The **church tower*** gives wonderful views over the town and its pretty setting. Behind the gate and tower, there's a fascinating **Musée de la Photographie****, with many examples of the work of several great photographers, as well as an impressive display of old cameras and early photographic equipment. Subject of several of the photos is Picasso, often with his wife Jacqueline and his children – they lived in Mougins from 1961 onwards in a house which the artist named l'Antre du Minotaure (the Minotaur's Lair).

Accommodation and restaurants in Mougins

Mougins is known throughout France for the large number and high prices of its restaurants, much favoured by holiday-makers staying in Cannes. It has some half-dozen good-quality but pricey eating places, including one real high-flyer, as well as many other mediocre places cashing in on the popularity of the place. The very best are pretty hotel-restaurant **Les Muscadins** €€–€€€ *(tel: 04 92 28 28 28; fax: 04 92 92 88 23)*, and the little *Relais et Château* hotel-restaurant **Moulin de Mougins** €€€ *(tel: 04 93 75 78 24; fax: 04 93 90 18 55)*, a couple of kilometres out of the village centre at Notre-Dame-de-Vie, on the D3, which is the only one of the Mougins' eateries currently sporting a Michelin rosette.

Best of the cheaper eating places in the village, both offering excellent cooking and value, are **Le Feu Follett** €€ *(tel: 04 93 90 15 78; fax: 04 92 92 92 62)* and **Le Bistrot de Mougins** €–€€ *(tel: 04 93 75 78 34; fax: 04 93 75 25 52).*

ST-PAUL***

St-Paul Tourist Office *Maison Tour, rue Grande (part of the fortifications at the village entrance); tel: 04 93 32 86 95; fax: 04 93 32 60 27; e-mail: artdevivre@wanadoo.fr*

P No visitors' cars are allowed in the village. Park at the edge either in car parks or by the road and walk in.

Also known as St-Paul-de-Vence, this ancient hilltop fortress-village originally guarded the frontier of France which followed the Var valley. It remains beautifully preserved. The high, imposing **ramparts** of the village, with their walkway, are quite spectacular from afar and must be entered on foot through Porte de Vence. Within the walls, St-Paul is stunningly picturesque, despite the twee touristy shops. Focal point is the Provençal fountain – simple, yet adorned with an ornate central urn – in Grande Rue beside an arcaded former *lavoir*, public wash-house. Climb up to the early Gothic **church****, which contains extraordinary art treasures, including a Tintoretto, and fine 12th- to 15th-century craftsmanship. The treasury displays a document signed by Henri III. The entertaining **Musée d'Histoire Locale*** (Local History Museum) tells the dramatic story of the village in a series of tableaux

Musée d'Histoire Locale (Local History Museum) € *place de la Castre; tel: 04 93 32 53 09. Open daily 1000–1700 (1800 mid-Jun–mid-Sep). Closed Dec and holidays.*

La Colombe d'Or €€€ *place du Général de Gaulle; tel: 04 93 32 80 02; fax: 04 93 32 77 78; www.la-colombe-dor.com.* Come in for a meal or drink at this delectable, discreet little hotel-restaurant and you can admire original works of the many famous artists who used to frequent the place; you're also likely to see film stars, authors and politicians at the other tables. And the food? Patchy and overpriced.

Le Hameau €€ *route de la Colle; tel: 04 93 32 80 24; fax: 04 93 32 55 75; e-mail: lehameau@wanadoo.fr.* Though 1km out of the old village, this is one of the loveliest, most pleasing places to stay at St-Paul, with attractive little rooms, garden and terrace at moderate prices.

with life-size chararacters, together with photographs of famous visitors in recent times.

St-Paul was a great favourite of Picasso, Braque, Signac, Chagall (who died here), Modigliani and other artists. Millions of francs' worth of their works hangs on the walls of the prestigious **Auberge de la Colombe d'Or**, where – when the *auberge* was just a bar and the artists unknown – they offered paintings, sculptures, mobiles, anything instead of money, for meals and drinks. When you see the bill today, you'll be tempted to do likewise.

Outside the village, the large **Fondation Maeght**✦✦✦ complex (€€ *route de Pass-Prest; tel: 04 93 32 81 63. Open Jul–Sep 1000–1900; Oct–Jun 1000–1230, 1430–1800*), reached up a winding little road off the D7D, is one of the leading French modern art museums, with works by Miró, Chagall, Braque, Picasso, Léger, Kandinsky, Bonnard and Giacometti.

Right
St-Paul-de-Vence

VALLAURIS*

ⓘ Vallauris Tourist Office *square du 8 mai 1945; tel: 04 93 63 82 58; fax: 04 93 63 95 01.*

ⓘ Musée National Picasso 'La Guerre et la Paix' € *(including Musée Céramique) place de la Libération; tel: 04 93 64 16 05. Open 1000–1230, 1400–1800 (1830 Jun–Sep). Closed Tue and holidays.*

Frankly not a particularly agreeable spot, this working-class town makes nothing of its Picasso connection. Long noted for ceramics and pottery production, it attracted the artist when he wished to explore the artistic possibilities of that medium, and he came here to work and learn at the Madoura pottery. Beside the scruffy old quarter, the **Musée National Picasso 'La Guerre et la Paix'*** is barely signposted. Picasso once lived and worked in this 16th-century manor house that used to be a Lérins priory. Inside, three of its walls display Picasso's gigantic *War and Peace*, which is arguably not one of his best pieces. Also in the château is the **Musée Céramique***, a ceramics museum with work by Picasso and others. In the main square stands his more interesting bronze *Man and Sheep*.

VENCE**

ⓘ Vence Tourist Office *place du Grand Jardin; tel: 04 93 58 06 38; e-mail: information@ville-vence.fr*

ⓘ Château de Villeneuve € *place du Frêne; tel: 04 93 58 15 78. Open Tue–Sun 1000–1230, 1400–1800; in summer, no midday closing.*

Chapelle du Rosaire *avenue Henri Matisse; tel: 04 93 58 03 26. Open Tue and Thu 1000–1130, 1430–1730. Also open by arrangement and sometimes on other days. Closed 1 Nov–15 Dec.*

ⓞ There is a daily market in town.

ⓒ Traditional Festival: Easter; **Classical Music:** July.

At its centre the busy, art-loving town of Vence has a walled medieval **Vieille Ville** of exquisite lanes and alleys and fine old houses, now thoroughly polished and restored. Parts of the original ramparts can be seen, and five gateways survive. The focal point of the town is just inside the 15th-century Peyra gateway, where place du Frêne, with its huge ash tree *(frêne)*, joins place du Peyra – once a Roman forum, now a charming square with a fountain. Alongside is **Château de Villeneuve** and its looming 13th-century watch-tower. The beautifully decorated and restored château now houses the Fondation Emile Hugues and is used for major exhibitions of 20th-century art. At the very centre of the old quarter, the ancient cathedral stands on the site of the Roman temple it originally replaced. Out of town, there's a marvellous little church – the **Chapelle du Rosaire*** – which was entirely designed and decorated by the painter Matisse. Tiny, pure white and perfectly peaceful inside, it is an exquisite jewel of tranquillity. Matisse considered it his greatest masterpiece. When should you visit? Matisse commented, 'The most favourable season [to visit the Chapelle] is winter – and the best time, it is eleven in the morning.'

Accommodation and food in Vence

Auberge des Seigneurs €€ *place du Frêne; tel and fax: 04 93 24 08 01.* The whole of the old quarter is packed with pizzerias, snackbars, bistros and other inexpensive eateries. With more style than most of the others, this 17th-century inn stands right on the main square by the château and main gateway into the old town. It's a laid-back, good-humoured *restaurant avec chambres* with just half-a-dozen rooms.

Diana €€ *avenue Pollus; tel: 04 93 58 28 56; fax: 04 93 24 64 06.* Just outside the old town, this unusual and likeable modern hotel has attractive rooms with kitchenettes – and the washing up is included in the price. There's a garden and terrace.

Villa Roseraie €€ *avenue Henri Giraud; tel: 04 93 58 02 20; fax: 04 93 58 99 31.* Out of the centre, this stylish, well-equipped little country house has an attractive garden and terrace and a good restaurant.

Suggested tour

Total distance: About 90km, or 155km including the three detours.

Time: 1 long day or 2 shorter days for the whole route including detours, with a quick look at the museums. The drive, without stops, could be done in about 2 hours, traffic permitting. Note that the route can be done equally well from Nice.

Links: From Mougins to Grasse you're travelling on the Route Napoléon (*see page 174*).

Route: Start from **Cannes** (*see page 212*). Leave town on the road to **MOUGINS** ❶. Continue to **Grasse** (*see page 179*). From Grasse leave town on the D2085 (avenue Victoria, signposted Nice and Vence). At Châteauneuf Grasse turn on to the D2210 (direction Vence), passing beautifully located **Le Bar-sur-Loup** among its orange groves and fields of flowers. There's an impressive 16th-century castle at the heart of the village.

Detour: Before Le Bar-sur-Loup, the D3 leads off to the left on a scenic drive to **GOURDON** ❷. Continue on the D3 into superb scenery. After 7km, turn right on to the D6 and double back south again, this time through the narrow, plunging **Gorges du Loup**, the rocky landscape strangely carved with bowl-like hollows and cascading waterfalls – you pass Cascades des Demoiselles, Saut du Loup and Cascade de Courmes. The D6 rejoins the main route at **Pont du Loup**.

Continue across the River Loup at Pont-du-Loup, and stay on the very scenic D2210 which just skirts the edge of appealing **Tourrettes-sur-Loup**. It's worth pulling off the road here to take a look around this exceptionally picturesque medieval village. Follow the road into **VENCE** ❸. Turn on to the D2 for **ST-PAUL** ❹. There's a minor road, the D2, that runs directly from St-Paul to the **Hauts-de-Cagnes** area of **CAGNES-SUR-MER** ❺, but if you miss it the village can also be quickly reached on the D7. From Cagnes, head down to charmless **Cros-de-Cagnes** on the coast.

Detour: You're close to **Nice** (*see page 232*) at this point and could choose to head into the city from here.

The whole of the 15km on the N7 from Nice to Antibes, through tacky

Musée de l'Automobile €€
chemin de Font de Currault, off the D135; tel: 04 93 69 27 80; fax: 04 93 46 01 36. Open Jun–Sep 1000–1900; Oct–Mar 1000–1800.

Villeneuve-Loubet Plage and **La Brague** (passing a dozen campsites), is an unappealing ribbon of road, rail and stony beach too close to each other, but things shortly improve. Follow signs for 'Cannes par N7'. You do need to stay on the N7, as the railway line impedes access to and from the coastal N98. After passing child-oriented leisure parks **Aquasplash** and (bigger and better) **Marineland**, look out carefully for the badly signposted little right turn for **BIOT ❻** and turn here to visit the village and its nearby sights. Return to the N7, which runs right into **ANTIBES ❼**. Leaving town, follow signs for 'Le Cap par les Plages' to travel down the east side of **Cap d'Antibes**, with good sea views. After a beach stop, take the Cap road all the way, now following signs to Juan-les-Pins. The road eventually quits the peninsula and quite abruptly enters the hectic traffic and crowds of **JUAN-LES-PINS ❽**. Follow the coast road N98 round the bay into **Golfe-Juan**, close to the fringes of Cannes.

Detour: A couple of kilometres inland from Golfe-Juan is **VALLAURIS ❾**. About 4km beyond the cramped, crowded roads of this busy town, just past the *autoroute* A8, a little turning (Chemin de Font de Currault) leads into the **Musée de l'Automobile** with vintage cars, films and the history of the automobile and a 1939 garage.

Either return to Cannes via Golfe-Juan or re-enter the city directly from Vallauris on the D803.

Nice

Ratings

Entertainment	●●●●●
Museums	●●●●●
Restaurants	●●●●●
Shopping	●●●●●
Street life	●●●●●
Architecture	●●●○○
Children	●●●○○
Sightseeing	●●●○○

Despite everything, the Promenade des Anglais is still magical. Despite the highway that runs beside it, that majestic azure sweep of the Baie des Anges and the immense sidewalk with its mimosas and palms still take the breath away. For 200 years Nice has been the 'Queen of the Riviera'. A dynamic, sophisticated capital of the Côte, an ancient worldly wise city where high life and low life meet and squalor lives round the corner from style. When the British gentry built their promenade, this was the Italian Riviera (Nice joined France in 1860), and from the slatted shutters and ochre façades to the Mafia-linked local regime an Italianate feel remains. Down by the sea, it's as beautiful as ever. The dazzling blue bay, the intricate Old Quarter and the colour-splashed flower market have fascinated the greatest painters of our times, giving the town its close links with modern art.

City tours

A Tourist Train drives the streets of the Old Quarter and up to the Château, starting from Jardin Albert 1er on Promenade des Anglais. Qualified guides are available for private guided tours. Contact the tourist office for details or see the website: *www.guides-french-riviera.com*.

ⓘ Main office/railway station *gare SNCF, avenue Thiers. Open summer Mon–Sat 0800–2000, Sun 0800–1200; winter Mon–Sun 0800–1900.*

Beach *5 Promenade des Anglais. Open summer: Mon–Sat 0800–2000, Sun 0800–1200; winter Mon–Sat 0900–1800.*

Tourist information by phone, *tel: 0 982 707 407 (34 cents/minute).*

Arriving and departing

The N98 runs through the city by the coast (part of it is the Promenade des Anglais). The N7 passes through town as a faster highway a few blocks inland from the sea. Several exits from *autoroute* A8 serve Nice.

Parking

There is plenty of street parking, including along the Promenade (maximum stay 2 hours), and a dozen car parks near the sea.

Musée Matisse
Musée d'Archéologique
Les Arènes

Cimiez

Avenue de Flirey
Bd Prince de Galles

Sainte
Rosalie

Avenue de Brancolar
Avenue de Valrose
Avenue St-Lambert
Avenue Borriglione
Avenue Valrose
Avenue Edith
Boulevard de Cimiez
Corniche
Boulevard Pasteur
Quai Mal Lyautey

Rue Michelet

Boulevard de Cessole
Boulevard A Raynaud

Place
Charles de
Boulevard Joseph Garnier Gaulle

Musée Marc
Chagall

Bd Villebois-Mareuil
Avenue des Arènes de Cimiez

Avenue de Pessicart
R.A Binet
R Comboul

Avenue P Arène
Boulevard Gambetta
Rue Vernier
Avenue Malausséna
Rue Marceau
Tunnel Malraux

Rue Trachel

Palais des Arts du
Tourisme et des
Congrés Acropolis

Boulevard Risso

Bd du Parc Impérial
Cathedral
Russe St Nicolas

Boulevard Carabacel

Boulevard du Tzarewitch

Avenue Thiers
Avenue Durante
Av Mal Foch
Boulevard Dubouchage
Avenue Gallieni
Rue Barla

Avenue G Clemenceau

Rue Berlioz
Rue Gounod
Rue Rossini

Place
Garibaldi

Rue de Châteauneuf
Médecin
Musée d'Art
Moderne

Rue Cassini
Rue Ségurane

Rue F Passy
Rue A Karr
Rue Gioffredo

Boulevard François Grosso
Avenue des Fleurs
Boulevard Victor Hugo
Rue du Mal Joffre
Rue Masséna
Avenue Felix Faure
Promenade
du Paillon

Boulevard Gambetta
Sacré
Coeur
Place
Masséna
Boulevard J Jaurès
Vieille
Ville
St-Jacques

Rue Dante
Rue de France
Cours Saleya
Château

Musée des
Beaux-Arts
Rue de France
Musée Masséna
Jardin
Albert Ier
Musée Raoul Dufy
Quai des États Unis

Tour
Bellanda

Promenade des Anglais
Quai Rauba Capéu

Baie des Anges

| 0 | | 400 metres |
| 0 | | 400 yards |

ℹ Nice-Ferber
*Promenade des Anglais;
tel: 04 93 83 32 64; fax: 04
93 72 08 27. Open summer
Mon–Sat 0800–2000, Sun
0800–1200; winter
Mon–Sat 0800–1900.*

**Nice Côte d'Azur
Airport** *Terminal 1; tel: 04
93 21 44 11; fax: 04 93 21
44 50. Open daily all year
0800–2200.*

**Tourist Office e-mail
enquiry service**
info@nicetourisme.com

Regional Tourist Office
*Comité Régional du
Tourisme, 55 Promenade des
Anglais; tel: 04 93 37 78 78;
fax: 04 93 86 01 06;
www.guideriviera.com*

Site of the Visitors and
Convention Bureau:
www.nicetourisme.com

Nice web sites Official
site of the City of Nice:
www.nice-coteazur.org

Schedules, airport
information and facilities at
Nice Airport: *www.nice.
aeroport.fr*

Markets

Cours Saleya – for flowers and fresh produce (daily except Monday).
Cours Saleya – antiques market (Monday).
Place St-François – freshly caught fish (every morning except
Monday).
Quai Papacino – flea market at the port (daily).

Festivals

Carnival February (including Shrove Tuesday): The two-week Nice
Carnival is a major Riviera event.
Feast of the Gourds April: painted pumpkins at Cimiez.
May Festival: weekend folklore and festivity at Cimiez.
Nice Jazz Festival July: two weeks of jazz focused on the amphitheatre
at Cimiez.

What's on

Pick up a copy of *Le Mois à Nice* from tourist offices or hotels for all
this month's events listings.

Shopping

Avenue Jean Médecin is the main thoroughfare, with scores of
ordinary local shops and a shopping mall, Nice-Etoile. Place Masséna
is a lively focal point, with a Galeries Lafayette. More interesting,
stylish shopping can be found in the old quarter in rue St-François-de-
Paul (parallel to the seafront), rue Droite and around Ste-Réparate
cathedral. Look out for perfumes, including Eau de Nice mimosa-
scented toilet water, Nice olives and olive oil, and the local Nice wine
Le Bellet. Most shops close Sunday and Monday.

The Pinecone Express

Have a day out to Digne-les-Bains (see *Route Napoléon, page 177*) on the
little narrow gauge Train des Pignes, the 'pinecone train', which takes a
route through scenic, hilly backcountry on the 3-hour trip to Digne. There
are several trains daily, and you can get off at any station to explore or
hike. Call Chemins de Fer de la Provence, *4 bis rue Alfred-Binet, Nice; tel: 04
93 82 10 17.*

Above
Book market, Nice

Art-Pass

Nice has several major museums, and there are scores more to visit along the Côte d'Azur. Consider buying an **Art-Pass** (*Carte Musées Côte d'Azur*). This bargain-priced card allows entry to 60 leading Riviera museums, monuments and gardens. Valid for either three or seven days, it's available from Nice tourist office, some Riviera tourist offices, and certain stores in Nice and other towns. For information, *tel: 04 93 13 17 51*.

♺ Cimiez is to the north and east of the town centre: take boulevard de Cimiez or avenue des Arènes. Approaching Cimiez directly from the *autoroute*, follow 'Pasteur', then 'Cimiez'.

🅿 There is parking in avenue du Monastère, round the corner from the Parc des Antiquités and Musée Matisse.

Sights

Cimiez✦✦✦

Rising in the northeast section of the town, Cimiez (pronounced 'Cimié', originally *Cemenelum*) must once have been very grand, before the broad boulevard de Cimiez, gently climbing the hill, became full of buses and cars. Queen Victoria stayed here – a statue of her at the top of the boulevard records the event. The district, though still upmarket, has little to recommend it today except for two

Parc des Antiquités
avenue Monte Croce.
Open Apr–Sep 1000–1200,
1400–1800; Oct–Mar
1000–1300, 1400–1700.

Musée d'Archéologique
€ *160 avenue des Arènes; tel:*
04 93 81 59 57; fax: 04 93
81 08 00. Apr–Sep 1000–
1200, 1400–1800; Oct–Mar
1000–1300, 1400–1700.
Closed Sun am, Mon, holidays,
16 Nov–5 Dec.

Musée Matisse € (free for
under-18s) *164 avenue des*
Arènes de Cimiez; tel: 04 93
81 08 08; fax: 04 93 53 00
22; www.musee-matisse-
nice.org. Open Apr–Sep
1000–1800; Oct–Mar
1000–1700. Closed Tue and
holidays.

Musée Marc Chagall €
avenue du Docteur Ménard;
tel: 04 93 53 87 20; fax: 04
93 53 87 39. Open Oct–Jun
1000–1700; Jul–Sep
1000–1800. Closed Tue.

Above
The Franciscan monastery, Nice

exceptional art museums and the important **Parc des Antiquités***. More colloquially known as Les Arènes (the arena), this Gallo-Roman site at the top of Cimiez hill is arranged as a pleasant little park. The ruined outer wall of the arena itself, relatively small and oval-shaped, stands beside the road. It's used for events and shows, large and small, throughout the year. Inside the gardens, the interesting 1st- to 3rd-century Roman ruins include extensive Roman baths, among the best examples in France. Overlooking the gardens, the **Musée d'Archéologique*** displays numerous finds from Classical Cimiez and Nice, which was founded by the Greeks in the 4th century BC, and named *Nikaia* after the goddess of victory, Nike. Also in the gardens, entered from below ground level, is the **Musée Matisse****. After the modern underground area, the museum continues upstairs in a fine, beautifully adapted 17th-century mansion. The museum displays hundreds of Matisse's works, showing the many different moods and stages of his art. Most pleasing are the exquisite line drawings and bright gouaches. His working model of the chapel at Vence (*see page 229*) is on show, and some of his personal effects, together with photos of the artist at work. Follow avenue du Monastère round to Cimiez cemetery, where Matisse (1869–1954) and his fellow Nice artist Raoul Dufy (1877–1953) are buried. Beside it is the Franciscan **monastery***, with three works by 15th-century artist Louis Bréa. Lower down boulevard de Cimiez, the **Musée Marc Chagall**** is the leading collection of the work of this lyrical, dreamy painter. The major works here, including stained glass and a mosaic, as well as Chagall's art

Musée des Beaux-Arts € *33 avenue des Baumettes; tel: 04 92 15 28 28; fax: 04 93 97 67 07. Open 1000–1200, 1400–1800. Closed Mon and holidays.*

Musée Masséna (or Musée d'Art et d'Histoire) € *65 rue de France and 35 Promenade des Anglais; tel: 04 93 88 11 34; fax: 04 93 82 39 79. Open 1000–1200, 1400–1800. Closed Mon and some holidays.*

Musée Raoul Dufy € *77 quai des Etats-Unis; tel: 04 93 62 31 24. Open 1000–1200, 1400–1800. Closed Sun am, Mon, some holidays.*

Château *Tel: 04 93 85 62 33. Open 1000–1800/ 1900/2000 (depending on season). A lift takes visitors up the hill.*

books and sketches, particularly emphasise his interest in Biblical and Jewish themes, his love of rich blues and his ability to transform the world into mysteries.

Promenade des Anglais and the seafront✦✦✦

The Anglais were the British gentry who flocked to the Riviera every winter. In the 1820s they built a promenade alongside the new quarter where they were constructing villas (the main road at that time was rue de France, a block inland). And even though their majestic, elegant promenade is now merely the sidewalk for a multi-lane divided highway, it's still a wonderful, inspiring introduction· to the city. Forget the traffic. The broad walkway between the roadway and the sea is still shaded with palms, backed with glorious pre-War buildings. The stony beach below, though, is almost the worst on the Riviera: visitors in those days weren't interested in sand or suntans, though gentlemen might take a dip in the sea (this was in winter, remember) for the sake of their health. Off the promenade at the far western end, the **Musée des Beaux-Arts**✦ (or Musée Jules Cheret) houses a considerable collection of Italian and French paintings of the 17th and 18th centuries and 19th-century paintings and sculptures. Much closer to the centre stands the great pink-domed Hôtel Negresco (*see page 239*). Just beyond it, **Musée Masséna**✦ (or Musée d'Art et d'Histoire), occupying the opulent Villa Masséna, uses the finest artworks to illustrate the history of Nice from medieval to modern times. There is religious art, with painting, sculpture, jewellery and tapestries, as well as arms, documents and an important library. After the Ruhl Casino and the tourist office, the road passes in front of **Jardin Albert 1er** and **place Masséna**, the pleasant gardens and busy square which cover over the Paillon river.

Technically, the Promenade des Anglais ends here, and the newer section continuing east is the Quai des Etats-Unis, though in practice there's little difference. Just where the promenade edges below the **Vieille Ville**, the **Musée Raoul Dufy**✦✦ displays an excellent collection of the paintings and other works of this artist (1877–1953) associated with Nice and the Riviera. The seafront ends at 19th-century Tour Bellanda, a copy of the medieval bastion which once stood here at the foot of the **Château**✦ – not a château at all but a prominent headland projecting into the sea between the beach and the port. Delightful shaded paths run around and to the summit of the hill. Certainly there was a fortress here once, destroyed in 1706; a few ruins remain, including those of an 11th-century cathedral, with wonderful views.

Vieille Ville✦✦✦

Lying at the very end of the coastal promenade and at the foot of the high château headland, Le Vieux Nice, as it is often called – literally, Old Nice – is a haven for strolling, shopping, exploring or lingering over a coffee. In the south of the quarter, almost beside the sea, **Cours**

Musée d'Art Moderne et d'Art Contemporain
Promenade des Arts; tel: 04 93 62 61 62; fax: 04 93 13 09 01. Open 1000–1800, closed Tue and some holidays.

Saleya is a wonderful indoor and outdoor market-place. Its daily flower market sets up a magnificent array of colour and fragrance between café tables. Among the lanes and little squares are several remarkable churches, containing some fine artwork and craftsmanship, notably the Chapelle de la Miséricord, Eglise St-Jaques at the centre of the district, the Ste-Réparate cathedral, Eglise St-Sépulcre and St-Martin et St-Augustin. The last three all have superb baroque interiors. The triangular old quarter is bordered on the north and west by the wide, green **Promenade du Paillon,** which covers the Paillon riverbed and cuts the district off from the newer town centre on the other side. Several museums have been placed along the Paillon promenade. Most distinguished of them is the **Musée d'Art Moderne et d'Art Contemporain❖❖** (Museum of Modern and Contemporary Art), a world-famous exhibition space, museum and permanent display of avant-garde art since the 1960s.

Below
The beach, Nice

Accommodation and food

The tourist office hotel reservation service can find and book a hotel for you. Web site for Nice hotel searches: *www.hotel.coteazur.org /eng_search1.htm*

Hôtel Negresco €€€ *37 Promenade des Anglais; tel: 04 93 16 64 00; fax: 04 93 88 35 68; www.hotel-negresco-nice.com*. This wonderfully frivolous and opulent pink-domed Riviera palace is such a landmark, such a legend and such a visual treat, that you tend to forget that it is also somewhere to stay – if money is no object. Its restaurant, too, **Chantecler €€€**, is one of the gastronomic greats of southern France.

Hôtel La Pérouse €€€ *11 quai Rauba-Capéu; tel: 04 93 62 34 63; fax: 04 93 62 59 41*. There are several hotels along the stretch of waterfront at the foot of the Château, at the eastern end of the Promenade and within minutes of the Vieille Ville. They tend to be good value, with exceptional views. This is one of the very best – superb value, with comfortable rooms.

Hôtel Windsor €€€ *11 rue Dalpozzo; tel: 04 93 88 59 35; fax: 04 93 88 94 57*. A solid, good-quality hotel, attractively furnished and equipped, with lovely garden and good value. Three blocks from the Promenade des Anglais.

L'Univers de Christian Plumail €€€ *54 boulevard Jean-Jaurès; tel: 04 93 62 32 22*. Well placed at the edge of Vieux Nice, close to the city centre, this outstanding gastronomic restaurant with its traditional ambience and french windows makes an excellent setting for chef-proprietor Plumail to express all his skill and enthusiasm for Provençal cooking.

Restaurant Zucca Magica €–€€ *4bis quai Papacino (port); tel: 04 93 56 25 27*. This idiosyncratic harbourside vegetarian restaurant has won praise from France's food commentators. Enjoy imaginative, delicious cooking of fresh, seasonal produce straight from the market.

On the menu

Pissaladière – a native Nice snack of a pizza-like base covered with a topping of stewed onions decorated with a lattice of anchovies and olives.

Salade niçoise – salad with anchovies, egg, olives and tuna.

Pan bagnat – salad niçoise in a bun.

Ratatouille – a Nice speciality, the savoury, olive-oily stew of tomatoes, aubergines, peppers and courgettes.

Right
The Promenade des Anglais, Nice

Suggested walk

Total distance: About 4km, and a bus ride.

Time: The main walk will take between 2 and 3 hours and the bus detour about 20 minutes return.

Route: Start at the market-place, Cours Saleya, in **VIEILLE VILLE ❶**. Walk down to the seafront boulevard and turn left toward Le Château. Reaching Tour Bellanda, take the *ascenseur*, or lift, to the top of the hill – or if you prefer, walk up. Wander down from the hilltop heading inland, towards the old church of St-Martin et St-Augustin. Continue into beautiful Piedmontèse place Garibaldi, marking the northern point of the old quarter. Beside it, in **Promenade du Paillon**, is the large **Musée d'Art Moderne et d'Art Contemporain**.

Detour: Walk a few paces to avenue Desambrois and turn along here for boulevard de Cimiez. Catch a bus (number 15, 17, 20, 22 or 25) up this modern avenue to **CIMIEZ ❷**. Walk up if you prefer. After visiting the museums, return to place Garibaldi.

Walk along Promenade du Paillon into place Masséna, and to the **Jardin Albert 1er**. Reaching the seafront, turn right on to **PROMENADE DES ANGLAIS ❸**. Walk as far as you like, beside the sea, but at least as far as **Hôtel Negresco**, the greatest landmark of the Nice waterfront. Pause to visit the museums, then return along the

Musée Matisse
Musée d'Archéologique
Les Arènes

Avenue de Firey
Avenue de Brancolar

Bd Prince de Galles

2 Cimiez

Sainte
Rosalie

Corniche
Boulevard Pasteur
Quai Mal Lyautey

Rue Michelet
Avenue Borriglione
Avenue St-Lambert
Avenue Valrose
Avenue Edith

Boulevard de Cessole

Boulevard A Raynaud

Boulevard de Cimiez
Bd Villebois-Mareuil
Avenue des Arènes de Cimiez

Place Charles de Gaulle
Boulevard Joseph Garnier

R A Binet

Av R Comboul

Musée Marc Chagall

Avenue de Pessicart

Rue Vernier
Avenue Malausséna
Rue Marceau

Tunnel Malraux

Avenue P Arène

Boulevard Gambetta

Rue Trachel

ℹ

Palais des Arts du Tourisme et des Congrés Acropolis

Bd du Parc Impérial

Boulevard Carabacel

Boulevard Risso

✝ Cathedral Russe St Nicolas

Avenue Durante

Av Mal Foch

Boulevard du Tzarewitch

Avenue Thiers

Boulevard Dubouchage

Avenue Gallieni

Rue Barla

Avenue G Clemenceau

Rue de Châteauneuf

Rue Berlioz
Rue Gounod
Rue Rossini

Médecin

✉

Place Garibaldi

Rue Cassini

Boulevard François Grosso

Rue F Passy

Rue A Karr

Rue Gioffredo

Musée d'Art Moderne

Eglise St-Augustin

Rue Séguranne

Avenue des Fleurs

Boulevard Gambetta

Boulevard Victor Hugo
Rue du Mal Joffre

Rue Masséna

Avenue Felix Faure

Promenade du Paillon

Rue Dante

Sacré
✝ Coeur

Rue de France

Place Masséna
Boulevard J Jaurès

Vieille Ville
ℹ

✚ St-Jacques

Musée des Beaux-Arts

Rue de France

3

Promenade des Anglais

Musée Masséna

Hôtel Negresco

Jardin Albert Ier

Cours Saleya

Quai des États Unis

Château

Tour Belland

Quai Rauba Capéu

Baie des Anges

0   400 metres
0   400 yards

The Riviera Corniches

Ratings

Entertainment	●●●●●
Restaurants	●●●●●
Scenery	●●●●●
Beaches	●●●●○
Children	●●●●○
History	●●●●○
Shopping	●●●●○
Roman remains	●●●○○

From Nice to Menton, craggy mountains of the Maritime Alps plunge crazily into the azure sea. The water's-edge Corniche Littoral roadway, carved out two centuries ago for a Prince of Monaco, and two upper Corniche roads clinging to precipitous slopes, give thrilling views of this dizzyingly spectacular scenery. On the coast, from gentle Menton, where lemons and oranges grow, to glitzy Monte Carlo is all Gold Card country, where the super-rich come by yacht and private plane to spend a few days dining, gambling and partying. Then comes a stretch of seafront devoted more to hideaways than holidays (a second home by the sea at Beaulieu or on the secretive little peninsula of St-Jean-Cap-Ferrat, for example, would be heavenly). Rising above this sybaritic extravagance the dramatic landscape remains aloof, the sky and sea a sublime blue and the Corniche one of the most glorious drives in Europe.

What's a Corniche?

The Oxford Encyclopaedic English Dictionary: 1. a road cut into the edge of a cliff, etc. 2. a coastal road with wide views.

Chambers' Dictionary: (French) a coast road built along a cliff-face.

Collins-Robert French-English Dictionary: cliff road.

Petit-Larousse: Portion de versant, verticale ou à pente abrupte [vertical or steep mountain slope].

At their start in Nice, the three Riviera Corniche roads are separate exit points from the city. La Grande Corniche merges with La Corniche Moyenne at Cabbé just west of Roquebrune, and then with La Corniche Littorale 4km later at Cap Martin, 7km from the Italian frontier.

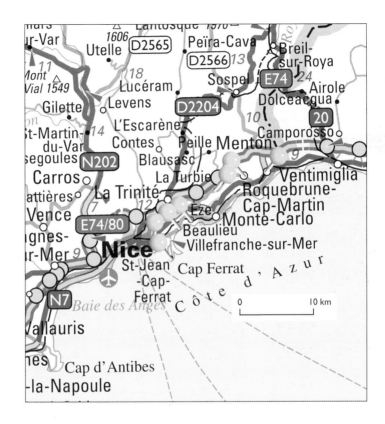

The Corniche roads

Fire warning

Signs all along the route warn about the risk of fire. Fires start quickly here and can be devastating. The fire of 1986 caused extensive damage to Riviera property and vegetation, which has not yet recovered.

La Corniche Littorale (Coastal Corniche) or La Corniche Inférieur (Lower Corniche): this road at the foot of the mountains clings to the coast, passing through all the resorts. It is the oldest of the roads, and is today the N98. Traffic can be a problem.

La Corniche Moyenne (Middle Corniche): built in the 1930s between the Grande and Littorale corniche roads, it was intended to ease traffic flow on the other two. A wider, faster road, it's now the N7. It gives fantastic coastal views – sometimes obscured, but there are sidewalks and many viewpoint lay-bys.

La Grande Corniche (Great Corniche) is *the* Corniche, built by Napoleon as a military road following the Roman highway *Via Julia Augusta*. A spectacular route, winding high among dense vegetation with beautiful mountain views, it by-passes all towns (except La Turbie) and is now the D2564. There are frequent light mists.

BEAULIEU-SUR-MER*

ⓘ Beaulieu-sur-Mer Tourist Office *place G Clemenceau; tel: 04 93 01 02 21; fax: 04 93 01 44 04; e-mail: tourisme@ot.beaulieu-sur-mer.fr, www.ot-beaulieu-sur-mer.fr*

↻ The N98 runs straight through the town.

ⓟ By the port.

ⓜ Villa Kérylos €€ *Impasse Eiffel; tel: 04 93 01 01 44. Open 1000 or 1030 to 1800, 1830 or 1900 according to date.*

This resort town is noted for its mild climate and handsome sheltered position, with the Alpes-Maritimes descending in cliffs all around. It's a long established Riviera favourite, with an Anglican church and many fine villas. Along the seafront, mimosa, plane trees and palms grow, and there are lush gardens. Opulent *belle-époque* mansions include private houses as well as luxury hotels. A curve of beach and a tiny harbour lie within little Baie des Fourmis. At the tip of the bay, the unusual **Villa Kérylos**** is a perfect imitation of an authentic Greek villa of Classical times: it was built in 1900 for archaeologist Théodore Reinach, and was even decorated with genuine ancient Greek artefacts. On the other side of this little headland, there's a large yacht harbour. Ordinary shopping streets rise inland from this sumptuous coastal scene, and at the back of town there are even some decent 1- and 2-star hotels.

Accommodation and food in Beaulieu-sur-Mer

Two grand, expensive hotels, both famous for their classic luxury and refinement and their outstanding restaurants, stand on the Beaulieu waterfront between the beaches (boulevard Maréchal Leclerc): the extremely elegant and stylish **Métropole** (€€€ *tel: 04 93 01 00 08; fax: 04 93 01 18 51; e-mail: metropole@relaischateaux.com; www.lemetropole.com*), standing in its beachside gardens, and the even pricier, even more abundantly equipped **La Réserve de Beaulieu** (€€€ *tel: 04 93 01 00 01; fax: 04 93 01 28 99; e-mail: reserve@wanadoo.fr; www.reservebeaulieu.com*), with its exceptional spa facilities.

Hôtel Havre Bleu €€ *29 boulevard Joffre; tel: 04 93 01 01 40; fax: 04 93 01 29 92.* Simple, clean and comfortable family hotel in a Victorian house set well back from the sea on the N98.

EZE***

ⓘ Eze Tourist Office *place Général de Gaulle; tel: 04 93 41 26 00; fax: 04 93 41 04 80; e-mail: eze@webstore.fr, www.eze-riviera.com*

Beware of fire: the area around Eze was particularly badly hit in the 1986 fire.

A classic *village perché* (*see page 262*), tiny fortified Eze stands atop an extraordinary pinnacle which holds it hundreds of metres above the sea and surrounding country. Commercially, the whole place has been a huge success, a 'must-see' attraction, with thousands of visitors wandering the picturesque narrow lanes, alleys and stairways of the old village – ironically, its seemingly unassailable position now attracts rather than deters invaders. The old houses have become arty little shops, and everywhere the village has been lovingly prettified, painted and adorned with flowers. It's a dramatic, towering site, with La Corniche Moyenne passing by it on the inland side. Though dating

Chapelle des Pénitents Blancs
Open by arrangement with the tourist office.

Jardin Exotique € *rue du Château; tel: 04 93 41 10 30. Open 0900–1200, 1400–1700; except Easter–Jun 0900–1200, 1400–1900 and Jul–Aug 0900–2000.*

Below
Eze

mainly from the 14th century, the village started out as a Ligurian settlement, subsequently Roman. In the Middle Ages it was successfully taken by the Saracens, but recaptured, rebuilt and refortified. Today, it is entered through a fine 14th-century gateway. A tangle of lanes wanders to the **Chapelle des Pénitents Blancs**✧, of the same period, decorated with enamelled panels. The village curves around the lofty site of its ruined castle, where the remains are encircled by the **Jardin Exotique**✧ cactus garden. The views from here are breathtaking – it's even possible to pick out Corsica on the horizon.

The steep mule track from old Eze to Eze-Bord-de-Mer on the coast is now marketed as Sentier Frédéric Nietzsche, because the writer is said to have been inspired when he took this walk (about an hour each way).

The N7 (Corniche Moyenne) skirts the foot of the village. Free car parks are provided here, and you must walk up – motor vehicles are not allowed in the old village.

Many of the Eze boutiques have original, high-quality products. At the foot of the village, Parfumerie Fragonard (see Grasse, page 179) have a showroom and shop selling their perfumes at low prices.

Accommodation and food in Eze

Restaurant le Troubadour €€€ *4 rue Brec, tel: 04 93 41 19 03.* Tucked away in an atmospheric backstreet of the old village, this is a small, family-run restaurant specialising in rich gastronomic dishes with truffles, lobster or foie gras.

Château de la Chèvre d'Or €€€ *rue Barri; tel: 04 92 10 66 66; fax: 04 93 41 06 72.* Eze is just the place for peaceful height-of-luxury hotels with top gastronomic restaurants! One of several, the Chèvre d'Or is in a fantastic garden setting in the pedestrianised old village, with beautiful coastal views. It's a luxurious *Relais et Château* hotel with just about the best dining in Eze.

Hermitage du Col d'Eze €–€€ *On Grande Corniche, 500m from Col d'Eze; tel: 04 93 41 00 68; fax: 04 93 41 24 05.* In a cool, silent, spectacular location at a Grande Corniche high point, much favoured by walkers, here is good, comfortable accommodation at a modest price. The hotel is closed in Dec and Jan, and the restaurant from mid-Oct to mid-Feb.

MENTON❖❖

Menton Tourist Office *Palais de l'Europe, 8 avenue Boyer; tel: 04 92 41 76 76, fax: 04 92 41 76 78, e-mail: ot@villedementon.com; www.villedementon.com*

The N7 passes right through the town. Exit 59 from autoroute A8 is 4km from Menton.

There is parking on the waterfront between the two beaches.

Musée Jean Cocteau *€€ Bastion du Port; tel: 04 93 57 72 30. Open 1000–1200, 1400–1800. Closed Tue and holidays.*

A covered and open-air general market take place daily except Mon at Esplanade de Carei; there's a second-hand market on Fri in place aux Herbes.

Until it became part of France in 1860, the town's name was Mentone, for centuries a possession of the Grimaldis of Monaco (though from 1848 to 1860 it declared itself an independent republic). Once one of the most prestigious Riviera resorts, sedate Menton was the favourite winter haunt of many aristocratic and well-to-do Victorians, visited by Queen Victoria herself in 1882. It has lost a lot of that gloss but still has some charm. The climate is famously mild – the best on the Riviera – and Menton's most enduring image is of its lemon and orange trees, growing on steep terraces behind the town. Its long seaside **Promenade du Soleil❖** runs beside a narrow pebble beach backed by a busy road lined with apartment blocks and cafés. Behind this strip is the town centre, including still-grand avenue de Verdun, divided along its length by the **Jardin Biovès❖** gardens with fountains, exotics and citrus trees, soaring Maritime Alps at one end, the casino at the other. The promenade curves to a little headland where the Bastion du Port, a 17th-century fortress of the princes of Monaco, was completely restored by the artist and writer Jean Cocteau using much of his own original design and workmanship; it is now the **Musée Jean Cocteau❖**. On the other side of it extends a second bay, with the better Les Sablettes beach and a port flanked by the quai Napoléon and the Jetée Impératrice Eugénie, perfect for strolls.

Rising steeply behind this bay is the lovely Italian **Vieille Ville❖❖**, the mainly 17th-century old quarter of steps, alleys and mansions; dominated by the delightfully ornate St-Michel's church with its

On the menu

Pichade – Menton's *pissaladière*, a little tart of onions, tomatoes and anchovies, with parsley.

Socca – different from the *socca* of Nice, these are another version of baked savoury chick-pea cakes.

decorative campanile. Rue St-Michel, pedestrianised and lined with citrus trees, and pretty place aux Herbes, are focal points between old town and new town. Where rue St-Michel meets bustling main street avenue Félix Faure, turn right to find Menton's attractive 17th-century Italian town hall, where the **Salle des Mariages (Wedding Room)**✦✦ is decorated with a wonderful, allegorical mural by Jean Cocteau.

To the east, Menton merges into up-market **Garavan**, which has a luxurious marina. It's a place of sumptuous, elaborate, pre-War villas and gardens, including several open to the public. The waterfront Promenade de la Mer continues almost to the Italian border. In the other direction, Menton merges with the town of **Roquebrune-Cap-Martin**. Promenade du Soleil extends all the way to **Cap Martin**, a quiet wooded haven of tranquillity, though it, too, is covered in large villas.

🏛 **Salle des Mariages, Hôtel de Ville** € *rue de la République; tel: 04 93 10 50 00. Open Mon–Fri 0830–1200, 1330–1645. Closed holidays.*

📞 **Ferries and excursions:** From quai Napoléon III, Vieux Port – departures to Monaco, St-Jean Cap Ferrat, Villefranche, St-Tropez, San Remo (Italy). Not daily. Less frequent in winter. Operated by CNT line; *tel: 04 93 35 51 72.*

🎵 **Chamber Music Festival:** summer classical music festival attended by world-famous performers, held in place St-Michel. About 12 concerts, usually in Aug.

Fête du Citron: a brilliant, joyous Carnival that pays homage to the lemons and oranges of Menton, using thousands of them to create lavish designs, decorations and, for the final procession, spectacular floats. Mid-Feb–mid-Mar, always including Shrove Tuesday.

Accommodation and food in Menton

Hôtel Chambord €€ *6 avenue Boyer; tel: 04 93 35 94 19; fax: 04 93 41 30 55.* One of the best of the town centre hotels, in the heart of things just by the Jardin Biovès and the tourist office, and a few minutes to the Promenade du Soleil. Spacious well-equipped comfortable rooms at reasonable prices.

Royal Westminster €€ *1510 Promenade du Soleil; tel: 04 93 28 69 69; fax: 04 92 10 12 30.* In a relatively inexpensive Riviera resort with dozens of undistinguished town centre hotels, and only a few moderately grand establishments along the Promenade du Soleil, this well-modernised turn-of-the-century luxury seafront hotel represents excellent value.

Au Pistou € *9 quai Gordon Bennett; tel: 04 93 57 45 89.* This atmospheric little place not far from the port offers good traditional Provençal and Italian cooking at affordable prices. Closed Mon.

Weather report

Thanks to its sheltered position, Menton has the warmest winters on the Riviera, and is the only place in France cultivating oranges and lemons. Citrus fruits die if the temperature falls even briefly below -3°C. At Jardin de Maria Serena, an exotic garden in Menton's suburb of Garavan, the temperature has never been below 5°C, even though in 1990 snow fell during the Lemon Festival – for the first time on record.

ROQUEBRUNE✣✣✣

ℹ Roquebrune Tourist Office *218 avenue Aristide Briand, Roquebrune-Cap-Martin; tel: 04 93 35 62 87; fax: 04 93 28 57 00; e-mail: office-du-tourisme-rcm@wanadoo.fr*

⮂ The old Roquebrune is reached by a turning off the N7 about 4km west of Roquebrune-Cap-Martin. The N7 continues straight through Roquebrune-Cap-Martin.

🏰 Donjon (Château de Roquebrune) € *Tel: 04 93 35 07 22. Open daily (except Fri in winter) 1000–1200, 1400–1730 (1900 in summer). Closed 1 May and mid-Nov–mid-Dec.*

P There is parking in place de la République.

◐ Passion procession: this two-hour religious procession on the afternoon of 5 Aug has remained unchanged since first enacted on 5 Aug, 1467.

Entombment of Jesus procession: at 2100 on Good Friday a traditional, solemn procession of 60 people representing characters at the entombment of Jesus walk through the village, which is illuminated by traditional oil lamps using shells.

A picturebook *village perché* (*see page 262*), the medieval fortress village clings high on a rocky spur. Although hundreds of tourists swarm up and down its stepped alleys and precipitous arcaded lanes, and the old houses have become twee craft shops and art galleries, the village has unquenchable charm. Its aura of history is intoxicating. Originally, the whole of the walled village and its awesome **donjon✣✣** (keep) comprised a single castle, built to hold off Saracen raiders, and its massive ramparts were entered through six gateways. Constructed in the 10th century, it's the only example in France of a castle built in the Carolingian period. A possession of the ruling Grimaldis of Monaco, they 'modernised' the keep in the 15th century and much of it survives unchanged. The odd Tour Anglais at one corner, though, is just a sham – added in 1911 by a wealthy English visitor who had purchased the castle. Just outside the village on the Menton side, stands the **Olivier Millénaire (Thousand Year Old Olive Tree)**. If it truly is 1000 years old, this is one of the oldest trees in the world.

Old Roquebrune is part of the *commune* of **Roquebrune-Cap-Martin**, down by the sea some 4km away, which forms part of the modern ribbon development heading west along the coast from **Menton**.

Long before mass tourism and modern transport made Roquebrune a popular excursion, the village was the favourite away-from-it-all hideaway of British prime minister Sir Winston Churchill.

Accommodation and food in Roquebrune

Vista Palace Hotel €€€ and **Le Vistaëro Restaurant €€€** *On La Grande Corniche, 4km from Roquebrune; tel: 04 92 10 40 00; fax: 04 92 35 18 94e-mail: vistapalace@webstore.fr*. Exceptional, unforgettable style, luxury and, most of all, views make this one of the best places to stay or eat on this route. Rooms are modern, light and open, with terraces or balconies looking across the sweep of the coast. There's a lovely garden and the restaurant is outstanding.

Au Grand Inquisiteur €€ *18 rue du Château; tel: 04 93 35 05 37*. Up a steep stairway in the old village, inside the château's rustic former farmhouse, this popular, capable place offers good Provençal cooking with touches of the richer Gascony cuisine.

ST-JEAN-CAP-FERRAT✣✣

ℹ St-Jean Tourist Office *59 avenue Denis Semeria; tel: 04 93 76 08 90; fax: 04 93 76 16 67.*

The Cap Ferrat peninsula is a secretive enclave of very grand houses hidden amongst lush vegetation and high walls – it's more like a smart city suburb than a seaside community. The millionaire residents enjoy seclusion, peace and quiet, a gentle climate and gorgeous sea views.

St-Jean can only be reached from Pont St-Jean in Beaulieu-sur-Mer.

There is plenty of waterside parking in St-Jean.

Fondation Beatrice Ephrussi de Rothschild (or Musée Ile de France) €€ *Chemin du Musée, Cap Ferrat; tel: 04 93 01 33 09; fax: 04 93 01 31 10. Open 15 Feb–1 Nov 1000–1800 (1900 in Jul–Aug); 2 Nov–14 Feb weekdays 1400–1800, weekends and school holidays 1000–1800.* There is an elegant tea room in the villa, open every summer afternoon for light refreshments.

Parc Zoologique €€ *Cap Ferrat; tel: 04 93 76 04 98. Open 0930–1900 (1730 Sep–May).*

One substantial *belle-époque* property open to visitors is now **Fondation Beatrice Ephrussi de Rothschild****, the superbly located Italian-style villa which the Baroness left to the state. The house is a sort of museum, with the Baroness's eclectic, eccentric collection of over 5000 works of art, including medieval and 16th-century tapestries, Renaissance religious art, Impressionist paintings, a huge quantity of Dresden and Sèvres porcelain, scores of 18th-century art works and decorative items, and a section devoted to Far Eastern art. Enclosing the villa are glorious gardens. Just down the road, the King of Belgium's Villa des Cedras has become an exotic **Parc Zoologique*** and tropical gardens. **St-Jean****, the peninsula's harbour village, is a prestigious yacht marina edged by attractive Italianate ochre-washed buildings, though here you may also see just a few ordinary homes and apartments.

It's possible to walk beside the sea right around the Cap on a series of linked footpaths, walkways and promenades.

Accommodation and food in St-Jean

Top-of-the-range luxury hotels on Cap Ferrat, all with acclaimed restaurants, include **Grand Hôtel du Cap Ferrat** €€€ *71 boulevard Gén. de Gaulle; tel: 04 93 76 50 50; fax: 04 93 76 04 52*; **Royal Riviera** €€€ *3 avenue Jean Monnet; tel: 04 93 76 31 00; fax: 04 93 01 23 07*; and **La Voile d'Or** €€€ *La Port de Plaisance; tel: 04 93 01 13 13; fax: 04 93 76 11 17*.

LA TURBIE**

La Turbie Tourist Office *Mairie (town hall), place Neuve; tel: 04 92 41 51 61.*

La Grande Corniche passes through the village.

There is parking in place Neuve.

Le Trophée des Alpes (and Musée) € *In village; tel: 04 93 41 20 84. Open Apr–Sep daily 0930–1800, Sep–Mar daily excluding Mon 1000–1700. Closed holidays.*

The only village on La Grande Corniche stands high in a mountain pass with stunning views over Monaco. Ancient and atmospheric, with a turbulent history, it straddles the *Via Julia Augusta* at the Roman frontier between Italy and Gaul. It has several reminders of the Roman period, by far the most important of which is the Tropaea Augusti, locally called **Le Trophée des Alpes*****. Built in 6 BC to commemorate Augustus's success in crushing all the local peoples of the Maritime Alps, it was an immense, gleaming white monument – a great square base, circular colonnade and conical top – holding high a 6-m tall statue of Augustus at this lofty border crossing point visible from afar. The names of the humiliated tribes were listed on the stonework. Smashed by the local peoples after the Roman withdrawal some 400 years later, it was turned into a fortress in the 13th century, and blown up in 1705. Even so, it still remained an imposing enough spectacle to be partly restored in 1933, with great care and sensitivity, up to about 35m – and leaving off the vanished statue of Augustus. The **Musée du Trophée des Alpes**, nearby, has a permanent display about the monument.

VILLEFRANCHE-SUR-MER**

ⓘ Villefranche Tourist Office
square François Binon; tel: 04 93 01 73 68; fax: 04 93 76 63 65; e-mail: ot@villefranche-sur-mer.com; www.villefranche-sur-mer.com

⊘ The N98 (La Corniche Littorale) passes through the centre of town, and the N7 (La Corniche Moyenne) passes along the edge of town.

Ⓟ There's car parking on the waterfront.

Chapelle St-Pierre
€ *At the port; tel: 04 93 76 90 70. Open Jul–Sep 1000–1200, 1600–2030; rest of year 0930–1200, 1400–1800 (1700 in winter, 1900 in spring). Closed part of Nov and Dec.*

⬤ There are markets on Wed, Fri, Sun and holidays.

Villefranche, almost within the outskirts of Nice, is a fascinating, attractive little harbour town on a hill so steep that some streets tunnel beneath houses in other streets! Sturdy, well-proportioned Italian buildings in ochre shades or pastel pinks and yellows, arranged around squares and paved lanes and the picturesque quayside, seem more a work of art than a town. Don't miss it. Its long history has been all about protecting its strategically sited port, and a 16th-century **Citadelle*** in excellent condition still keeps guard. Inside its ramparts are the Villefranche town hall and an open-air theatre, together with assorted minor museums and collections. The walls of quayside **Chapelle St-Pierre**** are entirely covered with frescoes by Jean Cocteau. Perhaps because it is also a naval port, Villefranche is not so exclusive,

Right
Villefranche

The Fête de St-Pierre takes place on the first weekend in July.

and accommodation, restaurants (there are lots, mostly specialising in fish) and shopping are more reasonably priced than others in neighbouring towns. There are local festivals at various times throughout the summer, and a couple of good modern art galleries here, too.

Accommodation and food in Villefranche

Hôtel La Flore €€ *boulevard Princesse Grace de Monaco; tel: 04 93 76 30 30; fax: 04 93 76 99 99*. This well-equipped little family-run hotel at the edge of town has modern, attractive rooms and good service.

Hôtel-Restaurant Welcome €€–€€€ *1 quai Courbet; tel: 04 93 76 27 62; fax: 04 93 76 27 66; e-mail: resa@welcomehotel.com*. Despite the modern-sounding name, this agreeable little quayside hotel is 100 years old and occupies a former 17th-century convent. It's an ideal location to watch the comings and goings at the picturesque port, and its restaurant serves excellent fish dishes.

Suggested tour

Total distance: 65 km; 10-km detour.

Time: About 4 hours' driving. Allow a full day, or 2.

Links: At Nice the route connects with the Nice to Tende tour (*see page 262*) and (via a detour) Cannes to Nice (*see page 220*). For the city of Nice, *see page 232*. For Monaco–Monte-Carlo, *see page 254*.

From behind the port in **Nice** take boulevard de Riquier and boulevard de l'Armée des Alpes, or avenue des Diable-Bleus, into boulevard Bischoffsheim, leading to boulevard de l'Observatoire. This is the start of the **Grande Corniche**. At this stage it loops around Mont Gros and its Observatory and, turning back towards the sea, climbs **Col des Quatres Chemins**. There are already fantastic views, first one way, then the other, giving sweeping vistas over the Pré-Alpes de Nice, then Cap Ferrat and beyond. The **Belvédère d'Eze** is a viewpoint from which you can see way over to the Italian Alps. Anyone interested in space exploration might like to visit **Astrorama**, an 'astronomical study and observation' centre housed in an old gun fort up a long access road on the left about 1.2 km after the Belvédère. **Col d'Eze** (512m) commands an immense vista (there's an inexpensive hotel on the road just here, *see Eze, page 246*). Take the D46 turning just here, which plunges hair-raisingly downhill to the Moyenne Corniche at **EZE**. Head east out of Eze and take the left fork which climbs again (less steeply this time) back up to the Grande Corniche.

The Grande Corniche then reaches the only town along its length, **LA TURBIE ❶**. Beyond, it passes **La Vistaëro** viewpoint and runs downhill. Take the left turn to visit **ROQUEBRUNE ❷**. Soon after

Wintering on the Riviera

The very word *Riviera* brings to mind a lazy, sunlit elegance, a reputation won in the 19th century when Europe's upper class used to travel to the Italian Mediterranean for weeks at a time. There was no French Riviera then, and even Nice was considered to be 'in Italy'. After the development of railways, they would catch a luxurious sleeper train south at the drop of a top hat. Tourists then were exceptionally wealthy, came mainly in winter, didn't like sand, didn't want a tan, and lived in the grandest style imaginable. 'Sea bathing' was only for invalids, and beaches were strictly for the sea birds. People didn't sunbathe either – a tan was terribly low class. Even in winter, ladies guarded against this awful risk with pretty parasols. However, although everyone remained modestly dressed, they wore special cool holiday outfits and loved to stroll along the elegant promenades. During the summer months all the great beachside hotels, lavish, luxurious and polished, were closed for the season!

A lot has changed. If a hundred years ago it was all painfully select, now it's painfully crowded. Some eight million visitors come here each year. Still, the Riviera keeps its cachet, its charm and its undeniable beauty. The drift down-market came with the many artists and writers, celebrities and *nouveau riche*, who discovered that they too loved the Riviera in winter. The Côte d'Azur didn't catch on as a summer destination until as recently as the 1960s. It's still a favourite wintering place for the super-rich. Before or after summer's peak, during school terms, the resorts are relaxed. The air is exquisite, temperatures are at comfortable levels, millionaire yachts are moored at the quaysides, the squares and markets and outdoor tables are not jammed with foreigners. It's even possible to find a parking place on the seafront boulevards.

rejoining the road, it merges with La Corniche Moyenne, N7, and descends into the resort town of **Roquebrune-Cap-Martin**. Continue 4km on the N7 into **MENTON ❸**.

Turning west again, drive out of Menton on the N7, through modern **Roquebrune-Cap-Martin**, cutting across the top of green, secluded **Cap-Martin** peninsula with its villas, after which the N7 becomes La Corniche Moyenne.

Right
Cap Ferrat

Stay on the N7 to by-pass **Monaco-Monte-Carlo** (*see page 254*). Just after the cliffs of the Tête de Chien (556m, on the right), a left turn leads down to La Corniche Littorale (the N98) at Cap d'Ail. The road runs close to the sea, passes through the coastal developments of so-called **Eze-Bord-de-Mer** (*see Eze*), to reach **BEAULIEU-SUR-MER ❹**.

Detour: It would be easy to miss **ST-JEAN-CAP-FERRAT ❺**. To make a little tour of this posh peninsula and its sights, while travelling through Beaulieu look out for the D25 on the left (by the railway line and bridge Pont St-Jean). This minor road thens skirts around the Cap, returning to Beaulieu at the same point.

Only a short distance separates Beaulieu from **VILLEFRANCHE-SUR-MER ❻**. It's just 6km back into Nice.

Getting out of the car: The Promenade du Soleil clings to the water's edge all the way from **Menton** to **Cap Martin**. A coastal path, **Promenade Le Corbusier**, then makes its way up the west side of Cap Martin, clinging to the pale rocky shore and its woods of Mediterranean pine. It was named after the concrete architect Le Corbusier (real name Edouard Jeanneret, 1887–1965), a frequent visitor, who drowned off this shore. The Irish poet W B Yeats (1865–1939), another Cap Martin fan, also died here. The footpath continues all the way into **Monte-Carlo** (*see page 254*).

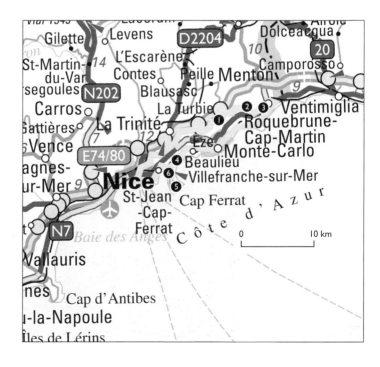

Monaco

Ratings

Entertainment	●●●●●
Restaurants	●●●●●
Shopping	●●●●●
Street life	●●●●○
Architecture	●●●●○
Children	●●●○○
Museums	●●●○○
Sightseeing	●●○○○

A precipitous mountain slope plunging into a rocky sea, Monaco is a curious, privileged anomaly. Many visitors wonder why this incongruous mini-state, tax-haven and glittering bolt-hole for the idle rich isn't part of France. The answer is simple: the Princes of Monaco were once an important power in Provence and Italy, and when Napoleon swept up all the other fiefdoms, counties and independent domains of Provence and Nice in 1860, he balked at taking Monaco from the Princes. However, the Grimaldis, Monaco's royal family, remain one of the great aristocratic names of Europe, and Monaco (though under 2 sq km) has become one of the wealthiest spots on earth. Unlike other chic resorts, here there's no pretence – this time it's *real* wealth. There's little to do but stroll, shop, people-watch and enjoy life. Yet Monaco is beautiful, the setting is awe-inspiring, and there's nowhere better to order a bottle of champagne.

Facts and figures

- All driving laws, road signs, drink-driving limits, etc, are the same in Monaco as in France, but enforcement is much stricter.

- Monaco has one policeman for every 100 residents, and 24-hour police surveillance of the entire area of the Principality, including the interiors of most public buildings.

- Monaco has its own internet code – .mc – and its own international phone code – 377.

- When phoning from outside Monaco, prefix all numbers with 00-377.

- The people of Monaco are called Monégasques. Of the 30 000 population, fewer than 5000 are native Monégasques. Only they can vote, and they are completely exempt from all taxes.

- The average air temperature of Monaco for the year is 16.31°C.

- There are on average 310 sunny days and 1583 hours of sunshine per year.

Avenue de Verdun

Boulevard d'Italie

Boulevard du Larvotto

Boulevard des Anciens
Combattants d'Afrique du Nord

N7

Boulevard de la Turbie

Moyenne Corniche

Avenue de Prof Langevin

Boulevard de la République

Boulevard du Général Leclerc
Boulevard de France

Boulevard des Moulins

Avenue de Grande Bretagne

Boulevard du Larvotto

Avenue Princesse Grace

**Musée
National** ■

**Forum
Grimaldi**

N7

Avenue de Villaine

Avenue de Villaine

Carref.
du Portier

Monte-Carlo

Avenue P Doumer Prolongée

Rue des Martyrs de la Résistance

Rue Bellevue
Rue Bel Respiro

Boulevard Princesse Charlotte

Av Princesse Alice

Casino

Av de Monte-Carlo

Pointe
Focinane

Ch de la Turble

Boulevard de Suisse

Avenue de la Costa

**Centre de
Congrès Auditorium**

N7

Rue Jean Boulin

Ste-Dévote ✝

Avenue d'Ostende
Quai des Etats-Unis

Moyenne Corniche

Bretelle Aureglia

Rue Grimaldi

Boulevard Rainier III

Boulevard du Jardin Exotique

Boulevard de Belgique

Rue Grimaldi

Boulevard Albert 1er

Rue
Suffren Reymond

Rue

la Condamine

**Port
de Monaco**

Quai Antoine 1er

Avenue de la Quarantine

**Théâtre du
Fort Antoine** ■

…ée d'Anthropologie
Préhistorique ■

Jardin
Exotique

Boulevard Rainier III

Place du
Canton

Avenue de la Porte Neuve

**Palais
du Prince**

Monaco-Ville

…ard du Jardin Exotique

Avenue Pasteur
Avenue Pasteur

Boulevard Rainier III

Avenue de Fontvieille

Fontvieille

Rue Emile de Loth

Avenue Saint Martin

**Musée
Océanographique**

Rue du Gabian

Avenue Prince Héréditaire

Av des Papalins

Port
de Fontvieille

✝
Cathedral

Avenue des Castelans

Quai des Sanbarbant

**Stade
Louis II**

Av des Papalins

**Parc Paysager
de Fontvieille**

Avenue du 3 septembre

Port de
Cap d'Ail

0		200 metres
0		200 yards

Monaco – the facts

Monaco consists of five small districts:

- Monaco-Ville, the old town on 'The Rock';

- Monte-Carlo, the larger new town, including the beach area to the east;

- La Condamine, the harbourside district which links Monaco-Ville and Monte-Carlo;

- Les Moneguetti and Les Révoires, the steep slope rising from Monaco-Ville to the French border; and

- Fontvieille, the more recent district west of Monaco-Ville, extending into the sea.

Some streets in Monaco are almost directly above others. Large, efficient, clean public lifts and escalators quickly connect certain streets and squares.

Tourist office

2A boulevard des Moulins; tel: 92 16 61 16; fax: 92 16 90 00. Mon–Sat 0900–1900, Sun 1000–1200. Summertime tourist information kiosks are set up at the railway station and main sites.

Web sites

- *www.monaco-tourism.com/index.html* – Monaco's official US-based tourism site.

- *home.vicnet.net.au/~monacofr/* – Website of the Friends of Monaco in Australia.

- *www.monaco-congres.com/* – official site about Monaco for congress attendees.

- *www.monte-carlo.mc* – useful commercial site about Monaco.

Monaco information in UK *Tel: (Freephone) 0500 006 114; e-mail: monaco@monaco.co.uk*

Monaco information in North America *Tel: (800) 753-9696 or (212) 286-3330; e-mail: mgto@monaco1.org*

Arriving and departing

Monaco is accessible directly from *autoroute* A8. The N7 (La Moyenne Corniche) skirts the northern edge of Monaco: sideturns give access to the Principality. The coastal N98 (La Corniche Littorale) runs right into Monaco-Ville. Access to parts of Monaco is reserved for residents of Monaco and the Alpes-Maritimes.

Caravans are not allowed to stop anywhere in Monaco.

Parking

Street parking is difficult. Entering the town, follow the prominent signs to the large, reasonably priced underground car parks. Walking distances are small, so it doesn't matter which car park you use.

Excursions and tours

- **Azur-Express** An entertaining little tourist 'train' runs around Monaco-Ville and between Monaco-Ville and Monte-Carlo Casino. *Daily 1030–1200, 1400–1800. Closed Nov–Jan. Tel: 92 05 64 38.*

- **Boat trips** Pleasure boats (some with glass bottoms) leave Monaco's port for trips around Monaco, along the coast, or to the Iles de Lérins (*see page 214*). All year. *Tel: 92 16 15 15.*

Prices and seasons

Prices are sky-high all year (*see Accommodation and food, page 258*). The time not to visit is during Formula 1's most prestigious annual event, the Monaco Grand Prix, during the second week in May.

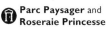

Parc Paysager and **Roseraie Princesse Grace** *Open daily till sunset.*

Musée des Timbres et des Monnaies € *Les Terrasses de Fontvieille; tel: 93 15 41 50. Open daily 1000–1800 (1700 in winter).*

Musée Naval € *Les Terrasses de Fontvieille; tel: 92 05 28 48. Open daily 1000–1800.*

Collection des Voitures Anciennes € *avenue Prince Héréditaire Albert; tel: 92 05 28 56. Open all year excluding Nov, daily 1000–1800.*

Centre d'Acclimatation Zoologique € *Les Terrasses de Fontvieille; tel: 93 25 18 31. Open Mar–May 1000–1200, 1400–1800; Jun–Sep 0900–1200, 1400–1900; Oct–Feb: 1000–1200, 1400–1700.*

Jardin Exotique €€ *62 boulevard Jardin Exotique; tel: 93 15 29 80. Open daily 0900–1900 (1700 or 1800 in winter). Closed 19 Nov and 25 Dec.*

Grotte de l'Observatoire *Entry via Jardin Exotique, boulevard Jardin Exotique; tel: 93 15 29 80. Open daily 1000–1800. Closed 19 Nov and 25 Dec.*

Musée d'Anthropologie Préhistorique *Entry via Jardin Exotique, boulevard Jardin Exotique; tel: 93 15 80 06. Open daily 1000–1800. Closed 19 Nov and 25 Dec.*

Sights

Fontvieille and Le Jardin Exotique**

Fontvieille is Monaco's new district, a great technical achievement, with homes, businesses, sports stadium and entertainment complexes, built into the sea on an artificial platform of rock covering 22 hectares. In the process a new yachting harbour was also created. Garden lovers should see the beautiful **Parc Paysager**, and in particular **Roseraie Princesse Grace***, its rose garden with over 3500 varieties dedicated to Princess Grace of Monaco (the former film star Grace Kelly) who died in a car accident in 1982.

On the inland side, close to Monaco-Ville, a series of museums will appeal to 'collectors' of all ages: the exhibits in the **Musée des Timbres et des Monnaies*** places the emphasis on stamps and money issued by Monaco; the **Musée Naval*** displays hundreds of remarkable model ships, and the **Collection des Voitures Anciennes*** is a superb, polished array of historic motor vehicles. Overlooking the sea, the **Centre d'Acclimatation Zoologique*** is Monaco's zoo. Rising up the steep slope behind, the cactus garden of the **Jardin Exotique*** overlooks Fontvieille. Opening off the gardens, **Grotte de l'Observatoire*** is a fascinating, once inhabited system of caves. There's more about prehistoric man – and animals – of the region in the **Musée d'Anthropologie Préhistorique***, accessed through the gardens. There is a joint ticket for the Jardin Exotique, l'Observatoire and Musée d'Anthropologie.

Monaco-Ville***

A Greek temple once stood on 'the Rock' (*Le Rocher*), dedicated to Heracles Monoikos, and the name stuck. The original town of Monaco was the strangest of perched villages, a medieval fortress atop a rock soaring from the Mediterranean, its château a possession of Emperor Barbarossa. In the 13th century, the noble Grimaldi family of Genoa acquired it and have held it ever since as the capital of their tiny independent state. Dominating the Rock today is the small 13th–17th century **Palais du Prince**** (Prince's Palace) within its robust fortifications. Inside, guided tours show off sumptuous rooms, decorated with priceless artworks, frescos, marble, tapestries and fine furniture. Part of the palace is a **Musée Napoléonienne***, a museum of Napoleonic memorabilia (including one of his hats), though more entertaining is the **Changing of the Guard**** in the courtyard outside (daily at 1155). In summer the guardsmen are cool in crisp white, in winter sombre in dark uniforms. Behind the Palace, the **Vieille Ville*** (Old Quarter) is a small area of attractive shaded streets. Past princes are all buried in its **cathedral**, which has a Louis Bréa **altarpiece*** and a distinguished collection of paintings. Pink and white **Chapelle de la Miséricorde**, nearby, contains the Recumbent Christ sculpture that heads Monaco's Good Friday procession. The Rock is a tourist area, with souvenir shops,

Palais du Prince (Prince's Palace) €
Tel: 93 25 18 31 Open Jun–Oct only, 0930–1830 (1000–1700 in Oct), Jul–Aug 0900–2000. Palace closed if royal family present.

Musée Napoléonienne
€ Palais du Prince; tel: 93 25 18 31. Open Jun–Sep 0930–1830; Oct–Dec 1000–1700; Dec–May Tue–Sun 1030–1230, 1400–1700. Closed some holidays.

Monte Carlo Story €€
Parking des Pêcheurs; tel: 93 25 32 33. Open daily. Multivision shows every hour 0930–1245, 1345–1830 (timetable may change; call to check).

Musée Océanographique (Oceanography Museum) €€€ avenue St-Martin; tel: 93 15 36 00; fax: 92 16 77 93. Open Apr–Jun and Sep 0900–1900; Jul–Aug 0900–2000; Oct and Mar 0930–1900; Nov–Feb 1000–1800. Closed on Sun pm of Grand Prix.

Opera House in the Casino, place du Casino; tel: 92 16 23 00. Open daily all year from 1200.

Musée National de Monaco € 17 avenue Princesse Grace; tel: 93 30 91 26; www.monte-carlo.mc/musee-national/anglais.html. Open Easter–Sep daily 1000–1830; Oct–Easter daily 1000–1215, 1430–1830. Closed hols and during Grand Prix.

Jardin Japonais avenue Princesse Grace. Open daily 0900 to 1 hour before sunset.

a waxworks, the **Monte Carlo Story**✶ and other attractions. On its southern cliff face, Monaco's best attraction is the **Musée Océanographique**✶✶✶ (Oceanography Museum), one of Europe's leading marine science and sea life museums. Below ground level, its magnificent **aquarium** has around 350 different species. The Museum also houses a meteorological and seismological observatory, and its terrace gives panoramic coastal views.

Monte-Carlo✶✶✶

Prince Carlo III created this new zone in 1866, and it's named after him. This is the 'high life quarter', the Monaco of glamour and glitz, with the grand hotels and the fantastically opulent **Casino**✶✶✶, focal point of ostentation and plutocracy. Stand outside, by the immaculate palm and flower gardens in front of the building, and simply admire the lavish gold-coloured façade of this temple to Mammon, created in 1879 by Charles Garnier, who also designed the famously gaudy Paris Opera House. Inside, visit his gorgeous Salons Européens and Salons Américains, with their slot machines, roulette and gaming tables, and the extravagant Pink Saloon bar, where strange ceiling frescos depict nudes smoking cigars. Pay the fee and – if properly dressed – you can enter the even more splendid Salons Privés, the real Monte-Carlo casino of legend and fortune. A grandiose staircase leads down to an exclusive night-club. In the same building is Garnier's prestigious **Opera House**✶✶, an auditorium in similar taste. Heading along the coast, Garnier also built the villa which now houses the **Musée National de Monaco**✶ or Musée des Poupées (doll museum), which is a collection of hundreds of dolls and toys from the 18th to 20th centuries. Many are *automata*, dolls which move, entertaining and eerie. Further along, the **Larvotto** area is Monaco's little beach resort. A surprising discovery here is the 7-hectare **Jardin Japonais**✶, a perfectly tranquil, authentic Shinto garden – nothing could be further in spirit from the rest of Monaco.

Accommodation and food

The grandest hotels of Monaco – L'Hermitage, Loews Monte-Carlo and Hôtel de Paris (*see below*) – are sights of interest in their own right, historic landmarks on the world map. Their restaurants, too, include some of Europe's best. Though there is little budget accommodation in Monaco, lower prices can be found just across the French border in neighbouring Beausoleil. When dialling Monaco hotels from outside the Principality, remember to prefix numbers with 00–377.

Hôtel de Paris €€€ *place du Casino; tel: 92 16 30 00; fax: 92 16 69 21.* You've arrived. Spend the night if you can afford to. If not, have a meal, or a coffee, or if even that's too much, just stand and stare. An equestrian statue of the Sun King in the magnificent domed entrance hall sets the tone. Step back more than a century, when this was the grandest of the Riviera hotels patronised by Europe's monarchs – there

Casino € *place du Casino; tel: 92 16 23 00; www.casino-monte-carlo.com. Open daily all year from 1200, except Salons Privée, from 1500. Passport required. Entry to over-21s only. No casual dress in Salons Privée (men: jacket and tie obligatory after 2100).*

In addition to Monte-Carlo Casino, there are three other casinos and several private gambling salons in the same area.

were often several staying here at the same time. No need to describe the rooms, which combine the majestic, palatial style of those days with ultimate modern comfort ... it's the best money can buy. Top suites are over 100000F a night, even the cheapest rooms are about 2000F. The hotel's **Le Grill** €€€ and the grander, more famous **Le Louis XV** €€€ are reckoned the best in Monaco, among the best in France.

Hôtel Helvetia € *1bis rue Grimaldi; tel: 93 30 21 71; fax: 92 16 13 34.* Surely among the cheapest accommodation in Monaco, simple but comfortable rooms, friendly welcome, but on a main road.

Café de Paris €€ *place du Casino; tel: 92 16 20 20; fax: 92 16 38 58.* Italian food is good at this huge, historic *belle-époque* brasserie right beside the Casino.

Restaurant Polpetta €€ *2 rue du Paradis; tel: 93 50 67 84.* Plenty of places in Monaco serve authentic Italian food, and that's one way to eat well at modest prices in the Principality. This convivial, likeable, home-from-home restaurant has found favour with visiting Italian stars.

Hotels in Beausoleil The border between France and Monaco runs along boulevard Général Leclerc, and several simple but adequate inexpensive hotels can be found on the French (odd-numbered) side of the street, including **Hôtel Diana** (€ *tel: 04 93 78 47 58; fax: 04 93 41 88 94*) and **Hôtel Boeri** (€€ *tel: 04 93 78 38 10; fax: 04 93 41 90 95*). It's 5 minutes' walk to the Casino.

Shopping

Boulevard des Moulins, the main street of Monte-Carlo, is lined with ready-to-wear designer outlets, shops and cafés. At one end, where it meets avenue de la Costa, Les Allées Lumières are up-market shopping galleries. The Casino area is the place for jewellery, luxurious fashions and accessories. Rue Grimaldi is the busy main shopping street in La Condamine. Several hotels have extensive shopping centres, especially the Métropole. The Fontvieille shopping centre is one of several indoor shopping centres in the Principality. For souvenirs and traditional Monagèsque and Provençal products, look in Boutique du Rocher, avenue de la Madone, and the streets of the Vieille Ville. There is also a daily market on place d'Armes.

Suggested walk

Total distance: About 4.8km, or 6km including the detour.

Time: The walking will take about 2 hours. Allow a long day to include visits to the sights. Remember not to reach the Casino before 1200.

Links: Monaco lies off the Riviera Corniches tour (*see page 242*).

🅿 **In Monaco-Ville:** Parking des Pêcheurs.

Parking in Fontevieille and Le Jardin Exotique: Parking Sous-sol du Stade Louis II or Parking Centre Commercial de Fontvieille.

In Monte-Carlo: There are several car parks, but for the casino area, it is convenient to park in Beausoleil (in France) and take the 5-minute walk into Monaco. For Larvotto, use the Plage du Larvotto car park.

Start at MONACO-VILLE ❶, at **Parking des Pêcheurs**. Here you can see the **Monte Carlo Story** and, coming out of the car park, it's convenient to visit the **Musée Océanographique**. From the museum, walk through the **Jardins St-Martin**, where romantic, shaded paths through tropical vegetation on the cliff edge give some lovely sea views. Walk round to the **Cathedral**, into the narrow streets of the **Vieille Ville**, and to place du Palais for the **Palais du Prince**. Leave the Palace on its right, go on to Rampe Majeur, the slope leading down the north side of the Rock to **place d'Armes**, Monaco's market-place.

From place d' Armes, walk round to **Les Terrasses de Fontvieille** for the zoo and the Fontvieille museums. We are now in **FONTVIEILLE ❷**. It's a few minutes' walk, along avenue des Papalins (opposite Les Terrasses), to the **Roseraie Princesse Grace** rose gardens in the Parc Paysager. Return to the Terrasses de Fontvieille and place d'Armes.

Retracing your steps, walk along **rue Grimaldi**, the main street of the La Condamine area, lined with orange trees, to place Ste-Dévote. Here is the 19th-century **church of Ste-Dévote**, dedicated to Monaco's Corsican patron saint and standing on the remnants of an older church. Walk along avenue de la Costa to chic Les Allées Lumières and boulevard des Moulins and turn right into place du Casino. Ahead of you, beyond lovely gardens, is the ornate **Casino** and on one side, the Hôtel de Paris.

Detour: Continue along boulevard des Moulins as far as the lift (*ascenseur*), which you take down to avenue Princesse Grace. Just here is the **Musée National**, the doll museum. Turn back along avenue Princesse Grace (ie towards the Rock), pausing at the **Jardin Japonais** on the left. Further along the avenue, turn right to take avenue des Spélugues back to the Casino.

From place du Casino, go down avenue de Monte-Carlo and avenue d'Ostende to the La Condamine **yacht harbour**. Follow the attractive promenade which runs beside the quay, then climb again (on avenue de La Quarantaine) to **Fort Antoine**, a handsome corner fortress on the Rock, overlooking the port. The Fort is now a theatre, a pleasant spot for an annual summer season of outdoor concerts. It's a short walk from here to Parking des Pêcheurs.

Who broke the bank at Monte-Carlo?

In the gaming rooms of Monte-Carlo Casino, kings, sheiks and emperors, film stars and tycoons have lost fortunes. Since it was opened in 1879, many flamboyant characters have earned an entry in the Casino's memoirs, such as the ultra-glamorous Mata-Hari, whose response when a fellow gambler slipped his arm round her waist was to take out a revolver and shoot him in the chest (she was politely asked to leave). One visitor in 1891 was the high-flying Charles Deville Wells, a well-known crook, whose three days of almost uninterrupted winning at the Casino tables netted him 4 million francs – equivalent to hundreds of millions today. Despite a thorough investigation, no evidence was found that he had cheated on this occasion. He went down in legend as The Man Who Broke the Bank at Monte-Carlo, the 'bank' being the maximum 100 000F pay-out at each table.

Boulevard des Anciens Combattants d'Afrique du Nord

N7

Boulevard de la Turbie

Avenue de Verdun

Boulevard d'Italie

Boulevard du Larvotto

Musée National

Moyenne Corniche

Boulevard de la République

Boulevard du Général Leclerc

Boulevard de France

Boulevard des Moulins

Boulevard du Larvotto

Avenue Princesse Grace

Forum Grimald

Avenue de Prof Langevin

Avenue de Grande Bretagne

Jardin Japonais

Carref. du Portier

Avenue de Villaine

Avenue de Villaine

N7

Monte-Carlo

Pointe Focinane

Avenue P Doumer Prolongée

Rue des Martyrs de la Résistance

Rue Bellevue

Rue Bel Respiro

Boulevard Princesse Charlotte

Casino

Hôtel de Paris

Centre de Congrès Auditorium

Ch de la Turbie

Av Princesse Alice

Av de Monte-Carlo

N7

Avenue Pasteur

Rue Jean Bouin

Boulevard de Suisse

Avenue de la Costa

Moyenne Corniche

Ste-Dévote
†

Avenue d'Ostende

Quai des Etats-Unis

Bretelle Aureglia

Rue Grimaldi

Boulevard du Jardin Exotique

Boulevard Rainier III

Boulevard de Belgique

Port de Monaco

Rue Suffren Reymond

Boulevard Albert I er

la Condamine

Rue Grimaldi

Théâtre du Fort Antoine

usée d'Anthropologie Préhistorique

Boulevard Rainier III

Quai Antoine I er

Avenue de la Quarantaine

Avenue de la Porte Neuve

Monaco-Ville

Jardin Exotique

Place du Canton

Palais du Prince

Rue Emile de Loth

ulevard du Jardin Exotique

Avenue Pasteur

Avenue Pasteur

Boulevard Rainier III

Avenue de Fontvieille

Fontvieille

Av des Papalins

Port de Fontvieille

Rue Emile de Loth

Avenue Saint Martin

Cathedral
†

Musée Océanographique

Rue du Gabian

Avenue Prince Héréditaire

Avenue des Castelans

Quai des Sanbarbant

0   200 metres

0   200 yards

Stade Louis II

Av des Papalins

Avenue du 3 Septembre

Parc Paysager de Fontvieille

Roseraie Princesse Grace

Port de Cap d'Ail

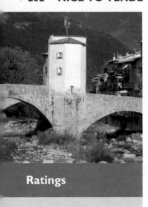

Nice to Tende

Ratings

History   ●●●●●
Scenery   ●●●●●
Villages   ●●●●●
Walking   ●●●●●
Children   ●●●○○
Sightseeing   ●●●○○
Restaurants   ●●○○○
Shopping   ●●○○○

The Nice backcountry and the Maritime Alps behind the Côte d'Azur are among the most enticing Provençal landscapes, unspoiled yet civilised. By road up to Tende is spectacular, whether you take the difficult mountain routes from the French Riviera or drive first to Ventimiglia in Italy and take the faster road which soon crosses the frontier into France again. On the Italian side, as on the French, the soaring, rocky hinterland is thrilling. The special flavour of these southern, sunlit Alpine slopes changes at the end of the tour as the higher altitudes are reached at last. Then the Mediterranean suddenly feels far away and the mountains become simply mountains, lofty and majestic. The peaks have an awesome appeal; yet there's a special magic in the warmer, more human Mediterranean slopes, a vivid landscape between snow-covered peaks and sun-drenched beaches, reaching to the perfect blue of both sea and sky.

ℹ Main tourist office for the Haute Roya (Upper Roya) region: 1 place Gen. de Gaulle, Tende; tel: 04 93 04 73 71; e-mail: info@tendemerveilles.com; www.tendemerveilles.com. Open daily except Sun and Thur all year. May–Sep 0900–1200, 1400–1800; Oct–Apr 0900–1200, 1300–1700.

Road information tel: 04 93 04 74 64.

Weather tel: 08 36 68 10 20.

Villages Perchés

Although 'Perched Villages' exist right across the coast and hinterland of Provence, the landscape of the Nice backcountry made them especially numerous here. These spectacular medieval villages, usually fortified, were built high on narrow peaks to prevent attacks by Saracen raiders. The strange cramped space and steep setting gives characteristic features: houses clustered one higher than the next, stepped alleys, narrow arcaded lanes and passageways that pass beneath houses.

BREIL-SUR-ROYA✦

Tourist Office
Mairie (town hall),
place Biancheri;
tel: 04 93 04 99 76;
www.breil-sur-roya.fr

Ecomusée du Haut
Pays €€ *Tel: 04 93*
04 99 76. Open Jun–Sep
only: daily except Tue
1000–1200, 1530–1830.

Breil makes a good base on the main road for walkers and others exploring the surrounding forests and mountains. The wide Roya, dammed here, flows through the busy little mountain town. The picturesque old centre on the east side, with remnants of its historic fortifications, two ruined gateways and a watch tower as well as many medieval buildings, is impressively located below steep slopes, and has a 16th-century altarpiece in the church. The **Ecomusée du Haut Pays**✦, highlighting the region's local culture and history, covers public transport in the region, including the old mountain tramway to the Riviera.

Saints' festivals – two fêtes in the second half of Aug. *La Stacada*: every 4–5 years the people of Breil celebrate boisterously with a medieval costume festival their successful 18th-century rebellion against the feudal custom of *droit de seigneur* (by which the local lord assumes sexual rights over all the women in his territory).

Accommodation and food in Breil-sur-Roya

Hôtel-Restaurant Castel du Roy €€ *route de Tende; tel: 04 93 04 43 66; fax: 04 93 04 91 83.* This quiet, comfortable little hotel in riverside gardens 1km out of town is a well-equipped *Logis* with an excellent and inexpensive restaurant. Mar–Oct only.

LUCERAM❖❖

Eglise (church) *Generally open. For guided visit, tel: 04 93 79 51 87.*

Perched between two ravines among surrounding slopes in the woodland below the soaring peak of Cime du Gros Braus (1330m), the old centre of this pretty, very Italian village is a maze of steps

On 24 Dec shepherds and other villagers from the surrounding district come to the church in Lucéram with Christmas offerings in a colourful old ceremony to the music of traditional instruments.

and arcaded alleys. There are several remarkable **medieval houses**. The village has a long history. Originally a Roman town, in the Middle Ages it became a well-defended independent district. Its 13th-century tower is still a landmark. The 15th-century **church**❖❖ contains an exceptional group of 15th- to 16th-century altarpieces by Louis Bréa and his students. The church treasury too has several fine examples of craftsmanship of the same period. The chapels of St Grat (1km south) and Notre-Dame de Bon Coeur (2km north) have 16th-century frescos.

PEILLE❖❖

Peille Tourist Office Tel: 04 93 91 71 71. If closed, information from the Mairie (town hall); tel: 04 93 79 90 32.

There is parking on place de la Tour, off the D53.

A fine example of a *village perché*, the delightful medieval streets and houses of Peille cluster on the crest of a little hill topped by the ruins of the château. Several buildings are 14th century and older – look especially along rue St-Sébastien. The 12th-century church, with its Romanesque belfry, has a picture of the village as it was at that time, as well as a 16th-century altarpiece and a font said to be some 1600 years old. Views from the village reach right across to the Baie des Anges.

Accommodation and food in Peille

Belvédère Hôtel €–€€ *3 place Jean Miol; tel: 04 93 79 90 45; fax: 04 93 91 93 47.* Reservation (by post) is advisable as there are just five rooms in this friendly, family-run hotel with wonderful views. Good, unpretentious restaurant with inexpensive set menus.

PEILLON❖❖❖

Peillon Tourist Office At the Mairie (town hall); tel: 04 93 79 91 04.

There is a big local fête every Aug.

The single gateway entrance to this exquisite, compact perched village is locked and bolted each night. Within the fortifications, tiny alleys and stairways climb between the ancient houses. The place looks like a film set of the Middle Ages, except that it has been charmingly prettified with flowers. Look in the Chapelle des Pénitents Blancs for remarkable, still-bright frescos by Canavasio.

Accommodation and food in Peillon

Auberge de la Madone €€–€€€ *tel: 04 93 79 91 17; fax: 04 93 79 99 36.* An oasis of tranquillity and comfort at the foot of the Peillon hill, standing in its gardens with wonderful views of the village above. The food is first rate, strongly Provençal and not expensive. Rooms are nicely arranged with fine old pieces of furniture. The pricier rooms at this excellent hotel and restaurant are those with balconies.

Next page
Peillon rooftops

SAORGE✢✢

ℹ **Saorge Tourist Office** *at the Mairie (town hall); tel: 04 93 04 51 23.*

There is a Sat morning market.

The fortifications, belfries and tall, ancient houses of Saorge, clinging to the rocky slope, make a magnificent sight from across the Roya at the end of the narrow, winding Gorges de Saorge. The village stands among a ring of hills that made it unassailable in the Middle Ages, and even now it is hard to approach. Within the village, tortuous stepways and alleys thread between attractive 15th-century houses. Despite its remoteness, the parish church of St-Sauveur has several good pieces of 16th- to 18th-century religious art, and a fine Genoese organ specially made in 1847 and brought here on the backs of mules from Nice. Among olive trees, just above the village on the south side, Franciscan monks are again installed in their 17th-century monastery.

SOSPEL❖❖

ℹ️ **Sospel Tourist Offices** at Le Vieux Pont; tel: 04 93 04 15 80; and in centre at boulevard de la 1ère DFL; tel: 04 93 04 18 44; fax: 04 93 04 19 96.

🏛️ **Fort St-Roch €** Open 1400–1800 for 1½-hour tours; Jul–Sep daily excluding Mon; rest of year Sat and Sun only. Closed Nov.

🛒 There is a weekly Thu market.

This historic and picturesque village, lying in a pleasant sun-warmed hollow among the hills, is built around a fortified, cobbled 11th-century bridge where travellers used to be charged a toll to cross the River Bevera. Sospel was once an important town and a bishopric, and the church used to be a cathedral. A large 15th-century corner tower and a gateway survive from powerful ramparts that once enclosed the little town. In the old centre, place St-Michel is an attractive arcaded square; the church and chapel contain fine altarpieces by Louis Bréa. Several streets have fine old houses with carved lintels and doorways (look especially along rue St-Pierre, rue de la République and place St-Nicolas), and everywhere there are richly carved fountains – the grandest is in place de la Cabraïa.

Proof enough that the strategic site appealed even to the modern military mind is **Fort St-Roch**❖, a 1930s barracks and operations centre, built mainly underground just outside the village. A guided tour takes you along 2km of underground corridors to see artillery, store rooms, kitchens and more, as well as a museum of the wartime Alpine Army.

Accommodation and food in Sospel

Hôtel-restaurant des Etrangers €€ 7 boulevard de Verdun; tel: 04 93 04 00 09; fax: 04 93 04 12 31. This comfortable family-run hotel on the south side of town, looking down over the river, has gardens, pool, sauna and more. Terraces give great views, and its enjoyable restaurant is great value for money. Closed 20 Nov–20 Feb.

TENDE❖❖❖

ℹ️ **Tende Tourist Office** 1 place Gen. de Gaulle, tel: 04 93 04 73 71; www.tendemerveilles.com

🏛️ **Musée des Merveilles €** avenue du 16 Sept 1947; tel: 04 93 04 32 50; www.museemerveilles.com. Open daily excluding Tue. 1 May–15 Oct 1030–1830 (till 2100 on Sat). 16 Oct–30 Apr 1030–1700. Closed 12–24 Mar, 13–25 Nov, and some holidays.

Tende is a very pretty little hill town of narrow streets and arcades, dark stone-slab roofs and balconied houses seemingly stacked one on another, with a strange Byzantine-looking church rising over all. Until the last war the town used to be in Italy – a tactful war memorial doesn't make it clear which side the dead were on – and for historic reasons the railway line from Nice does not terminate here on the frontier but continues straight under the mountain crests to the Italian town of Cuneo. Not surprisingly, many Tende locals still consider themselves Italian. The town was Roman, became a medieval frontier fortress, and in modern times something of a transport hub for the mountain region. The ruins of its old defences stand a little above the town. Most intriguing of all is its mix of Mediterranean and mountainous, Riviera and Alps. It's a popular base for exploring the **Mercantour** (see page 272) and for excursions to the **Vallée des**

Merveilles. The **Musée des Merveilles**** in the village deals with the theories, archaeology, the rock drawings themselves and the legends concerning the Vallée, as well as the wider culture and lifestyle of the mountains. Another good walk from here is along the mountain road to Italy. It's closed to vehicles now (they take the 3-km tunnel) and affords fantastic views.

Fête de St-Eloi: mid-Jul; traditional festival with local dances, music and cavalcade with muleteers.

Fête des Bergers: Aug traditional shepherds' fair.

Accommodation and food in Tende

There are several *chambres d'hôtes* and *gîtes* in the area. For details ask at the tourist office.

Le Cheval Blanc € *18 rue Maurice Sassi; tel: 04 93 04 62 22.* One of few places in the town which rise above the basic level, this simple little inn is adequate and inexpensive. No credit cards.

VALLEE DES MERVEILLES**

The best approach to the Vallée is from the D91, a turning off the N204 at St-Dalmas-de-Tende.

Vallée des Merveilles Contact the tourist office or the Musée des Merveilles in Tende for details of guided excursions. Guided tours leave Refuge des Merveilles at 0730, 1100 and 1500 daily in Jul–Aug. Tel: 04 93 04 68 66.

Refuge des Merveilles €€ *On the GR 52. Tel: 04 93 04 64 64. Reservation advisable.*

This stormy, secretive valley, high in the Mercantour mountains on a tributary of the Roya, at the foot of Mont Bégo (2872m), is famous for tens of thousands of strange little drawings carved on its jumbled rocks. There are thousands more in the narrower, adjacent Vallée de Fontanalbe, and even a few scattered about outside the two valleys. The pictures, resembling a child's stick men, date mostly from the Bronze Age (1800–1500 BC) and repeat certain motifs and ideas again and again, especially horns, hands, weapons and tools. What do they mean? No one knows. A multitude of unprovable theories purport to explain them, and you will be told with some certainty by guides and at the Musée des Merveilles in Tende that the local Ligurian tribes worshipped the Bull-God and Earth-Goddess and that Mont Bégo was a sacred pilgrimage site for their religion. An understanding of the drawings is not helped by the fanciful names some of them have been given, for example The Sorcerer, emblem of the museum.

The walk to the Vallée is rewarding even without the added interest of the rock carvings. The surrounding landscape of lakes and mountains is wild and spectacular. Here and there are larch forests, while much of the scene is lit up by glorious displays of early summer flowers.

The Vallée des Merveilles and Mont Bégo lie within the **Parc National du Mercantour** (*see page 272*). Within the Park, the following are forbidden: pets, fires, camping, waste disposal or removing any plant or natural object.

Suggested tour

Total distance: Main route 80km and a detour of 52km, with a proposed 12-hour walk.

Time: The main drive alone takes 3 hours without stops. Allow 1–2 days for the route, or 3 if you decide to do the detour and the walk to the Vallée des Merveilles. The roads can be slow, steep and winding in places. Several villages invite a leisurely stroll, or a pause to admire fine views, so allow time.

Links: At Nice the route connects with the Riviera Corniches (*see page 242*) and, via a detour, Cannes to Nice (*see page 220*).

Left
Peille

An Italian corner of France

It's not just proximity to the border that makes this area seem so Italian. Tende became part of France only under the peace treaty of October 1947, when the upper valley of the Roya (together with the Mercantour summit region) passed from Italian to French rule. The city of Nice itself, parts of the Riviera and the old County of Nice became French less than a century before, in 1860.

To Tende by train
The Nice to Tende line is one of the most dramatic rail journeys in Provence, and an acclaimed engineering feat. The little train inches up the vertiginous narrow-gauge track that crosses gorges, twists and turns and tunnels through hills. At one point the train turns full circle as it spirals up inside a mountain, emerging to see the same track where it had just run far below. The line continues beyond Tende to Cuneo, in Italy.

Route: Start from **Nice**, leaving the city centre on the main road north on the east side of the Paillon, heading towards the *autoroute* A8. At a major junction close to the *autoroute*, take 'Sospel' on either of two roads, the D2204 or D2204B, one each side of a railway line. The route follows this rail track for much of its distance (for a rail alternative to driving, see *To Tende by train, below*). Out of Nice, the two roads merge and pass under the railway line and over the River Paillon close to its confluence with the River Paillon de Contes. Just here, turn right on to the D21 to **PEILLON** ❶, which lies off the road. Leaving Peillon on the D21 again, follow the Paillon stream, then turn right up the D53, driving 7km up this wiggly steep little road to **PEILLE** ❷.

Detour: Perched village enthusiasts could continue past Peille on the D53 to the junction with the D22, where you turn left on this scenic mountain route for 9km to reach Ste-Agnes. Return to Peille.

Head back down from Peille to the D21, turn right and continue down through the Peillon Gorge to the junction with the main road, the D2204, at the old village of **L'Escarène**. A 7-km drive up the D2566 from **L'Escarène** leads to **LUCERAM** ❸. If you stay on the D2566 for another 7km, you reach the little mountain resort of **Peïra-Cava**.

Return to **L'Escarène**. The D2204 climbs in a succession of hairpins towards the **Col de Braus** (1002m). The road now begins its equally winding descent around Mont Barbonnet into **SOSPEL** ❹. The road begins to climb again, first to the Col de Pérus (654m) and then to the more spectacular **Col de Brouis** (879m). Follow the road down from here to its junction with the N204. This is the busier road to Tende from Ventimiglia in Italy, also a magnificent route (*see The quick way to Tende, below*). Turn right here to enter **BREIL-SUR-ROYA** ❺.

Heading north up the N204 from Breil-sur-Roya, the road – quite straight and easy now, though sometimes busy – follows the River Roya through the dramatic **Gorges de Saorge**. Turn right at the end of the

The quick way to Tende

Autoroute A8 makes a quicker, shorter drive along the Riviera, tunnelling through mountain ridges, with coastal views to rival **La Grande Corniche** (*see page 242*). There can be queues at the border checkpoint. On the Italian side the road becomes the A10. Leave at the Ventimiglia exit and take the S20, a picturesque main road following the Roya valley. Crossing the frontier again, the road becomes the N204, continuing through **BREIL-SUR-ROYA** to **TENDE**.

gorge to get into the village of **SAORGE** ➏. Returning to the main road, the N204, continue through more Roya river gorges, all the way to St-Dalmas-de-Tende, the main starting point for the excursion into the Vallée des Merveilles.

Getting out of the car: Using Tende as a base, take a day out to visit the **VALLEE DES MERVEILLES** ➐.

It's another 4km into **TENDE** ➑. Returning from Tende, take the same route back as far as Sospel, then the scenic D2566 for 15km to *autoroute* A8. Travel on the *autoroute* back into Nice.

To the Mercantour

Ratings

History	●●●●●
National park	●●●●●
Scenery	●●●●○
Walking	●●●●●
Sightseeing	●●●○○
Restaurants	●●○○○
Shopping	●●○○○
Children	●○○○○

Are we still in Provence? Here winter temperatures plunge way below freezing – there are ski resorts – while in summer, Riviera locals come up to take a break from the crowds, traffic and heat. The high mountains of the Mercantour and its borders make a refreshing break, too, from the worldliness of the Côte: up here life is simple and the majestic landscapes dominate everything. Villages boast of an ancient chapel and a finely painted medieval altarpiece rather than a grand restaurant and a modern art museum. Strangely though, we *are* still in Provence. There's a bright southern feel in the air, even at this altitude the sun's warmth gets under the skin and anyway, Mediterranean beaches are just an hour or so away by car. In summer, the austere, peaceful hills and valleys appeal to walkers. In winter, you can ski Isola 2000 and be in Nice an hour later.

Mercantour National Park

This rugged mountain wilderness of 68 500 hectares extends along the high-altitude Provençal Alps close to the Italian border. Much of the distance, the Park runs across the border to merge with the Italian Alpe Maritimi National Park on the other side. The whole park is crossed by several footpaths, notably the GR52A, which traverse its entire length. Walkers spend the nights in the many refuges positioned along the trails. The main appeal is mountain scenery, with altitudes ranging from 500m to over 3000m. Eagles and occasionally vultures may be seen soaring above the territory. At lower altitudes within the Park, red deer, roe deer and blue hare may be seen. Higher up, ibex, moufflon and chamois are fairly common. Wolves have been sighted in the park since 1989, and are probably few in number but increasing. Rather than attempt to kill the animals, shepherds have been urged to keep sheep penned at night and protect them with a Pyrenean Patou – a traditional breed of sheepdog especially capable of driving away wolves.

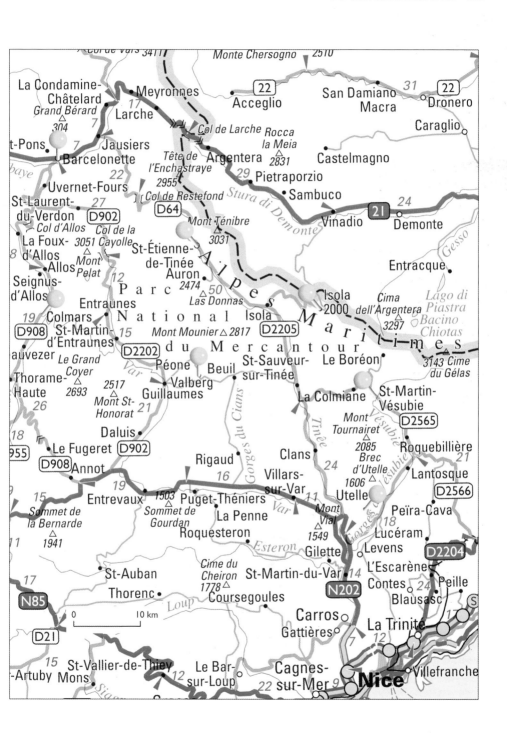

ⓘ Mercantour National Park

Head Office *23 rue d'Italie, 06006 Nice; tel: 04 93 16 78 88; fax: 04 93 88 79 05; e-mail: mercantour@ wanadoo.fr*

Web: *www.freinet.org/ creactif/ecolones/cyber/parc. htm* is a useful and entertaining web page (in French) about the Mercantour put together by a local school. *www.parc-mercantour.com* and *www.parcsnationaux-fr.com/mercantour/default.htm* are two official websites about the Parc.

Mountain refuges: *Club Alpin Français des Alpes Maritimes, 1 avenue Mirabeau, Nice; tel: 04 93 62 59 99.*

ⓘ Tourist offices
Village tourist offices in the region may keep intermittent hours and are generally not open daily. Information is usually available from the Mairie (town hall) during normal office hours. Larger town and resort tourist offices generally open *Mon–Sat 0900–1200, 1400–1800, except Jul–Aug daily 0900–2000.*

Road information *tel: 04 93 04 74 64.*

Weather check This route can be blocked by snow at any time from Nov–Jun. *The one-day tour option (page 278), is generally clear all year round.*

Weather for Alpes Maritimes: *tel: 08 36 68 02 06.*

Weather for Alpes des Haute Provence: *tel: 08 36 68 02 04.*

ℹ Five-day forecast for high altitudes: *tel: 08 36 68 04 04.*

🔍 Vallée des Merveilles For access to the southeastern Mercantour and **Vallée des Merveilles**, see Nice to Tende (*page 268*).

🍴 On the menu Miel de Lavande (lavender honey), charcuterie, chestnuts, and Génépi – the local liqueur.

Italian summits

Only after World War II, with the peace treaty of October 1947, was this area passed from Italian to French rule. When the County of Nice was joined to France in 1860, under Napoleon III, he unaccountably decided to let Italy keep the upper valley of the Roya and the mountain summit region of the Mercantour. The Italian king, Victor Emmannuel II, had specially asked that he could keep the high altitude regions for chamois hunting.

BARCELONETTE❖

ℹ Barcelonette Tourist office *place Frédéric Mistral; tel: 04 92 81 04 71; fax: 04 92 81 22 67; e-mail: info@barcelonnette.net; www.barcelonnette.net*

Mercantour Information Office (summer only) *Maison du Parc, 10 avenue de la Libération; tel: 04 92 81 21 31. Open mid-Jun–mid-Sep only.*

Musée de la Vallée *10 avenue de la Libération; tel: 04 92 81 27 15. Open Jul–Aug 1000–1200, 1500–1900; rest of year Wed, Thu and Sat pm only.*

🛒 There are Wed and Sat markets.

The most northerly town in Provence, 'Little Barcelona' takes its name from the time when the Counts of Provence were also Counts of Barcelona. Some traces of its old fortifications remain. It's a pleasant, peaceful town beautifully placed among flowery meadows and mountains, and a good base for walks, or trips into the Mercantour National Park, which has an office here. The **Musée de la Vallée**❖❖ tells all about the district and its history, including its curious Mexican connection (*see feature on page 276*).

Accommodation and food in Barcelonette

Hôtel Azteca €€ *3 rue des Frères Arnauds; tel: 04 92 81 46 36; fax: 04 92 81 43 92.* One of several 'Mexican villas' which have become unusual up-market guest-houses and hotels, this is a very comfortable hotel furnished with several Mexican artefacts.

Restaurant La Mangeoire Gourmande € *place Quatre-Vents; tel: 04 92 81 01 61; fax: 04 92 81 56 13.* Ambitious local restaurant in a beamed restored barn, sometimes achieving heights of cuisine, this is the best eating place in town.

Left
Rock outcrop

Little Mexico in the Alps

'Little Barcelona' is better known as Petit Mexique, thanks to a peculiar turn of fate. In 1805, enterprising local lads Jacques and Marc-Antoine Arnaud went to Mexico to make their fortune. As it turned out they made millions, eventually founding the London and Mexico Bank. Inspired by their luck, generations of young men from the Barcelonette area went to Mexico – where they soon dominated the textile trade. While few became millionaires, most made a good living and later returned to their native land to build lavish *haciendas* (actually most of their villas are a wild hotchpotch of styles) in the mountains of Haute Provence. Several of the so-called 'Mexican houses' can be seen around Jausiers, 9km away, the native village of the Arnaud brothers. The emigration continued for over a century, until the 1950s. Barcelonette has formed close ties with Mexico, and there's a Mexican craft store in the town.

COLMARS✦✧

ℹ Colmars Tourist Office / place Joseph Girieud; tel: 04 92 83 41 92; e-mail: colmarslesalpes@ wanadoo.fr; www.verdon-provence.com/hautverdon.htm

Fort de Savoie € Jul–Aug daily guided tour at 1030. To visit at other times, ask at tourist office.

◓ Markets takes place on Tue and Fri.

◐ Les Oralies de Haute Provence in Oct is a regional festival of period costume, traditions, crafts and folk arts.

Clustered together within indomitable ramparts among the green pastures and woodlands of the upper Verdon valley, Colmars has become a pleasing low-key summer and winter mountain resort. Two fortresses once guarded this strategic valley town on the border between Provence and Savoy. Then Vauban, the great 17th- to 18th-century military architect charged with the task of defending France's borders, decided that wasn't enough. He ringed the little town with defences, and linked the forts with the ramparts, creating an extraordinary, impregnable site in the countryside. When Napoleon was about to launch his war against Italy, his army waited here for the order to attack. Entered through two fortified gates, Porte de Savoie and charming Porte de France, the town is thoroughly picturesque, with narrow streets, little squares, tall old houses and fountains. The older **Fort de Savoie✦** can be visited in summer.

ISOLA 2000✦

ℹ Isola 2000 Tourist Office Immeuble Le Pelevos; tel: 04 93 23 15 15; fax: 04 93 23 14 25; e-mail: info@isola2000.com; www.isola2000.com

In the high peaks of Mercantour, this state-of-the-art ski resort is just over an hour's drive from the Riviera. It's also an excellent, if rather charmless, base for summer visits into the national park, with numerous footpaths – you're almost certain to see chamois. You can even cross from here into the Italian national park on the other side of the mountain crests.

St-Etienne-de-Tinee*

ℹ St-Etienne-de-Tinée Tourist Office *in the village; tel: 04 93 02 41 96.*

ℹ Musée des Traditions and **Musée du Lait** € *Tel: 04 93 02 41 96. To visit either museum, call at tourist office.*

Apart from the beautiful high, tranquil countryside of green pastures and terraced hillsides, the main attraction in this likeable little town are its fine old churches decorated with 17th-century altarpieces and frescos. Rising above the rooftops is the attractive Italian Romanesque belfry on the parish church. Two little museums, **Musée des Traditions*** and **Musée du Lait***, deal with aspects of traditional rural life in the mountains. The town is popular with hikers as a base for some great mountain treks.

St-Martin-Vesubie*

ℹ St-Martin-Vésubie Tourist Office *place Félix Faure; tel and fax: 04 93 03 21 28.*

Impressively sited among high mountains, and standing on a plateau between the valleys of two streams, St-Martin-Vésubie is the place where these tributaries come together to form the Vésubie river. Drinkable natural springs here include the Ciardola, likened to Evian. Cross the valley and take the winding little road high up to neighbouring village **Venanson** for an excellent view over the St-Martin and surrounding peaks, and take a look at the frescos painted in 1481 on the walls and ceiling of Venanson's church of St-Sébastien.

Accommodation and food in St-Martin-Vésubie

Hôtel La Châtaignerie €€ *tel: 04 93 03 21 22; fax: 04 93 03 33 99; e-mail: hotel-lachataigneraie@raiberti.com.* There's a warm, enthusiastic welcome at this peaceful 2-star *Logis* hotel. There is a swimming-pool, and low-priced set meals. May–Sep only.

Utelle*

⊘ There is a colourful, unusual, historic local festival on 16 Apr. The Madonna of Utelle pilgrimages take place on 15 Aug and 8 Sep.

Perched high on its hillside ledge, the once-fortified village of Utelle has plenty of Provençal mountain charm. Its church and chapel, standing close to one another, both contain excellent carved wooden altarpieces. A zigzagging road leads higher up the hill to the Madone d'Utelle sanctuary, first built in AD 850 by Spanish sailors in gratitude to the Madonna for saving their lives in a storm. Rebuilt nearly a thousand years later, it is still a place of worship and thanksgiving.

Accommodation and food in Utelle

Hôtel-Restaurant Bellevue Martinon €–€€ *route de la Madone; tel: 04 93 03 17 19; fax: 04 93 03 19 17.* Out of the village on the road to the sanctuary, this straightforward country restaurant offers decent local cooking. It's also a small, unpretentious hotel with simple, comfortable rooms and good views.

VALBERG✧

ℹ **Valberg Tourist Office** 4 place du Quartier; tel: 04 93 23 24 25; e-mail: ot@valberg.com; www.valberg.com

Mercantour Information Office Parc National du Mercantour, Centre Accueil Valberg. 1 rue St Jean; tel: 04 93 02 58 23.

Valberg is a pleasant summer and winter mountain resort, still with a touch of the rustic village at its heart. It's a great jumping off point for trips into the Mercantour, and there's a park information office here. Many enjoyable mountain walks and drives head off in all directions, notably the dramatic Gorges du Cians and Gorges de Daluis, and atmospheric mountain villages like nearby Péone.

Accommodation and food in Valberg

Adrech de Lagas €€€ tel: 04 93 02 51 64; fax: 04 93 02 52 33, at the nearby village of Peone, and **Chalet Suisse** €€ tel: 04 93 03 62 62; fax: 04 93 03 62 64, are two of the town's better hotel-restaurants, both good value, the one a little more down-market than the other.

Suggested tour

Total distance: Main route 80km and a detour of 52km, with a proposed 12-hour walk.

Time: 3 days. The roads can be slow, steep and winding in places. Several villages invite a leisurely stroll, or a pause to admire fine views or to see medieval frescos and altarpieces, so allow time. In winter, the route is impassable due to snow.

Option for a 1-day tour: Follow the route to **St-Sauveur-sur-Tinée**. Take the D30 to **Beuil**, 24km west, and rejoin the route for the **Gorges du Cians**. Follow the route from there back to the starting point on the N202, a total distance of 115km.

The fast N202 from **Nice** is not part of this route but gives the most convenient access to it. Start 24km north of Nice Airport (via St-Martin-du-Var) by turning off the main N202, just after **Plan du Var** on the east side of the Var river, on to the D2565. Straight away you are plunged into the **Gorges de la Vésubie**. The road is low down in this most spectacular stretch of the Vésubie valley just before it meets the Var. The rocky sides of the narrow, tight ravine are streaked with natural colour. At St-Jean-de-la-Rivière, turn left on the D32 for the winding climb to **UTELLE** ➊.

From St-Jean-de-la-Rivière, the D2562 heads out of the gorge between high rocky escarpments, and carries on through Lantosque.

La Route des **Grandes Alpes** One of the great summertime mountain drives in France crosses the Alps from Menton, on the Riviera, to Thonon, on the shores of Lake Geneva. Created by the prestigious Touring Club de France in 1909, the well-marked route follows a mix of roads from main highways to steep, narrow mountain roads. Clinging to the high-altitude frontier with Italy, most of the route is usually snow-covered between Nov and Apr.

Detour: Two kilometres after Lantosque, turn right on to the D70 to enter the Fôret de Turini region. Follow the road up to Col de Turini (1604m), then on the D2566 to **Peïra-Cava** a delightful base for not-too-difficult hillwalks to the top of Cime de Peïra-Cava (1582m). Beyond it, the road reaches Lucéram on the Nice to Tende route (*see page 264*). Return on the same road.

Passing below Roquebillière, the road goes through Roquebillière-Vieux. Just after, a little turn on the right leads 4km up to the tiny old spa, **Berthemont-les-Bains**. From Roman times till today, rheumatism sufferers have sworn to the powers of its hot (30°C) sulphur-rich waters, which are radioactive. The D2565 climbs into a fresher countryside of green pastures and forests of chestnut and pine among higher peaks – the area is known as Suisse Niçoise – just before entering **ST-MARTIN-VESUBIE ❷**.

From St-Martin stay on the D2565, now following signs to Barcelonette. With some steep hairpins and broad views the road reaches the tunnel beneath **Col St-Martin** (1500m); the little ski resort of **Colmiane** is just on the other side. It then descends through a high pleasant green landscape of woods and open pastures – this area is called the Valdeblore. **St-Dalmas-de-Valdeblore** has a simple 11th-century Romanesque church standing on an older crypt, and decorated with 16th-century altarpieces. Rising on a high point to the right of the road, the chapel in the tiny village of **Rimplas** has superb views. Meeting the D2205 and the valley of the River Tinée, turn right for **St-Sauveur-sur-Tinée**, a picturesque old mountain town of steep narrow streets and lanes and tall houses, with an altarpiece from 1483 in its church.

Stay on the D2205 heading north for some 12km through the bare, rocky **Gorges de la Valabre** to reach the beautiful Romanesque bell tower at the edge of the village of **Isola**. The left turn here skirts the village and passes the 100m-high **Cascade de Louch** waterfall.

Detour: At the bell tower, or from the village of Isola, take the D97 for a steep 17-km climb up the valley of the Guerche to **ISOLA 2000 ❸**.

Continue on the D2205C in the Tinée valley as it flows below mountain crests. The snow-capped mountains on the right, marking the Italian frontier, reach about 3000m. **Auron**, signposted to the left of our road, is a pleasant, popular little resort village whose Romanesque church is decorated with 15th-century frescos. It has become a favourite among Riviera locals for summer and winter mountain breaks. Carry on into **ST-ETIENNE-DE-TINEE ❹**.

We are now going to tackle the 50-km **Route de la Bonnette**, the highest road in France (check weather and road conditions first). The D2205 first climbs in the impressive rocky valley of the pouring Tinée stream. At the Pont Haut, take the right road, the D64, passing the **Cascade de Vens** waterfall (on the right). After Pra hamlet, the road starts to wind tortuously upwards, passing a ruined army barracks. **Col de la Bonnette** (2802m) is the high point of the road.

Getting out of the car: Park the car at the Col and take the footpath which climbs to the summit of Cime de la Bonnette, 2862m high. It's only a 30-minute walk there and back, and the phenomenal panorama over the Provençal Alps is well worth it.

The road starts the descent by passing the **Notre-Dame-du-Tres-Haut** chapel and the old Restefond barracks and running steeply downhill to **Jausiers**. The bizarre turn-of-the-century neo-Gothic **Château des Magnans**, before the village, is a first sight of the 'Mexican houses' built by this district's well-to-do returning emigrants. At Jausiers turn left on to the D900 – part of the great Route des Grandes Alpes (*see page 279*) – for **BARCELONETTE ❺**. Stay on the D902, still the Route des Grandes Alpes, which leaves Barcelonette on the southwest side of town heading for the ski-resort of Pra-Loup, 9km away.

Instead of taking the turning for Pra-Loup, though, stay on the narrow D902 through woodland as it threads the Gorges du Bachelard. Various hamlets and roadside chapels are passed as the road climbs for several kilometres, next to the Bachelard almost all the way, eventually leaving the stream to reach the wide views of **Col de la Cayolle** (2326m). From the source of the Bachelard, the road crosses the pass to find the source of the Var on the other side. Having crossed back into the Alpes-Maritimes *département*, the road number changes to the D2202, and this narrow scenic road follows the Var stream down through rather barren terrain, passing the village of **Entraunes**, where the parish church has good 16th-century frescos. At **St-Martin-d'Entraunes**, further on, the countryside is greener and the church has fine Renaissance wood carving and an excellent 1555 altarpiece by François Bréa.

Detour: From St Martin d'Entraunes, take the very steep and twisting D78 which climbs over 1000m in 9km to the Col des Champs, then descends sharply into **COLMARS ❻**. Come back the same way.

Keep on the D2202 into the picturesque fortified village of **Guillaumes**, with a ruined château gazing over a meeting of rivers. Here, leave the Var road, taking instead the D28 to the ski resort of **VALBERG ❼**. Beyond is the dramatically sited **Beuil**, a pretty and historic village with an interesting church and chapel, built from the stones of its ruined Grimaldi fortress. Turn south here on the D28 to follow the River **Cians** into its narrow red-rock gorges. This is one of the most impressive stretches of road on the whole route. One of the highlights can only be seen on foot: at the **Grande Clue**, park after the tunnel and take the walkway back. At the end of this stretch of gorge, the little D128 clambers up the rock into **Lieuche**, a small village with an unremarkable church – until you look inside and find the remarkable polyptych altarpiece of 1499 by Louis Bréa. Return to the river road. After another section of narrow, moist, winding gorge road, you reach the N202.

Turn left. The road follows the Var to its confluence with the Tinée, the two rivers merging as they pour through the **Gorges de la Mescla** (*mescla* is Provençal for mixing). It's 7km down the N202 to the starting point of the route.

Language

Although English is spoken in most tourist locations it is courteous to attempt to speak some French. The effort is generally appreciated, and may even elicit a reply in perfect English! The following is a very brief list of some useful words and phrases, with approximate pronunciation guides. For food vocabulary, see page 17.

The *Thomas Cook European Travel Phrasebook* (£4.95/$7.95) lists more than 300 travel phrases in French (and in 11 other European languages).

- **Hello/Goodbye**
  Bonjour/Au revoir *Bawngzhoor/Ohrervwahr*
- **Good evening/Goodnight**
  Bonsoir/Bonne nuit *Bawngswahr/Bon nwee*
- **Yes/No**
  Oui/Non *Wee/Nawng*
- **Please/Thank you (very much)**
  S'il vous plaît/Merci (beaucoup) *Seelvooplay/Mehrsee (bohkoo)*
- **Excuse me, can you help me please?**
  Excusez-moi, vous pouvez m'aider s'il vous plaît? *Ekskewzaymwah, voo poovay mahyday seelvooplay?*
- **Do you speak English?**
  Vous parlez anglais? *Voo pahrlay ahnglay?*
- **I'm sorry, I don't understand.**
  Pardon, je ne comprends pas. *Pahrdawng, zher ner kawngprawng pah.*
- **I am looking for the tourist information office.**
  Je cherche l'office de tourisme. *Zher shaersh lohfeece de tooreezm.*
- **Do you have a map of the town/area?**
  Avez-vous une carte de la ville/région? *Ahveh-voo ewn cart der lah veel/rehzhawng?*
- **Do you have a list of hotels?**
  Vous avez une liste d'hôtels? *Vooz ahveh ewn leesst dohtehl?*
- **Do you have any rooms free?**
  Vous avez des chambres disponibles? *Voozahveh deh shahngbr deesspohneebl?*
- **I would like to reserve a single/double room with/without bath/shower.**
  Je voudrais réserver une chambre pour une personne/pour deux personnes avec/sans salle de bain/douche. *Zher voodray rehsehrveh ewn shahngbr poor ewn pehrson/poor der pehrson avek/sawns sal der banne/doosh.*

- **I would like bed and breakfast/(room and) half board/(room and) full board.**
  Je voudrais le petit-déjeuner/la demi-pension/la pension complète. *Zher voodray ler pewtee-dehjewneh/lah dermee-pahngsyawng/lah pahngsyawng kawngplait.*
- **How much is it per night?**
  Quel est le prix pour une nuit? *Khel eh ler pree poor ewn nuwy?*
- **I would like to stay for . . . nights.**
  Je voudrais rester . . . nuits. *Zhe voodray resteh . . . newyh.*
- **Do you accept travellers' cheques/credit cards?**
  Vous acceptez les chèques de voyages/les cartes de crédit? *Voos aksepteh leh sheck der vwoyazh/leh kart der krehdee?*
- **I would like a table for two.**
  Je voudrais une table pour deux personnes. *Zher voodray ewn tabl poor der pehrson.*
- **I would like a cup of/two cups of/another coffee/tea.**
  Je voudrais une tasse de/deux tasses de/encore une tasse de café/thé. *Zher voodray ewn tahss der/der tahss der/oncaw ewn tahss der kafeh/teh.*
- **I would like a bottle/glass/two glasses of mineral water/red wine/white wine, please.**
  Je voudrais une bouteille/un verre/deux verres d'eau minérale/de vin rouge/de vin blanc, s'il vous plaît. *Zher voodray ewn bootayy/ang vair/der vair doh mynehral/der vang roozh/der vang blahng, seelvooplay*
- **Could I have it well-cooked/medium/rare please?**
  Je le voudrais bien cuit/à point/saignant s'il vous plaît. *Zher ler voodray beeang kwee/ah pwahng/saynyang, seelvooplay?*
- **May I have the bill, please?**
  L'addition, s'il vous plaît! *Laddyssyawng, seelvooplay?*
- **Where is the toilet (restroom), please?**
  Où sont les toilettes, s'il vous plaît? *Oo sawng leh twahlaitt, seelvooplay?*
- **How much does it/this cost?**
  Quel est le prix? *Kehl eh ler pree?*
- **A (half-)kilo of . . . please.**
  Un (demi-) kilo de . . . s'il vous plaît. *Ang (dermee) keelo der . . . seelvooplay.*

Index

Acknowledgements

Project management (first edition): Dial House Publishing Services
Project management (this edition): Fay Franklin
Series design: Fox Design
Front cover design: Pumpkin House
Cover artwork: Studio 183
Layout and map work: Concept 5D
Repro and image setting: Z2 Repro (first edition); PDQ Digital Media Solutions Ltd (this edition)
Printed and bound in Spain by: Grafo Industrias Gráficas, Basauri

We would like to thank the following for the photographs used in this book, to whom the copyright belongs:

Front cover: Lavender fields near Sault, ImageState

Back cover: Pont du Gard, Ruth Tomlinson/RobertHarding.com

Bob Battersby (pages 5, 6, 25, 33, 34, 46, 52, 54, 60, 62, 64, 66, 69, 72, 74A, 74B, 80, 84, 90A, 90B, 93, 94, 97, 105, 108, 110, 113, 116, 118, 149, 156A, 156B, 158, 160, 167, 174A, 174B, 176, 178, 186, 188, 204, 206, 216, 218, 220, 223, 224, 225, 235, 236, 242, 245, 262, 264, 266, 267, 268, 272, 274 and 275)

John Heseltine (pages 3, 12, 13, 19, 20, 23, 28, 39, 50A, 57, 77, 78, 102, 115, 130, 136, 138, 141, 146A, 146B, 153, 154, 164B, 168, 180, 183, 190, 228, 240, 250, 252, 276 and 278)

Linda R Miles (page 70)

Pictures Colour Library (pages 30 and 100)

Neil Setchfield (pages 14, 27, 40A, 40B, 42, 50B, 120, 122, 125, 127, 150, 151, 164A, 196, 199, 200, 212, 215, 232, 238 and 254).

Feedback form

If you enjoyed using this book, or even if you didn't, please help us improve future editions by taking part in our reader survey. Every returned form will be acknowledged, and to show our appreciation we will give you £1 off your next purchase of a Thomas Cook guidebook. Just take a few minutes to complete and return this form to us.

When did you buy this book? ....
....

Where did you buy it? (Please give town/city and, if possible, name of retailer)
....
....

When did you/do you intend to travel in Provence?...
....

For how long (approx)? ....

How many people in your party? ....

Which cities, national parks and other locations did you/do you intend mainly to visit?
....
....
....
....

Did you/will you:
❏ Make all your travel arrangements independently?
❏ Travel on a fly-drive package?
Please give brief details: ....
....

Did you/do you intend to use this book:
❏ For planning your trip?   ❏ Both?
❏ During the trip itself?

Did you/do you intend also to purchase any of the following travel publications for your trip?
Thomas Cook Travellers: Provence ....
A road map/atlas (please specify) ....
Other guidebooks (please specify) ....

Have you used any other Thomas Cook guidebooks in the past? If so, which?
....
....

Please rate the following features of *Signpost Provence* for their value to you (circle VU for 'very useful', U for 'useful', NU for 'little or no use'):

The *Travel Facts* section on pages 14–23	VU	U	NU
The *Driver's Guide* section on pages 24–26	VU	U	NU
The *Highlights* on pages 38–39	VU	U	NU
The recommended driving routes throughout the book	VU	U	NU
Information on towns and cities, National Parks, etc.	VU	U	NU
The maps of towns and cities, parks, etc.	VU	U	NU

Please use this space to tell us about any features that in your opinion could be changed, improved, or added in future editions of the book, or any other comments you would like to make concerning the book:

....

....

....

....

....

....

....

....

Your age category: ❏ 21-30   ❏ 31-40   ❏ 41-50   ❏ over 50

Your name: Mr/Mrs/Miss/Ms ....

(First name or initials) ....

(Last name) ....

Your full address (please include postal or zip code):

....

....

....

....

....

Your daytime telephone number: ....

Please detach this page and send it to: The Project Editor, Signpost Guides, Thomas Cook Publishing, PO Box 227, Units 19–21, The Thomas Cook Business Park, Coningsby Road, Peterborough PE3 8XX, United Kingdom.

Alternatively, you can email us at: *books@thomascook.com,* **or** *editorial@globe-pequot.com* **for the US.**

We will be pleased to send you details of how to claim your discount upon receipt of this questionnaire.